Women's emancipation
movements in the
2004.

2005 11 30

WOMEN'S EMANCIPATION MOVEMENTS
IN THE NINETEENTH CENTURY

Women's Emancipation Movements in the Nineteenth Century

A EUROPEAN PERSPECTIVE

Edited by

Sylvia Paletschek and
Bianka Pietrow-Ennker

STANFORD UNIVERSITY PRESS

STANFORD, CALIFORNIA

2004

Stanford University Press
Stanford, California

Printed in the United States of America on acid-free,
archival-quality paper

Original Printing 2004
Last figure below indicates year of this printing:
13 12 11 10 09 08 07 06 05 04

Typeset by Heather Boone in 11/14 Garamond

Contents

Acknowledgments

The contributions in this collection were originally written for a conference at Stuttgart, Germany. Neither the conference nor the collection would have been possible without the support of several institutions and the dedicated work of many individuals. For financial support in organizing the conference we thank the DFG (Deutsche Forschungsgemeinschaft), the Baden-Württemberg Ministry of Science, and the Friends of Tübingen University. Although cooperation across national boundaries presented many difficulties, the editors were motivated to press on towards their goal by the lively discussions at the conference and by encouragement from many quarters. We regret that some of the participants who contributed papers to the conference were unable to make them available for publication.

Funding for editorial work was provided by the Committee for Research at the University of Konstanz, to which we are most grateful. Stanford University Press accepted the manuscript for publication, and we are indebted to its Director of Scholarly Publishing, Norris Pope, for his guidance.

Our thanks go to all who helped to bring this book into being. Among them we single out Karen Offen, who gave the project her energetic support from start to finish and stood ready with advice whenever it was needed. Without her help and encouragement this book would never have seen the light of day. We are also indebted to Gisela Bock of the University of Berlin for joining us in stimulating discussions on women's emancipation movements in Europe and contributing many valuable suggestions.

Margit Retzlaff, Natascha Vinokurova, and Charlotte Henze of the University of Konstanz provided vital assistance in putting this book into proper form. Helen Boeckh McNeill, Amy Jacobs, and Helen Schoop contributed translations. Our special thanks go to Mark Seidel, University of Tübingen, whose reliable and competent help in translating and editing were essential to the success of the project. To all of the above individuals we express our gratitude.

Contributors

Ida Blom is professor emerita at the Department of History, University of
Bergen, Norway. Her numerous books and articles explore national as
well as international comparative approaches to women's and gender
history, especially within the fields of national citizenship, reproduction,
and medical history. Her latest publications focus on gendering the
fight against tuberculosis. She is presently researching strategies in
prevention of venereal diseases.

Christine Bolt is professor of American history at the University of Kent at
Canterbury. Her publications include *The Anti-slavery Movement and
Reconstruction* (1969); *Victorian Attitudes to Race* (1971); *A History of
the USA* (1974); *Power and Protest in American Life* (coauthor with
A. T. Barbrook and Martin Robertson 1980); *Anti-slavery, Religion,
and Reform* (coeditor with S. Drescher, 1980); *American Indian Policy
and American Reform* (1987); *The Women's Movements in the United
States and Britain* (1993); and *Feminist Ferment* (1995).

Mineke Bosch is a historian and associate professor at the Centre for Gender and Diversity at the University of Maastricht. She divides her
interests between current policies on women and science and the history of the (international) feminist movement. In 1990 she edited and
wrote *Politics and Friendship: Letters from the International Woman
Suffrage Alliance*. In 1994 she published a major study on the history
of women, gender, and science in the Netherlands: *Het geslacht van
de wetenschap. Vrouwen en hoger onderwijs in Nederland 1878–1948*.
Recently she participated in the European Technology Assessment
Group on Women and Science, which published the report *Science
Policies in the European Union: Promoting Excellence through Main-
streaming Gender Equality* (2000) on behalf of the European Com-

mission. She is currently writing a biography of the Dutch feminist
Aletta Jacobs (1854–1929).

Linda Edmondson is a research fellow at the Centre for Russian and East
European Studies, University of Birmingham. She has worked mainly
on issues of women's rights and civil rights in Russian history and is
the author of *Feminism in Russia 1900–1917* (1984). More recently her
research has focused on issues of sexual difference and gender relations
in Russia. Her latest publication is the anthology *Gender in Russian
History and Culture* (2001). Her current project is a study of nationhood
and gender, comparing ideas about "Mother Russia" with images and
myths of nation in other European cultures.

Ute Gerhard is professor of sociology and director of the Cornelia Goethe
Centre for Women's and Gender Studies at the University of Frankfurt.
She is the author of numerous publications on women's rights, social
policy, the history of the women's movement, and feminist theory.
Her most recent books are *Frauen in der Geschichte des Rechts. Von der
Frühen Neuzeit bis zur Gegenwart* (Women in the History of Law. From
Early Modern Times to the Present) (1997); *Atempause. Feminismus als
demokratisches Projekt* (Breather. Feminism as a Democratic Project)
(1999); and *Debating Women's Equality. Toward a Feminist Theory of Law
from a European Perspective* (2001).

Bogna Lorence-Kot is a historian who teaches world history at the California College of Arts and Crafts. Her research and publications are on
Polish topics involving women and families in the eighteenth and nineteenth centuries. Her most recent study, a collaborative article on the
evolution of Polish kindergartens, is published in Roberta Wollons, ed.,
Kindergartens and Cultures (2000). She is currently working on a study
of two nineteenth-century Polish women.

Jitka Malečková is associate professor at the Institute of Middle Eastern
and African Studies at the Charles University in Prague. She has published articles (in Czech, English, French, and Turkish) on nineteenth-
century cultural and intellectual history of the Ottoman Empire and
on gender and nationalism in Central and Eastern Europe. Her book
Fertile Soil: Women Save the Nation is coming out in 2001 (in Czech).

Ulla Manns is a historian of ideas who specializes in the early women's
movement in Sweden. She is active as a scholar and teacher at the
Department of Gender Studies at Södertörn University College,

Stockholm. Her current research project is called "The Construction of Sisterhood: Ethics and Citizenship in Swedish Nineteenth-Century Feminism." She has published several articles about first-wave feminism, among them one from a historiographic perspective.

Mary Nash is professor of contemporary history at the University of Barcelona and director of the Research Unit on Multiculturalism and Gender. She has published widely on contemporary Spanish women's history and her research has also focused on cultural representations and multiculturalism. Her current research is on discourses of otherness in relation to immigrants and gender in the Spanish press. Among her recent books are *Rojas. Las mujeres republicanas en la Guerra Civil* (1999) and *Multiculturalismos y género: perspectivas interdisciplinarias* (2001).

Karen Offen is a historian and independent scholar affiliated with the Institute for Research on Women and Gender at Stanford University. Her most recent book is *European Feminisms, 1700–1950: A Political History* (2000). She has published widely in the field of French and European women's history, and the comparative history of feminisms. Currently she is editing a collection of articles on global feminisms before 1945.

Sylvia Paletschek is professor of history at the University of Freiburg. She has published books and articles on the women's movement in Germany in the nineteenth century, on women's and gender history, and on the history of universities and higher education. She is the author of *Frauen und Dissens. Frauen im Deutschkatholizismus und in den freien Gemeinden 1841–1852* (1990); "Adelige und bürgerliche Frauen (1770–1870)," in Elisabeth Fehrenbach, ed., *Adel und Bürgertum in Deutschland 1770–1848* (1994), pp. 159–85; "Wer war Lucie Lenz?" in *Werkstatt Geschichte* 20, 1998, pp. 31–58; and "Kinder, Küche, Kirche," in Hagen Schulze and Étienne François, *Deutsche Erinnerungsorte*, Vol. 2 (2001), pp. 351–65.

Bianka Pietrow-Ennker is professor of east European history at the University of Konstanz in southern Germany. She is a specialist on social and cultural history and international relations. In the field of gender history she has concerned herself with the beginnings of the Polish and Russian women's movements. See, for example, *Women in Polish Society* (1992), co-edited with Rudolph Jaworski, and *Russlands "neue Menschen." Die Entwicklung der Frauenbewegung von den Anfängen bis zur Oktoberrevolution* (1999). The latter book is soon to be published in Russian by the Russian State University of Humanities.

Jane Rendall is a senior lecturer in the History Department and the Centre for Eighteenth Century Studies at the University of York. She is interested in eighteenth- and nineteenth-century British and comparative women's history, and particularly in Scottish women's history. Her publications include *The Origins of Modern Feminism* (1985) and, most recently, with Catherine Hall and Keith McClelland, *Defining the Victorian Nation* (2000). She is currently working on a study of the gendered legacies of the Enlightenment in Scotland.

Florence Rochefort is a researcher in the Groupe de Sociologie des Religions et de la Laïcité (Centre National de la Recherche Scientifique, Paris) and is on the editorial board of the review *Clio: Histoire, Femmes et Sociétés*. She is a specialist on the history of feminism in France and in Europe. Her recent research has been concerned with feminism, gender, laicism, and secularization.

Judith Szapor holds an SSHRC postdoctoral fellowship at the University of Toronto and teaches European history at York University. She has published on early twentieth-century Hungarian intellectual history and women's movements. Her book, *The Possibilities and Impossibilities of This Semi-Century: The Life of Laura Polanyi, 1882–1959*, will be published by the University of Toronto Press.

Eleni Varikas teaches political history and theory in the Department of Political Science at the University of Paris 8. Her most recent books are *With a Different Face. Gender, Difference and Universality* (2000) and *Les femmes de Platon à Derrida. Anthologie critique* (2000), co-edited with F. Collin and E. Pisier. She has published in the field of women's studies, gender politics, and exclusion. Currently she is working on the figure of the pariah.

Adam Winiarz teaches in the Department of Education at the Marie Curie-Sklodowska University in Lublin, Poland. He has recently published two articles in Polish: "Factors Determining Child-Rearing in Polish Families under Occupation" (2000) and "Education in the Grand Duchy of Warsaw and the Polish Kingdom (1807–1831)" (2001). He is currently awaiting publication, in English, of a co-authored book entitled *The Emancipation of Polish Women Through Education (1918–1989)*.

WOMEN'S EMANCIPATION MOVEMENTS
IN THE NINETEENTH CENTURY

PART I

Introduction

CHAPTER I

Concepts and Issues

SYLVIA PALETSCHEK AND BIANKA PIETROW-ENNKER

The following essays are the culmination of an international conference which was financed by the German Research Foundation (Deutsche Forschungsgemeinschaft), the Baden-Württemberg Ministry of Science, and the University of Tübingen. The participants, from twelve different European countries and the USA, were concerned with the origins and development of women's emancipation movements in Europe in the long nineteenth century. This anthology, along with Karen Offen's recently published monograph, is the first book to treat the beginnings of the women's movements from a broader European perspective.[1]

The so-called first wave of the women's emancipation movements and their forerunners covers the period from the Enlightenment and the French Revolution to the First World War. For many European countries, however, it is possible to speak of a continuous organization only from the end of the nineteenth century. Between about 1890 and the First World War, women's emancipation organizations existed in all European countries, although they evidenced various degrees of development.

From the turn of the century most European women's movements fought for women's suffrage. In most countries this goal was achieved quickly, within the first two decades of the twentieth century, aided by the fact that women were able to point to their services during the war and that many political systems changed after the war. New forces such as social democratic and liberal parties became influential and took up feminist demands for women's suffrage. The First World War was thus a turning point for the majority of European women's emancipation movements. Once women had achieved the franchise, many leading feminists became active in political parties and women who wanted to be involved in politics were no longer restricted to women's organizations to the same degree as before. As a result, according to recent research, in most European countries a certain stagnation in the feminist movements set in after 1918.[2] In some countries this standstill was reinforced by authoritarian and restorative political regimes in the period between the wars.

This anthology includes chapters on the British, French, German, Dutch, Swedish, Norwegian, Polish, Russian, Czech, Hungarian, Greek, and Spanish women's emancipation movements. These countries, which were selected for a synopsis, represent as far as possible the national, social, cultural, political, and religious diversity of Europe in the nineteenth century. Countries from northern, southern, western, eastern, and central Europe have been included. In contrast to the usual practice of comparative work on European history, which tends to focus only on the larger western European countries and usually stresses British and French developments with the occasional inclusion of German particularities, smaller countries are also included. Nevertheless, this book does not cover the entirety of European women's emancipation movements, although we have done our best to provide the broadest possible coverage. The movements which have been selected will have to stand for those which have not been treated here. Inherent circumstances, in particular the limited number and availability of specialists for the preparatory conference, were decisive when we made our selection.[3] A systematic elaboration which, for example, could have dealt with the relationships between European and non-European women's movements was therefore not possible. As one instance of such interconnections, however, the ties between the American and British women's movements have been included, because the American women's movement had a great influence on the international feminist movement.

In selecting the different national women's movements we have taken up the historiographical tradition of using the nation-state as a spatial frame of reference in recording history. With this there is a tendency to level regional differences within the feminist movements in a nation and to place the accent on nationwide parent organizations. In some cases the existence of a national women's movement is assumed at a point in time where a modern nation-state did not yet even exist and the national movement was itself in the stage of inception.[4] There are, however, reasons for using the nation-state as a frame of reference when writing about the history of women's movements in the nineteenth century. At that time there was in some cases a very close connection among nation, national movements, and the women's movements, in particular in those nations which were not independent and had no unified nation-state. The point in time in which organized women's emancipation movements evolved coincides with the formation of the modern nation-state. Gender and national identity were intertwined.[5]

Is it at all meaningful to choose Europe as a spatial unit and a frame of reference when making comparisons among women's emancipation movements in the nineteenth century? One can start from the fact that in spite of all the diversity of political, economic, social, religious, and cultural developments within the European states there was an important measure of closeness, of common interests and mutual influence in the course of their social development. Therefore, in spite of its heterogeneity, from a global perspective one can speak of a European culture which has been shaped since the Middle Ages by common religious, economic, and political traditions. In the nineteenth century all European states were confronted by the challenges of economic, social, and political modernization. The European women's movements were an important part of this process of radical change. A comparative look at developments in neighboring European countries provides the outlines of the conditions under which the women's movements arose and developed. This broadly based search for common denominators in the development of feminist movements in Europe may correct the dominant perceptions of an ideal type. For a long time the Anglo-American model has been considered axiomatic and exemplary while other developments have been seen as deviations from the norm.

After careful consideration we have chosen "women's emancipation movements" for the title of this book. Our original title, "women's movements in Europe," reflected, among other things, the German tradition of usage. Also, this title seemed too nebulous given the international discussion and the now broad diversity of research on nonfeminist women's organizations. The term "feminism" came into common usage only at the beginning of the twentieth century, when women's emancipation movements reached a peak in some European countries. Therefore, with respect to the time period under investigation, we decided to use the term "women's emancipation movement" because it includes the preparatory, organizational, and peak phases of the movement. "Women's emancipation" was also a term that had been in use since the beginning of the nineteenth century.

Women's emancipation is understood to mean the fight for self-determination and improvements in the legal, social, cultural, and political positions of women. Subsumed under this term are feminist as well as potential feminist discourses. Nor is it only women who are included in the terms "women's emancipation movement" and "feminist movement," but also men who were engaged in the cause of women's emancipation. Thus the term is broad enough to encompass the first indications of feminist demands, many of which originated within the area of male-dominated social, religious, or political movements.

During the 1970s, researchers characteristically defined women's emancipation movements or feminist movements as the organized efforts of women to achieve legal and political equality.[6] A broader concept of "women's emancipation movement," which was often used synonymously with the term "women's movement," became generally accepted in the 1980s. It stood for the "different historical and contemporary expressions of women's activities, social needs, and efforts in feminism and in policies concerning women."[7] The advantage of this more comprehensive concept is that today's definition of feminism does not obstruct historical perception, limiting our attention to the political demands of women. The disadvantage is that such a broad concept becomes diffuse and includes the entire range of women's organizations irrespective of their goals. Thus conservative and antifeminist women's associations are also included. This conceptual diffuseness reflects the fact that, historically speaking, there was a broad range of transitional areas among collective actions of women and those activities which were aimed at women's emancipation. For example, women who had been involved in benevolent associations could in the long run come to realize that the plight of poor women was caused by discrimination against women under existing civil and matrimonial laws as well as being due to their low levels of education and employment opportunities. This, in turn, could lead to the realization that basic improvements could only be achieved through the fight for women's emancipation. At the same time the organizational experience gained within such associations provided women with political and social skills which could then be effectively applied in seeking women's rights.

If one wisely adheres to a broad definition of the women's movement, then it is necessary also to be more precise and to make certain differentiations, to distinguish among feminist, potential feminist, and nonfeminist movements. The boundaries are often quite fluid. "Feminist" would describe a movement whose members are involved in emancipating women from social subordination and male dominance and who are trying to achieve a change in gender relations in the sense of expanding the leeway for action and the right of self-determination. Potential feminist movements are those in which feminist involvement could germinate and which could lead to feminist awareness.

Recently Karen Offen has vehemently supported the use of the term feminism to describe the women's emancipation movements of the nineteenth century: "What I am proposing here is that 'women's movements' in nineteenth-century Europe include an important subset of feminist and potential feminist movements. I am arguing that these movements, even before the words 'feminism' and 'feminist' go into circulation, but especially after, in the 1880s and 1890s, are integral to the history of feminism— the history, if you will, of challenges to male hegemony and authority."[8] The use of the term feminism makes it easier to distinguish and differentiate within the women's movements. It serves to give contour to a feminist tradition. The natural use of this term can contribute to freeing feminism from the negative connotations given by those who oppose emancipation and the women's movement.[9] The pragmatic advantages offered by this term, however, do not eradicate the problems which are associated with it.

The use of the term "feminist" to describe women's emancipation movements in the nineteenth century is disputed in research for several reasons. There is the risk that feminism will be defined in terms of our current understanding and that feminist action in other historical forms will not be recognized.[10] It is only since the 1890s that the term "feminist," originating in France, gradually came to be used self-descriptively in the women's emancipation movement.[11] As the chapters in this book will show, the term was naturally used in France, Britain, the U.S.A., Hungary, Spain, and Greece where, in fact, it was used by circles within the women's movement which ranged from the radical to the conservative Christian. The term nevertheless did not gain acceptance with many European women's movements. In central, eastern, and northern Europe it was not taken up, or if so, then only hesitantly. For example, in Germany the terms *Frauenrechtlerin* ("suffragette") or *Emanzipierte* ("emancipated woman") were used instead. In contrast to Anglo-American usage, the term "feminist" still carries a somewhat pejorative connotation today in Germany and some countries of eastern and northern Europe. It has the connotation of being "radical" and "antimale," thus giving it a somewhat different contextual meaning than the Anglo-American one.[12]

In this anthology the methodological approaches are reflected in the choice of terminology. Also, the chapters show the nationally different usage of terms which have evolved historically. The procedural approach of using terms in their historical sense has been complicated by the fact that these chapters are all in English. This translation problem extends beyond the matter of how the women's emancipation movements named themselves. The names of newspapers and organizations are also affected. Therefore, wherever it is necessary, the original term will be given along with the English translation.

As is already evident from the titles of the individual chapters, the authors have mostly chosen to use the terms "feminist movement" or "women's movement," depending on their native language and the historical name of the particular movement they are concerned with. In the chapters the terms "women's movement," "women's emancipation movement," and "feminist movement" are often used synonymously. However, they are sometimes also distinguished in order to describe the progression of a movement. Thus, for example, Jane Rendall calls her chapter "British Feminisms, 1860–1900" although she starts with the fact that the British women's movement "for the first time could claim the label 'feminist'"[13] between the turn of the century and World War I. Although Ute Gerhard describes the program of the General German Women's Association as "feminist," she generally uses the term "women's movement," which was preferred by nineteenth-century contemporaries in Germany. Mary Nash talks about the Spanish "women's movement" and simultaneously about the activists as "feminists." At the beginning of her chapter she warns about using a universal definition of feminism as she sees the danger in a perception that there are "'proper' paths to women's emancipation and 'correct' modes in the historical development of feminism." Feminism which did not fit into the pattern was labeled "backward, underdeveloped, or discordant with 'correct' patterns of feminism." Therefore, she says, definitions of feminism must be developed within the context of national and international historiography.[14] In the following we also use these terms synonymously in some cases. As in the chapters of this book, the meaning and definition of the terms used are only clear from their respective contexts.

We have organized the essays in this book according to chronological-spatial criteria. Karen Offen's chapter is the first in the book because she treats the conditions at the beginning of the women's movements in Europe at the turn of the eighteenth to the nineteenth century. The women's emancipation movement was first consolidated in Britain and in western and central Europe. Chronologically, the formation of women's movements radiated in concentric circles from western and central Europe to include northern, eastern, and southern Europe. Following the chronological-spatial pattern in which the movement spread, the chapters have been presented in this geographical order.

In order to attempt a systematic comparison of the situation of women's emancipation movements in Europe up until the First World War, the specialists were given a list of questions upon which they were to base their case studies. The catalog includes (1) dividing the women's emancipation movement into periods based on the social history of the respective countries; the main focus should be on the peak phase of the movement; (2) supporters of the women's emancipation movement including the categories gender, class, religion, region of origin, age, and family status; (3) the demands of the women's movements as well as their strategies in the individual historical phases, taking the self-perception of the movements and the concept of feminism into special consideration; (4) the different trends within the women's emancipation movements during the different phases; (5) the coalition partners; here it is also of interest to see which reform movements the women's movements were associated with, what role the women played within such movements, and what kind of opposition there was; and (6) the interplay between social change and the women's emancipation movements; of special interest here is whether or not there was a particular social development which marked the respective women's emancipation movements and resulted in peculiarly "national" characteristics. This questionnaire provided a structural working basis for the conference, though it became clear at the conference that it was often impossible, given the current state of research, to give a systematic answer on all points. The way in which the authors structured their chapters and placed their emphases was closely related to the different national historiographic traditions in women's research, although the methodological influence of the wide-ranging Anglo-American research on women and gender contributed a common point of reference.

At the conclusion of the chapters on selected women's emancipation movements, the editors offer a synthetic evaluation from a comparative perspective which is broken down into the following main points: history as an argument, division into periods, social supporters, fields of activity and goals, strategies, and women's emancipation movements within the context of social development. This concluding essay can be only a preliminary attempt at synthesis. Along with the chapters making up this anthology, it should provide a synopsis of research up to now on the subject and offer an incentive for more detailed and more intensive comparative examinations.[15] Such a study would need to include more countries and compare specific aspects systematically: demands for legal reforms, educational policies, the suffrage movement, strategies of legitimacy, self-perception, bilateral and international relations of the women's movements, the creation of traditions, and the importance of the nation for the women's movements of Europe.[16]

Our study of selected women's emancipation movements suggests the route for future research. These movements were situated in the context of sociocultural change in the long nineteenth century. Through their varied activities feminists helped to break down traditional hierarchies and promote the emergence of structures appropriate to a civil society. Over the long term, the women's emancipation movements did as much to transform society as such other major movements of the time as the labor movement or the various nationalist movements.

CHAPTER 2

Challenging Male Hegemony: Feminist Criticism and the Context for Women's Movements in the Age of European Revolutions and Counterrevolutions, 1789–1860

KAREN OFFEN

Symphonies customarily begin with overtures, and my task is to provide an overture for what will become a collective scholarly symphony in fourteen movements. We have come together to advance our historical understanding of women's movements of the so-called first wave, by systematic comparison of the (sociopolitical and cultural) conditions for their growth and development in late nineteenth- and early twentieth-century European societies. We propose to analyze their strategies, tactics, personnel, networks, and friendships, and to consider their respective characteristics and the obstacles they faced in specific linguistic, cultural, and national settings, even as we attempt to reach some general conclusions. It seems important at the outset, then, to offer several observations, at once historiographical and methodological, as to how we have arrived at our current understanding of these movements as well as about the vocabularies and conceptual frameworks we use to discuss them.

These remarks will be framed as a meditation on some pioneering English-language contributions to the comparative historiography on women's movements in Europe. The point here is not to generate a hegemonic historiographical narrative, but rather to acknowledge landmarks, raise issues, and pose questions that may guide discussion as we generate a new round of contributions based on a growing body of historical scholarship.

Several key book-length, though perhaps unorthodox, comparative works have contributed to my own understanding of (and approaches to) writing about the women's movements of Europe.[1] The first of these is Richard J. Evans's ambitious work, *The Feminists: Women's Emancipation Movements in Europe, America and Australasia, 1840–1920* (1977).[2] Evans characterized his work as a political history, not a social history, and as "a first attempt at comparative synthesis." Writing in a Weberian mode, Evans offered a "model" or "ideal type" movement against which various national movements could be measured, which he followed with a wide-ranging set of case studies. He equated "feminism" with the campaign for formal legal and political "equal rights," with a heavy emphasis on its adherence to the values of British liberalism and middle-class origins, a kind of combination of Enlightenment rationalism and Protestant individualism, as against Catholicism, authoritarianism, and feudalism.

Evans's study offered a deliberated response and a corrective to prior works that characterized feminism as primarily identifiable with socialism and sexual liberation. He argued that "feminism" (seen specifically as a movement for equal rights) was historically quite distinct from the women's liberation movement of the 1970s. The trajectory he traced for feminist movements in the nineteenth century was a linear narrative of "rise and fall," leading from economic and educational demands in the 1840s, based in "liberal individualism," to moral reform, to the vote, and back to economic claims, with a sequential shift in orientation from individualist claims to claims based on women's "difference" to acknowledgement of sex roles and emphasis on women's moral superiority.[3] According to Evans, radicalization of these claims then led to the campaign for woman suffrage, and ultimately to the self-destruction and demise of the movement in the 1930s.

At the time of its publication, Evans's account marked a major advance in comparative thinking about the history of feminism. Since Evans wrote, however, our scholarship has advanced substantially. We can now see holes in his argument along with flaws in his evidence. For one thing, his comparison was best informed about the British and German movements; his appreciation of developments on the European continent farther to the south and east was entirely inadequate. In particular, his coverage of the French case and its offshoots was derivative and superficial, reflecting the underdevelopment in the mid-1970s of published scholarship on French feminism. Moreover, in assessing Evans's contribution to scholarship on the German women's movement, Ute Gerhard incisively pointed out that he was "caught in a pre-fabricated understanding of politics," what we in the United States would call a "strict constructionist" understanding.[4] Politics, for Evans, was strictly about government, citizenship, and voting. Moreover, his model of "progress," of successive stages, of "rise and fall," now seems incapable of encompassing the complexity of feminist developments, given that they did not spring fully formed from Minerva's brow in the Europe of the 1840s. Despite its flaws, however, Evans's study and its broad survey of sources provided an important springboard for subsequent research, which has extended and drastically revised his portrait.

Three works of the early 1980s provided important correctives to Evans's account, though with little overlap. One of these was *Women, the Family, and Freedom: The Debate in Documents* (1983), in which Susan Groag Bell and I sought to provide a provisional synthetic reinterpretation, with accompanying documentary evidence, of the debate on the so-called woman question in Europe and the United States from 1750 to 1950.[5] This work offered a chronological collage, not a linear narrative. While part of our agenda was to demonstrate to North American readers how debates in the United States were related to what was going on in Europe, and to inform them of the breadth and depth of the European debate and movements,[6] another objective was to demonstrate how and in what specific ways the woman question lay at the heart of major issues in political and intellectual history, understood more broadly. We argued, against Evans, that the woman question was itself "political dynamite," which would transform our understanding of the history of the Western world between 1750 and 1950. We argued, too, that the conditions for the development (or nondevelopment) of women's movements were inextricably related to the context of so-called malestream political and intellectual history, a point to which I will return. *Women, the Family, and Freedom* provided a casebook in how-to-gender-history several years before the gendered approach suggested already in the mid-1970s by Natalie Zemon Davis had been nominated as "a useful category of analysis" by Joan Wallach Scott (and well before Georges Duby and Michelle Perrot argued in the recently published multivolume *Histoire des Femmes* that the history of women should really be written only as the history of gender).[7]

Another significant contribution in the early 1980s was the collection of articles (some of which were written by contributors to this book as well) published by Elizabeth Sarah, "Reassessments of 'First Wave' Feminism," in the British-based *Women's Studies International Forum* (1982).[8] Even as most of the articles focused on organized feminist "movements" of the 1880s–1920s, again informed by a kind of "rise and fall" paradigm, the editor of the collection raised a series of provocative questions about our notions of "movements," and how we might understand women's participation (or lack of participation) in them. Elizabeth Sarah problematized the linear chronology, especially in discussing "movements" beyond the framework of western Europe, and posed important questions about how we might portray feminist resistance more broadly. The articles themselves, singly and collectively, tore apart Evans's "equal rights" paradigm (even as it remained unmentioned) by showing how much more there was to so-called first-wave feminism and how many more issues were addressed than his approach had suggested.

In 1984 (1985 for the London edition) the British historian Jane Rendall published her masterful survey, *The Origins of Modern Feminism*, covering the earlier period, from 1780 to 1860, which Richard Evans had not addressed.[9] Rendall's well-contextualized study (which I discovered quite by accident in 1984 while browsing the women's studies shelves of a bookstore in Cambridge, Massachusetts, just after we had published *Women, the Family, and Freedom*) insisted on the importance of *women's culture*, of women coming together in association, and only *then* recognizing their common interests as women.[10] Her subject included the "women's movement" in its most capacious, "broad constructionist" sense. Certainly her insistence on the importance of the mother-educator model, on claims of equality in difference, based on the complementarity of male and female, and particularly on the importance of developments within a religious and philanthropic context, offered an important corrective preface to Evans's account of the subsequent period. Rendall's approach, which took seriously the work of Carroll Smith-Rosenberg and others who emphasized the importance of investigating women's culture, moved us well beyond exclusive concern with either "equal rights" or with the language of class conflict that had so typified earlier social-history approaches. Her findings complemented those of *Women, the Family, and Freedom*. It was the revelation of this strain of thinking and activism, with its call for women's rights based in foundations in women's culture and in women's relations to men, to family concerns, to the nation, and to society, that gave rise to my label "relational" feminism.[11]

Where our interpretations diverge, however, is in our understanding of "autonomy" as a dominant or primary goal in the works of the time, and in relating this to classical republican notions of citizenship and virtue, or to "natural rights" claims. Indeed, Jane Rendall placed a heavy general emphasis on women's aspirations to "values of self-determination and autonomy."[12] This emphasis, I think, marks *Origins* as a very British book, despite its inclusion of France. Calls for individual autonomy, or what we might also call "Liberty" with a capital L, phrased in a most eloquent but highly abstract manner do not seem altogether surprising in a culture, largely Protestant, whose marriage laws, particularly with reference to property and person, had subordinated wives (if not daughters) more thoroughly, far worse, and for more centuries than was true elsewhere in Europe. I would argue, however, that the cultural choice of abstract individualist arguments—or appeals to universal principles based in natural law—may, more often than not, and depending on local circumstances, have served to veil a still more penetrating critique of male hegemony. Liberty—from what? Freedom—from whom? Such individualist arguments often run in parallel with relational arguments, which involve naming the opponent and spelling out the terms of the conflict; thus an important task for historians of women's movements is to pay careful attention to analyzing the rhetorical mix, the absences and the presences within it, and the historical conditions that produce them. Jane Rendall's more recent work on the first stages of the English women's movement provides an exemplary close reading that can help to sort out such questions.[13]

There are other elements on which our understandings would seem to diverge, based in part on new evidence about the context beyond Britain, located since Jane Rendall published *Origins*. Her astute reconstruction of the role of women's history in the works of the eighteenth-century British and Scottish male historians was an eye-opener for many, and thanks to other scholars (notably Brita Rang, in the Netherlands, and Gianna Pomata, in Italy) we are learning more about its particulars.[14] This is but one aspect of a ballooning literature on the woman question, revealing strong challenges to male hegemony in earlier centuries, that shows up nowadays in studies of French women novelists in the seventeenth and eighteenth centuries,[15] in analyses of eighteenth-century children's literature, and in the new collection of articles, *Going Public: Women and Publishing in Early Modern France*, edited by Elizabeth Goldsmith and Dena Goodman.[16]

Based on these new findings, and on the recovery and republication of many additional primary sources, it is now possible to argue—as I am emboldened to do in my recent book, *European Feminisms, 1700–1950*—that the debate on the woman question was far more broadly and deeply anchored in Enlightenment thought, and indeed implicated in the realm of public opinion (the so-called public sphere) throughout Europe, than we had ever imagined. The debate/critique was by no means restricted to the works of the better-known philosophers we still study in political theory (and who are often articulate antifeminists, like Jean-Jacques Rousseau), but ran to an unprecedented degree through the eighteenth-century periodical and popular press of Europe. I argue that we need to reexamine and reclaim the Enlightenment for feminism.[17]

New evidence strongly suggests that our western European forebears had a thoroughly sophisticated understanding of gender, of the social construction of *genre masculin* and *genre féminin* (terms that are so used in eighteenth-century France, and not in reference only to grammatical constructions). Thus, Simone de Beauvoir's observation in *Le Deuxième Sexe* (1949) that "one is not born, but becomes a woman" would seem in fact to be a commonplace of French thought ever since the Enlightenment. That Anglo-American feminists in the 1970s and 1980s so insisted on the originality of Beauvoir's insight is a gauge of how lost to memory the Enlightenment critique of women's subordination had become. Gender, however, was what, in part, the consuming discussion over "education" and "culture" was about. What is more, writers both in England and in France (from Mary Astell to Olympe de Gouges) regularly utilized the contrast between slavery and freedom not only to speak about black slavery but to characterize the subordinate situation of women in marriage. Jane Rendall has suggested that by the mid-nineteenth century the various feminist movements reflected an "independent ideological force, which transcended national boundaries."[18] Based on recent works such as Constance Jordan's *Renaissance Feminism* (1990) and Londa Schiebinger's *The Mind Has No Sex?* (1989), and the excavation of much new documentation, we can now push these dates back several centuries.[19]

As we examine at close range the cultural context of nineteenth-century women's movements in Europe, what bears watching is how the influence of abundant French and English contributions to this debate during the eighteenth century stimulated discussion throughout other linguistic and national cultures on the Continent as the press developed, and particularly as French replaced Latin as the international language of educated Europeans. This is not to claim that these ideas traveled only in one direction, for there were certainly participants who published in German, Italian, Spanish, Dutch, and Danish, whose ideas had an effect on those writing in English and French. Having said this, however, it is fascinating to observe, for example, the way in which the arguments of the Cartesian ex-cleric François Poullain de la Barre (who coined the expression "the mind/soul has no sex," thereby transposing the Christian doctrine of equality of souls into secular terms) traveled around Europe, finding adapters in various other languages and cultural contexts.[20] It is also eye-opening to learn that the Danish/Norwegian playwright Ludwig Holberg (1684–1754), author of *Zille Hans-Datter's Tract in Defense of the Female Sex* (1722), had spent time in England as a young man and had been significantly influenced by the essays in the *Spectator* and by the social criticism of Daniel Defoe. It is remarkable, too, to read (even in translation) the eloquent response of the Swedish essayist and poet Charlotta Nordenflycht (1718–1763) to Rousseau, in the wake of his debate with Jean Le Rond d'Alembert in the late 1750s. It is intriguing to compare the arguments of the Spanish moralist Josefa Amar y Borbón (1749–1833) on the subject of women's education with those of her contemporaries in England and France, or to remark the apparent appropriation of arguments by the French author Jeanne Le Prince de Beaumont into the Dutch context by the novelist Betje Wolff. It is important to learn that published vindications of the rights of woman did not begin with Mary Wollstonecraft in England, but were stated and restated there throughout the eighteenth century. Only a decade ago those of us in the world of English-language scholarship on feminism knew next to nothing about these writers in other European cultures; the recent internationalization of feminist historical scholarship and our increasing possibilities for comparative analysis are a direct and splendid consequence of the internationalization of our networks.[21] Working together, we should be able to contribute further to the richness and refinement of knowledge about these past cultural interchanges.

One point of strong agreement between Jane Rendall's analysis and my own concerns the extreme importance of the French Revolution and, in particular, the counterrevolutionary backlash that ensued once women were written off or written out of the French Republic in 1793. In *European Feminisms*, I argue even more strongly for the enormous trans-European importance of the French Revolution for the debate over the relations of the sexes. There has been a lot of loose talk about the Revolution and the backlash with respect to its effect on women, but less comprehensive analysis than might be desirable of its content and significance.[22] With regard to the importance of the French Revolution and its aftermath, I want to make five further points:

1) The first point is that the feminist challenge to male hegemony reaches full flower well before industrialization takes place; it is not a consequence of industrial development, nor does it emerge from it, as was long claimed by a plethora of scholars who have studied only the nineteenth century and since. Indeed, the prior development of a critique of women's subordination

informs decisions made about the sexual division of labor, as well as the entire breadwinner controversy, during industrialization, and it shapes the direction the women's movements can take and the issues they address.[23]

2) Second, the notion of "women's sphere," and accordingly "women's culture" itself, became thoroughly and irrevocably politicized during the Revolution. The field of argument over women's subordination, their claims to citizenship and full legal equality, and the expression of differing views about the extent of their "roles" and the character of their prospective contribution to society—in short, a battle over sexual turf—was an open field, a fluid space, during nearly five years, from early 1789 to late 1793. Too often, the emphasis in scholarship has been on the results of 1793, not on the earlier debate. During this five-year period, many more participants engaged the issues of women's citizenship and, in particular, their relation to the family and to the state. In the early years of the Revolution, published petitions and tracts called not only for action to resolve women's grievances with respect to marriage, education, and the erosion of their privileges as guildswomen, but also for the representation of women *by women* in the Estates-General and National Assembly and even for "the abolition of the privileges of the male sex."[24] Revolutionary women established women's clubs and even women's marching and paramilitary groups, all of which were seen by some male critics, both at the time and in retrospect, as extremely dangerous to the extant sociopolitical order. These women made claims to full inclusion in society based on their roles as "citizen mothers" and as providers for their families. They were first shut out in 1791, then again in 1793 and 1795, precisely on the basis of separating "public" from "private" (or domestic). In other words, the act of attempting to confine or relegate women to household pursuits was a deliberate attempt to bind off and fortify a newly acquired male space from women's intrusion, and in some sense to hamstring, thwart, and channel the influence of "women's culture" itself. The language and arguments invoked were philosophical, but the effect was profoundly political. Henceforth, "women's sphere," "domesticity," and "public/private" were irrevocably politicized; as historians we cannot simply decide to get "beyond" these categories, at least not for the purposes of studying this period of history from a feminist perspective. To put it another way, one more familiar to French-language scholars and Foucaultians, women's culture necessarily operated within a "field" of power relations. But one does not need this kind of late twentieth-century terminology to describe what happened in the 1790s. We must not

lose sight of this extreme politicization, as we watch feminists (both women and their male allies) articulating their challenges to male domination and attempting to mobilize against it during the following century.

3) A third point concerns the transmission and reception of ideas. Literate people throughout Europe (many of them multilingual) were following with great interest this revolutionary debate about the sociopolitical relation of the sexes. Condorcet's *Plea for the Citizenship of Women* (1790) was read throughout Europe, as was Mary Wollstonecraft's *Vindication of the Rights of Woman* (1792), along with Talleyrand's *Report on National Education*, to which it was addressed. A *Defense of the Participation of Women in the Government of the Country* (1795) was penned by a certain P. B. von W. and published in Harlingen (The Dutch Republic), following his (the author speaks of "we men") reading of the Declaration of Rights that prefaced the French Republican Constitution of 1793. He argued against man's tyranny over women as evidence of their lust for power: "I do not know from which right we have taken the domination over women upon ourselves, since many a woman has been capable of governing her husband." And, he added, there was no reason why women could not also govern the state. This argument could be traced back to Poullain. A certain "Rosa Califronia (contessa romana)," in a tract published in Assisi (Italy) in 1794, remarked, "Have a look at the deadly theater of France, where the RIGHTS of MAN are extolled with much noise. How many benefits for the masculine sex! What system has ever been established for women and for their rights?" These are but a few of the many participants who challenged the subjection of women in the revolutionary era. We are discovering more all the time.[25] The French Revolution ensured that claims for the emancipation of women would be heard throughout Europe—and, indeed, throughout the world. Women's emancipation was henceforth truly "thinkable"—and hence fearsome.

4) A fourth point concerns the extent and range of the backlash. Fears generated by the Revolution also became the excuse for the articulation of claims that women's subordination was required for the benefit of society, the state, and male tranquility. From the dispassionate reasoning of a Talleyrand in the Legislative Assembly for a purely domestic role for women, in keeping with their new status of exclusion from citizenship in the 1791 Constitution, to the rantings of *Citoyen* Prudhomme against the presidents of the women's clubs in Lyon and Dijon in 1793, and the vituperative declamations of Chaumette and Amar against women in political life later that

year, it was only a step to the violent rhetoric of a Richard Polwhele about "unsex'd females," to Charles James Fox's ingenuous denial that the idea of women voting could even be imagined, or in the 1850s to Wilhelm Heinrich Riehl's *Natural History of the Family*, or Pierre-Joseph Proudhon's mathematical "proof" of women's inferiority to men. It also led to the restatements and more elaborate (and abstract) justifications of women's subordination in the philosophical treatises of Kant, Fichte, and Hegel, and in the sociomedical treatises of Cabanis, Virey, and many other physician-intellectuals. It led to a repudiation of the remarkable civil reform of marriage and property law due to the revolutionary assemblies by the Civil Code of Napoleon (1804), which deliberately inserted the claim that women must obey their husbands in exchange for their protection. It led to debates over whether women should be kept illiterate, so as to keep them in the kitchen.[26] Indeed, the European backlash against women was, by all accounts, fierce. Along with the Napoleonic Code, elements of what had become a virtual war over women's emancipation traveled throughout Europe and even into Russia and Egypt in the backpacks of the Napoleonic armies. The backlash was rendered explicit in the quarantine on the press, on association, even on freedom of speech (the so-called bourgeois liberties) by Metternich's post-1815 system for attempting to contain the French revolutionary virus. "Emancipated" women—from George Sand in Paris to Louise Aston in Berlin— would be specifically singled out for censure. The gendered intent and effects of these modes of repression—including repression of the very memory of earlier protests—need to be better appreciated.[27]

It is insufficient, then, simply to speak as some do about the period only in terms of the problem of the Universal Subject, or Reason, excluding women. Women were by no means excluded at the outset. What must be emphasized is that the challenge to male hegemony over women reached a high pitch during the French Revolution and that the pan-European backlash was exceedingly vicious. Controlling women seemed to become, in the aftermath, a virtually universal preoccupation. In France and England (1803) abortion was outlawed. In France secular laws would forbid women from publishing and from associating, and would even threaten their right to petition. In the USA biblical arguments would be used to curb women from speaking in public, but in France and Spain it even became permissible to denigrate women's writing.[28] In England and elsewhere, it became permissible to attempt to define women out of "production" and to insist on a "family wage" for men.

Medical men in France, England, the Netherlands, and Germany would insist on the importance of women's uteruses for conditioning their entire beings, including their brains.

It was in this highly politicized context that "women's culture" would be redefined and elaborated and would shape the nineteenth-century women's movements. It was in this highly politicized context that the education of women and their access to higher learning, to economic opportunities, and to a role in public (if not specifically "political") life would be articulated. It was in this highly politicized context that prescriptions for "women's mission" would be continually defined and challenged, and that Louise Otto would shape her vision of "the German woman" as against the French. "I believe a day will come," wrote Germaine de Staël in 1800, "when philosophical legislators will give serious attention to the education of women, to the laws protecting them, to the duties which should be imposed on them, to the happiness which can be guaranteed them. . . . If the situation of women in civil society is so imperfect, what we must work for is the improvement of their lot, not the degradation of their minds."[29] She could perhaps hardly imagine how terrified of women—of their sexuality, their fertility, their charm, their influence—the male political leadership of Europe could become. For some, it seemed that women, and especially those of France (long considered the freest in Europe), had to be controlled at any cost.

5) The fifth point concerns comparisons made of women's movements. Traditionally, when British or American scholars have written about the women's movement in France, it has suffered in comparison with those in England and the United States. This was certainly true in the 1970s scholarship of Patrick K. Bidelman, James F. McMillan, and Theodore Zeldin. Even Jane Rendall speaks of "defeat and difficulties in France" following the revolution of 1848.[30] And everyone in the English-speaking world who knows a little of French history is still mystified about why it took so long for women in France to get the vote.[31] Florence Rochefort's contribution to this book addresses the circumstances that conditioned the French women's movement from the perspective of French historiography.[32] But it seems to me that incomprehension of the French problem by earlier Anglo-American scholars has been based, to a very considerable degree, on a gross underestimation of the formal political obstacles placed before women's associational activity in postrevolutionary France, and again following the abortive 1848 revolution. The obstacles imposed in the German-speaking world were perhaps even

greater, as suggested by the Prussian king's 1850 "Decree protecting lawful freedom and order from the abuse of the rights of assembly and association," which was copied elsewhere and in 1854 incorporated into the protocols of the German Confederation.[33] Scholars of the German women's movement, from Amy Hackett to Ute Gerhard, have persisted in pointing this out. Consequently, in the post-1848 continental backlash, everywhere organized efforts turned away from "political" claims as such to a broad range of "social" and "economic" claims: legal reform; educational, economic, and professional opportunities for women; philanthropic activities to assist unfortunate women. The new labeling was deliberate, but it may have misled later scholars about the effective political content of these campaigns.

This brings us to the most recent contribution to the scholarly literature on the comparative history of feminism, the collection *Moving On: New Perspectives on the Women's Movement* (1992), edited by Tayo Andreasen et al.[34] This volume resulted from a 1990 conference organized by Danish scholars in conjunction with a funded "Women's Movement Project." No attempt was made here to establish a linear narrative; instead the contributors to this volume raise important theoretical questions about "*how* to study the Women's Movements." Introducing the collection, the editors pose the question "What is the Women's Movement—What is Feminism?" and they immediately invoke the debate provoked by my article, "Defining Feminism," in *Signs* (1988).[35] They then opt for a large-minded construction of what groups might be regarded as part of the women's movement, including groups that would not usually be considered "feminist," either in (to use my terms) "relational" or in "individualist" feminisms. However, these editors urge us to distinguish between "feminism" (ideology) and "women's movements" (activity), a distinction I think scholars must address.

The term "women's movements" also titles our conference, but our purpose (as expressed in the "Rationale and Goals") presents us with a somewhat more specific agenda. We have been convened to examine organized movements of women (and some men) who seek overtly to challenge and overturn one or more aspects of male hegemony, whether in terms of "women's rights," "women's emancipation," or some other formula. We are also called on to examine initiatives and strategies that occur in other organizational contexts, charitable, religious, professional, educational, which might lead to organized challenges to male hegemony. It looks to me as if we are talking about both the theory and practice of feminism.

We must confront the F word. "Feminism" has been a controversial term since its introduction into European discourse in the 1880s and 1890s. Is it still too dangerous today to define, embrace, and utilize it? If we don't claim it, we leave it to others to use against us.

Contrary to the editors of *Moving On*, and in the interest of Truth in Labeling, I would argue that it seems both useful to historical understanding and politically important to use the term "feminism" to encompass these organizational efforts as well as ideas, and to refer to these women's movements that challenge male hegemony as "feminist movements." One can then identify "feminist movements" as part of a broader grouping of "women's movements" but also as an intrinsic part of political history. Nor would this even be anachronistic. Indeed, the terms *féministe* and *féminisme* were already being used in France in the 1880s by Hubertine Auclert, and they spread throughout Europe and even to the Americas during the 1890s.[36] In the early twentieth century, other movements and their activists often tried to situate themselves with reference to these terms; in German and in the Scandinavian languages, both then and now, there is still resistance to the term "feminism." Even in French, *féministe* would soon be juxtaposed with *féminine*. Important questions remain to be answered about what connotations the words *féminisme* and *féministe* took on when they entered other languages, and about why there is no section in libraries for works on feminism.

While it is historically true that not all women's organizations or associational efforts can be called "feminist" (I think, for instance, of some very large and very conservative religiously affiliated women's groups, or women's auxiliaries such as the Primrose League in England), it is also historically correct to say (as Jane Rendall and I have both argued elsewhere) that feminist analyses and campaigns have frequently emerged in nonfeminist women's associations, just as they have from male-dominated contexts (such as dissident religions) that are not inherently feminist. In fact, until very recently, they almost always did. In my new book, rather than talking about "waves," I refer to these as "eruptions": much in the spirit of volcanic eruptions, given a fissure through which to escape or put under forceful pressure, the magma explodes. Gerda Lerner has written beautifully about such eruptions within the venue of medieval Catholic mysticism; in the North American context, one finds them in temperance, moral-reform, and antislavery societies, which very quickly spawned women's rights organizations. On the European continent such fissures open in the 1830s and 40s in Saint-

Simonism, in German Catholicism, and in Jewish reform efforts. By the late nineteenth century they emerge within Roman Catholicism as well as the organized workers' movement.

Both in *Moving On* and in our conference "Rationale and Goals," "Defining Feminism: A Comparative Historical Approach" is invoked.[37] In both I find some misunderstandings of my argument that need to be addressed. In the first place, "Defining Feminism" addresses the issue of *arguments* in our understanding of feminism far more than it does the issue of *movements*, although it was clearly the categorization of movements that prompted me to look more systematically at the arguments. The arguments often translate into, or provide the impulse behind, the accompanying organizational efforts—or attempt to rationalize or explain the objectives of organizational efforts—but they are not the same thing. At the same time, they are inseparable.

Second, I also tried to make it clear that I was not talking at the level of differing (and often conflicting) organizational strategies and tactics, but that I was attempting to locate feminism more generally at the level of overall sociopolitical goals, i.e., challenging and attempting to end male domination and women's subordination. My arguments were addressing questions pertinent to the history of ideas here, and to political history, broadly construed, though they are absolutely pertinent to the concerns of an all-encompassing "social history" as well. Perhaps the real point to be made is that writing the comparative history of feminism forces us to dissolve—or see through—those arbitrary barriers between political and social history, just as it obliterates the once-hallowed distinctions between "political" feminism (the campaign for the vote) and "social" feminism (all the rest of the issues), and to peer through the once-hallowed distinction between the notions of political and social altogether. We have to see these as parts of a whole: I prefer using the term "sociopolitical" to make this point.

The collection *Moving On* takes up issues concerning the public/private dichotomy and makes a strong case for looking more closely at women's culture, and especially women's everyday networks and communities. The inspiration here comes from questions that have arisen in the most recent ("second wave" and "third wave") women's movements. This is all very fine. But it seems to me that these questions continue to mute, if not to obscure, the historically important contexts in which earlier women's movements were born, including the most recent "wave." It is important to insist that since

1800, "women's culture" in European settings did not exist outside the bounds of politics, beyond the postrevolutionary politicization and European backlash of which I spoke earlier, however much antifeminist men (the Prudhommes and Proudhons) and the thoroughly antifeminist Mrs. Sarah Stickney Ellis might wish to insulate the domestic sphere. The "haven in a heartless world" was even then a deliberately created mirage. In addition, even as we focus on women's culture, as the culture surrounding women's movements, we need to acknowledge that there were many important *male* advocates of women's emancipation in virtually every European nation. Contrary to the claims of some recent authors, feminism is not an exclusively female challenge, nor has it ever been.[38]

Jane Rendall's essay in *Moving On* posed questions about how historians have responded to the problem of dichotomization of public/private, with respect to analyzing the nineteenth-century separation of spheres. She remarked four possible approaches: (1) the recovery and revaluation of the "private" world of women; (2) the move to insistence on the connection of public/private worlds;[39] (3) challenging binary oppositions as such; and (4) reinstating the public/private dichotomy, but along the lines of a Habermassian understanding of the "public" as a space for the formation of public opinion outside of governmental structures. Rendall then evaluated the importance of the public/private dichotomy for the history of feminism before the twentieth century.

Here several observations about vocabulary and conceptual frameworks may be useful. First, an aspect of the public/private problem that remains unmentioned by Jane Rendall or, to my knowledge, by any other contributors to the scholarly literature since Rosaldo and Lamphere first raised the point, is the important distinction made in Roman law between public and private. This *legal* distinction (which undoubtedly informs the Rousseauean distinction) was repeatedly invoked in France during the debates over women's role and place from the sixteenth century (notably by the political theorist Jean Bodin) through the French Revolution and well into the period we are considering; it was a living force throughout Europe. As historians we need to pay more attention to its force and, indeed, to the multiple connotations of "public" and "private." "Public" in this legal sense is not the same thing as "public" in the Habermassian sense (*Öffentlichkeit* in German, which has translated into French as *espace public* and into English, misleadingly, I think, as the "public sphere"). It is important to insist, too, that in earlier times the term "public" may not refer to the space of "production," nor is it interchangeable with the term "political"; this latter confusion mars the interpretation of Joan B. Landes, who has been severely called to order by U.S.-based historians of eighteenth-century France.[40] Nor does qualifying the term "public sphere" with the terms "bourgeois" or "liberal" contribute to clarifying the situation—at least not in the English language. Indeed, even the terms "republic" and "democracy" do not always carry the same meanings in languages other than English, nor do English-speakers use them in the same way. In early nineteenth-century Europe, republicanism was still a highly contested oppositional political current, and democracy, either political or social, existed nowhere. Only in 1848 did the brief French Second Republic establish universal *manhood* suffrage, a suffrage that quickly delivered the government of France over to a new authoritarian plebiscitary monarchy; even with the establishment of a parliamentary Third Republic in the 1870s, the French (and the Swiss) stood alone in a monarchical, authoritarian, and elitist Europe. Even the British, as Jane Rendall points out (*Suffrage and Beyond*), were not thinking in terms of democracy during the 1860s campaign for woman suffrage.[41]

A second point of clarification ensues, concerning the "equality vs. difference" conundrum that has so haunted feminist politics in recent times. Both in the introduction to *Moving On* and particularly in Rendall's contribution, I find some confusion with respect to the relationship between the dichotomy of equality and difference, on the one hand, and my own effort to name "individualist" and "relational" strains of feminist argument, on the other. Let me insist, lest anyone be further misled, that the two labels I chose should not be seen as coterminous or interchangeable with the terms "equality" and "difference"; indeed, my effort to find new terminology was born of frustration with what has been clearly identified as a false dichotomy, though it did not originate there but rather with the highly problematic distinction made in earlier scholarship (particularly in the United States) between political and social feminism.[42] Everybody nowadays seems to agree that there are two identifiable currents; efforts to distinguish them have created a new menu of vocabulary choices: "maternalism" and "womanism" are among the newest and most evocative contenders. I would consider maternalism and womanism particular expressions of a more general relational feminism.

The problem with the equality/difference distinction for historians is that in nineteenth-century Europe, and before, it is utterly meaningless. Indeed, one finds numerous examples of arguments for the most absolute equality of the sexes—political, legal, educational, economic—accompanied by great respect for the difference between the sexes and sometimes even a very positive celebration of womanly attributes. On the basis of this difference, women are arguing for full inclusion in society. There is no "contradiction," to use the fashionable term. They want equal rights, to be sure, but equal rights as women; "women's rights." The contemporaneous term "equality in difference" captures the complexity and nuance of this approach; my term "relational" underscores what is sociologically interesting about it. Sandra Stanley Holton, Eleni Varikas, Ann Taylor Allen, Anne Cova, Laurence Klejman and Florence Rochefort, Kari Melby, and many other scholars, working on various European cultures, are reviving evidence that supports my contention that relational arguments and approaches were dominant in the rhetoric and thinking of the later nineteenth century.[43] There may be a linguistic problem here: in English we have the concepts of equality and equity. In German, the term *Gleichheit* appears to mean both equality and sameness.

This is not to claim that individualistic arguments or universalist claims—human rights, for example, or claims for independence, for women's autonomy as individuals, as souls, as minds, irrespective of the societal implications of their sexed bodies—were not used in Europe; of course they were, particularly in the 1850s and 1860s, as the battle to end slavery in North America entered its climax and Russia emancipated its serfs. The important question is how they were used and what they meant in particular contexts. At what points, in which locations, and under what specific circumstances, for example, could one effectively invoke natural law or human rights on women's behalf? On what philosophical, religious, anatomical, and sociological convictions or assumptions do the concepts of autonomy and human rights hang? On what convictions—and fears—about sociopolitical order do relational arguments rest? Jane Rendall has convincingly demonstrated that even the highly individualistic rights arguments of the first generation of British suffrage advocates were framed within a firm commitment to altruism and duty; they exhibit a virtual allergy to selfishness and self-interest; they emphasize not right but duty.[44] Such arguments can be identified in France and Italy as well, and they are especially connected to a sort of Mazzinian discourse about rights, duties, patriotism, and nation. How different these arguments are from what we in the late twentieth century—or even French critics in the late nineteenth century—would associate with "individualism." What contexts provoke different argumentative mixes?

Kari Melby poses a different question. She suggests provocatively that the arguments used may not always be completely transparent or open with reference to the goals and interests of the speakers.[45] This suggestion, of course, raises some very interesting questions for our consideration: what is going on strategically when feminists use various types of arguments virtually in the same breath? How calculated are they? How transparent? Why are relational arguments (such as motherhood arguments) utilized almost exclusively in certain situations? In what cultural and political contexts can individualist arguments be introduced and made effective? What cultural and political work do they do? In particular, why do individualist arguments seem to show up so much more emphatically in the Anglo-American context? Do they function differently there than in the Russian context of the 1860s, where Bianka Pietrow-Ennker also argues for their predominance? Do they really have something to do with expressions of Protestant individualism, or with a deep moralism or ethical objective, as some would claim? Or is it rather that we used to see only these arguments because, in our own contexts, we found them more appealing (or perceived them as less "dangerous") than the relational ones that emphasize women's distinctiveness and insist on their sociopolitical contributions as mothers? How do we evaluate situations where both types of arguments are employed, but in differing proportions? How do we achieve a full reading of what is being said? How do we evaluate the rhetoric with respect to the actions? As historians, we must be alert to the problems posed by superimposing presentist rhetoric and concerns on historical materials. Too many misunderstandings have resulted— and still result—when scholars talk past each other, or use slippery or politically loaded concepts.

There are many other issues to discuss. How, for instance, should we understand the relationship of women's movements, or "feminist" movements, to nation-building efforts in a nineteenth-century continental European context? Surely, in Italy and in Germany, or among the linguistic minority groups of the Austro-Hungarian Dual Monarchy (Czechs, Hungarians, Ukrainians), the Russian Empire (the Poles, Ukrainians, Finns), or the Ottoman Empire (for example, the Greeks) we find variations on a theme as well as family resemblances.[46] Certain issues are not discussable, while others are; duties are almost always linked to rights. Some strategies that are commonplace in western Europe might be considered impossible farther to the east. What difference does it make, for instance, to be caught in the backwash of your neighbor's revolution when you have not had one of your own? What is the sociopolitical significance for women in linguistic minority cultures of the fact that children learn their mother tongue from their mothers? What happens to feminist impulses and organizational efforts in a repressive sociopolitical climate interrupted only by sporadic impulses toward liberalization? Where do the fault lines in the sociopolitical order open up, and when, and why? How do we map the fissures through which the magma of feminist claims will flow?

What I am proposing here is that women's movements in nineteenth-century Europe include an important subset of feminist and potential feminist movements. I am arguing that these movements, even before the words "feminism" and "feminist" go into circulation, but especially after, in the 1880s and 1890s, are integral to the history of feminism—the history, if you will, of challenges to male hegemony and authority. This history was severely resisted by the academy when it could no longer be suppressed or ignored. I propose that we reclaim it as an integral part of the history of European societies and that we do far more to make it known to succeeding generations.

To recapitulate, the history of women's movements—of feminist activism—in later nineteenth-century Europe cannot be understood without grasping the extreme importance (supported by much new evidence and scholarship) of the critique of women's subordination elaborated and spread throughout Europe by print culture and published debate during the Enlightenment. Nor can it be understood without knowledge of gender politics in the French Revolution and its pan-European counterrevolutionary aftermath, which included attempts at repeat revolutions and severe repression. Not only was women's overtly political activity deliberately repressed, but repeated attempts were made by fearful political leaders (male) to exclude women from political authority, to recontain and control them, and to bolster male authority in the family and the state against women's influence and against their claims to participate fully in society. What is more, historical memory of these debates and developments was increasingly excluded from historical accounts as the professional historical establishment itself developed within the universities.[47]

When Sigmund Freud posed the question "What do women want?" to Marie Bonaparte, he revealed how little he knew about the history of European feminism, about prior challenges to male hegemony. He was not alone. The historical evidence now available to us over the *longue durée* suggests that efforts to redress the balance of power between the sexes lie at the heart of the political and intellectual as well as the social, cultural, economic, and religious history of Europe. Women have aspired, like men, to be self-determining persons, not subject to a series of constraints, disabilities, or handicaps imposed on them as a sex by male-dominated authorities. But they have also aspired to accomplish this in ways that are woman-identified.

European societies are doubtless no more intrinsically sexist than those of other continents, but because of the early advent of print culture—to our everlasting benefit—they have left us an amazingly extensive published record of feminist contestation and agitation. This record, which has lain buried for too long, feminist historians are now uncovering, reconstructing, recuperating, and analyzing. We are all parties to that process of recovery and reappropriation. We must insist on its importance for understanding the patterns and phases of construction and contestation of male hegemonies over time. Moreover, we must do everything in our power to transmit its memory to future generations, to our daughters and granddaughters—and to our sons and grandsons. Women can't afford to begin again from Year Zero or from Square One.

PART II

Western and Central Europe

CHAPTER 3

Recovering Lost Political Cultures: British Feminisms, 1860–1900

JANE RENDALL

In 1894 Charlotte Carmichael Stopes began her historical work, *British Free-women. Their Historical Privileges*, with a chapter entitled "Ancient History and British Women." Citing Plutarch, Caesar, and Tacitus, she traced "the spirit of British womanhood" from its beginnings in the struggles of the empress Boadicea against the Romans to its conclusion in the admission of women into British universities.[1] The book was first published in shortened form as a pamphlet for the use of women's suffrage societies. Two years later, in 1896, Lina Eckenstein, drawing upon the histories of sexual politics studied in the Men and Women's Club of London in the 1880s, published her *Woman under Monasticism*, a "historical defence of celibacy and women's community."[2] In 1928 Ray Strachey, historian and participant in the first women's movement, began her fine history, *The Cause*, by arguing "we must not examine the position of women among savage peoples, nor in ancient civilisations; we must ignore the Middle Ages." Her view was clear. The impulse to "a genuine female revolt" came from "the doctrines and philosophies which inspired the French Revolution, and . . . received a further impulse from the economic changes of the Industrial Revolution." That is, "the real date for the beginning of the movement is 1792."[3]

In her excellent comparative article on the World Anti-Slavery Convention of 1840, which was held in London, Kathryn Sklar contrasted the conservatism of British women in the antislavery movement with the greater radicalism of American women activists, and called for a much closer analysis of women's political cultures and the larger settings of which they were a part.[4] It is a call which reflects the recent importance of broader historical concern with cultural history; and it also reflects the problems that may arise with too exclusive a focus on "women's culture" itself. The histories I cited, of Stopes in 1894, Eckenstein in 1896, and Strachey in 1928, illustrate the diversity of the ways in which each woman reconstructed her own history and her cultural and political traditions.[5] In this essay I follow Sklar in using the notion of women's political culture to look at the history of British feminisms, mainly but not entirely in the second half of the nineteenth century. Here I stress the national particularities of the British movement.

It is possible to identify three major phases in first-wave British feminism. The first lay in the developments in the political activity of women in different classes in Britain from the 1790s to the 1850s, including the work of individual women writers like Mary Wollstonecraft, Anna Wheeler, and Harriet Martineau. This first phase also included the involvement of women in utopian socialist movements and in the politics of male radicalism in the 1830s and 1840s. The second phase was that of the small and initially mainly middle-class campaigning organizations which grew up around the issues of legal and educational reform, employment for women, and the suffrage, from the mid-1850s to around 1900. In the final phase, a much larger and better-studied movement, which for the first time could claim the label "feminist," employed a far greater variety of strategies and of cultural politics on a number of fronts, but most dramatically in the suffrage campaign. A limited women's suffrage was won in 1918, and full adult suffrage in 1928.

In this essay my focus is on the middle phase, from the first appearance of an organized women's movement in Britain in the mid-1850s. Important initiatives in this phase included campaigns for reform of the marriage laws and the founding of the *English Woman's Journal.* From these initiatives came a wide range of informal groups and associations, campaigning on different fronts for improved education, more employment opportunities, moral reform, and women's full citizenship. So too came a number of feminist periodicals, speaking to different concerns of the movement. Organization entered a new phase in the 1860s with two new associations: first, the London Society for Women's Suffrage, founded in 1866, rapidly followed in a few months by the Manchester Society; and, secondly, the Ladies National Association for the Repeal of the Contagious Diseases Acts, established in 1869 by Josephine Butler to campaign against the regulation of prostitution in garrison towns. In 1869 women were granted the municipal franchise in England and Wales.[6] In 1866 the first English woman doctor, Elizabeth Garrett Anderson, was qualified and admitted to the medical register, and in 1869 the first women students to study at the University of Cambridge were admitted to the college founded by Emily Davies. In 1874 the Women's Protective and Provident League was founded to encourage women's trade unionism, and in 1883 the Women's Co-operative Guild was established with the specific aim of campaigning to improve the condition of women, appealing especially to married working-class women.

By the 1880s both political parties, Conservative and Liberal, had incorporated women's organizing abilities, from the early 1880s in local Women's Liberal Associations, and from 1884 in the admission of women to the mixed Conservative Primrose League. Both were split over women's suffrage. In the last two decades of the century new challenges emerged to a mainly middle-class movement. These challenges came from socialism and an emerging labor movement, and from new approaches to sexual politics. By 1897, the numerous splits among those working for women's suffrage were reconciled in the National Union of Women's Suffrage Societies; but, in spite of an environment that was considerably changed, by 1900 the political climate did not look promising for the granting of the parliamentary franchise to women.[7]

Three recent general interpretations of nineteenth-century British feminism have a biographical focus. Olive Banks's *Becoming a Feminist* in 1986 used the material she collected for her *Biographical Dictionary of British Feminists for 1800–1930*, on 98 women and 18 men, considered in four generational cohorts, to analyze the social and ideological origins of first-wave feminism.[8] Her major conclusion lay in the change over time that she found, in the shift away from the predominantly liberal outlook of the women in her first cohorts, towards the increasing inspiration of socialism and increasing proportion of working-class feminists; even so, however, working-class feminists in her Cohort IV, born between 1872 and 1891, were still only 23% of that cohort. Her analysis of 18 men in the women's movement remains one of the very few discussions of this subject. She found more male sympathizers in the earlier cohorts, with over half freethinkers and committed liberals. Banks's analysis was pioneering, though it could be argued that the selectivity of her small sample, covering a long period, meant that it would easily be overtaken by new research and more extensive biographical studies.

In 1990 Philippa Levine's *Feminist Lives in Victorian England* examined 194 nineteenth-century feminist activists, reconstructing their lives and networks, of family, friendship, religion, and politics.[9] She resisted interpretations cast in terms of masculine politics, of liberalism, and socialism. Late nineteenth-century English feminism was not, she argued, "a slightly charred phoenix rising from the still-burning ashes of individualism," a legacy of liberalism, the leftover business of 1789.[10] She stressed rather the strength of a feminist analysis rooted in a politics which challenged the rhetoric of separate public and private worlds, just as it challenged the different sites of male power. Her analysis of campaigns focusing on issues of sexuality and morality, against state regulation of prostitution, led her to agree with Judith Walkowitz in identifying the prostitute as the "paradigm for the female condition," as the "symbol of woman's powerlessness and sexual victimization."[11] Levine also stressed how far women's status in marriage was a central concern of the women's suffrage movement, reiterating that its meshing of public and private concerns demonstrated how far these women "recognised the primacy of gender as the motor of oppression." Levine, in her own words, sought "to examine the question of feminist agency."[12]

Barbara Caine's *Victorian Feminists* (1992) is also a biographical work, though one which explores the nature of Victorian feminism through the lives and work of just four prominent leaders, Emily Davies, Frances Power Cobbe, Josephine Butler, and Millicent Garrett Fawcett.[13] Caine engaged with Ray Strachey's interpretation of the history of the women's movement, and with the complex relationship between feminism and the liberal legacy of the Enlightenment. She stressed the significance of that inheritance—seen in the importance of John Stuart Mill to Victorian feminism, as in the impact of economic individualism—and wrote of its inability to confront the sexual basis of women's oppression. The limits of liberalism might rather be transcended through an exploration of Victorian domestic ideology itself, as the moral qualities of womanhood were projected beyond the domestic sphere into the political world. In addition, she located her four subjects within their rich cultural and, especially, their religious and literary contexts, illustrating very clearly the complexity of their lives and choices, and the significant differences among the four. In national political terms, for instance, Davies and Cobbe would call themselves Conservatives, Butler and Fawcett Liberals. All shared a common belief in the sexual differences between men and women, though Fawcett and Davies thought such differences greatly exaggerated. Within Caine's work, the choices between equality and difference, individualism and relationalism, remain of considerable importance.[14]

Each of these works has enhanced our knowledge of the nineteenth-century women's movement, its ideologies, networks, leaders, and activists, and I draw on them extensively for what follows. Yet I am not sure that any of them quite equips us for the kind of comparisons for which Sklar called. The problem seems to be, as Sklar puts it, that "it is not enough simply to look at women's motivations or institutions; we must also investigate how the male-dominated political environment encouraged or discouraged women's participation."[15] Such an investigation could allow us, while using these analyses, also to ask broader historical questions about the social, political, and intellectual developments which have fostered women's movements both nationally and internationally, and to trace more specifically what Alice Kessler-Harris calls the "intersecting circles" of loyalty and identity, which may cut across the politics of gender.[16] To study such intersections is not to exclude the possibility of female agency, but to identify its sites and its limits, to enhance our knowledge of the choices that could be made. I follow Janaki Nair's conclusion that our task is to understand "the complex ways in which women are, and have been, subjected to systematic subordination within a framework that simultaneously acknowledges new political possibilities for women, drawing on traditions of dissent or resistance while infusing them with new meanings."[17]

First I want to examine the different meanings attributed to citizenship in nineteenth-century Britain, meanings which could shift with the changing role of the state. Then I want to look at the sources of radical and dissenting identities, conventionally identified as the recruiting grounds of feminist activism. Finally, I consider alternative languages of collective identity and experience which might cut across the politics of gender and feminist analysis.

The mid-Victorian British state was, ostensibly, the product of a long series of reforms, though not, since the seventeenth century, of revolution or of transformative change. It was a state, as it still is, without a written constitution. It incorporated four very different strands of national identity and culture—from Scotland, Ireland, England, and Wales—into what has been interestingly called an "Anglo-British" whole, implying the English dominance of the polity.[18] The appearance of a reforming state could mask what was still the dominance at parliamentary levels of members of the landed classes. The period which saw the growth of a women's movement, from the 1860s to the First World War, was one of apparent change and the expansion of the male political nation, with new party organizations and, by the end of the century, the appearance of a political party based on labor. But such change was still limited. Roughly from the late 1860s to 1918, around 60% of adult men could vote in British parliamentary elections. Until 1918 the franchise still retained its historic basis in a property-based and residential qualification, and one authority has judged it to be by 1914 among the most limited in Europe.[19] However, from the early nineteenth century the piecemeal growth of institutions of local government in the great cities and larger towns of Britain had allowed the emergence of what José Harris has called "a very dynamic local and provincial culture, headed by an ambitious, dedicated, and sometimes highly intellectual urban middle class" coming to counterbalance national aristocratic and landed strength.[20]

The relationship between state and society was changing in the period which saw the emergence of a feminist movement. In the 1860s a division between state and civil society, between the public tasks of government and the private worlds of family, work, religion, and property, was still rhetorically accepted. While the role of government was never as minimal as some contemporaries suggested, it could still seem very limited to European observers. Slowly, in the later nineteenth century, piecemeal expansion in social policies and social responsibilities began to transform the role of that state, both locally and centrally. New responsibilities, for education and poor relief, for shaping the housing, the public health, and the environment of industrial cities were introduced and monitored by central government, enthusiastically administered by the more radical elements within local elites. Such policies gave Britain at the end of the nineteenth century the appearance of a more socially and collectively oriented society. At the same time, in the second half of the nineteenth century, British governments continued to consolidate, extend, and justify the British Empire, fighting continuous colonial wars, as well as maintaining informal economic dominance in many areas of the world. Though Britain lost industrial leadership in this period, she remained the dominant western trading nation. Harris points to the everyday implications of the nature of the state for British women and men: "Imperial visions injected a powerful strain of hierarchy, militarism, 'frontier mentality,' administrative rationality, and masculine civic virtue into British political culture."[21]

What models of citizenship then, in such a society, would appeal to and could be transformed by women claiming a share in the polity? Here I look primarily at three such models. In the 1860s, the oldest but still common view was of the vote not as natural right but as historic privilege, with its roots in an ancient, possibly Anglo-Saxon constitution. Such a privilege was historically based on the property of the head of household, the independent man. In the important debates about electoral reform in the 1860s, liberals and radicals put the case for the property qualifications to be lowered, and for that privilege to be earned in other ways, by, for instance, a recognition of men's property in their skills. Politicians sought in the 1860s to enfranchise the skilled respectable workman on this basis. Male working-class leaders made a case for the vote for the breadwinner of the household. Such constructions, based in property and in work, might seem to exclude the possibility of married women, who could own no property of their own, from claiming the vote. In language and raising issues that continued to resound throughout the nineteenth century, suffragists like Lydia Becker argued that, if women were entitled to have the vote on the same terms as men, they could qualify on two grounds: first, historic precedents for the political rights of propertied women stretching back to the early Middle Ages; and second, the respectability, moral character, and independence of women heads of household. Such arguments were strengthened and continued to be developed as women were given the local vote.[22]

Second, the impact of the ideas of the liberal John Stuart Mill on the women's suffrage movement was resounding, if ambivalent. Here I want to look at the ways in which he envisaged citizenship. In his *On Liberty* (1859), as in the *Subjection of Women* (1869), his goal was self-development, the highest cultivation of individual faculties, in all their variety and diversity, though such a goal was not for all and might exclude the uneducated, the pauper. Self-development rested on the freedom of the citizen—for only the citizen could experience the invigorating effect of freedom upon the character to the full.[23] Public duties offered enlarged horizons, social responsibilities, practical disciplines. There is in this kind of formulation not simply an egoistic individualism. Mill sought to encourage the fostering of individual character—and moral character was a very important concept to the educated classes of late nineteenth-century Britain—through civic virtue, even altruism. To Barbara Bodichon, the strongest argument for giving women votes was the influence that enfranchisement would have in increasing patriotism and a public spirit, "an unselfish devotedness to the public service." Such a view of citizenship offered more to feminists than did history-, property-, or labor-based claims: it did not necessarily exclude married women, nor was it incompatible with the sexual division of labor. Louisa Shore wrote of the angelic image of Victorian women that she "longed to take off these golden chains, open the hothouse doors, and turn the ethereal prisoner in to the free fresh air, to develop her moral and intellectual muscle."[24] It was the higher responsibilities of citizenship which were to provide this form of muscular character training. Such a view was to be reworked by different elements within the women's suffrage movement. The inculcation of individual moral character also defined the national character. Feminists could cast themselves as guardians of that national character, even of the nation's imperial responsibilities, justifying their claims in the face of a resistance often fuelled by a militarist imperialism.

By the 1880s, Sandra Holton has suggested, a further, third, conception of citizenship had gained ground among groups to the left of Mill, normally called the Radical-Liberals. This conception stressed work—both productive and reproductive—as the foundation of citizenship.[25] Such a view was at the heart of the work of the breakaway Women's Franchise League formed in 1889, influenced by the Americans Elizabeth Cady Stanton and Harriet Stanton Blatch. It was a view shared with a developing labor movement, committed to a socialism which rested upon the ideal of a cooperative commonwealth rather than upon class conflict. That vision might—though did not necessarily—unite socialism and feminism, as in Isabella Ford's pamphlet *Woman and Socialism* of 1904, which argued for both as the forces "making for the reconstruction and regeneration of society." She believed that middle-class women would use the vote to help the cause of women workers and bring about social reform, and that women workers needed the vote so that they could participate in the struggle for socialism.[26] From different directions, by the turn of the nineteenth century, it was possible for feminists in formulating their claim for recognition to turn towards the state as an agent of social change, although they remained hesitant and divided about mobilizing the forces of state intervention.[27]

I want now to examine how far feminists found the sources of their dissent within the oppositional frameworks of nineteenth-century Britain: particularly those of class, politics, religion, and nationality. Philippa Levine's careful analysis of the occupational background of her 194 female activists confirmed the middle-class preponderance, with 14% of the fathers of her sample in business of some kind, followed by 8% in the church and the law respectively, and 4% the daughters of military or naval personnel. A significant minority also came from landowning families.[28] Yet it is clearly not sufficient simply to identify feminist backgrounds as middle-class, especially given the problems in ascribing class status to women. It would, I think, be uncontroversial to suggest that one place to look for leaders would be just that "ambitious, dedicated, and sometimes highly intellectual urban middle class" of which José Harris has written, whose politics were very different from, and often defined against, the landed parliamentary elites. Dynasties of radical reforming families within major British cities—the Brights and Cadburys in Birmingham, the Wilsons in Sheffield, the Rathbones in Liverpool, the Peases in Darlington—were radical reformers across a wide front of issues. These might include women's issues both nationally and locally, as well as others such as the extension of the male franchise, temperance, and the enhancing of the civic goals of their city.[29] What we lack, unfortunately, are the local studies which might enable us to place activists within the women's movement in relation to such a culture. One recent thesis, on reforming and rescue movements in Birmingham, has spoken of the "female civic gospel" of the women activists of Birmingham, of women like Elizabeth Cadbury.[30] Such families were drawn from the upper levels of the urban elites, already by the 1850s upper-middle-class, often enjoying a gentrified lifestyle yet retaining a questioning view of the established political order and a profound social commitment. These groups provided important leadership and political strength.

Other women came from families of professional occupation, like the generations of the Davenport Hills of Bristol, who practiced law. Or they were academics and intellectuals, like those who participated in the Men and Women's Club. Or they were the daughters of Anglican clergy, like Emily Davies and Emily Faithfull. Their loyalties were sometimes of the same local kind, and sometimes they developed a metropolitan, even bohemian focus. They were joined by a small number from landed and even aristocratic backgrounds. Kate Amberley, an active women's suffrage campaigner in the late 1860s and early 1870s, had married into one of the greatest aristocratic families, the Dukes of Bedford, and found herself humiliated at the dining table of Downing St. for her feminist politics.[31] A generation later, Lady Frances Balfour, daughter of the Duke of Argyll, became active in different women's causes in the 1880s and noted in her autobiography that "no one in my social class had the least feeling for, or wish to know more about these unwomanly women."[32]

The groups identified so far have been upper- or middle-class. It remains extremely difficult to reconstruct the participation of lower-middle-class women, who had, for instance, participated in Chartist and Owenite movements and who barely make an appearance in Levine's 194.[33] What is interesting here is the comparison with the politics of male radicalism, to which the claims of the lower middle class and upper working class, the skilled workers, the heads of household, the respectable, were central. In Britain much debate has focused on what has been called by Dorothy Thompson, in a classic article, the withdrawal of working-class women from political activity from the mid-1840s.[34]

That withdrawal has continued to be identified with the shift of the location of male radical politics into the workplace and with the emergence of a leadership identified with skilled trade unionism. There were exceptions, like Emma Paterson, the founder of the Women's Protective and Provident League, the teacher's daughter who married a cabinetmaker. Within the upper working class as within the middle class, from the 1860s to the 1880s the dominant political current remained Radical-Liberal rather than socialist, appealing to nonconformist religion and "respectable" trade unionism. Though we still need to know much more about this period, women from the lower, middle, and upper working classes seem to have had little access to the meeting places, the networks, even the journals of this popular radicalism. It was an environment, a political culture, from which they appear to have been discouraged. One who tried to identify with it was a shoemaker's daughter, Mary Smith, first a servant, then governess and journalist, who founded a women's suffrage society in Carlisle in 1868 and left an autobiography and poetry.[35] She included in her *Progress, and other Poems* (1873) one called "Gladstone's Axe" and another called "Oliver Cromwell": both refer to significant figures in the pantheon of popular radicalism. "Gladstone's Axe," for instance, calls on the politician William Gladstone to cut down "dead unfruitful privilege" and "Overreaching Tyranny."[36] Yet Smith's life, revealing her exclusion from any formal political activity, suggests the difficulties of incorporating women's politics within more popular radical activities, as opposed to elite liberalism.

In the last twenty years of the nineteenth century, different, socialist voices were clearly to be heard (though it is important to understand how far socialist arguments in Britain drew upon radical and religious currents of opinion—national trade union organizations for women, like the Women's Trade Union League, tended to owe their foundation to the commitment and semi-philanthropic interest of middle-class women). But by the 1880s the emergence of stronger trade union organization, particularly in the textile industries, and of new socialist political groups allowed different voices to be heard.

They could be the voices of those Lancashire working women described by Jill Liddington and Jill Norris, like Helen Silcock, Selina Cooper, Sarah Reddish, and many others, who after activism in the textile unions became campaigning suffragists.[37] Their socialism, incorporating a dream of a new life, could encompass the language of religious conversion as well as that of class difference. Active women who united their feminism and socialism might, as did Isabella Ford of Leeds, also come from a Radical-Liberal background. By the 1890s the new Independent Labour Party, drawing upon a local socialist culture, provided a forum, and by no means the only one, within which socialist and feminist aspirations could come together. The party mingled millworkers with white-blouse schoolteachers and clerical workers, with leading figures like Isabella Ford and the educator Margaret McMillan, with Richard Pankhurst, active in the cause of women's suffrage since 1866, and with Emmeline Pankhurst, later founder of the Women's Social and Political Union. But within the Independent Labour Party also, the priority to be given to women's, as opposed to adult suffrage, was already questionable, as was the attitude of the party's policymakers to the family wage. A recent study has also suggested how a socialist group like the Social Democratic Federation, founded in 1884 and more closely linked to the politics of the Second International, equivocated on the "woman question," identifying feminism as a "bourgeois fad." The achievements of Clara Zetkin, whose speeches were reported in the paper *Justice* by Eleanor Marx, and of the women's sections of the German Social Democratic Party, were widely admired in this group. Nevertheless there was some marginal space for the exploration of women's issues: questions about work, the suffrage, and marriage. There was also space for women's activism through the organization of Socialist Circles. Still such spaces remained clearly marginal.[38]

As this analysis has already indicated, class was not the only source of identity and difference. Within the upper levels of the urban middle class as within other social groupings, there were marked differences in both political and religious loyalties. It is not, I think, particularly helpful to dwell here on party loyalties. As Levine has suggested in her examination of the party political loyalties of feminists and their families, Radicals and Liberals were far more numerous than Conservatives although there was certainly a small minority of the latter.[39] More important perhaps were the political strategies, drawn from reform-minded radical and liberal politics, which were adopted by the women's movement. The antislavery campaign, in which British women had petitioned government in unprecedented numbers, was an out-standing early example of such extraparliamentary and voluntaristic political activity.[40] Such strategies continued, offering middle-class women some limited opportunities for participating, if only in fundraising. Examples are the Anti–Corn Law League, formed to campaign against the corn laws which protected farming interests, the struggle against the Anglican monopoly on education, and the struggle against the payment of rates to the Church of England. All these activities helped to create a politics of pressure, what Brian Harrison has called "a genealogy of reform."[41]

The question which still requires much closer analysis lies in the religious roots of the women's movement in Britain. Here I look primarily at Protestant churches, both the established Church of England and nonconformist groups outside that establishment, with a long tradition of campaigning for civil rights, which by the mid-nineteenth century were largely achieved. These religious differences were complex, because there could be theological common ground between Anglicans and nonconformists, in the Protestant evangelical inspiration so fundamental to British cultural life from the late eighteenth century onwards. The impact of Protestant evangelicalism upon women's lives in the first half of the nineteenth century has generated an extensive literature which has tended to read that impact as both confining and empowering to women's lives.[42] Overall its legacy to the women's movement has been difficult to gauge. Within the commitment to activism could lie justification of a public role. The metaphorical resonances of the missionary impetus can easily be heard. When, in the 1850s, women active in the *English Woman's Journal* sought to contribute to the reform of their society, they tried to set up a Ladies Sanitary Mission. By the late nineteenth century evangelical women, drawing upon a powerful belief in their moral mission and their commitment to a purified society, were active on many fronts, including the rescue of prostitutes, the encouragement of social purity, and temperance movements. Yet relatively few were able to dissociate themselves, as did Josephine Butler, from the repressive and confining aspects of the mission. Of Levine's sample of 194, 21% of the total were known to be Anglicans, though the true figure was probably higher. Only a small number apparently came from the major evangelical nonconformist sects, though we need more research on this. From the largest such group, the Methodists, Levine mentions by name only Isabel Petrie Mills, whose family had many Quaker friends, and the deeply unorthodox and later freethinking Elizabeth Wolstenholme Elmy;

there were also a few Congregationalist women, including the social purity campaigner and suffragist Laura Ormiston Chant.[43]

More significant, and much in need of further investigation, is the role of two numerically very small Protestant nonconformist groups, the Quakers and the Unitarians, from which a quite disproportionate number of activists in the women's movement were to come. Levine found that 9% of her total were Quaker and 11% Unitarian—at 20% almost as many as from the established church. That figure needs to be set against the minute membership of both groups—approximately 15,000 Quakers and 50,000 Unitarians in England and Wales in 1851, in a population of 18 million.[44] We do not have any overall social analysis of such groups, though we know more of Quakers than of Unitarians. Both had roots which went back to the seventeenth century. The Quaker movement had an organizational base of separate male and female meetings (though the one was subordinate to the other), a female ministry, and a record of long formal exclusion from established institutions of public life. British Quakers had particularly close links with those in the United States. Unitarians, who denied the divinity of Christ, were theologically heterodox. In the eighteenth century they were in the forefront of the English Enlightenment and of discussion about women's education.[45]

Neither Unitarians nor Quakers went untouched by the nineteenth-century evangelical current, though the language of evangelicalism can obscure the significance of these liberal and rationalist approaches to social and political change. Socially both Quakers and Unitarians were a part of that urban elite middle class I have been sketching; they formed the most radical sections of the urban patriciate. Both groups preserved effective networks of family visiting and of countrywide contacts, which were easily mobilized in a good cause. John Stuart Mill found his Harriet Taylor in Unitarian circles. Unitarian money backed the *English Woman's Journal,* founded by Bessie Rayner Parkes and Barbara Bodichon, both from Unitarian families, just as it did Bedford College for Women.[46]

Sklar illustrated very effectively the greater conservatism of British Quakers than American Quakers. Yet in the British context, the strength of the Quaker contribution to the British women's movement is striking. New work by Sandra Holton on one of the most important archives in the history of nineteenth-century British feminism, that of the Clark family of Millfield in Somerset, has uncovered the strength of Quaker familial networks. These networks drew upon a long history of male involvement in radical politics as well as the close links of Quaker communities, especially in Birmingham, Bristol, and Edinburgh. Her reconstruction of the political culture of a group of leading Quaker and radical-liberal families—the Brights, McLarens, Priestmans, Estlins, and Clarks—is shifting our perceptions and disrupting more familiar images of homogeneity in the women's movement from the mid-nineteenth to the early twentieth century. The families which she has studied were active in antislavery and abolitionist campaigns, in the women's suffrage movement, and in campaigns against the regulation of prostitution. They worked for international peace and for temperance. Holton traces a continuity throughout the second half of the nineteenth century, through the many splits which took place in a radical, internationalist, and eventually militant stance within the women's movement.[47]

There are, however, other indications of the ways in which religious loyalties could inform feminist politics. The outlook of the Anglican Church was broad. Within Anglicanism it was possible to move in a more liberal direction, as did Emily Davies, who shifted from her evangelical upbringing to a more liberal form of Anglicanism. Besides its strong evangelical wing the church also contained an Anglo-Catholic wing, within which the growth of sisterhoods could provide a model of active philanthropy. The example of the female religious order as a model for female collective experience was one which brought about the conversion of more than one Protestant feminist—like Bessie Rayner Parkes and Adelaide Procter—to Catholicism.

Religious doubt and a search for personal faith might also be a powerful accompaniment to participation in the women's movement. Barbara Caine's fine exploration of the religious faith of Frances Power Cobbe shows how the search for a theistic religion led one politically conservative woman to a progressive and heterodox religious faith. At first an agnostic, Cobbe questioned the literal truth—and of course the chronology—of the Christian Bible, leading her to see new possibilities: a rational Deity whose social prescriptions were adapted to particular stages of society and whose intentions were for a progressively developing universe and a constantly improving faith. The *Englishwoman's Review* carried several articles by clergy outlining why God might support women's suffrage in the nineteenth (though not in the first) century.[48]

And there were certainly those like Elizabeth Wolstenholme Elmy and Annie Besant, whose feminist activity was coupled with an uncompromising challenge to orthodox Christianity, a challenge which might also bring a libertarian defense of free unions. The union between Elizabeth Wolstenholme and Ben Elmy, and Wolstenholme's pregnancy, was greeted with hostility by most leaders of the women's movement, who eventually persuaded her to go through a civil marriage ceremony.[49] Some supporters of women's suffrage— Harriet Law, Kate Watts, Mary Reed—were to emerge from the small secularist movement.[50] And Annie Besant's journeys through Fabianism and secularism to the Theosophical Society point to one continuing theme: the search for alternative forms of spirituality.[51]

There were of course further sources of division within the British feminist movement. So far I have treated the term British in this context as unproblematic, although, of course, it is not. There are important distinctions to be drawn among the different political formations of Scotland, Wales, and Ireland, largely omitted, for lack of research, from the biographical studies I have been citing, and those of England. The women's movement in Scotland has been much better studied over the past five years, that of Wales rather less so.[52] The Irish movement has its own complex history which cannot be addressed here. The Scottish movement did in some respects parallel the English, its leaders in the 1860s in Edinburgh and Glasgow including members of that broad circle of middle-class Quaker families, active in antislavery politics, which Holton has traced. It also however mobilized the working-class Jessie Craigen, who in the 1870s addressed audiences of working people. In April 1872 she spoke to an open-air crowd in Glasgow, said to be over 1,000, "chiefly working men of the most intelligent type."[53] Yet political legislation for Scotland was not uniform with that for England, and women in Scotland first enjoyed the municipal vote in 1882, thirteen years later than in England. The religious history of Scotland is very different from that of England, and to my knowledge it has not yet been studied from the perspective outlined above.[54] Though research is still at an early stage, there is little indication of the women's movements of Scotland or Wales expressing a sense of national difference. Though Scottish heroines of the past might be invoked as well as English ones, this was consistent, especially in the absence of strong nineteenth-century Scottish nationalist sentiment, with identification with the British movement. In this there was a marked contrast with Ireland, where the developing women's movement was to have a complex relationship with Irish nationalism.[55]

Third, I also want to look at alternative sources of collective identities claimed by feminists, which could also, invisibly, exclude and divide. Denise

Riley and Patrick Joyce have written of the imagining of "society," "the people," and "democracy" as collective subjects in this period, and Benedict Anderson has written of "the imagined community" of the nation.[56] Such visions were intrinsic to the women's movement. Riley has identified new meanings given to "society" and the "social" as essentially related to the understanding of middle-class women as potential agents of social improvement and of working-class women and families as the objects of their action and attention. To Barbara Bodichon, in 1866, the call for the vote meant the development of the individual woman's sense of public responsibility through "an active interest in all the social questions—education, public health, prison discipline, the poor laws and the rest—which occupy Parliament."

In her major study of women in local government in the nineteenth century, *Ladies Elect*, Patricia Hollis argued that elected women "invariably and inevitably" spoke "the language of separate spheres," carrying a "philanthropic portfolio," claiming for themselves the tasks for which they were specially qualified, and identifying their constituency as women, children, the old, the sick, and the poor. Such themes are not entirely uncontroversial and have been questioned: can we accept that such a homogeneity existed among women drawn from very different political backgrounds, Conservative, Liberal, and Labour? We may, however, have to accept the prevalence of a "universalist language increasingly employed by all parties," which could mask real divisions between women and their interests.[57]

I would argue, however, that such appeals to the "social" functions of women did not prevent them from imagining their participation in "the people" and "the nation," as described in Benedict Anderson's *Imagined Communities*. So the participation of women in local government could be rewritten also as a part of the history of the nation's liberties, in the narrative of a golden age when women enjoyed a lost power, one at the heart of the British constitution. Feminists, like male radicals, might appeal imaginatively to an Anglo-Saxon past. Mary Smith of Carlisle included in her book a poem on the Anglo-Saxon "Ethelflaed Queen of Mercia," clearly the female equivalent of that Anglo-Saxon King Alfred, who was constantly invoked by male radicals.[58] Lydia Becker in 1879 suggested that "women have, and always have had, coeval rights with men in regard to local franchise" and that "political freedom begins for women as it began for men, with freedom in local government."[59] The commitment to the nation's history and to the place of women within that history was one traced throughout the women's periodicals of the period, the *English Woman's Journal*, the *Englishwoman's Review*, and the *Women's Suffrage Journal*.[60] But, as in Charlotte Carmichael Stopes's *British Freewomen*, and in spite of Stopes's own Scottish background, it was a history recounted almost entirely in English terms.[61]

Such themes were perfectly compatible with an interest in and openness to other European nationalisms—most notably, for the British movement, that of Italy. Anne Summers, in her important study of British military nursing, *Angels and Citizens* (1988), suggested the importance of confronting the "man's world," of noting the ways in which notions of citizenship shifted in Europe during the years between 1848 and 1871. During this period the relationship between soldiers and civilians changed, war became the business of whole populations, and the map of Europe was transformed.[62] In Britain there was no military history of conscription or of universal male military service. The British army, based on long-term professional soldiers policing the empire, could seem remote, especially from liberal domestic opinion. But this was changing. The glorification of women who went as nurses to the Crimean War was followed in the short term by the individual voluntary nursing of British women, and the foundation of voluntary relief societies, in the wars of Italian unification and in the Austro-Prussian, Franco-Prussian, and Turco-Serbian wars. These women went as individuals, yet they helped to establish the possibility of war service for women. As Summers suggested, "the nation state at war supplied a working definition of civic need and responsibility,"[63] with links between war nursing and claims for equal citizenship established by the 1870s. Her study traced the legacy of such claims onwards to the support of significant sections of the women's movement for mass mobilization in 1914. Sandra Holton, Jill Liddington, and others have stressed the association of many feminists with international and national women's peace movements across Europe as well as the United States. Yet it seems important also to consider, with Summers, the argument that the service of the state in war and peace could command women's loyalty to the nation, even if in the still ambiguous figure of the war nurse.

There was of course a further aspect to the imagining of the British nation, and that lay in identification with its empire. The frameworks of identification here are complex. The British women's movement had its strongest roots in powerful nonconformist communities which frequently set themselves in opposition to a militarist imperialism. At the same time such communities could also be those with strong economic links and with commitments to what was perceived as the progress of "humanity." So one of the most significant precursors of the women's movement, the antislavery and abolitionist struggle from the 1830s to the 1860s, which created, as Clare Midgley has argued, an extraparliamentary female political culture, was contradictory and ambivalent. It drew upon that radical challenge to slavery which had inspired in the United States the politics of Elizabeth Cady Stanton and the Grimké sisters. But Sklar in her valuable comparison has also pointed out the different social, political, and economic significance of slavery in each society. British women's daily lives for the most part did not involve contact with black people or slaves, nor did campaigning women experience the social and political consequences faced by American women. British activists used, as Clare Midgley has demonstrated, a language of sisterhood in their representation of female slaves, highlighting the powerlessness of mothers, the sexual exploitation of women. It was not, however, the language of the transatlantic middle-class Quaker sisterhood. It had its roots partly in a maternalist rhetoric of responsibility, partly in the evangelical spirit of Christian mission, and, perhaps most powerfully, in a broader form of cultural imperialism, a vision of the transforming potential of Western civilization, uniting the expansion of commerce with the coming of Christianity. Antoinette Burton has traced this vision of the "white woman's burden," of a benevolent, enlightening empire, responsible for the situation of its colonized women, with particular reference to India, as an important and continuing constituent within the British feminist movement. Vron Ware and Antoinette Burton have, for instance, pointed out how Josephine Butler, identifying the figure of the Indian prostitute as the passive victim of British imperialism and militarism, saw her as degraded also by cultural backwardness, "to be led into a position of greater freedom and light" by British women like herself.[64] By the later nineteenth century, British suffragists were operating within a cultural climate of a popular imperialism and more explicitly racial discourses.

Josephine Butler's position can be contrasted with that of Millicent Fawcett. A question that preoccupied Fawcett was the situation of Ireland and the possibility that it would be granted Home Rule by the British government in the 1880s. Millicent Fawcett believed in what her biographer has called the "civilizing mission" of England and a "sensible imperialism of mutual benefit to England and Ireland alike," and identified with the maintenance of British authority and denial of even modified measures of Home Rule.[65] She broke with a Liberal Party moving in the direction of Home Rule in 1888, and with other liberal women founded the Women's Liberal Unionist Association. She became an active and highly patriotic speaker on platforms which both defended the union between England and Ireland and supported women's suffrage. Increasingly she cast women's suffrage in support of the order and stability of the nation, and she was to carry that support into her approval of Britain's participation in the Boer War in South Africa in 1899. Antoinette Burton, who has done so much to mark out the imperial dimensions of British feminism, has most recently argued strongly that British historians need to remap their subject. They have to unite internal and external others, home and empire, to understand the intercultural exchanges—imperialist, nationalist, gendered—which shaped the languages and practices of the women's movement.[66] That exchange is a constant theme throughout the period I have discussed, as later, whether in the meetings between British feminists and Indian nationalists or in the examples of the achievement of women's suffrage in New Zealand in 1893, followed by the Australian states.[67]

Much more work clearly needs to be done on the extensive imaginative and cultural sources of feminist identities in this period. Feminists cast themselves within different narratives, whether of a mission to "other" peoples and "other women," or in a nostalgic mood for the recovery of a golden age of matriarchy, or as leading actresses in the evolution of a progressive world drama. Such narratives were shifting and many commentators have identified, conveniently, the 1890s and the turn of the century as marking a significant challenge to the feminisms I have traced here. These challenges were over, first, the relationship between middle-class feminists and new kinds of socialist and labor politics. Demands were for protection of working women and of wives and mothers. They entailed a shift towards accepting the possibility of constructive intervention by the state, in line with the "new liberalism" of the period. Even so, some of these diversities were already present among Radical-Liberals. As Holton has shown, such groups were already preparing for more militant forms of action, action which both looked towards European socialism and prefigured the foundation of the Women's Social and Political Union in 1903. The challenge to an older feminism came also from new forms of sexual politics by the 1890s. The two might be associated, as in the case of Edith Lanchester, a middle-class woman socialist and member of the Social Democratic Federation, whose determination to live in a free union with her working-class lover and consequent imprisonment by her family won no support from established feminist societies in 1895.[68] More generally, and in a variety of ways, the claims of women to be sexual, and to redefine sexuality, in fiction, in marriage, in the right to celibacy and in the right to lesbian partnerships, were being heard in the decade before 1914, perhaps most of all in the journal *The Freewoman.*

Much more is known of the feminist cultures of the period after 1900, more about their many organizations, their visual appeal, and the different local contexts in which women's movements have been studied. Yet there were, as Holton and others have stressed, many continuities with the earlier period. For the history of nineteenth- and twentieth-century feminisms it may be helpful to reflect on the relationship between the British women's movement and the shaping of the nineteenth-century nation-state. Anne Summers has looked at the way in which women's public activity in the early nineteenth century was modeled on the demands of minorities, on religious and secular sects, and on pressure groups, and has contrasted this with the claims made in the second half of the nineteenth century for a stake in the politics of the whole: the secular nation-state, its military governance, its imperial responsibilities, and its domestic and social frontiers. A fuller understanding of nineteenth-century feminisms, which draws upon the insights of cultural history, must see them as both agents and subjects in social and political processes. One way of viewing British women's movements is to see the ways in which they were a part of, and themselves shaped, different challenges, often in a spirit of modernity and progress, challenges to so much that remained of a British *ancien régime*, whether in the name of the liberal nation-state and empire, the cooperative commonwealth, or the international order of humanity. Feminist political cultures were fractured, split by differences, allowing fragmentation and choices. They did represent, in Nair's words, frameworks which "simultaneously acknowledge[d] new political possibilities for women, drawing on traditions of dissent or resistance while infusing them with new meanings."[69]

CHAPTER 4

History and Historiography of First-Wave Feminism in the Netherlands, 1860–1922

MINEKE BOSCH

INTRODUCTION

In her opening speech to the Congress of the International Woman Suffrage Alliance in Amsterdam in 1908, Carrie Chapman Catt pointed to the curious fact that "caricaturists in all lands show suffrage leaders carrying umbrellas." Though I am a bit suspicious about the suggestion of universality in "all lands," there is no doubt that many of the issues and images, strategies and arguments of proponents and opponents of feminism traveled easily from country to country. This testifies to a common cultural heritage called "western," consisting of a common body of philosophical and political thought, which made the exchange of a feminist discourse possible. For Catt the universality of the image of the umbrella (which certainly deserves to be analyzed!) functioned as a key to her vision of a common cause shared by women irrespective of their national and other differences. In the business meetings behind closed doors the commonality of suffrage practices was not such an easy matter, and the formulation of IWSA policy was most often the result of long and difficult disputes.

I was again reminded of the gap between IWSA rhetoric, stressing the similarities among national suffrage feminisms, and the difficult practice of overcoming differences when I first read the "Rationale and Goals" of this conference. For although I fully share the organizers' presupposition that there exists a common practice of women's history in "all lands," the guidelines offered for writing the papers made me immediately aware of the difficulty of finding an umbrella fit to cover the national histories. Such an umbrella, however, is a prerequisite for any useful comparison.[1]

I will discuss here only two points in the "Rationale and Goals" which are problematic from the perspective of a Dutch historian of feminism. The first is the suggestion that the new and European cross-country comparison should counterbalance the "western perspective" on historical feminism which stems from the restriction of recent comparative history to France, Germany, and the USA. According to the organizers the Conference should aim at "generalizations" which could also accommodate the "somewhat divergent strategies of southern or eastern Europe." Implicit in this statement is a criticism of Karen Offen's article "Defining Feminism," in which a general picture of "European feminism" is presented.[2] I am tempted to ask where the Scandinavian countries, as well as smaller countries like the Netherlands, Belgium, Luxembourg, and Switzerland, are positioned within this western versus southern/eastern division in European history. As much as histories from eastern and some southern European countries have been underrepresented in international feminist scholarship, so are the histories of the smaller western and northern European countries. The balance will not be redressed by the introduction of a division between western and eastern/southern feminism. From a Dutch (and I think any European national) perspective the "European experience" is something almost metaphysical, and by definition multiple.

A second point in the "Rationale and Goals" of the Conference which is troublesome from a Dutch perspective is the suggestion to concentrate our papers around the dual classification of "relational" and "individual feminism," which again, but now explicitly, makes Offen's proposal function in a way as the much-needed umbrella. As I will show, Dutch developments in the historiography of feminism do not favor this kind of classification and generalization, making it difficult to follow this suggestion. Obviously there is more needed for useful comparison than a comparable historical experience: a common historical practice in the form of shared theoretical and methodological starting points.

This leads to the conclusion that while I do wish to compare notes with colleagues from other European countries, especially since many of us share at least the experience of being on the periphery of "international" women's history, I think it is too early to attempt a "systematic comparison." In my opinion the first thing to do is to get to know each other's histories and contemporary historical practices. From this I think may follow a more workable agenda and maybe even a European research program. My essay is structured accordingly. In the first part I have aimed at a rather descriptive, informative overview of Dutch first-wave feminism, which gives an impression of periodization, the main organizations, leaders, and issues. The second part consists of a review of Dutch historiography of first-wave feminism since 1948 to analyze the interpretative traditions which have guided our research so far. Finally, in the epilogue I make some tentative but useful proposals for future comparison.

HISTORY OF DUTCH FIRST-WAVE FEMINISM, 1860–1922

Beginnings of Dutch Feminism, 1860–1889

There is a growing consensus that in the Netherlands the first wave of feminism started in the beginning of the 1860s, when two women, Elise van Calcar and Minette Storm-van der Chijs, climbed the platform to give lectures on women's education. They did so in order to influence the political debate around the important Law on Education, which was devised by the liberal statesman R. Thorbecke and was passed in 1863. A limited victory was won: though the newly founded *Hogere Burgerscholen* (HBS; Citizens' High Schools)—planned to give middle-class boys a general education as a preparation for a position in industrial society—kept their doors closed to the daughters of the middle class, the law proposed that private citizens could found girls' high schools. These would not give their graduates the same rights as the boys who finished HB schools, but they certainly could offer a better education than the existing "French schools." The first girls' HBS opened its doors in 1867. From 1871 state subsidies were given to such initiatives; then in 1887 the confessional parties succeeded in trading these off against their support for the new constitution.

In the late 1860s it is possible to speak of a broad and ongoing debate on better education for women which centered on questions such as the following: Which women should have secondary education? Was this education meant to prepare women for paid labor and/or family duties? If women should be prepared for labor, what kind of work could or should women do? And related to this: What should a girls' curriculum look like? At the same time the radical freethinker Multatuli published some *Ideën* (Ideas) on the women's question, while the term "emancipation" blew over from across the Atlantic Ocean, with its inevitable associations of women smoking cigars and wearing trousers. In 1870 John Stuart Mill's *Subjection of Women* was translated as *De slavernij der vrouw* (The Slavery of Women) and widely discussed. In the same year a brochure called *Gelijk recht voor allen* (Equal Rights for All) was anonymously published by a woman. After giving a survey of legal inequalities on the basis of gender, it demanded the abolition of marital power.

In the 1870s this debate was intensified and practical steps were taken. In 1870 the first women's periodical, *Ons Streven* (Our Striving), was founded by Betsy Perk, who left the editorial board after the first issue due to differences of opinion. In the same year she started another journal, *Onze Roeping* (Our Calling). Betsy Perk was also initiator of the first women's organization, *Arbeid Adelt* (Labor Ennobles), which aimed at selling at bazaars the needle and art works of impoverished ladies. Again a disagreement occurred, in part to be attributed to differences of opinion about principles. Perk refused to sell these works anonymously; her ambition was the recognition of labor as a worthy manner of life. Other members of the board, however, wanted to guarantee anonymity and set out to found the organization *Tesselschade*. The next year Betsy Perk went on a famous lecture tour with the impressive writer and actress Mina Krüseman (Oristorio di Frama), who was for some time part of Multatuli's circle and had just published a book, *Marriage in the Dutch Indies*, which dealt with the immorality of marriage conventions and advocated a free, love-based marriage. The two got an enormous amount of attention, in large part for Krüseman's partly autobiographical story "The Sisters," in which the convention of "waiting for a man" was criticized. After the lecture tour the women parted in discord and disappeared from the feminist stage.

Also in the 1870s more women got better education. Though only one woman, Aletta Jacobs, entered the university, others applied for high school teacher's exams, for which they needed no preliminary training. They were among the first women to attend selected university lectures. Some of them became the first teachers at the girls' high schools, others social or feminist reformers, publicists, translators, or private scientists. Aletta Jacobs's sisters belonged in 1872 to the first group of women who got permission to follow the regular curriculum of the (boys') high school, a permission, however, which had to be given to every single girl by the Minister of Internal Affairs personally until 1906 and which was withheld when in the same town a girls' high school existed. In this period women also entered new jobs as assistant apothecaries, post-office workers, or nurses in a changing nursing profession. Quite a few novels appeared in which traditional women's lives were critically examined. Every new step women took was a reason for discussion: whether it was the right thing to do, and how it should be done. By and by, the question of gender popped up in every issue and every debate.

By the late 1870s, women were paying ever broader attention to the question of "the double standard of morality" as symbolized in the state regulation of prostitution. In 1878, the Protestant League against Prostitution was founded by a Protestant minister. In 1884, three upper-class women from circles of the *Réveil* (Protestant Revival), Marianne Klerck-van Hogendorp and her sisters, Wilhelmina and Anna van Hogendorp, founded the *Nederlandsche Vrouwenbond ter Verhooging van het Zedelijk Bewustzijn* (Dutch Women's League to Elevate Moral Conscience), which related the prostitution question to the women's question as a social question. Soon 700 members were registered, and in 1885 the first petition was addressed to the government asking for an abolition of trade in girls and women. It was signed by 15,000 people.

Dutch Feminism in the Roaring Nineties, 1890–1898

Though this league can certainly be seen as the first Dutch mass-based feminist organization, Wilhelmina Drucker's *Vrije Vrouwenvereeniging* (VVV; Free Women's Association) has until recently been taken as the beginning of the "organized" women's movement. This reflects the older equal rights paradigm in the historiography of feminism, about which I will speak later. The founding manifesto framed a revolutionary and broad program around questions of gender. After reference to Abbé Sieyès's brochure on the Third Estate (1789), it opened with the unambiguous sentences: "By right she [woman] should be equal to man. The Law should but recognize 'human beings' [*menschen*] without any comment." Therefore women were called upon to cooperate to gain entrance to all educational institutions, jobs, and professions on the same terms as men. Explicitly mentioned were public offices, professorships, and legal positions. The last three demands were the right to guardianship, the right to paternity action, and, for married women, the same right as the husband to have control over common possessions. Women should join together without "paying attention to color, status, or class," while the first duty of the organization was to promote relief of women's household tasks.

It may be that it was not so much the demands that were revolutionary as the language and the ambition to be political, without in any way being tied to one of the (also rather new) political organizations and parties: "free" meant free from political, dogmatic, class, or "any coterie's" affiliation. The VVV was founded at the beginning of the 1890s, which were lively in all aspects of social, cultural, and political life, and for the women's movement in some sense its most active and interesting phase. Wilhelmina Drucker and her co-founders came for the most part from the socialist (later anarchist) Social Democratic League. The first public meeting, however, announced two noble women from the Antiprostitution League to discuss another petition of 1890, asking for the right to paternity action. In 1893 the feminist journal *Evolutie* (Evolution) was founded, which under the editorship of Drucker and her friend Theodora P. B. (Schook-)Haver was an important mouthpiece of feminism, as well as the feminist lice in the fur of many movements (including the women's movement) until 1925.

Though suffrage was not mentioned in the VVV program, in 1893 Wilhelmina Drucker and her friends also took the initiative to found the *Vereeniging voor Vrouwenkiesrecht* (VvVK; Association of Women's Suffrage), after cooperation with socialist and radical liberals on the question of general suffrage had failed. Aletta Jacobs did not attend the first meetings, but soon joined the association. She had brought the question of women's suffrage to the attention of a broader public when in 1883 she had tried to register to vote on the grounds that she met the qualifications of paying a certain amount of tax. She fought her case to the High Court, but her request was denied. In 1887 a new constitution was adopted which explicitly excluded women from the right to vote. The first president of the VvVK was the rather inexperienced Annette Versluys-Poelman, who stood for a broad feminist program and led the association in the first nine years. In the 1890s one main question ran through the suffrage association: Should women campaign only for suffrage, or should they make alliances on many other issues? The question was resolved only when Aletta Jacobs took up the presidency in 1903.

But 1903 was not the 1890s anymore, and feminism was changing, through its proliferation of organizations, its manifold actions, its broad scope of themes and demands, and its multiple alliances. These alliances, which gave full respect to differing opinions and sympathies, left an imprint of deeply felt unity on all women who became involved at that time. Among the new feminist organizations were the women teachers' association *Thugatêr* (named after one of the "Ideas" of Multatuli), the *Vrouwenbond* (Women's League) in Groningen, and the Rotterdam-based *Vereeniging ter*

Behartiging van de Belangen der Vrouw (Association for the Promotion of the Interests of Women). The latter was founded by two important feminists, Martina Kramers and Marie Rutgers-Hoitsema, who were both socialists and admitted Neo-Malthusians. Last but not least, the clearly upper-class *Comité ter Verbetering van den Maatschappelijken en Rechtspositie der Vrouw* (Committee for the Amelioration of the Social and Legal Position of Women) was founded in 1895, in which women like Jeltje de Bosch Kemper sought the cooperation of men, preferably members of Parliament.

The new organizations also started new periodicals. The VvVK published a *Maandblad* (Monthly Journal); the Groningen League of Women, Thugatêr, and the above-mentioned committee joined forces to edit *Belang en Recht* (Interest and Right); the journal *De Vrouw* (Woman) appeared as the organ of a Dutch-Flemish cooperative project by women in the Netherlands and Belgium.

In the midst of this ongoing segmentation and differentiation of feminism in organizations and publishing activities, which of course all defined their own identities against and with reference to each other, two events took place which testify to the unity of the women's movement. The first of these was the publication of the didactic novel *Hilda van Suylenburg* by Cécile Goekoop-de Jong van Beek en Donk in 1897, which generated a tremendous response.[3] Testimony to the importance of this novel is the primary role it plays in virtually all recently published dissertations, for its wealth of opinion on matters as diverse as office labor, higher education, marriage, and questions of morality. The novel brings together all the different viewpoints and arguments which played a role in feminist thought and action of that time, and it makes for fascinating reading. Though it borrows many conventions of the naturalist novel, it subverts at the same time its major frame by making the protagonists healthy, rational women—women doctors!—instead of ailing, apathetic women. Even more radical is its subversion of the central political metaphor of the time, society as a sick body in need of cure by intervention of doctor-politicians. The author instead points to the women's question as the heart of the social question, and stresses the role of women and morality in solving the many social problems of the time.

The central story is the *Bildung* of Hilda van Suylenburg, a rich young orphan who comes at the age of eighteen to live with a family in The Hague, where she is expected to lead the social life of the leisure class. She is saved from a "good match" as well as growing nervousness by the woman doctor

Corona van Oven, who takes her on visits to her patients and introduces her to poverty and injustice. Thus the reader is confronted with an irresponsible gambling husband who spends the money of his wealthy wife, an unwed mother, neglected children who are taken into hiding by courageous women who defy unjust laws, and an impoverished widow whose son spends the little family money left on a student life worthy of his noble birth, thereby preventing his sister from having any education at all. In the end Hilda decides to take up the study of law, which makes her into the first female student of law in the Netherlands. Indeed, her example was followed immediately after the book was published, when the first two women students enrolled in the faculty of law. The happy end shows Hilda as a beautiful wife and mother of a new-born son. She combines domestic duties with writing pamphlets on the necessity of women's labor organizations and giving legal advice to women. It is most interesting that the question of how "women's emancipation" should be defined runs continuously through the book, ending in the statement: "Indeed, one cannot find a formula for it, because the idea of emancipation encompasses too much, and is too encroaching, to be defined in a few words."

The book provoked a stream of reaction, and during the next few years protagonists of the novel would be mentioned in discussions as if they were real persons. It certainly brought women's emancipation to the forefront of cultural, social, and political debate, which made very fertile soil one year later for the second event of the 1890s to show so vividly the unity of the women's movement, the *National Exhibition of Women's Labor*. To contemporaries the two events were bound inextricably: Cécile Goekoop-de Jong van Beek en Donk was president of the organizing committee, and the premises of the exhibition were put at the committee's disposal by Cécile's husband, Adriaan Goekoop. The initiative for the exhibition was taken in 1895 by a few women from the Groningen Women's League in imitation of similar events in Chicago (1893), Brussels, and especially Copenhagen. The exhibition took place between July and September 1898 and attracted 90,000 visitors. It wanted to show all the labor that women did, thereby also changing traditional ideas about what women could and should do. Although most of the organizing women had diverse middle-class backgrounds, they were proud of the cooperation among women of different confessional groups, and they certainly showed an active interest in the labor and labor conditions of working-class women. Symbolic in this sense was a sculpture which hung above the entrance depicting a woman wheeling stones in a wheelbarrow. One section the organizers took great pride in was the industry section, which showed machines and women doing mechanical work. Also there was a "horror table" which showed sewing products like richly embroidered evening dresses and the ridiculous prices paid for this work. Near this was a table which displayed the "working attributes of the accomplished girl," a tennis racket, theater tickets, and some music. The mouthpiece of the exhibition was the weekly *Vrouwenarbeid* (Women's Labor), which under the direction of Johanna Naber, later the movement's major historian, reported about the fourteen congresses which were held. The first of these was opened by the second woman doctor in the Netherlands, Catharine van Tussenbroek. In her speech "The Lack of Life Spirit in Our Young Women and Girls" she argued for economic independence of women regardless of marriage. For contemporaries this performance seemed like an incarnation of Corona van Oven, especially for the eloquent formulation of "spiritual motherhood" at the end.

The image of differentiation and cooperation, diversity and unity, in Dutch feminism during the 1890s may be exaggerated. There certainly were dissenting opinions before the exhibition, and notable absentees, for instance in the person of Aletta Jacobs. The issue of women's suffrage played only a marginal role in the exhibition's discourse. In the next decade, however, there was a growing tendency to identify and institutionalize differences among groups of feminists and to divide the women's question into clear-cut issues which demanded unequivocal choices: politics or reform, words or deeds, socialism or feminism, labor or suffrage, difference or equality. An important mediator of this development was the growing antifeminist backlash in terms of social Darwinist theories promulgated by sociologists (like S. R. Steinmetz), psychiatrists (like W. H. Cox), and famous medical professors (like C. Winkler), as well as the growing political opposition on the part of the socialist party. These oppositional voices came to the surface when feminism became a visible presence in social, cultural, and political life.

Dutch Feminism and the Unifying Force of Women's Suffrage, 1900–1922

In the first two decades of the twentieth century the feminist landscape changed again under the influence of a growing suffrage movement which after about 1908 became the central force of the women's movement. At first the differentiation of the 1890s seemed to continue. In 1898 with the profits of the Women's Labor Exhibition a *Nationaal Bureau voor Vrouwenarbeid* (National Bureau of Women's Labor) was founded, which undertook research and gave information on the subject of women's labor. In the same year the Dutch affiliation of the International Council of Women came into being. Especially in the first ten to fifteen years it functioned as an impartial and central meeting point for all women's organizations. According to Johanna Naber the growth of the suffrage movement had an important basis in these meetings. In between the sessions Aletta Jacobs pleaded her case and thus made allies of other women's organizations. In 1904 the National Council of Women hosted the largest and most memorable conference of its existence to discuss the "Children's Laws," which according to the assembled feminists should contain changes in the legal regulations of marriage, parenthood, and custody. When, in 1903, a new Labor Law was about to be discussed in Parliament, Wilhelmina Drucker, Anna van Hogendorp, and Marie Rutgers-Hoitsema founded the *Nationaal Comité in zake Wettelijke Regeling van den Vrouwenarbeid* (National Committee for the Legal Regulation of Women's Labor). Its purpose was to prevent all kinds of local protection measures, as well as "Royal Decisions" (ministerial decisions which are not laws and therefore not discussed in parliament). When in 1910 such a law was drafted by the confessional State Secretary (Minister) Heemskerk, in which he proposed to dismiss married women teachers and state employees under the age of 45, this committee initiated a *Comité van Actie tegen het Ontwerp Heemskerk* (Committee of Action against the Heemskerk Law). In 1912, after two years of local agitation, a large national protest meeting was held at which all women's organizations were represented; the law was shelved and later withdrawn.

Although the struggle against special labor protection for women time and again was able to mobilize the various sections of the feminist and women's organizations, it took place more and more in the shadow of the suffrage movement. From the time Aletta Jacobs took over the presidency in 1903, the VvVK started to grow and the vote became the symbol for everything related to the women's question. The vote also stood for the unity of women and their demands. Instead of a diversity of equally important issues, bound together by an open definition of "women's emancipation" (as in *Hilda van Suylenburg*), a hierarchy of feminist issues originated, with women's suffrage at its ever more undisputed top. The vote became the key to open all doors and remove all sex barriers in the most unexpected and disparate places.

Important for the success of the suffrage movement was a kind of professionalization (an example being the strong leadership position of Aletta Jacobs). Important too was internationalization, which now emphasized contacts with the USA more than those with other European countries. Especially the 1908 congress of the International Woman Suffrage Alliance in Amsterdam was instrumental in the growth and acceptance of the women's suffrage movement in the Netherlands. An event in some ways traumatic was the split in the suffrage movement when in 1907 a group of women left the Alliance to found the "more moderate" *Nederlandsche Bond voor Vrouwenkiesrecht* (Dutch Suffrage League). The secession was attended by rather bitter polemics, in which the women of the League legitimated their action in terms of "difference versus equality" arguments. But although the leaders of the League and the Alliance no longer cooperated, the rank and file of the two organizations had less difficulty doing so: many women (and some men) were members of both suffrage organizations.

From 1908 suffrage propaganda became more visible and the political argumentation and agitation more influential. More and more political parties adopted an explicit policy on women's suffrage, and the socialists began to interpret "general suffrage" to include women. In 1912 the first large demonstration took place, followed by other mass events such as the exhibition *De Vrouw 1813–1913*, which attracted many visitors. The outbreak of World War I only temporarily distracted the public from suffrage propaganda; in 1916 political pressure was renewed. In 1917 the constitution was changed, and women got the right to be elected. In 1919 the "Jacobs Law" ensured women active suffrage; in 1922 women for the first time cast their votes.

HISTORIOGRAPHY OF DUTCH FEMINISM

From Mother to Daughter: Feminist Historiography before Women's History

Much of what I've related can be found in the book *Van moeder op dochter: het aandeel van de vrouw in een veranderende wereld* (From Mother to Daughter: The Contribution of Women to a Changing World), which appeared in 1948.[4] This large, richly illustrated volume is a comprehensive overview of women's life and the women's movement from 1789 to 1948. The title page lists four authors and an editor, Dr. W. H. Posthumus-van der

Goot, who in 1935 had been one of the founders of the *Internationaal Archief voor de Vrouwenbeweging* (International Archive for the Women's Movement; hereafter IAV). There were two reasons for publishing the book in 1948: The immediate cause was a large exhibition organized on the occasion of Wilhelmina's fiftieth Queen's Jubilee; it thus stood in a tradition of projecting feminist hopes and drew strength from the visible representation of women's power.[5] The second and more lasting reason for the publication of *From Mother to Daughter*, however, was the wish to compensate for the great loss of knowledge about the women's movement brought about by the death of several prominent feminists, among them two cofounders of the IAV, Rosa Manus and Johanna Naber, and the loss of books and archives from the IAV as a result of the German occupation from 1940 to 1945.[6]

The book is divided chronologically in three main parts: The Development in the Nineteenth Century (1789–1898); Entrance in Society (1898–1928); The Last Twenty Years (1928–1948). In their choice of 1898 as an important turning point, the editors pay their respect to Johanna Naber's vision of history.[7] The book gives information on "pioneers," especially in the fields of women's education, social reform, women's labor, and suffrage politics, and it describes innumerable "first women." Though the scope is broad, the accent falls definitely on *public feminist political action* in the period between 1898 and 1918. Special attention is also given to the 1930s, a time of increasing pressure to prohibit (married) women's labor. The book thus reflects the "equal rights paradigm" which informs most historiography of feminism before women's history started to develop as a discipline, through the efforts of many suffrage movements to preserve national heritage. Nevertheless, the last part of the book also gives attention to the new, often explicitly nonfeminist women's organizations (of housewives and of Catholic, Protestant, and Jewish women), which were formed around 1920. Moreover, every main part has an opening section called "Foreground and Background of Women's Life," consisting of information on domestic life in a changing world, as illustrated by color plates of fashion, household improvements, and interior decoration.

Looking back, one cannot but admire the project and conclude that the main goal, to preserve the memory of the women's movement in the face of tremendous loss, was reached. Thus, when in the 1970s young feminists and students of history began to turn to the history of their movement, they found this book and also a small and almost dormant IAV, which nevertheless was able to serve as an excellent center of feminist collecting and collective memory. Most of these students, however, had mixed feelings for this classic. Though there was certainly admiration and gratitude for the abundance of facts, the book was said to be inaccurate, too descriptive, and too much based upon the "contribution concept" of women's role in history. It was too much of an old-fashioned history, focusing on leaders and organizations and offering too little analysis.[8] Also it was considered too subjective and bourgeois in its undervaluation of socialist women and their organizations; the authors were unable to cope with an important concept like ideology. The most severe criticism was delivered in the (more or less editorial) introductory article to a special issue entitled *The First Feminist Wave* in the *Jaarboek voor Vrouwengeschiedenis* (Yearbook of Women's History), where the book was criticized for its lack of conceptual framework and its failure to define feminism and the women's movement.[9]

In view of this mixed reception it is justified to ask what this new generation (my generation) of feminist historians has done differently, and how their (our) supposedly more vigorous theoretical outlines have contributed to deeper insight into the history of the Dutch women's movement.

Historiography of Dutch Feminism after the Emergence of Women's History

Given the importance of Marxist/socialist influences in feminism in the 1970s it comes as no surprise that the first well-documented contribution to the history of first-wave feminism was contained in a 1973 study of the attitude of the *Sociaal Democratische Arbeiderspartij* (Social Democratic Workers Party: SDAP) to the women's question.[10] (The study got a worthy follow-up in 1983 when Ulla Jansz published a book on the women's organization in the SDAP (after 1945: PVDA), which concentrated on the dynamics of gender politics within the party.[11]) This 1973 publication took the antagonism between the (bourgeois) women's movement and the (proletarian) labor movement as a matter of fact, and so did another, published in 1977 and entitled *Vrouwen, kiesrecht en arbeid* (Women, Suffrage, and Labor).[12] In this study, the result of the first women's history class in the Netherlands, the women's movement was self-evidently identified as a bourgeois movement. Though there were remarkable similarities with *From Mother to Daughter* with respect to periodization, and especially with the idea that agitation for better education, la-

bor reform, and social reform inevitably led to greater awareness of legal discrimination and to political action for women's suffrage, there was also a remarkable difference: the whole period of religiously inspired reform activities
before the 1870s was neglected. A few years later this new periodization—
which was obviously linked to a definition of feminism as "organized action"—was validated in an article in the *Jaarboek voor Vrouwengeschiedenis.*
Here Nancy Cott's hypothesis of women's religious networks as a preliminary
stage of feminism was tested for the Netherlands' Reveil and proved wrong.[13]

Also new with respect to *From Mother to Daughter*, however, was the effort
to explain feminism in terms of structural causes, characteristics, and effects.
Thus in the introduction to *Vrouwen, kiesrecht en arbeid*, the nineteenth-
century division between public and private is sketched as the outcome of old
patriarchal values and the development of capitalism. The origin of organized
feminism is explained as the result of a growing gap between the bourgeois
ideal of femininity as domestic idleness and economic deterioration. Marriages were delayed and a spinster problem occurred. More important was the
effort to describe the women's movement in terms of "ideas on the position
of women." Here a basic division within first-wave feminism between "ethical feminism" and "rational feminism" was identified. According to the authors, ethical feminism stressed the importance of "true femininity" as the basis of social change, and was supported by the majority of feminists. Rational
feminism, on the other hand, advocated an idea of the "human above the
sexes" and was adhered to by only a handful of feminists. The terms "ethical"
feminism, "rational or dogmatic" feminism, "moderate" feminism, and "ultrafeminism" had occurred systematically in 1907 only when the split in the
suffrage movement took place. They were made into a basic classification in
the history of feminism some time later by "ethical feminists" in the *Encyclopaedisch Handboek*, which appeared between 1914 and 1918.[14] The authors
of *Vrouwen, kiesrecht en arbeid* thus reinforced this division, stating that it was
indeed historically justified to project the terms back in time.

The conclusion of *Vrouwen, kiesrecht en arbeid* was devoted to a comparison with present-day (1970s) feminism and to the question why the first
feminist wave did not succeed.[15] The early feminists were taken to task for
their focus on juridical change (juridism) instead of a change of mentality,
and thus for the fact that they restricted their efforts to changing the position of women instead of striving for the liberation of women. A second

mistake first-wave feminists made was their "traditionalism," as reflected in the influential notion of ethical feminism. This conclusion, in its focus on what unites and what divides "them" from "us," reflected the general characteristic of identification in most early women's history. The attempts to pursue a more theoretical or "scientific" approach succeeded at the same time in relativizing the "equal rights paradigm" by attracting attention to the importance of difference arguments in the history of first-wave feminism.

Identification, as well as the effort to amend inherited views of feminism, also informed the historical research which in the early 1980s tried to apply the concept of women's culture to a definition of (historical) feminism. A book like *Politics and Friendship* focused on the construction of an international sisterhood through personal "bonds of womanhood" within the International Woman Suffrage Alliance.[16] This certainly reflected contemporary definitions of feminism. The explicit turn to primary sources in the history of feminism, however, at the same time reflected the wish to avoid premature conclusions based on hierarchies of historical importance and well-known ideological divisions. Indeed, the concept of women's culture encouraged the use of such primary sources as letters and autobiographical material, which brought to the surface all kinds of unexpected alliances: between suffrage feminists and social reformers, between socialists and "bourgeois" feminists, and between (rational) equality and (ethical) difference feminists. These alliances upset the traditional divisions and value judgments of good and bad, real and would-be feminists.

Until about 1985, when the special issue of the *Jaarboek voor Vrouwengeschiedenis* (Yearbook of Women's History) on first-wave feminism appeared, most of the research into historical feminism was concerned with attempts to revise long-standing historical interpretations and to expand the definition of feminism. Articles appeared on feminist attitudes toward sexuality, birth control, prostitution, antifeminism, girls' education, and aspects of women's labor. A remarkable number of biographical studies focused on very specific contextualized views of feminism.[17] I will discuss here three articles which had a special impact. In the first article Petra de Vries points out the political importance and strategic value of the notion of "spiritual or social motherhood," which had its basis in conceptions of women's (biological and moral) difference in historical feminism. She not only identifies but also rehabilitates the use of difference arguments in feminism in the face of traditional neglect and repudiation.[18] The second article, by Marijke Mossink, examines the use of historical arguments in the (nasty) contemporary feminist debates on good (equality) and bad (difference) feminism.[19] Mossink returns to the source of the distinction between ethical and rational feminism in 1907 and concludes that it served only to legitimate the split in the suffrage movement and that the terms should be regarded as weapons in the struggle for hegemony in feminist politics. Never before nor after was such a clear distinction to be found between individuals or groups of feminists, since equality and difference arguments most often were used by both. Moreover, she emphasizes that neither "ethical" nor "rational" arguments could be judged as conservative or radical on the surface, since their effect had to be studied in context. The third article, by Myriam Everard, deals not with the equality-difference split, but with the socialist-bourgeois feminist division.[20] On the basis of a selection from the personal correspondence of Annette Versluys-Poelman, Everard concludes that "real class differences" were not what lay at the root of the hostility of SDAP leaders towards the VvVK, but rather the fact that socialists and feminists had to attract followers from the same social groups.

It should be noted that this "revisionist" work was often inspired and strengthened by research from other countries. Thus Petra de Vries mentions the influential German article by Irene Stoehr on the subject of "spiritual motherhood," while Marijke Mossink draws parallels with Ellen DuBois's interpretation of the origins of the American women's suffrage associations.[21] The special issue of the *Jaarboek* opened with a review of international historiography on the subject of first-wave feminism.

The efforts to deconstruct the old historical oppositions, especially between ethical and rational, and difference and equality feminism, were reinforced by the more general and theoretical debate on equality versus difference in women's studies and women's history. Important in the Dutch context were articles by Mieke Aerts, Joan Scott, and Gisela Bock.[22] The first combines a plea for the contextual study of gender construction (instead of taking the categories of men and women for granted) with an effort to overcome the equality-difference dilemma in the history of feminism. Aerts argues that difference and equality arguments had common origins in the *Polarisierung der Geschlechter* (polarization of the sexes), as the late eighteenth-century construction of gender was called by Karin Hausen. The historical construction of women as different from men had not only excluded women from history, politics, and the public sphere, it had also given them a basis for an identification "as women." Arguments of equality and difference were just two sides of the same coin, both of which contributed to modern womanhood and to feminism. This conclusion parallels Scott's exhortation to "take heart from the history of feminism, which is full of illustrations of refusals of simple dichotomies and attempts instead to demonstrate that equality requires the recognition and inclusion of differences."[23]

Recent Historiography of Dutch Feminism

The first scholar to apply these ideas in a history of first-wave feminism was Ulla Jansz in her dissertation *Denken over sekse in de eerste feministische golf* (Thinking about Gender in the First Feminist Wave), 1990. In its focus on the history of feminism this book may be seen as the first serious attempt to replace (or "rewrite," according to a favorite expression of the author) *From Mother to Daughter*. Though Jansz also sets out to deconstruct the oppositions between Christian-inspired and liberal feminism[24] and between socialist and bourgeois feminism, her true target is the dichotomy between equality feminism and difference feminism as useful classificatory terms in the history of feminism. Using numerous examples she shows that feminism and feminists are not to be differentiated on this basis, and that more important differences among feminists are to be found in ideas on the division of labor, and especially on the collectivization of household tasks, class position, and marital status. Her historical evidence supports Aerts's and Scott's earlier theoretical insights into the equality-versus-difference dilemma.

This important attempt at rewriting the history of Dutch feminism received a lot of attention and, of course, attracted some critical reactions. Berteke Waaldijk, for instance, pointed at Jansz's rather ahistorical reading of equality and difference arguments in a much more diverse historical language, which in a sense made all differently located debates into one discourse.[25] Therefore, instead of historicizing feminism the book was again set into the mode of identification and molded history to the contemporary desire to deconstruct equality versus difference. Myriam Everard opposed the book for its colorless picture of feminism, a picture that ruled out all the fascinating differences between feminisms and feminists—which, at least in part, did reflect contrasting conceptions of difference (and equality).[26] Someone like the radical and obstinate Wilhelmina Drucker clearly had uncompromisingly adhered to the idea of sexual difference as socially constructed, and this set her apart (though it did not isolate her) from other contemporaries. Her opponents reacted with repeated reproaches of masculinity or third-sex allusions. Such allusions were rooted in definitions of natural difference, and they certainly had their impact on feminist debate. In addition to this I argued that deconstructing the opposition of equality versus difference did not so much mean upgrading arguments of difference and making all arguments of equal weight, but rather reinterpreting the dichotomy between the terms.[27] Opponents of feminism had erected this dichotomy by interpreting equality demands as the feminists' wish to become men, which linked up to their notion of natural difference. This made the feminists' choice into one of either-or between equality arguments and difference arguments, a choice which many of them refused—but not all of them. The effort in 1907 and later of "ethical feminists" to introduce just such an opposition and to put equality feminism (rational feminism or ultrafeminism) uncompromisingly in opposition to difference feminism was certainly detrimental to feminist argumentation.

My criticism appeared as part of my dissertation, which focused on the discourse on women and gender in higher education and science in the Netherlands. Though the women's movement as such was not the subject of my dissertation, it played an important role in my research as an active agent of major debates regarding gender definitions. And this is how most of our knowledge of first-wave feminism developed in the second half of the 1980s: in academic dissertations which did not focus on feminism or the women's movement as such, but did deal with aspects of these subjects in the context of a special domain of gender construction. Thus, as one of the first *promovendae*, Selma Sevenhuijsen examined the debates on "the (patriarchal) order of paternity," which brought feminist interventions with respect to unwed motherhood and feminist campaigns for the recognition of paternity to light.[28] Francisca de Haan, in her doctoral thesis on the construction of office labor as "women's work," investigated the feminist struggle against definitions of labor put forward by labor organizations and the government.[29] A broader scope on the construction of women's labor as "different" from men's labor, or simply labor, was provided by Corrie van Eijl.[30] As a part of this process, her dissertation also threw light upon the history of the National Bureau of Labor.

Because of (or notwithstanding) this sideways glance at first-wave feminism, these studies all reinforced the idea that the first feminist wave was more than a history of organizations, leaders, ideology, and demands which culminated in the suffrage movement. For me the most fascinating dissertation in this respect has been Marianne Braun's *De prijs van de liefde* (The Price of Love), which deals primarily with matrimonial law.[31] Braun shows convincingly that along with the issues of labor, the "double standard of morality," education, and suffrage, the issue of men's marital power ran through all feminist actions, and that all feminist questions had matrimonial law aspects. She uncovers the intrinsic relation between the private and the public and between personal relations and political practice by showing both the political aspects of civil law and the legal (marital order) aspects of politics. Thus she throws an unexpected light on some well-known historical developments. For instance, she convincingly argues that the strong feminist reaction to protection of women's labor (which started with the Labor Law of 1889) should be explained not so much in terms of general feminist demands for "equal rights" but rather in terms of specific feminist objections to the doctrine of "the weaker sex," which after 1838 in part legitimated marital arrangements with the argument of "protection." Thus far such protection had not been extended to unmarried women, for in contrast to their married sisters they were not *personae miserabilis* (though they certainly lacked some of the personal rights which were thought necessary for protection). Protection of women's labor, however, brought all women, and therefore also unmarried women, under the protection of the state.

Braun then goes on to show how this shift from marital power to state power also had positive effects, especially on the women's suffrage struggle. She depicts this struggle as an unrelenting campaign against notions of suffrage based on (male) heads of families. This included a principled opposition to proposals, mostly by liberals, for unmarried (or widowed) women's suffrage, since these were rooted in the existing marital order. This suffrage policy was helped by such unintended side effects of state protection (as well as other laws), which slowly undermined the "sovereignty" of fathers and husbands. In the end this led to a political upgrading of married women and to genuine individual suffrage instead of suffrage based on a doctrine of heads of families. Here is where the specific feminist contribution to the history of general suffrage lies.

Historical Feminism between Social and Political History

Apart from these intriguing results, there is another reason to give Braun's dissertation close attention: her effort to connect the history of feminism to political history. Braun not only constructs an unexpected and fascinating image of historical feminism, she also shows that feminism had an impact on the main political issues of the period: the social question and general suffrage. In addition, feminism influenced those who in traditional history are seen as the main actors of the period: the liberals, the socialists, and the confessional parties. And this is quite exceptional. For if this review of the historiography of feminism in the Netherlands allows for a conclusion, it is that although our knowledge about past feminisms has been enriched enormously in the last twenty years, in comparison with *Van Moeder op Dochter* the new knowledge is fragmented. In a way "the subject is lost": there are— except for Ulla Jansz's book—no book-length studies of first-wave feminism, or aspects of it. Especially striking in this respect is the absence of any synthetic history of the women's suffrage movement.

There are several reasons for this state of affairs. In the first place, feminism and women's studies in general in the Netherlands have responded quickly and thoroughly to the poststructural criticism of identity politics. All the above-mentioned dissertations in women's history testify to the paradigm shift from a humanist, subject-oriented, and emancipatory "women's history" to a discourse-oriented, deconstructive, and poststructuralist "women's and gender history." Linked to the enthusiastic response to poststructuralism is, I think, a general willingness (or necessity) to integrate women's history in the historical discipline.[32] The main policy among women's historians has been that feminist history should make a difference in existing historical knowledge in the first place, and not just mark out a special women's history domain or concentrate on special themes like the history of feminism. The accent is now on questions about "how gender works" in well-defined discursive contexts, with the aim of convincing colleagues of gender's importance as a central category of historical analysis in any field.

Another reason for the tendency to decenter the subject of feminism, and especially the history of the suffrage movement, is to be found in the (gendered) opposition between political history and social history. It was in part this opposition that put women's history in the vicinity of social history. This development was reinforced by the broad definition of politics in the feminist motto of the time: "the personal is the political," which found its way to women's history in various ways. Some time later this broad definition survived the turn to poststructuralism by way of Foucault's insistence that politics is related not so much to state power, but to dispersed and local power struggles in various discursive and institutional contexts. This explains not only why our view of historical feminism is fragmented, but also why historical feminism is less related to "state politics" than to what might be called a kind of social politics.

A good illustration of this tendency is given by Maria Grever's recent dissertation on the feminist historian Johanna Naber.[33] Grever not only contextualizes Naber's biography in such a way as to decenter the subject, she also puts Naber primarily in the perspective of the emerging historical profession. That is to say, she emphasizes the context of a social history of science instead of—for instance—the political struggle for civil, social, and political citizenship. Though in this study, more than in any other, the point of departure is in (suffrage) feminism as a social and political movement, Grever clearly favors a conception of politics as a professional struggle over power. This resulted in an excellent book, which in itself justifies the choice of perspective. Another perspective could have been taken, however, as is demonstrated by a separate article that appeared almost simultaneously with the dissertation; here Grever connects Naber's work to feminist conceptions of female citizenship. The same tendency to conceive of feminist politics in a broad sense is to be found in a special issue of the *Jaarboek voor Vrouwengeschiedenis* on feminism and representation.[34] In this issue one article explains the political aspects of the fairy tales which Wilhelmina Drucker wrote; another points to the feminist or political dimensions of Elise van Calcar's spiritism.

Thus, while historical feminism has been analyzed as being everywhere, suffrage feminism has almost been lost from sight. Nevertheless there are signs of change. In the past few years the challenge to "go political" has been taken up again. Scholars are turning their attention to the more traditional realms of political history, though certainly with the aim of historicizing and politicizing the concept of politics by putting it in a gender perspective. A starting point for this development was a seminar called "Feminist Perspectives on Political History," which resulted in the publication of a special issue of the *Jaarboek voor Vrouwengeschiedenis* (1991).[35] In this issue the authors took up such central themes of political history as the construction of notions of citizenship, the cold war, and the formation of national identity, with the aim of showing the gendered dimension of various political discourses.

At the same time an attempt to relate the women's suffrage movement to wider political discourse, with a keen eye for its gendered dimensions, was made by a political historian, Henk te Velde.[36] In his article te Velde connects the importance of "difference" or "relational" arguments in the heyday of suffrage feminist politics to the gendering of political discourse in general under the influence of the social question. It is not in any way new to see the "social question" as the major force behind the democratization of western societies and the organization of the modern state at the end of the last century. Te Velde, however, expands the argument by demonstrating how the social question introduced a concept of "care" in politics. This definitely was a gendered concept. At first women's suffrage demands were generally posed in terms of personal rights, and they were supported by social or radical liberals (and some socialists) with the argument of self-protection through self-representation, which especially unmarried women needed. At the same time—that is, in the 1880s and 1890s—within feminism the concept of "social or public motherhood" began to be used to legitimate women's role in public. This definition of women's role was seen as the key to a solution of the social question. The novel *Hilda van Suylenburg* exemplifies this development. In this period "public motherhood" was in the first place connected to social reform and more hesitatingly to legal change or political rights. This accent shifted after 1900, when the social question began to play an ever larger role in parliamentary political discourse directed to redefining the role of the state. Now it became possible for the suffrage movement to use the concept of public motherhood to enter the parliamentary political debate. Aletta Jacobs more than once pointed to women's housekeeping qualities in the public realm. The liberal defense of women's suffrage changed likewise, stressing the special qualities of women with respect to care. Around 1910 it was suggested for the first time in Parliament that married women, rather than unmarried women, should have the vote in the first place. It therefore seems right to state that women's suffrage was won in the sign of motherhood, but that this had less to do with a special European tradition of "relational" feminism or with the more general attractiveness of difference arguments for a wider public, and more to do with "the emergence of new entities after the Enlightenment and their implicatedness with the collectivity of women—like the idea of "'the social.'"[37]

EPILOGUE

This review of recent contributions to the history of Dutch first-wave feminism will explain why I could not follow the suggestion to adopt Karen Offen's definition of feminism, which stresses a division in "relational" and "individual" feminism. In the first place this would have resurrected the old dichotomous classification which can already be detected in the 1977 publication *Woman, Suffrage and Labor* and which for good reasons has been left behind.[38] A greater obstacle is the underlying conception, which attributes to the historian a special authority in defining or identifying feminism and which makes historical truth the basis or essential condition for contemporary feminist politics.[39] Moreover, Dutch historical evidence has not in any way confirmed the conclusion that Ellen Key "had a profound impact on the theory and practice of the European women's movement" or that the term feminism "referred far more often to the 'rights of women' than to 'rights equal to those of men.'"[40] Nor has it confirmed the well-known qualification of "European feminism" as relational, as opposed to Anglo-American individualist feminism. In the Netherlands the official dictionary definition of feminism still emphasizes "equal rights," and the historical image of Ellen Key is still, and rightly so, related to antifeminist agitation in Holland as well as Key's refusal to discuss feminism with Aletta Jacobs when she was on a lecture tour in Holland.

Maybe cross-country comparisons should not aim so much for universal truths and generalizations. It is perhaps more important to comprehend the local and contextual aspects of our nationally organized histories and to see similarities and differences among these. This view tallies with a conception of history which respects strangeness and difference more than sameness and identification. Within this frame I would suggest selecting very specific limited subjects, such as feminists' preoccupation with prostitution, paternity action, labor legislation, or suffrage. Similarly, one could investigate feminists' reception of books or their own literary production. If the goal is to compare "feminisms at large," the comparison should rather be guided by such synthetic themes as state and empire building, constructions of citizenship, or the meaning of nationalism. In this context one should also look at how feminists use or oppose the related gendered discourses. Here it would be interesting to analyze the various national feminist reactions to events which had international reverberation.

But maybe even the goal of comparison should be given less emphasis and we should strive for a real international exchange of our local and national histories in order to improve the flow of information and promote mutual understanding. This might be an even better road to a varied and multinational conception of feminism and gender struggle, and it might thus become easier to accommodate the many different experiences of women from "all lands" in an increasingly unified Europe.

CHAPTER 5

The French Feminist Movement and Republicanism, 1868–1914

FLORENCE ROCHEFORT

Why include the French feminist movement in a collective work on women's movements in Europe? Was there a "women's movement" in France in the second half of the nineteenth century? When we consider the various groups composed of women or the different ways in which women became involved in the public sphere in France at the time known as the Belle Epoque, are we really dealing with a "women's movement"? In fact, the term is commonly used to designate the much more recent feminist mobilization of the 1970s, which facilitated the assimilation of the two movements, feminist and women's. The fact is that in France during the first twenty years of the period under consideration, the movement for women's rights was characterized by the joint participation of women and men. And while many associations made up of women came to support this movement and its cause, others, such as some groups of Catholic women, came into existence specifically to oppose them. My object, then, is more appropriately designated the history of the *feminist* movement in France, and we may begin by observing that at the turn of the twentieth century that movement displayed extraordinary vitality. It came into existence at the end of the 1860s in the tide of republican opposition to the Second Empire of Napoleon III and began to acquire strength in the 1880s, as the monarchical threat to the Republic receded. As we shall see, it reached a high point between 1897 and 1900. It then gathered new strength just before World War I around the single demand for the right to vote: in July 1914, France's first and only major demonstration for women's suffrage was held—in honor of the philosopher Condorcet (1743–1794). The movement cannot be reduced to the demands its proponents made, however. While revealing their own aspirations and vocations to a number of individuals and providing them with opportunities for self-realization, it gave women a political identity within the French Republic, consolidating them as a social group composed of people with common interests. The movement comprised numerous groups; numerous were their political and social initiatives and their newspapers, and in the 1890s they began acquiring a considerable audience. Fascinated by the themes and issues raised by the movement, Belle Epoque French society (though it might come out ardently for or against a given manifestation of *la femme nouvelle*) adopted the word *feminist* into its daily vocabulary and male and female feminists began attracting the interest of novelists, sociologists, jurists, historians, and politicians.

Long ignored by historians in this century, the movement was first taken seriously by specialists of the workers' movement. Predictably, their analytic grids could not register the richness of the phenomenon; for socialists in the 1960s, the movement was just as pejoratively "bourgeois" as it had been for their predecessors near the end of the nineteenth century. The new perspectives opened up in the 1970s by the discipline of Women's Studies have enabled us to change this prejudice. First there was the revolution in methodology that consisted in acknowledging the feminist movement as a historical object in its own right. Here the pioneer work was done by Americans: Karen Offen, Patrick K. Bidelman, Charles Sowerwine, Claire Goldberg Moses, Marilyn J. Boxer, and, working together, Steven Hause and Anne Kenney.[1] In French university studies, Eleni Varikas's doctoral thesis on the beginnings of a feminist consciousness in nineteenth-century Greece[2] and the one I co-wrote and defended with Laurence Klejman on feminism in France[3] broke new ground. In our work on the feminist movement in France from 1868 to 1914, Klejman and I sought not only to prove the existence of such a movement—which had been quite ignored by historians of the Third Republic—but also to demonstrate its intrinsically political character: resituating the movement in its rightful political and ideological context, that of French republicanism, enabled us to show its idiosyncrasy. At its height the movement appears somewhat nebulous, and in identifying main characteristics we must be careful not to efface its diversity. I have chosen to present here only aspects specific to this movement, those that facilitate a comparative approach. What was particularly French about French feminism were its ties to the Republic, the passage from gender consciousness to feminist commitment, and the specific developments in the movement around the turn of the century. Before feminism allied itself with what proved to be the enduring force of republicanism, the history of French mobilization for women's rights was a discontinuous one, tied to moments of revolution.

FEMINIST MOBILIZATION BEFORE 1868

The debate on the difference between the sexes runs through all historical periods in France. As early as the fifteenth century, Christine de Pizan (1364–1430) wrote *La cité des dames,* her brilliant plea in favor of recognizing men and women as equal. But we must be wary of attributing such distant origins to the feminism of the Belle Epoque. It is not as though a feminist heritage had been transmitted from generation to generation through the centuries—the history of feminism followed no such continuous or progressive line. In fact, up until today that history has been characterized by the repeated forgetting, obscuring, and rediscovery of the complex historical problem of equality between the sexes.[4] The *querelle des femmes* itself, however—as opposed to people's consciousness of it—follows a virtually continuous chronology and produced numerous theoretical manifestos against inequality. In some cases the authors rediscovered the little-known body of texts and existing "official knowledge" on the question; each then drew up his or her own outline of "women's history." Women's activism, on the other hand, was not at all continuous. And we must distinguish between women's participation in important collective events—they have always played a role in such events, though it has long been neglected or caricatured by historians—and their collective coming to awareness of how they were oppressed as a sex. The two phenomena are of course closely related—the first facilitated the second—and they are sometimes confused with one another. We can say that from the end of the eighteenth century through the first half of the nineteenth, the history of feminism closely follows the great revolutionary events of 1789, 1830, and 1848.

The demand for sexual equality logically followed from the new truths of the French Revolution, namely those of natural right and equality before the law. In the name of the universal principles of the *Déclaration des droits de l'homme et du citoyen,* certain important figures, among them the philosopher and scholar Condorcet and the *femme de lettres* Olympe de Gouges (1748–1793), together with a few anonymous petitioners, spoke out against the effective inequality of the sexes and women's exclusion from political citizenship. Women revolutionaries, both *bourgeoises* and *femmes du peuple*, began organizing clubs and taking action to champion the Revolution. Though they had only rarely spoken or written overtly in favor of women's rights,[5] they nonetheless fell victim to the repression of the *Terreur*, which condemned without distinction political activism and demands for equality. The delegates to the Convention of 1793 pronounced their opposition to women's political rights and made all women's clubs illegal. The Napoleonic Civil Code of 1804 then confirmed women's exclusion from political life and abolished all civil rights that had been granted by revolutionary legislation. Single women did not have the right to appear in court, serve as witnesses in common civil procedures, or be legal guardians; and married women lost all their rights: declared civilly inept and subject to their husbands' will, they were comparable in status to minors, criminals, and crazy people. Women's subjection within the family was harshly criticized by such utopian socialists as Charles Fourier and the Saint Simonians; women's emancipation was at the core of their program for social regeneration.

Following the July Revolution of 1830, several newspapers began to appear that were devoted to the cause of women's emancipation.[6] One focused on legal equality, another on instituting schooling for girls; the most revolutionary of all were the Saint Simonian women. Protesting against the male-dominated hierarchy of the group itself, they affirmed the need to speak out *themselves* for the cause of their emancipation. In 1832 two working women, Désirée Véret (1810–1890) and Marie-Reine Guindorf, founded *La Femme libre*, in which they forcefully denounced the oppression of working women and wives and asserted women's moral superiority to men. In their conception, women's emancipation remained closely tied to that of "the people." Quickly muzzled by the authorities, the Saint-Simonian women also suffered from the internecine conflicts that characterized the movement and the existential risks involved in their break from traditional morality. Claire Demar, a radical who favored free love and the abolition of marriage, committed suicide with her male companion in 1833. Other women, such as Jeanne Deroin (1805–1894) and Eugénie Niboyet (1796–1882), turned toward Fourierism and were just taking up the struggle for women's emancipation when revolution broke out anew in 1848. With the advent of the short-lived Second Republic, women's clubs were formed once again, but while universal male suffrage was instituted, no official attention was paid to demands for political equality between the sexes. The clubs were quickly prohibited, as they had been in 1793, and with Napoleon III's coup d'état of December 2, 1851, many militants for the women's cause were forced into exile or silence. It was under the Second Empire (1852–1870), however, that a feminist movement closely associated with republican ideals first came into being.

FEMINISM AND THE REPUBLIC

During the first years of the Second Empire no collective action was possible, but a few women of letters did manage to publish texts in favor of sexual equality. Juliette Lamber (1836–1936) sought to refute Proudhon's misogynist theories, and in 1860 Jenny P. d'Héricourt (1809–1875) published *La Femme affranchie: réponse à MM Michelet, Proudhon, E. de Girardin, Legouvé, Comte et autres innovateurs.* Julie Daubié (1824–1874), the first French woman to receive the baccalaureat, published a study entitled *La Femme pauvre,* while the novelists Angélique Arnaud (1797–1884) and André Léo (1824– 1900) (the pseudonym of Madame Champseix) denounced women's condition within marriage, somewhat in the manner of George Sand.[7] One of the most important thinkers on women's situation (though her plays and pamphlets reached only a small audience) was Maria Deraismes (1828–1894). She was particularly interested in the causes of women's effective inequality, and her work, which dissociated feminist thought from both Christianity and socialist utopianism (with its own particular religiosity), from misogynist positivism on the one hand and Jules Michelet's philogynist mystifications on the other, enabled thought on sexual equality to develop more richly, while the priority she gave to the concept of right helped identify women's emancipation as an autonomous cause. When Napoleon III declared public meetings and debate legal once again in 1868, it was immediately clear how that cause had matured: this time many of the women's groups formed were openly dedicated to obtaining women's rights. They composed a movement that survived the Third Republic and remained active up until 1940;[8] it led to the founding of the National Council of French Women in 1901, an institution that still exists. At the time, mobilization first took the form of open meetings where people heatedly discussed opinions for and against women working. A handful of men and women who had gathered around the woman novelist André Léo focused their efforts on a project for women's schooling. Meanwhile republican Freemasons, among them Léon Richer (1824–1911), organized public talks, thereby offering Maria Deraismes the chance to speak before an audience. Richer and Deraismes focused on obtaining civil and social rights for women. On April 10, 1869, Richer launched a new newspaper called *Le Droit des femmes*. The groups organized around the paper emphasized education for girls and the defense of *la femme* as a "human person with a right to be free and autonomous." They formulated precise proposals for reforming all articles in the Civil Code that made women civilly inferior to men, including in their demands the right for women to work, receive equal pay for equal work, and initiate paternity searches. The new militantism was accompanied by a renewal of theory, as is clearly shown in the thinking of Maria Deraismes.

Born in 1828 into a cultivated, bourgeois, Voltairean family, Maria Deraismes had enjoyed an intellectual education—with particular focus on art and philosophy—that was quite exceptional for a woman of her time; she continued to build on it all her life. When the opportunity presented itself to express her views in public, she hesitated at first: women of the time simply did not expose themselves to the general view, and she feared collective disapprobation. But she was appalled by Barbey d'Aurevilly's misogynist article on the "blue-stockings," as women writers were pejoratively called, and finally decided to speak out. Early in her series of talks her erudition and oratorical talent won the enthusiasm of her listeners. After presenting her views on independent morality and positivism, on the *principes* and *moeurs* of her time, she moved on courageously to the question of women. Deraismes's demonstration was ambitious: by retracing what she called "the history of Eve through Humanity," she meant to expose the workings of the system of male domination in all domains of life: the law, mores, the family, society, even the theater. "Let me repeat: women's inferiority is not a fact of nature but a human invention, a social fiction," she declared, deconstructing, we might say today, the religious, scientific, and historical discourses of her time.[9] She even went so far as to denounce the way wives were put on a pedestal: "this way of exalting your maternity is nothing more than a means to bring you down: you only count for something because you have the honor—sometimes—of engendering a man." In her conclusion she proclaimed that "in spite of formal differences, woman and man are absolutely identical with and equal to each other." This provocative affirmation of identity did not signify that the two sexes were undifferentiated, rather that women might define themselves by means of new criteria: "We want at last to be what we are and not what is made of us."[10] Maria Deraismes identified women's struggle in women's terms, without making concessions to the normative definition of the female or the feminine. It might be said, therefore, that she avoided the paradox of reproducing existing gender identities in the discourse of contestation.[11] Though Deraismes never again treated the issue as audaciously as in these first talks (her later commitment to the republican political cause did not permit it), her particular feminism circa 1869 constructs a dialectic of equality and difference which present-day feminism should not be allowed to render unintelligible. According to Maria Deraismes, once preconceived definitions and mythologies of femininity and femaleness were demolished it was up to women themselves to construct their identity. At the core of her demonstration is a clear concept of the female individual and her natural right to equality, a concept which leaves open—and dynamic—the question of individual identity.

Few later texts, however relevant and innovative, attain the depth and scope of Maria Deraismes's thinking; her talks represent republican feminist thought at its most fully developed. Though they were not published until 1890 and cannot be considered founding texts in the same way as Simone de Beauvoir's *Deuxième sexe*, she and the persons who first shared her commitment, particularly Léon Richer, had a profound influence on the period.[12] Maria Deraismes provided French feminism under the Third Republic with an individualist and rationalist foundation which it has never lost, despite the fact that in the years following her active period public feminist argumentation tended to be based instead on philanthropic and maternalist values. It seems important to note that French feminism was not any less individualistic than feminism in Protestant countries. In fact, the gradual diversification of arguments may be explained by both the nature of French republican thinking and the influence of American feminism. Like republican political thought of the same time, thinking in the 1860s about women's emancipation detached itself from utopian socialism and Christian idealism, keeping exclusively to the ground of right. Women's emancipation was no longer systematically linked to the emancipation of the people (except in the minds of the socialists) but came instead to be theorized as an autonomous object. And feminism's project, once revolutionary, became reformist in intention and tone. It was promulgated by republicans who had been deeply affected by the failure of the Second Republic and the trauma of Napoleon III's coup d'état. Among the different groups struggling for the establishment of a secular liberal democracy, feminists, for whom equality between the sexes was a necessary condition of any improvement in the distribution of wealth, power, and knowledge, were—and knew themselves to be—a minority. And they formulated their demand for sexual equality in the same universalist terms as those that had been formulated during the French Revolution—by Condorcet. Relations between men and women were indeed analyzed in terms of power—domination and subjection—but the critique of the real inequalities oppressing women also cited their subjection as individuals and human subjects. In the name of progress and reason, democratic principles of equality and liberty should, the feminists believed, direct the lives of men and women in both the public and private spheres. The singularity of the French movement lies in how it linked its fate to that of the Republic. But while the Republic seemed the only regime capable of guaranteeing equality for men and women, the feminist understanding was that it could only actually attain democratic legitimacy if it applied that principle of equity. French feminism of the period was therefore an example of what may be called republican utopianism.

The republicans in power, on the other hand, prisoners, for the most part, of positivist teachings, remained generally hostile to the feminist approach to relations between the sexes. Women were to be associated with the republican project only as wives and mothers of future citizens, not as freestanding individuals. And the Third Republic developed a concept of gender that was fully in keeping with this perception and policy. Though it did reinstitute divorce in 1884, the family was to remain outside the domain of democratic values; indeed, the father's absolute authority over wife and children was presented as essential to social and political equilibrium. The texts no longer evoked women's "absolute" inferiority but postulated instead the "complementarity" of the sexes: woman was considered inferior to man in the public sphere and superior to him in the private sphere, specifically as a reproducer. And as long as she was organically linked to the family and the "race," she could under no condition be perceived as a person.[13] The feminist movement, by contrast, defended the interests of women as persons and envisioned an original project for democratic society in which the two sexes, mixed and acting together, would play a fundamental role. Their demand to make women a part of all strata of public life did not call for dispossessing men or for any kind of exclusion but rather for power sharing and the reorganizing of society in such a way as to abolish gender boundaries. The expressed will for integration rather than conquest made the feminist project appreciably different from the political forces—now considered classic—that were establishing themselves at the time. It concerned not only women but the relations between the sexes and the organization of society at large. For this reason it seems difficult to apply the terms "individual" and "relational" here.[14] In fact the two types of argument are closely related; moreover, it seems to me that feminism's concerns are always relational, in the sense that the man/woman relation is at the core of feminist thought even when its principal aim is to conceive of woman as an individual. This enables us to better understand the activism of feminist men as well as the difficulty of communicating such a complex message.

By instituting freedom of expression and association, the Third Republic made it easier for the feminist movement to develop and grow. The various partisans of feminism were linked ideologically, politically, and in some cases by personal sentiment and passion. Despite their many disappointments, those fighting for women's rights continued to believe in the perfectibility of the regime. "It is not the Republic, but republicans, who are against us," Maria Deraismes affirmed.[15] Most of them were active in the Freemasons or other anticlerical, free-thought movements, and at moments when reactionary forces threatened the Republic—namely in the parliamentary crisis of May 16, 1877, and during the Dreyfus affair near the turn of the century—they were quick to show their support of the regime. Republican values constituted the movement's ideological cement; there was no place in it for anyone who did not stand behind the "pacte laïque."[16] Christian, that is Catholic, feminists, for example, could no longer belong—supposing they wished to—after their leaders chose the anti-Dreyfusard camp. And the fact that republican values were under such intense attack from the extreme right made them a ground of consensus for a large range of political sensibilities, from moderate socialism to conservative and even nationalist republicanism.

From 1898 to 1914 what is known as the "radical" Republic was characterized by great political and reformist dynamism, and most feminist militants felt a party to its actions. This is one factor explaining why, contrary to what happened in Germany, French socialism did not play a major role in pre-1914 feminism; the socialists' hostility toward feminism as bourgeois is neither more nor less significant. In fact, the women designated by socialists as "bour-geoises" were for the most part situated well to the left on the political spectrum. When, in 1908, spurred by the Second International, the polemic between socialism and "bourgeois feminism" got under way, it did not bring about a major schism within the feminist movement; for feminists it remained possible to have a twofold commitment—to feminism and to socialism—and many chose to do so. For socialists, however, things were more complex. To these potential allies of the feminists, it seemed sufficient to have voted as a group in favor of the principle of women's equality; they were against any independent feminist movement. In fact, as much as the ideas defended by the feminists, it was their very existence as an autonomous force that excited socialist hostility. It was quite enough that women should demand rights; to go so far as to organize themselves into a movement was tantamount to setting off a war between the sexes. A few marginal attempts at forming feminist socialist groups failed, and their instigator, the socialist Louise Saumoneau (1875–1950), soon abandoned the field.

Feminism's felt proximity to the republican state raised a strong hope within the French movement of one day seeing women integrated into public life. The vote for women was not made an overt cause for fear of endangering the regime (once again, people had unpleasant memories of how universal suffrage as instituted in 1848 had put Napoleon III in a position to violate and abolish it three years later). And though feminists were disappointed in the "wicked stepmother" Republic that refused to grant women their rights, outright rebellion was never declared against government representatives; diplomacy and negotiation were almost always preferred to open confrontation. The feminists' objective was to convince parliamentarians that their ideas were sound and that they could be useful collaborators, all the while maintaining their autonomy as a movement and affirming political neutrality within the republican framework. The movement sought to transform the republican state in such a way as to integrate women. We should note that the feminist approach to the state as neutral arbiter contributed to the development of the welfare state.

There were, however, some notable exceptions to this policy, a few openly provocative voices. Hubertine Auclert (1848–1914), the pioneer of political enfranchisement for French women, was frankly combative: she denounced the "minotaur state" and the "all-for-show Republic." Once a follower of Léon Richer and Maria Deraismes, Auclert had became convinced that no reform would be possible until women had the right to vote. She broke with the tactic of "little steps," and her *franc tireur* methods prefigure those of the suffragettes.[17] She refused to pay taxes until such time as "Français" would also signify "Française" in the Constitution (for which action all her personal belongings were seized by the state) and called for boycotting the national census. But while attracting press attention, Auclert did not rally the feminist movement to her tactics. Between 1868 and 1889, in fact, the small groups that composed the movement, each made up of a small number of men and women, chose instead the tactic of "reasonable" pressure. The French League for Women's Rights, founded in 1882 by Léon Richer, actually constituted for a time a kind of feminist lobby around members of parliament. Their purely legislative program was sober and low-profile; projects for libraries, welcoming or meeting centers for women, and free legal counsel all remained dead letters, for either lack of funding or simply lack of supporters. Indeed, the feminist movement was not much more than a small minority lobby until 1889, when it began to develop a much wider female base.

PROGRESS IN GENDER CONSCIOUSNESS

The consolidation of the republican regime, which began in 1879, and the first great reforms in favor of freedom of the press, assembly, association, and education facilitated the development of collective gender consciousness among French women, a consciousness, that is, of belonging not only to a biological sex but to a social gender. The development of industrial urban society, and the progress of notions of individualism and egalitarianism facilitated—in France as in all western countries—the development and expression of a kind of female individualism.[18] Making primary and secondary education available to girls and opening employment in white-collar service professions to women greatly advanced the process. By favoring girls' education and insisting that in raising their children "mothers of citizens" were fulfilling a public responsibility (though in the private sphere), the republican state quite unintentionally built a bridge between the two spheres it meant to keep strictly separate. And republican wives and mothers began demanding greater recognition for their public role. The move from consciousness of gender to feminist consciousness was not systematic, but it was helped along by the existence of a movement which, between 1878 and 1889, maintained a high profile, namely by holding international conferences. For women who had already run up against the limits of republican policy with regard to gender, the feminist movement was a valued interlocutor. And for women with an imperious need to realize themselves as individuals, it offered considerable opportunities and excited great hopes. The feminist leader Adrienne Avril de Sainte Croix (1855–1939) thus defined feminism as "the modern manifestation of woman's own coming to awareness of her female individuality."[19]

The fact that for republican women gender consciousness was evolving into fully feminist consciousness is reflected in certain women's initiatives of the period. In 1879 Louise Koppe (1846–1900), described by a contemporary as "a girl and a workman's wife," possessed of only a rudimentary education, founded a new kind of women's newspaper, *La Femme de France*. The paper refused all male collaborators and was written and edited by a "humble committee of mothers and housewives who know better how to love, sew, and spin than to wield a pen against the scoffers of our day."[20] Its ambition was to provide women with a place in which to express themselves and exchange ideas on the "question of women" without wasting their time on such things as "fashion and pleasures." Though the editors announced no departure from existing conceptions of gender, they sought to bring women to a consciousness of "[their] dignity, [their] value as members of society,"[21] and they denounced male arrogance. Louise Koppe believed more in social regeneration through the exaltation of women's natural superiority and maternal function than in legal reforms. This familialist, of-the-people feminism thus represented a return to themes dear to the Saint-Simonians. But while at first she positioned herself at the margins of the movement for women's rights, Louise Koppe became interested in and ultimately made use of its arguments, and eventually she too began to call for equal rights.

Ten years later, in 1889, on the occasion of the International Congress of Feminine Works and Institutions, another group of women, representing the generally Protestant milieu of female philanthropy, began collectively speaking out and demanding recognition for their social role. The philanthropists' discourse was one of wives and mothers utterly devoted to the Republic; it was in perfect conformity with republican gender logic. This was likewise reflected in their support of a legislative measure forbidding women to work at night. It was on this ground that a serious clash took place between "protectionist" philanthropists and the feminist groups led by Maria Deraismes and Léon Richer, a clash that resulted in the holding of two separate congresses on the feminine condition:[22] the latter group, firmly opposed to the new legislation, refused to participate in a congress headed by the "protectionist" MP Jules Simon. Still, the women philanthropists had no desire merely to "fulfill their duties" and keep silent. They meant to speak up themselves and get public recognition for their activities in the public sphere, to express themselves as representatives of the female gender and to be heard. This was the first sign of a feminist consciousness, one that had radically evolved: the vast majority of women philanthropists rallied to the struggle for women's rights. In so doing they agreed to position themselves on political ground. They did not, however, abandon their particular approach to women's questions, an approach that valorized the specificity of women, following either an essentialist philosophy that underlined natural, biological differences or a differentialist one stressing cultural differences.

The evolution among Protestant women philanthropists from gender consciousness to feminist consciousness is exemplary.[23] Their charity and organizing work gave them detailed knowledge of women's condition and moved them to denounce women's legal inferiority. Meanwhile the *chrétiens sociaux*, in this case left-leaning Protestants particularly concerned about social issues, gradually became receptive to feminism in their struggle against prostitution—a problem, of course, that directly concerned relations between the sexes. Between 1889 and 1901, the year the National Council of French Women was established, the most advanced philanthropists were gradually won over by egalitarian argumentation; they were also greatly stimulated by the example and encouragement offered by English and American women. Those among them who were more in favor of solidarity than charity and believed in prevention as much as treatment pulled the troops toward feminism. The word itself had entered people's vocabulary by the end of the 1890s and no longer scared people. The success of Jeanne Schmahl's (1846–1915) group, the "Avant-Courrière," founded in 1893, whose political stance and strategy were openly moderate, reassured the philanthropists and others: feminist commitment was no longer synonymous with marginality or subversion. With the exception of the issue of political rights, the platform developed by women philanthropists at their 1889 congress (International Congress of Feminine Works and Institutions) hardly differed from that announced by the more progressive group at the International

Congress on Women's Conditions and Rights. The following year, under pressure from American feminists, the two groups came together and founded the National Council of French Women, opening a new phase in the history of the French movement.

The Catholic milieus, on the other hand, remained thoroughly hostile not only to feminism but to the "radical" Republic—understandably so since it had launched a veritable anticlerical offensive and would, in 1905, decree the separation of church and state. When in 1896 Marie Maugeret (1844–1928) founded a group and a newspaper—*Le Féminisme chrétien*—that attempted to reconcile Catholicism and feminism, she was perceived by the Catholic mainstream as a radical and remained isolated. (It should be noted that her rightist political positions and her anti-Semitism and anti-Protestantism at the time of the Dreyfus affair made any collaboration with non-Catholic feminists unthinkable.) Social-minded Catholics focused on the problems of working women without evoking the issue of equality between the sexes. They were particularly receptive to the antibourgeois "workers' power" movements, which for their part unconditionally condemned the women's rights movement. Catholic women philanthropists refused any role in the National Council of French Women, though overtures were made to them. Their submission to the Catholic hierarchy and absolute acceptance of the church's patriarchal concept of the family were clearly manifest in some of the small groups they founded. But Catholic culture is not alone to blame for Catholic women's inability to attain gender consciousness before 1914: precluded as they were from assuming the collective identity of wife and mother generated by the anticlerical, "enemy" republican state, passing from sex to gender was more difficult for them.

TURN-OF-THE-CENTURY DEVELOPMENTS IN THE FEMINIST MOVEMENT

With the philanthropists and significant numbers of middle-class urban women coming over to the cause, the movement acquired the female base it had been lacking. Now it had a dependable network of women and could claim a higher degree of representativeness. The new activists brought new ideas and new groups to support those ideas: the movement took on a different look. The avant-garde, which had been sexually mixed, evolved into a movement composed of women. Men were not excluded, but they were no longer accepted as leaders, and some new groups were made up exclusively of women.

A new generation of leaders took over from the pioneers, whose influence began to fade. Léon Richer withdrew in 1892 for health reasons, and in 1894 Maria Deraismes died. Their last joint project was to organize the International Congress for Women's Rights, held in 1889. Deraismes spent the remainder of her energies fighting for women to be admitted into the Freemasons; she herself had been initiated in 1882, but the lodge that had accepted her retracted after being condemned by the Grand Orient de France. She remained firmly committed to the project of integrating women into republican institutions, and in 1893 founded a Freemasons' lodge, "Le Droit Humain," that welcomed men and women together. Hubertine Auclert, who incarnated the second generation of feminists, left Paris in 1888 to follow her male companion to Algeria; she thus gave up her leadership position in the movement. Her regularly transmitted articles, in which she courageously denounced the condition of Arab women—"ces Françaises africaines"—subjected to Muslim law,[24] had virtually no resonance in a milieu in which the question of female solidarity beyond the borders of the West had not yet been raised. She returned to Paris in 1894, deeply shaken by her widowhood, to discover that her newspaper *La Citoyenne* had been taken over by Maria Martin. Undaunted, she took up the pen once more. With the new group she organized in 1902, she continued her suffragette activities until her death in 1914.

The new generation of the 1890s was more diverse than its predecessors. In addition to Eugénie Potonié Pierre (1844–1898), Aline Valette (1850–1899), and Léonie Rouzade (1839–1916), all strongly drawn to socialist and solidarity doctrines, there were important political moderates such as Jeanne Oddo-Deflou and Jeanne Schmahl, who sought to attract women of the *grande bourgeoisie* and the aristocracy. Spiritualist, Christian, and socialist currents developed. But though sensibilities had grown more varied, there was no intention of surrendering the autonomy of what was now openly known as the *movement féministe*. The word "feminism," which had been used by Alexander Dumas fils in *L'Homme-femme* (1872) to ridicule partisans of the women's cause and then by Hubertine Auclert in a positive way to designate her own struggle, began to circulate in the 1890s.[25] It was adopted by a new radical group founded the day after the 1889 conference: Marya Chéliga (1853–1927) declared in her *Bulletin de l'Union universelle des femmes* dated April 15, 1890, that the union was "openly and independently feminist." Eugénie Potonié Pierre, president of Solidarité des femmes, included it in the title of the group she organized at the end of 1891: *Fédération des sociétés féministes* (the meeting held by the federation in Paris in 1892 was entitled General Convention of Feminist Societies). In becoming part of the language, feminism also came to be identified as something sociological, both a subject of study itself and a source of sociological information about women. Larousse's *Revue encyclopédique* of 1893 included an entry on feminism under the heading "sociology"; then in 1896 the editor published a supplement on the feminist movement throughout the world. From that time forward, as French society focused on social questions and discovered the *question des femmes*, feminism was considered a legitimate subject of intellectual debate—a debate in which antifeminists did not fail to make their (loud) voices heard. As surprising as it may seem today, feminism actually became something of a fashion, at least in Paris. The talks given on the subject by the historian Léopold Lacour (1854–1939) and the writer Jules Bois (1871–1941) at the Théâtre de la Bodinière attracted new audiences. All the important newspapers and most reviews began publishing a "feminism" column which discussed not only developments in the movement but all subjects that could be deemed of concern to women. Feminist theses became the matter of novels and plays, and though their dénouements did not always advance the cause of women's emancipation, the intrigues at least served to expose the contradictions and archaism of the laws, especially those applying to married women. And when the feminist activist Avril de Sainte Croix was requested in 1906 by the publishing house of Giard and Brière to write a book on feminism for their "series on political doctrines," it was clear that feminism had been recognized in French society as a real subject of debate. Nothing in the immediately succeeding periods equaled this publishing event.

LA FRONDE, A FEMINIST DAILY

Though resistance against equality remained strong, the movement managed, while remaining conspicuously autonomous, to make women visible in the public space and to make people conscious of some of the inequalities to which they were subjected. Then on December 9, 1897, a new feminist daily newspaper entitled *La Fronde* came out—headed, managed, written, and typeset entirely by women. *La Fronde* continued to be published until September 1903. The newspaper's contribution to women's—and feminism's—visibility in the political life of the Third Republic—where, it should be remembered, the press was the main forum for debate—was of crucial importance.

For five years, *La Fronde* enabled republican women's voices to be heard in the public space; it was an incomparable tool in the struggle for equality. The only experiment of its kind in its time, it illustrates both the integrationist aspirations and the subversive tendencies of French feminism at the turn of the century. *La Fronde*'s founder, Marguerite Durand (1864–1936), was representative of those active women who had come to feminism only recently and in unusual ways. Won over to the women's cause at a convention in 1896—which she had gone to with the intention of writing an ironical account—Marguerite Durand had already had professional and political experience. She was born out of wedlock in 1864 and was brought up in a convent. Theater classes at the Conservatoire led to a career as an acclaimed actress at the Comédie Française; she then left the stage to marry Georges Laguerre, a lawyer, with whom she got involved in the Boulanger adventure and founded a newspaper called *La Presse*. She was divorced a few years later and began writing a column for *Le Figaro*, then under the direction of Antonin Périvier (with whom she had a child).[26] In founding *La Fronde*, Marguerite Durand sought both to open the profession of journalism up to women and to defend women's rights. Refusing male participation was what gave the newspaper credibility: as Durand explained, "excluding male collaboration was not a way of ostracizing men; it's just that if there had been a single man on the paper, people would have said that it was run by men."[27] Durand's strategy proved effective. For the first time journalism—investigative reporting rather than "armchair" opinion journalism—became a career accessible to women. By hiring only women, *La Fronde* obtained the right for them to attend parliamentary debates and city council meetings, to set foot in the stock exchange, and to investigate all aspects of public life. Marguerite Durand's team was as serious and talented as that of any other important daily of the period, and the newspaper soon acquired the nickname "*Le Temps* in petticoats."[28] Indeed, its function was twofold: next to feminist articles defending women's rights and information presented from an explicitly female and feminist point of view, there was general information presented in the same tone and terms as in newspapers written and edited by men. The intention was to prove that women could do as well as men in a field that had traditionally been forbidden them, all the while acquiring power as a means of feminist expression. When the Dreyfus affair broke in December 1897—almost immediately after the newspaper's founding (Emile Zola's celebrated text "J'accuse" was published in *L'Aurore* in January 1898)—*La Fronde* came out resolutely in favor of Alfred Dreyfus. The fate of the Jewish army captain unjustly accused of espionage by the army mobilized public opinion of the time and divided the French into two irreconcilable camps.

When publication of *La Fronde* ceased after five years of existence, Marguerite Durand's assessment was intensely negative. After announcing that the newspaper was closing down for financial reasons, she portrayed the venture as one "tremendous bluff" that she alone had sustained all along: "Feminism has not paid. It did not subscribe, it did not keep *La Fronde* alive; it did not read it, recommend it, disseminate it, or buy it," she bitterly complained.[29] No doubt Marguerite Durand felt she had been abandoned by a movement which, behind the scenes, had sharply criticized her worldly manners, expensive tastes, and the life she led as a "free woman" with many lovers. It is also probably true that feminists did not have the financial means to support such a project, as is specified in numerous schoolteachers' letters to the editor. *La Fronde*'s existence was in fact made possible by exceptional circumstances and it should not lead us to overestimate the activist capacities of French feminism. Marguerite Durand seems to have preferred to let people believe that it was thanks to her blond hair and pearls rather than reveal the name of her secret sponsor—for from the start *La Fronde* had been financed by the Baron Gustave de Rothschild; Durand was almost certainly his mistress—a demonstration once again of how close the ties were between the feminist and republican causes. Moreover, this particular "Dreyfusard" manifestation on the part of the French Jewish milieu has hardly been taken into account by historians of the affair. The pro-Dreyfus camp thus recognized feminism as a political agent and as the "spokesperson" for women.

Though women and feminism may have been used in the Dreyfus affair, the feminist movement undeniably profited from the association. During its short existence, *La Fronde* gave republican women a genuine collective political identity and a real presence in the political landscape. It was a breath of air and life not only for women and feminists in the capital but all over France; indeed, it incarnated for a time the French feminist movement. And it proved women's abilities even to those (women) who did not share its political opinions. While making feminism acceptable and attractive to many women who would have been repelled by "traditional" activism, the paper also initiated many political actions: it launched petitions, organized the Congress of 1900, was active in founding women's unions, and supported strikers. Many of its campaigns were successful: women lawyers were authorized to plead cases; women won the right to be admitted to the École des Beaux Arts; Madeleine Pelletier (1874–1939) obtained the right to take the selective examination held to fill positions of *médecin aliéniste* (the contemporary equivalent of psychiatrist) for the city of Paris. Almost all women and women's groups that wished could express themselves in the paper, communicate their thinking, report on the actions and activities they were involved in, or simply announce where and when their meetings were held. *La Fronde* was a unique experience that demonstrated how much legitimacy feminism could acquire within the Republic. The end of the Dreyfus affair put an end to the paper, which lost a great deal of money. But the movement outlasted *La Fronde* and became more and more diversified.

HETEROGENEITY AND MARGINALITY

In the early twentieth century, the feminist movement was a highly fragmented one. Newspapers and groups remained its backbone, though the first rarely survived after the money ran out; the groups—about fifty of them, calling themselves leagues or societies—enjoyed a longer life span. Geography explains why groups proliferated in the rest of the country; the fragmentation that characterized the movement in Paris was due to the fact that each of the various leaders, many only recently won over to feminism, meant to run her own organization. Madeleine Pelletier was exaggerating when she affirmed that the leaders were mere "generals without armies," but it does seem that small structures suited the activists best. The groups differed from each other in their theoretical and strategic preoccupations and choices; their special concerns were sometimes expressed in their names, such as the "study group on French feminism," which concentrated on legal questions, or the "Women's Jury," whose principal complaint was that

women were not allowed to serve as jurors and whose primary activity was
to rejudge contemporary legal cases. The Avant Courrière limited its program of action to getting two laws passed, one recognizing women's right to
serve as witnesses for official administrative and notarial documents (right
obtained in 1897), the other giving married working women the right to use
their salary as they saw fit (right obtained in 1907). But joining one feminist
group instead of another was often less a matter of strategy than one's sensi-
bility and personal affinity with the leader in question.

This heterogeneity makes it extremely difficult to establish a typology of feminist currents. Though right/left political divisions did exist, they cannot account for the particular dynamics of the movement, any more than the opposition bourgeois/proletarian can. French feminism's recruits came from the
middle classes; they were often women with modest incomes. Primary school
teachers, white-collar employees, and women with small private incomes were
among the most receptive. Some blue-collar women joined the movement—
Gabrielle Petit (1860–1936), Jeanne Bouvier (1865–1964), and the women
typesetters of *La Fronde*—but they were a small minority. In the French workers' movement, the Proudhonian tradition continued to exert a strong influence on people's thinking: the unions were hostile to the idea of opening
membership to women and the socialists were simply not interested in the
question. Personalities from the grand bourgeoisie and the aristocracy (in the
second category, the Duchess of Uzès [1847–1933]) were few and far between,
and lack of financing remained a crucial problem throughout the period.

The archives do not provide enough information to undertake a sociological study of the group members (men or women); the leaders, on the other
hand, are fairly well known to us. They resembled each other only in that they
were all strong, ambitious personalities, power-wielders whom the feminist
cause had in many cases enabled to "find themselves." The mere act of joining the movement was already a transgression in Belle Epoque society, one
whose consequences not all women were strong enough to assume. In
Catholic France, with its firm attachment to patriarchal values, the feminists,
like their leaders, were likely to belong to a minority—Protestant, Jewish,
"free-thinking." Among the "personalities" who led the groups there were also
a fair number of émigrées: Marya Chéliga and Madame Orka were Polish;
Maria Martin (1839–1910) and Jeanne Schmahl English; Madame Bezobrazov
Russian. In addition, there was a German, Kathe Schirmacher (1865–1930),

and a Swiss, Emilie de Morsier (1843–1896). Feminist leaders could be born out of wedlock, divorced, unmarried. What so clearly characterized the leaders no doubt also applied to most of the troops (especially given that before 1914, as we have said, all Catholic women's groups were thoroughly hostile to feminism). A feminist woman's social marginality might have been reinforced by specific misfortunes or simply by the experience of working life.

The male feminists of the period are even less known to us. In most cases they were husbands, companions, or relatives of women activists. Often couples were active together, or the husband openly supported his wife's commitment. As for those men who made women's rights a lifelong cause, it is hard to say what they had in common. Political affiliation was not really a deciding factor. What is clear is that each seemed out of place in his own social or professional milieu. Men's feminist commitment did not involve any collective coming to awareness, but implied rather a desire for egalitarian and harmonious relations between men and women. And whereas a woman's feminist consciousness was often due to some painful experience of the injustice of women's "fate," a man's consciousness tended more to develop out of a special individual relationship with a woman. The statesman René Viviani (1862–1925), for example, learned very young about the struggle for women's rights from his mother; he worked for the cause as a member of parliament and minister and throughout his life. The public man drew his convictions from private experience.

The distinction between a moderate and radical wing (the second is to be understood in opposition to the first and the word is used here as it is in the typology of German feminism) does not do justice to the movement's diversity, but it does enable us to define certain major differences. First it should be noted that the two did not correspond precisely to existing political labels: occasionally (though this was exceptional), nationalists such as Jeanne Oddo-Deflou or the Bélilon sisters belonged to the radical wing. The two wings were perhaps most visibly divided on the issue of tactics. The moderate wing sought to persuade through peaceable methods—primarily legislative—whereas the radicals spoke their minds directly, wore their convictions on their sleeves, were incautious and imaginative, choosing to shock in order to convince—they were not above creating a scandal to get public and press attention. There was also a significant difference in the degree of emancipation sought. For a time the moderate wing was hostile to political emancipation, not only because of its allegiance to the Republic but also because it did not want to shock public opinion. But in time it let itself be persuaded of the justice of the suffragist cause: the National Council of French Women—incarnating the moderate position—ended up participating fully in the struggle to obtain the vote for women; it was particularly active in this cause from 1909 to 1914. Finally, people had differing ideas about freedom. The movement offered no single model of the "new woman" or the "new man," appropriating instead the rallying cry of the Protestant feminist Felix Pécaut: "Woman, dare to be!" (Helen Brion [1882–1962], a primary schoolteacher who spent her life assembling material for a never-published *encyclopédie féministe*, later adopted this slogan.) The crucial thing was to refute all prejudices that put women in a position of inferiority so that they might then experiment to discover their individuality. The objective was to offer each person the means to realize her chosen identity in practice, whatever that choice might be. But feminists were not free of dogmatism since the choices themselves were often incompatible. The multiple subgroups and alliances within the feminist movement reflect these different and often divergent female identity choices. And the oppositions were often irresolvable. There was, for example, no common ground between women like the "doctoresse" Madeleine Pelletier, who wore men's suits and favored women's "masculinization," and the journalists from *La Fronde*, who demanded the right to be "feminists in lace." But moderate feminists were not the only ones to stop short at the idea of women having free control over the biological function of maternity. The idea's most illustrious defender was probably Nelly Roussel (1878–1922). In her original, free-thinking, neo-Malthusian feminism, birth control was a fundamental tool for women's self-realization. But even though Roussel valorized maternity as a "creative function," many women were appalled by the very idea of sexuality unlinked to reproduction. More shocking still was Madeleine Pelletier's open defense of women's right to abortion and sexual emancipation.[30] Most moderate feminists condemned abortion in the name of women's "maternal mission."

Within the radical wing there were different analyses of women's oppression and divergent positions on whether and how men and maleness should be accused. Johann Jakob Bachofen's theories about an original matriarchy found some supporters, including Jeanne Oddo-Deflou, who translated a part of his writings. Positing an original matriarchal system made it possible to demonstrate that men had seized power and to show the present system as patriarchal. Accusing men as the dominant social group led to criticizing "male nature" and what was seen as men's natural selfishness and egotism. All feminists condemned prostitution and the double moral standard that applied in sexual relations: most often these were seen to result from the reprehensible male sexual nature. While lesbianism remained taboo, women sometimes publicly demanded the right to refuse all sexual contact with men—as a means of self-protection. With this came a valorization of virginity, chastity, and female purity, though few went so far as Arria Ly (1881–1934) to develop a theoretical justification for this particular choice. Madeleine Pelletier, who agreed with Ly, nonetheless advised her for strategic reasons not to publish her ideas. Women activists were more explicit on the matter in their private correspondence. The feminist and socialist Caroline Kauffman (1840?–1926) sent a woman friend a poem entitled "Hymne à Phallus" in which she satirized phallic power and denounced the transmission of venereal disease by unfaithful husbands (she herself had become ill this way). Most feminists, however, chose to attack the system of oppression rather than men themselves; they defended an ideal of harmonious relations between the sexes. Nelly Roussel spoke of feminism as a "doctrine of happiness [that aims at realizing] the general interest," enabling "each person to develop fully in the direction of his [or her] aspirations." Léopold Lacour called feminism "Comprehensive Humanism."[31]

FEMINIST CULTURE

Despite its members' profoundly divergent sensibilities and analyses, the feminist movement was a cohesive one, as is demonstrated not only by its program of action but also by its cultural implications. For both moderates and radicals, the Republic had not satisfied the hopes it had raised in its "daughters," and the feminist movement was appealed to in some degree to compensate for this failure. At the turn of the century the feminist movement was a place where a woman could do many things. She could find free legal aid; she could organize a press campaign to enable her to accede to a particular profession or to sit for a selective examination to further her education or start a career; she could discover knowledge and references that were not to be had elsewhere. It was a privileged locus of female sociality outside the private sphere, a place where identities could be forged and lived. The newspapers, groups, and various cultural initiatives, such as Marya Chéliga's feminist theater, provided many women with an unprecedented opportunity to present and publicize their writings, thinking, and artistic creations, or simply to come out from the shadows and break the silence. French feminist culture was dedicated to promoting the creativity and constructive actions of all women, whether feminist or not, and of the few men actively engaged in the struggle for equality between the sexes. In the feminist *Petit Almanach illustré*, published in 1906, all the male and female Christian saints were replaced with "saints" of feminism: here "newly famous women" shared the page with "feminologists" and "feminists" of both sexes.[32] Reforming the French language so as to give feminine forms to the names of professions newly accessible to women was high on the feminist agenda. Use of the terms "Madame" and "Mademoiselle" and of the patronymic was also challenged. Opinions were divided on this and other questions, and there was never unanimity about how such issues should be resolved; what was clear was the felt need to shake up social codes pertaining to gender and to make all that was female visible, particularly in those areas where new definitions of femaleness were being developed.

Another priority was to preserve the memory of battles already fought and ensure the transmission of acquired knowledge and understanding. History and memory were considered essential to integrating women into the public sphere. Helen Brion painstakingly collected articles about women and the women's movement in the hopes of one day publishing an *encyclopédie féministe*. Marguerite Durand and Marie-Louise Bouglé assembled archives, books, and documentary material that would make it possible to retrace the history of feminism under the Third Republic. Instituting *lieux de mémoires* by erecting monuments or simple plaques within the urban space in honor of former important militants was also a way in which this fundamentally political feminist culture sought to express itself. The feminist movement meant to inscribe its conception of gender difference within cultural, symbolic space.

Did the inventiveness of French feminism during the Belle Epoque bear fruit? And how can we measure its impact? From a purely legislative point of view, the progress achieved did not measure up to feminist hopes. Still, republican politicians were now more kindly disposed to the militants and their projects for reform. In fact, considerable parliamentary action was taken on women's issues. Early on in the twentieth century, women obtained the right to serve as witnesses for notarial documents and to accede to professions such as medicine and law. The question of granting them political, civic equality was not put to parliamentary vote, but it was discussed with increasing seriousness. Though the 1907 law giving married working women the right to use their salary proved extremely difficult to apply and thus did not have much impact on women's real lives, it did represent a crack in that formidable patriarchal legal edifice, the Napoleonic Code.[33] In 1909 the *Chambre des députés* (French lower house of parliament) delivered a report in favor of granting women the right to vote in municipal elections. We might even say that in the person of René Viviani, MP, then government minister, there existed a kind of state-led feminism—moderate of course, but radically different from the conservative thinking that characterized the French *provinces*. Several feminist personalities were in regular, friendly contact with government representatives and used their influence to obtain subsidies for specific projects or get parliamentary hearings scheduled on questions of concern to women. It must be remembered that the highly conservative Constitution of the Third Republic granted the Senate the power to veto all laws passed in the Chambre des députés. And the republican elite continued to favor a strict definition of gender and the strict separation of public and private spheres. Finally, the anticlerical radicals, a rising political force, remained hostile to granting the right to vote for fear most women would follow the dictates of their priests. Though the feminist movement remained cut off from the broad mass of Catholic France, it nonetheless managed to incarnate new ideas about collective and individual gender identity that brought together values of equality and freedom and fueled a debate that cut across all French society.

On the eve of World War I, the struggle for the right to vote began to take priority over identity-related demands; the war and the new political issues of the period known as the *entre-deux-guerres* accentuated this tendency. The feminist movement no longer had a monopoly on women's political commitment, and it would not lead the ultimate fight to integrate women into the public space. The demands of French feminists had lost that slightly utopian dimension which, however fragmentary and contradictory it may have been, constituted one of French feminism's major resources at the turn of the century.

Translated from French by Amy Jacobs

CHAPTER 6

The Women's Movement in Germany in an International Context

UTE GERHARD

> I am not writing a history of the German women's movement.
> That already exists, as a whole and in monographs. What doesn't
> exist is an image of the diverse forms of personal womanhood
> [*Frauentum*] that were caught up by the movement and supported
> it, an image not of the programs, organizations, work, and achieve-
> ments, but rather of the characteristic vital impulse [*Lebensdrang*]
> from which everything emerged. . . . the actual reality of the move-
> ment. And exactly this is what is carried off with time, and in this
> empty space an uninformed posterity places shadows of abstraction
> and calls them, perhaps, "the feminists" [*die Frauenrechtlerinnen*].[1]

INTRODUCTION

This short epigraph, extracted from a description of the German women's movement, includes several words that are typically German, a little old-fashioned, and thus very difficult to translate, and yet it reveals some characteristics that may be illuminating in an international comparison. Moreover, because it accentuates the "actual reality of the movement," beyond "programs, organizations," etc., it is interesting to historians concerned with the inner functioning of a movement, its peculiarities, its social and cultural networks, and its self-image.

To experts, the author is easily recognizable because of her pensive and somewhat bombastic style. But for now, the author is of no importance, and to know her might evoke biased reaction. In my opinion, these kinds of biascs toward the German women's movement of the turn of the century are a real problem in any presentation or comparative discussion. Of course, I am not talking about the common prejudices which women's movements, women's issues, and feminists always face in patriarchal societies. Not only are we used to such resistance, but it is in some ways the elixir of life for every feminist, the *conditio sine qua non* for feminism and a women's movement. Rather, I am thinking of the many blind spots and rash judgments of the experts, who could and should actually know better.

To begin with, let us look at research on social movements in general. German research on social movements, which has been expanding since the 1980s, has misinterpreted or played down the fact that the women's movement has as long a history as the labor movement. Raschke, for instance, prefers not to classify the historical women's movement as one of the "'great' historical movements" because it pursued "only thematically limited" goals.[2] The reproach of "particularity"[3] has likewise led scholars to underestimate the social relevance and politically explosive nature of the new women's movement and to subsume it under the new civil rights movements.[4] Only recently have concessions been made. The new women's movement has been called the "most durable and momentous new social movement" after the ecology movement;[5] it has even been chosen as the subject of systematic comparisons among countries (USA, France, Germany).[6] However, with very few exceptions, the German women's movement has not been included in comparative studies in English-language feminist research,[7] because these comparisons are usually based on a small number of English-speaking authors.[8] Indeed, the language barrier is a problem also for other European countries with vigorous women's movements around the turn of the century.

Considering these deficits it is all the more regrettable that evaluations are often rash and inappropriate. Examples are Chafetz's and Dworkin's cross-national examinations of historical women's movements around the world.[9] Apart from the fact that the schematizing of "merely" ameliorative as opposed to feminist women's movements is carried to extremes,[10] the justification for a scale evaluation based only on the analysis of English-speaking literature is dubious:

> It is likely that in some societies movements existed concerning which no English-language sources were available to us. Most such cases have been incipient, as historians publishing in the sources available to us appear to

have done a rather substantial amount of research in first-wave women's movements in recent years and are unlikely to have missed larger movements.[11]

This is why the German women's movement until 1914 is judged to be merely "incipient," whereas contemporaneous movements in Sweden, Denmark, the Netherlands, and the United Kingdom are labeled "intermediate" or "mass" movements.[12]

A further reservation that plays a role in historiography on the German women's movement concerns feminist research itself. Even though historians of women and gender have explored a wide spectrum of issues, produced an abundance of new knowledge, and discovered numerous historical documents, historical investigation of the women's movement has long remained the concern of a few experts who—in addition—have often worked in isolation or in contexts lacking institutional security and resources.

Historical analysis of the women's movement developed parallel to women's history itself, from early compensatory and contributory research to gender history as social history.[13] It began with quite traditional and partial issues. The focus was either, from a political science perspective, on the history of organizations and associations, with special attention paid to leading personalities,[14] or, from a sociohistorical perspective, on living and working conditions,[15] improvement of education and professional work,[16] and problems of sex and gender relationships (for example, prostitution and sexual reform).[17] In addition, there appeared resource books and anthologies about diverse aspects of the history of the women's movement, reprints of documents, series, and biographies.[18] Investigative priorities followed political orientation or sympathies, which is why the proletarian movement was examined first and most thoroughly, whereas the bourgeois or liberal women's movement and even more so the radical movement did not draw attention until much later.

Only with the more recent and detailed studies, which deliberately went beyond dominant concepts of political science, did the focus shift to women's self-esteem and to a different understanding of the political as personal. These studies were specifically interested in border-crossers between the fronts and between different wings of the so-called bourgeois and proletarian women's movements. They explored women's personal relations, their way of seeing themselves, their social and intellectual networks, and the culture of the movement.[19] It became obvious that these factors constituted the prerequisite and the practical basis for the mobilization of women. In this approach a connection was also made to international feminist and sociological movement research, which raises a lot of these questions under the label of resource mobilization theory. The emphasis here is on social and sociostructural conditions, the activists or supporters of a movement, communication structures, forms of action, mobilizing ideas, preexisting networks, and "cycles of protest."[20] With this latter concept the connections and discontinuities between the different phases, the "long waves" between the old and the new women's movement, can be systematically analyzed.[21] Investigators working from this perspective formulate research issues and hypotheses of medium range, leaving the "great" social theories behind. Although this approach regards social movements as indicators *and* producers of social change and thus views history as changeable, at the same time it bears in mind the need to analyze concrete conditions: "political opportunity structures," changes in social structures, and differences in the availability of new resources that increase the likelihood of collective action.[22]

On the other hand, research on the topic of women's friendships and relationships from a more sociohistorical point of view, which has brought forth fruitful and theoretically controversial results within Anglo-American research,[23] can be regarded as stimulating as well. This work has emphasized the relevance of a "women's sphere,"[24] a "women's support network,"[25] "bonds between women,"[26] and women's friendships and politics,[27] without denying the mobilizing effect of differences and controversies among women.[28]

Without trying to present a complete profile of the women's movement of one country in a single contribution, I will at least try to outline what appear to me to be the fundamental characteristics of the German movement in its most vital phase, around 1900. To paraphrase the epigraph, "[Here] I am not writing a history of the German women's movement; it already exists."

HISTORICAL AND POLITICAL CONDITIONS— QUESTIONS OF PERIODIZATION

The history of the German women's movement begins with the *Vormärz* and around the revolution of 1848. This is not a continuous process of development. On the contrary, it is a history of repeated setbacks, halts, and painful and courageous new beginnings. In order to describe its course, I will divide this first wave of the women's movement until the First World War into three phases:[29]

1. The beginning of the movement until 1850, followed by a quiet time until the mid-1860s. During the latter years all democratic endeavors, especially women's organizations, were suppressed.

2. The period from 1865 until the end of the 1880s. These years saw the prolonged development of a network of women's organizations in the bourgeois realm, the "insect work of local organizations," as Bäumer mockingly remarked in her historical review.[30] Proletarian women suffered under the restrictions of the Anti-Socialist Laws, which were in effect until 1890. We thus witness a long period of incubation.

3. The period between 1890 and 1914. In 1890, with the end of the Bismarck era, the "virus of women's emancipation"[31] was finally able to flourish and spread into new initiatives and organizations. Now the woman question, as one that concerned all realms of political and private life, was put on the political agenda. This period is to be seen as the peak, the heyday of the old women's movement. Although organizational expansion was not yet complete, there was an intensity of public attention and debate that we can hardly imagine or want to admit to today. An indication of this—and more thorough press analyses can prove the point[32]—is the fact that on the occasion of the International Women's Congress in Berlin in 1904, the portrait photograph of Marie Stritt, chairwoman of the *Bund Deutscher Frauenvereine* (Federation of German Women's Organizations), adorned the cover of the biggest mass magazine of the time, the *Berliner Illustrierte Zeitung.*

These three phases will now be described in more detail in order to consider how appropriate it is in each case to speak of the existence of a movement.

Beginnings, 1848–1865

In the historiography of the first women's movement, the 1848 beginnings are generally attributed to one particular woman, the pioneer and "mother of the German women's movement," Louise Otto.[33] Otto was the first to bring women's issues to the attention of the newly constituted public of the *Vormärz*. Without minimizing her accomplishments, recent feminist studies have collected a great variety of new evidence for the existence of a first movement, a "collective actor."[34] The beginnings seem rather inconspicuous: anonymous letters to editors, political poetry, novels of social criticism, and scandals about particular "emancipated" women like Louise Aston, which became political issues. There were also new forms of female resistance. The press, which from 1843 on increasingly resisted political censorship, was a crucial medium for mobilizing support and calling attention to women's issues. For the first time there existed a political women's press, principally the *Frauen-Zeitung* (edited by Louise Otto from 1849 to 1851), and other publications.[35] The importance of women in the free-religious movement of the so-called German Catholics and the free Protestant parishes has been brought out convincingly and in great detail by Sylvia Paletschek.[36] Not only did women enjoy equal recognition and participation within this free-thinking movement, but the commitment to religious reform hit at the heart of traditional femininity. Women's emancipation and the critique of religion had the same social and political meaning.[37]

For further evidence of a growing social movement one can point to the strong participation of women in the liberal-democratic movement and to the increasingly expanding net of women's organizations with political goals. The Democratic Women's Associations were a part of this, as were the organizations for women's education, which were intended to enable women "to fulfill their duties not only as housewives but as citizens of the world and of the state."[38] In addition, there were female labor associations and welfare organizations that supported families of victims of persecution and families of prisoners.[39] Finally, one must mention the kindergarten movement, which adhered to Fröbel's concept of a democratic education that would reconcile class differences.[40]

Women were motivated to organize by an experience typical for feminists of the modern age and a paradox: on the one hand, their involvement with the democratic movement and their political alliance with leftists and democrats; on the other, simultaneously, disappointment at being excluded from equal participation, constitutional rights, and human rights. Of particular importance was the fact that the constitution drawn up in 1848 at the Church of St. Paul (Frankfurt) proclaimed equal citizenship for male Germans only. The political significance of this early phase of the women's movement can at the same time be seen in the strict state repression and its long-lasting consequences: the Press Laws, which explicitly forbade women to edit newspapers (for example, the Saxon Press Law called "Lex Otto"), and particularly the *Vereinsgesetze* (Laws Restricting Associations), which forbade women and minors in most states of the German Confederation to found political organizations or to take part in political gatherings (in effect in Prussia and other territories until 1908). This ban on political action, which was maintained for over two generations, tremendously hindered the German women's movement.

The Period between 1865 and 1890

The change of sovereign and government in Prussia and the dawn of a new era at the beginning of the 1860s, with the amnesty for political prisoners of 1848 and the loosening of press censorship, led to a resurgence not only of the Social Democratic labor movement. The women who had been active around 1848, led by Louise Otto and Auguste Schmidt, decided in 1865 to convene "a conference of German women of the different cities and states." The *Allgemeiner Deutscher Frauenverein,* or ADF (General German Women's Association) represented a bold venture, because even though German unification "was still a dream," these women wanted to represent "the whole of Germany."[41] "Women's days" were to be held regularly, in rotation in different cities, in order to found local women's organizations. Though the sensation stirred by the *Leipziger Frauenschlacht* (Leipzig women's battle) was tremendous, and in the beginning everything developed swiftly, after the founding of the German Kaiserreich in 1871 there was resistance and stagnation.[42]

Still, this organizational new beginning was the seed of all further initiatives and the starting point for practical self-help: a special newspaper (the *Neue Bahnen,* from 1866 until 1919); many petitions to the Reichstag and the government; surveys and publications; and the founding of a network of associations. The most important claims to be fixed in statutes were the right to work outside the home—a possibility only for middle-class women[43]— and the improvement of education for girls and women. What marked the ADF as feminist was its principle of self-help and self-determination and its conscious independence from male participation and decision-making. In contrast, other women's organizations, soon to be much more successful, took up the question of women's work as a social problem instead of as a question of woman's emancipation. Examples are the *Lette-Verein* and the membership-strong *Vaterländischer Frauenverein* (Patriotic Women's Organization) under the vice-rectorship of Empress Augusta.

Whereas the meetings of the ADF were considered harmless by state authorities, much greater difficulties arose with the organizing of working-class women's interests. Until 1870, the ADF and certain women from the bourgeois spectrum tried to take working-class women under their wings, for example in the Berlin *Verein zur Fortbildung und geistigen Anregung der Arbeiterfrauen* (Organization for Further Education and Intellectual Stimulation of Working Women).[44] In the 1870s, however, the paths of the middle-class women and the female labor movements parted, parallel to the separation of the labor movement and liberalism. The female labor movement was oppressed by the existing laws in two ways, an experience that shaped the class-struggle politics of the German women's movement. It suffered under the *Vereinsgesetze* (Laws Restricting Associations) and the *Sozialistengesetze* (Anti-Socialist Laws). According to Hilde Lion, this was a political battle marked by "disruptions and closings of organizations, trials, bans on publications, arrests, and expulsions of leaders."[45] Characterizing this epoch of the women's movement, Twellmann writes:

> In 1889, at the end of the epoch treated here, the middle-class women's movement had still not yet succeeded in becoming an influential factor in public life; but it was able to gain a foothold thanks to its "practical" activities over the decades. . . .
>
> However, the significance of this work should be estimated not only on the basis of scarce successes; what is more important is that these necessary demands were well thought-out, well formulated and well justified to their own members and the public. In the midst of an economic and social transformation process, the organizations of the women's movement thus gained significance as an "intellectual center of leadership," applying an ordering and planning focus that took care to remember that the "woman question" included more than the question of earning a living, but rather touched on every aspect of human life as "an issue of humanity."[46]

Upturn around 1890

The revival of the women's movement around 1890 was made possible by political change: the dismissal of Bismarck, the abolition of the Anti-Socialist Laws, and a new willingness to work towards the peaceful resolution of social conflicts. At the same time, there were growing contradictions between traditional women's roles and conditions in the capitalist economy. A number of new political organizations emerged, both within and outside the women's movement. But the movement was well prepared for change. It had networks, organizations, and media at its disposal, and it had already fostered an awareness of injustice. A new generation of women was pushing into professional life, bringing new resources, demands, and expectations. In the late 1880s the leaders of the bourgeois and the proletarian movements simultaneously but, it seems, independently of each other identified the main areas of injustice and developed strategic concepts in the educational and occupational spheres. Helene Lange published her *Gelbe Broschüre* (Yellow Brochure) in 1887, a petition to the Prussian ministry of education written in the tone of a manifesto. In it she sharply criticized Prussian educational policy, specifically the educational institutions for girls. Lange linked her liberal concept of emancipation—"knowledge is power"—with the demand for participation in the shaping of social conditions. This was in a nutshell the program of "spiritual motherhood." In 1889, at the founding congress of the Second International in Paris, Clara Zetkin gave her highly acclaimed speech to the world public about the necessary connection between socialism and women's issues. This became the basis of socialist theories of women's emancipation.[47]

As if all of a sudden the locked gates had been opened, a variety of new initiatives and organizations in addition to the ADF came into being, in fact often from the circle of women active in the latter. The new organizations took up diverse problems of gender relations, generating new discussions around a common point of reference, the "woman question." They developed new ways of exerting influence and new forms of propaganda (papers, association launchings, projects by women for women, lecture tours, and public gatherings). Some of the most important organizations were:

The *Verein Frauenwohl* (Organization for Women's Well-being) in Berlin, founded in 1888 by Minna Cauer, brought together many women who would later become leading activists.

The *Allgemeiner Deutscher Lehrerinnenverein* (General German Association of Female Teachers), founded in 1890 by Helene Lange and Marie Loeper-Housselle, promoted new ideas about female education and work.

The *Kaufmännischer Hilfsverein* (Association for Female Employees), run by Minna Cauer after 1889, offered its members help in finding work within the realm of new occupations typical for women, and help in furthering their education and obtaining legal aid.

The *Verein Jugendschutz* (Association for the Protection of Youth), founded in 1889 by Hanna Bieber-Böhm, marked the beginning of an organized morality movement, from which the radical abolitionists later separated.

Once before, within the context of the Social Democratic movement at the beginning of the 1880s, Gertrud Guillaume-Schack, inspired by Josephine Butler, had tried to bring female labor organizations into the struggle against prostitution. She was expelled from the country, and as an exile in London she continued her activism in the abolitionist movement.

The *Mädchen- und Frauengruppen für soziale Hilfsarbeit* (Girls' and Women's Groups for Social Services), initiated by Jeanette Schwerin in 1893 and led by Alice Salomon after 1899, served as a cradle for the professionalization of female social work by combining practical work with a profound theoretical education.

The *Rechtschutzverein Dresden* (Dresden Legal Aid and Protection Agency), founded in 1894 by Marie Stritt, not only offered free legal advice but also was a pioneer in feminist legal work (in 1914 there existed 97 legal protection agencies by women for women).

In 1894 these associations united under an umbrella organization, the *Bund Deutscher Frauenvereine*, or BDF (Federation of German Women's Associations). The stimulus for this came from the outside. Three activists accepted an invitation from American women to visit the general assembly of the International Council of Women (ICW), held in Chicago on the occasion of the World Exposition in 1893. They came back with the idea to "strengthen women's philanthropic organizations through organized cooperation." The federation, modeled after the American National Council, aimed to "benefit the family and the people" (paragraph 2 of the statutes). With their "charitable" and "moderate" orientation the Germans followed the pragmatic principle of the ICW, to engage only in duties "all can heartily agree upon."[48]

For this reason, the BDF was tainted with a structural defect that was very controversial and much discussed: it excluded the female labor organizations of the Social Democratic party; it did not invite them to the first meeting. This circumspection not only was in keeping with the Laws Restricting Associations, as the majority of those involved repeatedly assured the public,[49] but it also reflected and strengthened the class differences that dominated turn-of-the-century society in the Kaiserreich.

The female labor movement, which even after the abolition of the Anti-Socialist Laws was still judged to be "political" by the state and thus continued to be prohibited and oppressed, gave itself a new structure in 1889 (in the "Zetkin era"). It installed so-called women's agitation commissions, which without statutes, membership lists, or chairwomen tried to undermine the

Laws Restricting Associations. The newspaper *Die Gleichheit*, edited by Clara Zetkin since 1893, became their propaganda instrument. Zetkin knew how to use it effectively as a means of conditioning and indoctrinating her followers and as a weapon in political struggles.

In 1888 the ADF had apologetically declined an initial invitation by American women on the occasion of the foundation of the ICW in 1888: "In Germany we have to work with great tact and by conservative methods. . . . The difference between our position and that of our American sisters is largely due to the fact that you live in a republic, we in a monarchy."[50] The beginning of the new phase in the 1890s was marked by a new opening to the outside; the connection with the international women's movement was now used to promote the aims of German women.[51] And yet, the political climate of the Wilhelmine empire still was a hindrance.

THE ACTIVISTS OF THE WOMEN'S MOVEMENT: SOCIAL STRUCTURE AND MOBILIZING NETWORKS

To give substance to the "shadows of abstraction" which—as stated in the opening quotation—represented feminists (Frauenrechtlerinnen) to an "uninformed posterity," I would now like to inquire very concretely into the functioning of the movement. First I will present the results of a modest study of the social background of the supporters and leading activists. The empirical base is a sample of 40 activists in the women's movement around the turn of the twentieth century.[52] As preliminary as the particular categories and classifications may be, the information thus gained includes some surprises. The results seem valid to me because Christina Klausmann, in her local study of the women's movement in Frankfurt/ Main,[53] a much more detailed examination, comes to very similar findings.

The percentage of women who can be defined as belonging to the middle class according to their family origins (85% compared to 10% proletarian and 5% aristocratic) is hardly surprising. The high percentage of Protestants in contrast to Catholics was also to be expected, although it needs to be stressed that these figures are not quite reliable because of the high number of people that cannot be classified in terms of confession. However, what is remarkable is the high percentage of Jewish women (25%). As Klausmann has shown, the figure is even higher in Frankfurt, at over 40%.

In my opinion, the figures about marital status are also rather surprising. There was a high percentage of married women (40%), and of the 45% of women recorded as single almost half (20%) were known to have lived in a long-term relationship with a woman. Furthermore, we must give up our usual idea that the bourgeois protagonists represented nothing more than a club for elderly ladies. The figures show that 27.5% were between 20 and 30 years old when they joined the movement and that 67% were between 30 and 40 years old. That is, more than 90% were as young at the beginning of their involvement with the movement as the activists of the new women's movement. It seems that the images available from the period around the turn of the century, as well as the memories of an already aged movement, have influenced our imagination. In terms of profession, the high percentage of teachers is a well-known fact.[54]

The regional distribution does not give much insight at first, although it reveals that the regional focus of activity shifted from Saxony to Berlin beginning in the 1890s. But these findings also reflect the fact that national research has focused too strongly on the women's movement in Berlin. Local studies of other big cities thus change the picture,[55] and we know hardly anything about the women's movements in the provinces.[56]

Klausmann, who has investigated the social structure of the women's movement in Frankfurt by examining the membership lists of the ADF, has found remarkable differences between the main activists and those at the grass roots. While the majority of the main activists were single, two thirds of the more passive members were married. It is also striking that the already high percentage of Jewish women in the Frankfurt ADF (41.35%) was exceeded by their percentage among the main activists (43%).[57]

Future studies will have to provide more such structural data. Completely new insights into the functioning of the movement have been gained through research into organizational forms, informal networks of personal relationships, and methods of public relations. In her content analysis of the major nationwide newspapers Ulla Wischermann has collected a great variety of internal information on lecture tours, public relations work (such as reading circles and discussion events with nonmembers), social gatherings, cultural events, and women's clubs.[58] All of this shows that the women's movement had a very special but in no way separate culture, and it indicates that mobilization and mutual support were organized through a female support network. It is also interesting that there seems to have been a division of work between the nationwide and the regional organizations. While the nationwide organizations were responsible for programmatic decisions and political orientation, it was the task of the local organizations to carry out the practical work and to create the public space for consultation and encounter.

In order to grasp the "reality of the movement," the epigraph says, it is not enough merely to take into consideration the "programs, organizations, work, and achievements." One must also look at what bound the women together, for "in the big community that gathered, there were numerous circles, of very different character." In this survey of the three phases of the women's movement, these circles and networks have repeatedly been mentioned. They carried the movement through "doldrums"[59] and setbacks, and at other times they provided the impetus for new activities. For example, the "women of 1848" were among the founders of the ADF in 1865. From this group, and especially from the "nest" of the *Höhere Töchterschule* (high school for young women) in Leipzig, run by ADF chairwoman Auguste Schmidt, a later generation of women emerged. Schmidt's most important student was Clara Zetkin, who never denied these roots and her admiration for the "red democrat" Louise Otto.

Another example is the Berlin circle around Henriette Schrader-Breymann, who was Fröbel's niece and follower and the wife of a liberal member of the Reichstag. Schrader-Breymann had connections with the Prussian Princess Royal Viktoria, an Englishwoman—note again the influence from the outside—and with those who signed the *Yellow Brochure*. From this circle the Verein Frauenwohl was recruited. Mention should also be made of the completely different and unconventional artists' scene in Munich, whose main protagonists were Anita Augspurg, Sophie Goudstikker, and Ika Freudenberg. This group was shaped by a creative avant-garde, including such writers as Helene Böhlau and Lou Andreas-Salomé.[60]

These examples will be sufficient to emphasize our main thesis:[61] Below the traditional forms of political and social organization there was an informal network of women's relations and friendships that had an important influence on political theory and practice.

EMANCIPATION DEMANDS AND CONTROVERSIAL ISSUES

To begin with, a comment on the term "bürgerlich" (bourgeois) may be helpful. In German it has a double meaning. On the one hand, following

Marxist terminology, it is a class term, and the majority of supporters of the
bourgeois movement were members of a privileged social class. It was in this
sense that Clara Zetkin spoke disparagingly, and from a perspective of class
struggle, of "bourgeois feminists," reflecting the class conflicts of the German Kaiserreich. On the other hand, historically, the term refers to modern
societies that are dedicated to the principles of enlightenment, rule of law,
and democracy. These liberal and socioliberal societies are called "civil societies" in English. Dedicated as they were to social reform and individual
emancipation, bourgeois women used the term for self-definition. For example, on the occasion of the aristocrat Lady Aberdeen's election as president of the ICW, their leaders declared: "The German women's movement
is a thoroughly 'bourgeois' one and as a women's movement rejects all mere
charity work by the aristocrats, the conservatives, and the Church."[62] In this
way they dissociated themselves from conservatives, ultramontanists, and
monarchists in the German Kaiserreich and at the same time showed their
opposition to their republican sisters abroad.

From the point of view of liberal or bourgeois women, the women's
movement had developed from two driving forces: on the one hand industrialization, which forced women out of the family's restricted realm and
created the women's issue as one of earning a living, and on the other the
spiritual forces. In her programmatic document *Die Frauenbewegung in
ihren modernen Problemen* Helene Lange speaks of "the rights of the individual in opposition to society as a whole and in opposition to conditions
set by external forces."[63] She continues: "What we consider to be the real
core of the women's movement is the struggle to bring this process of individualization to a conclusion."[64]

But the crucial point was how this process of individualization was to be
special and different for women, and this issue was contested among the different currents in the bourgeois spectrum. Helene Lange and Gertrud
Bäumer represented the majority of the bourgeois moderates, in contrast to
the radicals or left-wing activists like Minna Cauer, Anita Augspurg, and Helene Stöcker, who combined the claim for women's suffrage with international campaigns for peace and sexual reform. Lange went far afield in order
to ground her theory of gender difference, as we would call it today. Let us
follow her briefly as she dissociates herself, with regard to the American
women's movement, from the "unconditional idealism that voices its absolute
demands without concern for historically grown circumstances . . . "[65] She
inquires into the effects of the individualist theory in Germany and refers to

romanticism as "the period of great spiritualization" that "woke spiritual powers" in women and created a "favorable climate for female individuality." "And that is why we perceive female personality in German culture as fully grown when the spark of spiritual life was carried over from the bare fields of Enlightenment to the world of emotions, of personal inner life."[66]

For Lange, this was where the roots of a highly differentiated gender philosophy were to be found. Hers was a philosophy that pretended to resist drawing boundaries and marking essential differences between the genders in terms of Rousseau's theory of gender roles.[67] Yet this philosophy saw women as having a special cultural mission in modern societies. Accordingly, in 1905 the program of the ADF stated that the goal of the women's movement was "to bring the cultural influence of women to its fullest inner bloom and to free, social effectiveness."[68] The road to the realization of this goal was seen in a fundamental reform of education for women and girls. Education was to be organized by women themselves and lead to qualified professions insofar as they were compatible with motherhood. Charitable work by women was regarded as a way to enhance their cultural influence so that it would be acknowledged by the state as indispensable. And, last but not least, "keeping matrimony holy" remained "the essential guarantee for the physical and spiritual well-being of posterity."[69]

This emancipation program, which was understood as moderate by most of its supporters,[70] was enhanced via the concept of "spiritual motherhood." This notion expressed the real and intrinsic duty of women.[71] The moderates comprehended the dilemma that came with adjustment, with merely equalizing men's and women's rights:

> If one were to add to the male scholars . . . a few female ones, who
> borrowed their ideas and views of things from men, this would be of
> no benefit to science. . . . If women were to enter working life in free
> competition with men, without social ideals appropriate to their female
> ways of thinking and feeling, nothing would be gained.[72]

The radicals were liberals, and they were also radical individualists, because their demands for equality and autonomy also applied specifically to matrimony and family relations. This meant self-determination in the realm of sexuality too, and it extended to all social and political controversies that the women's movement around the turn of the century had taken up: prostitution, patriarchal matrimonial law, discrimination against illegitimate motherhood, and abortion. The moderates, in contrast, put strict limits on the liberation of women in matrimony and in sexual relationships. For them the conflict between individual rights and motherhood was solved with a class-specific edge to it: for the "majority of women" motherhood was held to be not only "the real cultural contribution of women to society"[73] but their duty, their destiny, or—as Bäumer called it—"their tie to the cosmos."[74] "One learned to grasp women not solely as individuals but as *organs* of the people as a whole, as agents that had to fulfill their *specific* functions and duties."[75] Sexual liberty and self-determination were, from this perspective, "anarchistic feminist thinking."[76] Here the term "feminist" is obviously used polemically.

One of the major differences between the radicals and the moderates was their different perception of legal issues in the struggle for emancipation. For the radicals the struggle for rights was not only a question of pace or of method, as was sometimes asserted; for them laws represented a crucial lever and a starting point for mobilization. Although they too saw the woman question as a cultural issue, they held it to be primarily a legal issue to be solved politically. As Augspurg, the leading jurist of the radicals stated:

> Whatever a particular woman achieves and gains in art, science, industry, and in general recognition and influence: it remains something private, personal, temporary, isolated—it is always characterized as exceptional and tolerated as such, but it has no right to exist and thus cannot become the rule, cannot influence the general public.[77]

In a similar manner to present-day feminists in their debate about equality and difference, the moderates argued that the radicals, by giving priority to legal issues, "held out their hands for men's rights."[78] Yet we have to keep in mind that women *were* legally inferior at that time and had no experience of the failure of legal equality. Because women's rights campaigns started from a positive idea of femininity,[79] these activists believed that by achieving equal participation in government and politics they would be able to bring about fundamental social and political change. This was their motive for initiating the struggle over rights at the turn of the century, in which they opposed the Civil Code for its neglect of women's rights (especially in matrimony), fought against state-regulated prostitution, and raised the issue of the vote. From the beginning, the radicals oriented themselves along the lines of the western women's movements; that is, they were less nationally and more internationally focused. They provoked controversy not only through their propaganda methods but also through their lifestyles and appearance. Despite the big stir and trouble they raised, even within the women's movement itself, they never gained majority support, and they failed to overcome the strict division between the bourgeois and proletarian women's movements that had opened up even within their own ranks.[80]

The question of whether the proletarian women's movement should really be defined as a women's movement was raised many times and was answered negatively by the bourgeoisie. At least it was not an independent women's movement, since it defined itself largely as part of the labor movement. Indeed, socialist emancipation theory demanded equality between women and men, and for the female worker this meant participation in production so that she could "go into battle with the proletarian, side by side."[81] The message that Zetkin conveyed to her comrades was that "only together with women will socialism triumph."[82] Although she repeatedly polemicized against "feminist mawkishness about harmony" in the controversies around the turn of the century, in reality the female workers, like the Social Democrats, supported demands for equality in matrimonial law and family law and fought for unrestricted voting rights. A specific German edge in Clara Zetkin's position was her attitude toward family and motherhood. Her sociopolitical about-face between 1889 and 1892, from a strict rejection of protection for mothers to a demand for such protection, led to irritations and controversies among the supporters of the Socialist International in other countries. Finally, one has to mention the diverse border-crossers between feminism and socialism (for example, Oda Olberg and Wally Zeppler), who were marginalized as revisionists during the Zetkin era but who could have built bridges.[83]

STRATEGIES AND ORGANIZATIONS

In various respects, the issue of strategy has already been mentioned, and there is extensive literature available on this aspect of the history of the women's movement,[84] so I take the liberty to be very brief now. Three directions of the women's movement have been characterized by a chronicler as follows:

> The Social Democratic women emphasize the problem of women's economic dependence, those on the bourgeois left [the radicals] focus on the fight against legal and political oppression, and those on the right [the moderates] see lack of spiritual and intellectual freedom as the strongest shackle. Needless to say, this comparison provides only a very rough measure of differentiation, and sometimes the roles can be reversed.[85]

Paralleling this division there were at the time various federations or umbrella organizations. The charitable and moderate organizations came together in the *Bund Deutscher Frauenvereine*, or BDF (Federation of German Women's Associations), part of the ICW; the more radical groups and the suffrage organizations formed the *Verband Fortschrittlicher Frauenvereine* (Federation of Progressive Women's Associations) in 1899; finally there were the organizations and activities of the proletarian women's movement (women's agitation commissions, women's conferences, and, from 1910 on, international women's days).

Of course, by reducing politics to the respective organizations of the women's movement one encourages schematic classification according to party affiliation or degree of adherence to feminist principles. There is much evidence to justify keeping the women's movement as a whole in mind: the border-crossers; the joint conferences (for example, the International Congresses of Women in Berlin in 1896 and 1904); the various, often surprising linkages (like the tentative communication between Minna Cauer and Clara Zetkin); and those who changed sides (the most prominent was Lily Braun). Marie Stritt, an important initiator of the rights movement, an internationalist, and chairwoman of the BDF from 1899 to 1910, stood up for the unity of the women's movement.[86] Her forced resignation and Gertrud Bäumer's inauguration in 1910 indicated an obvious shift in power in favor of the conservatives and moderates.

The role of confessional women in the spreading of ideas should not be underestimated, even if they often seem to be absent from this spectrum. With the exception of the Catholic women, they were organized under the umbrella organization of the BDF and at times exerted a great influence on its policies. In 1899 Protestant women formed the *Deutsch-Evangelischer*

Frauenbund, or DEF (German Protestant Women's Organization). Against the one-dimensional hypothesis that they strengthened the conservative and, later, national orientation, Doris Kaufmann argues for a much more balanced view: "The Deutsch-Evangelischer Frauenbund for the first time gave women who were faithful to the church the opportunity to . . . work for women's rights without having to leave the religious context. "[87] But even though the DEF was an important agent of propaganda and persuasion within the confessional movement, it embodied a "retarding element" within the women's movement as a whole.[88]

The formation of the *Katholischer Frauenbund Deutschlands,* or KDF (Catholic Women's Association) had a similar effect. Because of the "religious indifference"[89] of the BDF, the Catholic association refused to join it. Yet it understood itself as part of the women's movement and cooperated in issues of women's education and legal rights. In contrast to the Protestant association, the KDF did not disapprove of the issue of the woman's vote, and it agitated within the church for women's voting rights in the congregations.

Despite ideological contrasts, double membership of many women was not unusual on the level of associations. This holds true especially for the Jewish women's movement, which formed the *Jüdischer Frauenbund* or JFB (Jewish Women's Alliance) on the occasion of the General Assembly of the ICW in Berlin. Many Jewish women were also prominent in the bourgeois women's movement. According to president Bertha von Pappenheim, the JFB united goals of the women's movement "with a distinct feeling for Jewish identity."[90] But there is nothing to gloss over: from 1919 on at the latest, anti-Semitic prejudices and incidents burdened sisterly solidarity.

PECULIARITIES: A PRELIMINARY AND PERSONAL RÉSUMÉ

On the whole, the women's movement in these years was characterized by controversies and dogmatic confrontations, both between bourgeois and proletarian women and between moderates and radicals. But that does not mean that discord among women and their competing organizations diminished the movement's influence and success; rather, in my opinion, these controversies attest to the vitality and relevance of the movement and its activities. Specifically, because of the growing strength of social democracy in the German Kaiserreich, class differences were just as great a barrier to joint political action by women as were differences in attitude towards matrimony and family, morality and suffrage. These differences reflect deeply rooted perceptions of the world that in the face of so much structural resistance could not be altered within one generation. Taking that into consideration, the social change initiated by this movement in the realms of education, professional work, and politics was enormous.

Compared to the protagonists of women's movements in other countries, those in the moderate and radical wings of the German women's movement were all acutely aware of and articulate about differences. But while the radicals, with great personal commitment, worked to strengthen their connections and strove for internationalism in the "great community of women" despite the war, the moderates were interested in retaining and cultivating German uniqueness, inwardness, and depth of feeling towards *Frauentum* (womanhood). That is why I can now reveal the identity of the author I cite in the epigraph: it was Gertrud Bäumer, a strong promoter of these notions. She described the functioning of the women's movement very adequately in my opinion, which is why I cited her, but the sentence that is most typically German seems at the same time problematic to me. It reads: "What doesn't exist is an image of the diverse forms of personal *Frauentum* that were caught up by the movement and supported it." This notion of *Frauentum*—it becomes clear in many other contexts—not only stands for uniqueness, but also—in its reliance on German culture—provides a reason for national arrogance. This indicates that gender difference and national difference played equally important roles and were insurmountable barriers in Bäumer's politics.

Finally, the scholarly attention given to diverse feminisms, and specifically to European "relational feminism,"[91] has in many ways rehabilitated the concept of social or spiritual motherhood. I agree to that, but nevertheless want to raise doubts about its glorification. In the philosophy of the moderates especially, it is obvious that the bourgeois concept of motherhood remained a class concept that provided different recipes for the female laborer, the "mass of women," and the educated, bourgeois mother.[92]

Connected with this was a problematic relation to law and a curtailment of human rights for women,[93] including an antidemocratic, organic notion of the state. These ideas not only applied to women but were part of the mainstream political and legal theories in the German Kaiserreich. In this constitutional theory the state was not based on a social contract between equals but was understood as a "social organism" with very different and hi-erarchically organized members and a typical division of labor.[94] It is a mat-ter of debate whether this concept of the state paved the way for an anti-in-dividualistic understanding of rights and for an ideology of community that was one of the roots of National Socialism. Without wanting to take part in the highly contested debate on a German *Sonderweg*, I see a connection be-tween this thinking and Bäumer's problematic analysis from the year 1933. To her, in the end, it did not matter in what kind of a state women lived—"monarchic, democratic, or fascist."[95] This almost incomprehensible indif-ference towards the legal constitution of the state was dangerous, as we know today. However, it corresponded with Bäumer's approach to the poli-tics of feminism, which was based on gender difference as essential and un-deniable. In 1904 she had argued:

> Modern feminism, which does not put human rights first, but rather the right to love and motherhood, tends to understand the exclusion of women from the community and the state as a division of labor that complies with the intrinsic nature of women and with which she can thus be satisfied.[96]

Since then, with the Weimar Republic, opportunities for women to partici-pate as citizens had changed fundamentally. In 1933, Bäumer criticized the "immature parliamentary system" and even expressed contempt for the principles of democracy. Such thinking leads to a muddled, self-annihilating conception of feminism. In my understanding, feminism (today, if not his-torically) is a democratic project that necessarily aims towards equality and equal freedom for both men and women, and this includes equal responsi-bility for the constitution of the state. The feminist understanding of equal-ity presupposes that all individuals, men and women, are different and do not have to become the same in order to enjoy equal rights. This equality principle recognizes and enables gender differences as well as other differ-ences. However, it is a means to promote justice, for it has to be critical of social inequality in general—not only with respect to women.

PART III

Northern Europe

Modernity and the Norwegian Women's Movement from the 1880s to 1914: Changes and Continuities

IDA BLOM

SETTING THE SCENE

"A modern woman is a woman who, in contrast to women of the past, understands that the fate of her children is mainly decided by society, and that her work is pointless and may be in vain if she does not take part in forming the society in which she lives."[1] This was the opinion of a well-known Norwegian author, Bjørnstjerne Bjørnson, who wrote in the journal of the Norwegian women's movement at the end of the nineteenth century. The quotation places the women's movement in the general process of modernization and democratization. Women's traditional loyalty to children and the family was, in this perspective, seen as vain as long as it was not combined with active participation in the democratic development of society. What characterized Norwegian society around 1900? What was the setting within which the Norwegian women's movement operated?

Norway was still mainly an agrarian country. The primary sector dominated the economy, and towns were still small. Two-thirds of the well over two million inhabitants lived in an agrarian setting. The rich were few, and although there was a gulf between the lives of the wealthy and the poor, social differences were smaller than in most European countries. The nobility was practically nonexistent and most people managed to eke out a meager livelihood. Except for the Lapp minority in the north of the country, the population was ethnically homogeneous. The dominant religious denomination was Lutheran.[2]

However, changes were imminent. Industrial enterprises had started growing, and hydroelectric power would soon start transforming the economy. Agrarian society was in the process of transformation, technologically, eco-

nomically, and demographically. Thousands of people migrated to the growing towns, and many continued migration to the USA.

Political changes were also on the way. The growing working class was organizing at the end of the 1880s, so the middle-class parties, Conservatives
and Liberals, were facing a new opponent. Simultaneously, the wisdom of
upholding the political union with Sweden was being questioned. The national conflict grew in intensity and led to the dissolution of the union in
1905. The process of building the Norwegian nation was entering a new and
important phase, generating demands for democratic reforms, general suffrage for men and women, and more democratic election systems.

The birth of the Norwegian women's movement has been dated to 1884,
when *Norsk kvinnesagsforening* (the Norwegian Women's Rights Association)
was established. It seems more than a coincidence that this was the same
year as the Liberal and Conservative Parties were formed, the principle of
parliamentary rule was accepted (albeit only after hard political struggles),
and the vote was extended to include new groups of men. Three years later
the Social Democratic Party was formed. The women's movement thus was
part of a general modernization and democratization of political processes;
it was part of the flowering of new and older associations at the local and national level. Since the 1840s women had joined mixed-gender missionary societies and teetotaling and philanthropic associations, and they had formed
"women-only" associations within these fields.

The modern world changed the role of family and household, and it
strengthened the possibility for a single individual to survive outside such
collectivities. Organizations supplemented and sometimes replaced earlier
local and family-based loyalties, weakened by structural changes in society.
The women's movement was one answer to new demands on both sexes
made by industrialization and urbanization. Demographic changes resulting
from the migration of young men to towns and out of the country added to
the women's problem of finding a livelihood through marriage, while at the
same time the growth of industry and of the service sector offered paid work
to an increasing number of young women. A number of functions which in
an agrarian society belonged to the family and household were gradually
moved into the public sphere of schools, factories, offices, hospitals, and
shops. In short, industrial society worked to change the meaning of gender,
gradually accepting women in the public sphere, even in arenas until then

perceived as clearly masculine. The opposite movement, men invading former feminine arenas, was rare, but did happen, perhaps most conspicuously when male doctors took up the female profession of midwife.

This process did not take place without battles about how to define femininity and masculinity, especially within the middle class. Though such battles certainly were also fought among working-class people, the need for class solidarity seems to have dampened working-class gender confrontations. Part of the agrarian population was also touched by discussions of how to define gender relations in a changing society, although to a much lesser degree.

The history of the early women's movement in Norway has yet to be written. A very early contribution, and still the most comprehensive, was written in 1937, written by a female historian outside academia.[3] It deals mainly with the middle-class women's organizations, and sketches developments within working-class women's organizations mostly when the two wings of the movement touched each other. Since the 1970s a large number of studies of individual organizations and of problems central to the women's movement, such as prostitution, protection of women workers, female trade unions, and family planning, have been published,[4] but the flowering new field of women's history has not produced a comprehensive portrayal of the early women's movement as such.

It therefore seems timely to ask what changes were promoted by the women's movement around the turn of the century, and what continuities remained uncontested. First of all, how should the concept of the "women's movement" be defined? There has been disagreement among historians.[5] A narrow definition may demand a clear opposition to gender hierarchies, maybe even a consciousness of women's identities as socially and historically constructed. This would make the women's movement a very narrow phenomenon indeed, and would present obstacles to attempts at understanding the complexity of women's lives. On the other hand, accepting almost any organized female activity as an expression of the women's movement would not make sense either.

I will suggest a fairly broad definition, which will encompass organized activities aimed at changing gender relations and improving women's conditions. A broad definition will include internal splits and fights over goals and strategies, but it will allow attempts to recreate the rich diversity of women's ideas and actions in a period when they were facing a rapidly

changing society. A broad definition also means including professional organizations, such as trade unions and female branches of political parties.
Although both these kinds of organizations may be seen more as a result of
the women's movement than as part of the movement itself, I will include
them, without enlarging on them, since they were very actively involved in
efforts to create equal opportunities and to find solutions to problems of
special importance to women. I perceive organizations such as teetotaling
and religious organizations as stepping stones to the women's movement,
since they advanced women's participation in social and political problems,
taught them organizing abilities, and lowered the barriers between the private and the public.

THE FOREMOTHERS: THE LITERARY FEMINISTS

The women's movement started with foremothers. From the middle of the
nineteenth century, women started forming missionary and teetotaling organizations; and, at the same time, a "literary feminism" pointed to problems involved in redefining gender relations. As early as 1854–55, Camilla
Collett (1813–1895) depicted in a novel the degrading and exasperating position of young women who were bound by tradition to conceal their preferences and accept being married off to a husband not of their own choice.
Collett demanded that women start giving free expression to their feelings
and that their opinions be taken seriously. She saw an inner emancipation
and a change of attitudes as the prime goal. At the end of her life, after forty
years as a widow, she maintained that women should be offered the possibility of economic independence through paid work. Clearly influenced by
Josephine Butler's thoughts, she represented the ideal of the innocent and
modest wife as the counterpart of the prostitute, sacrificed to men's sexual
desires.[6]

In 1869 John Stuart Mill's *On the Subjection of Women* was published in
Danish. It was immediately taken to heart by Collett and a number of other
Norwegian women. Among them was Aasta Hansteen (1824–1908), who
strongly condemned the church for reinforcing women's subjection. In 1871
she published an article under her full name, venturing to sketch a theology
that did not discriminate against women. She was also the first Norwegian

woman to speak at a public meeting. Her very unconventional behavior was met with ridicule. She left for the United States and returned only after the women's movement had started up in Norway, when she was greeted as one of the important foremothers.[7]

The most outspoken female author of the time was Amalie Skram (1846–1905). Her first novel was published in 1885, the year after the Norwegian Women's Rights Association was established. Here, as in a number of her later novels, Skram castigated the double sexual standard and openly pictured female sexuality. This made her an easy target for opponents.

What may be termed the literary feminists included, however, literary men as well. Among the best known was Henrik Ibsen. Although he did not want to be seen as one of the proponents of new perceptions of gender relations, many of his plays show him to share a number of the ideas at the heart of the women's movement. He saw women as completely different from men: more noble, less egoistic, more in touch with ideals that he wanted to promote. But at the same time he found them to be subjected to male judgments and norms, bound to be overlooked and neglected in society. He hoped for "renewal" of society from two sources: workers and women. His play *A Doll's House* (1879) stimulated not only a Norwegian but international debate on gender relations, and gave important inspiration to burgeoning women's movements as far away as Japan.[8]

THREE PERIODS OF A DIFFERENT CHARACTER

The decades between 1884 and 1914 may be divided into three periods, each with a distinct character: the 1880s, the 1890s, and the time from the turn of the century until 1913.

In the 1880s the women's movement was established and the first battles over strategies and goals were fought. In the 1890s efforts turned to educating housewives and female servants; and cooperation and conflicts between the increasing number of organizations, not least between socialists and nonsocialists, complicated the situation. The 1890s saw the fight for the vote taking off, resulting in the first victory in 1901 and the achievement of general female suffrage in 1913. As the new century started, new areas of conflict reopened earlier battlegrounds. Between 1902 and 1909, laws to give special protection to working women were discussed, dividing bourgeois and working-class women. Discussions on reforms concerning unmarried mothers, lasting from 1901 until 1915, brought out opposing views of sexual morals, marriage, and social policies. I shall look at each of these historical phases at a time, outlining the demands of the women's movement and the varying perceptions of femininity and gender relations. I shall also point out conflicts and cooperation within the movement and describe its allies and opponents. Parallels to developments elsewhere spring to mind, because two main strategies in attempts to change existing gender relations are easily discerned: One strategy was built on natural rights, seeing women and men as humans with the same potentials and stressing gender equality. The other was built on gender difference, highlighting women's "otherness." It stressed that women and men had their gender-specific qualities and that both were needed in society. These different understandings of gender and the two different strategies should not be seen as opposed and competing phenomena, however. Rather they should be taken as closely interwove analytical categories, often coexisting within one and the same individual.

THE 1880S—THE FIRST BATTLES

Two Strategies: Different or Equal?

Norsk kvinnesagsforening (the Norwegian Women's Rights Association) was the result of an initiative taken by Gina Krog (1847–1916), in close cooperation and competition with Hagbart Emanuel Berner (1839–1920). The association's purpose was vaguely formulated as "working to obtain for women the rights and the place in society due to them."[9] Four areas were singled out as targets for the activities of the organization: women's education; better wages and more opportunities for working women; a law to safeguard the interest of spouses and protect married life; and better opportunities for women to be heard on questions of importance to society. The program was carefully designed to attract a wide membership and obviously mirrored the difference strategy. This has been seen as the result of Hagbart Berner winning over the more radical Gina Krog, who had insisted that women's suffrage be the fundamental goal of the association.

However, Gina Krog and a group of more radical women founded Norsk kvinnestemmerettsforening (the Norwegian Women's Suffrage Association)

only one year later, in 1885, to work for women's suffrage on the same conditions as for men. They remained loyal members of the Women's Rights Association, Gina Krog even assuming leadership of this organization for a short
while and editing the journal, considered its mouthpiece, *Nylænde*. The Suffrage Association worked in parallel with the more moderate Women's Rights
Association, and found supporters among men within the radical branch of
the Liberal Party. There was a great deal of overlap in membership as well as
in leadership of the two organizations. Members of both organizations came
from the liberal urban middle class (though men were not accepted as members of the Suffrage Association).

More than half of the founders of the Women's Rights Association came
from the capital, Kristiania (until 1924 the name of the capital, now Oslo).
Over half of the female members were married, and many of them were
joined by their spouses. They belonged to the upper middle class, and about
two-thirds of the male members had a university degree. Prominent liberal
politicians were among the members; most of the (mostly unmarried)
women who were gainfully employed worked in education. Associations for
women's rights were soon created in other major towns, such as Bergen and
Trondheim. Attempts to coordinate activities in a national organization were
unsuccessful, and the organization in the capital, well placed as it was to
lobby parliament and other important institutions, became the trend-setter.

The founding of the Women's Rights Association followed two strategies,
proposed by Hagbart Berner and Gina Krog respectively. Both leaders embraced John Stuart Mill's ideas, but Berner was mindful of creating an organization that would not break too sharply with what might be accepted by
the Liberal Party. He wanted to progress slowly and without challenging the
moderate part of his party too openly. He took as his model *Dansk Kvindesamfund* (the Danish Women's Association), which had been established in
1871 with a moderate program of ameliorating women's economic position,
omitting the suffrage claim. Amelioration, not equality, was the catchword.

Krog, on the other hand, was adamant that the strategy to obtain wom-
en's rights should demand full equality with men, nothing more, nothing
less. She rarely used the argument of women's special qualities, and immediately started criticizing the program of the Women's Rights Association for
being too modest. She raised the claim for women's suffrage on the same
conditions as for men and advocated separate property within marriage—an
important measure to secure married women the vote as long as men's suf-

frage rested on property rights. Krog found her model in the American National Woman Suffrage Association. She interpreted Elisabeth Cady Stanton
and Susan B. Anthony as proponents of human rights, grounded in natural
law. Equality between women and men was to her a question of justice, and
the vote could be obtained simply by specifying that the word "citizen" in
the constitution meant "men *and women*." This became then the goal of the
Norwegian Women's Suffrage Association of 1885. It put proposals for wom-
en's suffrage before parliament every year, wrote addresses and petitions, lob-
bied, and collected signatures.

The two founders had their respective followers. In the fall of 1884, the
Women's Rights Association had 274 members—153 women and 121 men.
Ten women founded the Women's Suffrage Association the following year—
the more radical wing of the women's movement was not numerous, but active, and its activities set the tone in the 1890s.

However, even the more moderate Women's Rights Association met with
much criticism in the mid-1880s. It was immediately perceived as an ultra-
radical organization. Conservative middle-class women—and men—kept
their distance. Some of them were already organized in *Kristiania Sede-
lighetsforening* (the Association for Better Sexual Morals), a mixed-gender organization led by men and established in 1882 by the conservative middle
class of the capital to combat prostitution. Inspiration no doubt had come
from Josephine Butler's activities in Britain, but it was welcomed by the Association for Better Sexual Morals. The Women's Rights Association was hesitant to take part in public discussions of sexuality. However, in 1887 its leader
Ragna Nielsen was provoked by a meeting discussing ideals of "free love," in
which traditional marriage bonds were criticized. Proponents of common-
law marriages clashed with defenders of "purity" and the same sexual morality for women and men—meaning sexual relations in marriage only. Some
participants maintained that the same sexual morality for women and men
would never be possible, due to gender differences in sexual urges. Gender
equality was characterized as nonsense, seeing that women's special biology
would never allow them to equal men. The women's movement was depicted
as consisting of puritanical, man-hating women, and as a derailment from
more important questions, such as the fight to promote socialism.

The discussions split the Women's Rights Association. Ragna Nielsen
wanted to stage a protest meeting. She represented a small minority who ac-

cepted women as sexually active individuals, fought the double standard, and demanded respect even for prostitutes. But the majority preferred "boycotting through silence." They declined to spend their time and effort on what they saw as theoretical debates about sexual morality, marriage, and celibacy; it was more important, they said, to seek solutions to practical problems, such as establishing girls' schools. The conflict became very intense and led to a change in the leadership of the organization.

The Women's Rights Association was fighting the image of a politically radical organization and was attempting to win support for its program within established political circles. No doubt the idea of getting involved in public discussions of such delicate matters as sexual morality frightened many women, who still signed articles on much less controversial subjects using pseudonyms. These women kept back from conquering public spaces, or at least carefully chose the spaces they wanted to conquer.

But the question of sexual morality cropped up again in the 1890s. Ragna Nielsen, who had resigned as leader of the association in 1888, was still a respected and popular person, due mainly to her activities in support of coeducation. She was reelected in the latter half of the 1890s and resumed her efforts to influence sexual mores. Soon she was strongly criticized for using the name of the association, without securing the acceptance of board members, in a petition to the Ministry of Justice to introduce whipping as a punishment for violence against women. She also managed to have the association protest an attempt to reinstate the hated visitation of prostitutes, this time not by the police but by health authorities. A mass meeting of the Women's Rights Association in cooperation with women from the Association for Better Sexual Morality resulted in a resolution to the *Storting* (Parliament) condemning visitation as a humiliation of women and as a measure without sanitary importance.

It proved difficult to unite members behind one definition of "better schooling for girls," one of the major items on the program of the association. Ragna Nielsen, who started the first coeducational college in Kristiania, strongly argued in favor not only of coeducation, but also of the same curriculum for girls as for boys, easing women's way to higher education. For her, as for Gina Krog, equal rights was the watchword. She was opposed by those who, like Edvard Hambro, a prominent member of the Bergen Association for Women's Rights and the director of a well-established school for boys, wanted to continue separate girls' schools with a curriculum favoring women's special vocation as wives and mothers.

The members of the association proved to be a disparate group, and heated discussions over a resolution demanding government action to improve the education of girls never led to a united stance. Some wanted to strengthen women as wives and mothers, while others insisted on fighting for equality between women and men.[10] The equality/difference dilemma seems very clear. The equality strategy called for far-reaching changes in gender relations and in perceptions of femininity and masculinity. The difference position also challenged male superiority and propelled women into the public arena, but in a slower and more circumspect way. This became even clearer in the 1890s.

THE 1890S—DISPUTED GOALS

Housewives

In 1890 a small group of women succeeded (for a short time) in establishing a special branch for housewives within the Women's Rights Association. The idea was that housewives treat servant girls more fairly by introducing written contracts and clearly stipulating working hours. This was an early example of women's participation in the formation of social policies, an attempt to improve working conditions for the biggest group of economically active women, the female servants (and tainted by an upper-class paternalistic approach which aimed to prevent servant girls from joining the growing socialist movement). It built on continuities in the perception of femininity by emphasizing the calling of housewife and mother, but it also signaled change by insisting on more education and training to fulfill this calling. Housewifery and mothering were no longer seen as biologically given.

The initiative was strongly opposed by Ragna Nielsen and others who gave priority to opening teacher-training schools to women, a goal that was reached in 1890. The efforts of Nielsen and her followers rested on perceptions of women as individuals with the same potential as men and therefore with claims to the rights and privileges enjoyed by men. Clearly, a double vision of femininity characterized the work of the association.

Efforts to educate women to become housewives were strengthened when two housewives (Frederikke Marie Qvam and Randi Blehr) took over association leadership in the middle of the 1890s. The association organized lectures and courses on cooking, sewing, and hygiene. It obtained financial support from the government to start a school in home economics. As a consequence of this shift in emphasis a proposal was made to change the name of the association to indicate a distance from efforts at emancipation and from confrontations with men, a strategy deemed to be against the interests of housewives. No wonder Ragna Nielsen and others strongly opposed this change of program, and they were successful in preventing a change of name. But the result was the birth of a new women's organization, *Hjemmenes Vel* (Association for the Welfare of the Homes) in 1898. This was later to become the second largest women's organization in the country.

The supporters of the equality strategy gave priority to policies concerning women's paid work outside the home. Cooperation with the Kristiania Lærerinneforening (Kristiania Female Teachers' Association), established in the 1860s, was frequent. In the 1880s, under the leadership of Anna Rogstad, who was also vice-president of the Women's Rights Association for most of the period up to 1913, the Teachers' Association changed from a forum for social gatherings to a professional interest group. Cooperation also developed with the Association of Female Shop and Office Workers, established in 1890 to fight for better wages and better working conditions.[11]

Working-Class Women Organizing

Contact was also established between the Women's Rights Association and the socialist movement. This was a continuation of attempts at building bridges between women of different classes, a policy started by a small group of female students who in 1883 formed the core element of what soon became the Women's Rights Association and the Women's Suffrage Association. Offering free educational courses to working-class women, they meant to share the knowledge they were themselves acquiring.

In January 1889, Carl Jeppesen, editor of the leading socialist paper, invited the Women's Rights Association to attend a meeting and to support a resolution stating that the most important condition for women's liberation was full economic independence. This was to be achieved through education, organization, and occupational training. Equal wages were an important goal, and the principle of solidarity between men and women of the working class was stressed.

This initiative might have been meant as an invitation to cooperation across class divides. The Labor Party was new and weak, and the tradition of cooperation with the Radical Liberals was still alive. Furthermore, the Second International had stated as principles for the socialist movement that women workers should be accepted as comrades in the struggle against capitalism, and that equal wages for equal work was part of the socialist program—Norwegian socialists were in tune with international trends.

However, for women workers the question of equal wages was a difficult one, knowing as they did that one of the main reasons for their entrance into the labor market was that they were cheap labor, and the question of women workers as competitors and as a means to depress wages remained unsolved.

The Women's Rights Association supported women workers when a strike, the first ever among female workers, broke out among female matchworkers in October 1889. Competition between socialists and the bourgeois Women's Rights Association immediately followed. Carl Jeppesen acted as leader of the strikers, but the association helped establish the first female trade union, the Female Matchworkers' Trade Union. Prominent members of the association acted as the first presidents. The strike also involved male workers who had very meager financial means, and could not afford a long strike. The female workers, supported from many sources, wanted to press on for less hazardous working conditions and higher wages. The board of the association tried to work out a compromise between the factory owners and the female workers, and were harshly criticized by Jeppesen. When, after seven weeks, the female workers decided to call off the strike, they gave as their reason the interests of male workers.[12]

This is clear evidence of conflicting loyalties within the women's movement. Cooperation among women across class boundaries challenged class solidarity. The question of conflicting loyalties, of class versus gender, became more important when the socialist wing of the women's movement started organizing.

If we see the women's movement as an attempt to raise women's consciousness of their value as human beings and to encourage them to take responsibility for their own lives, then female trade unions certainly belong. In 1890, when they had formed their own trade union, a female canvas-weaver (*seildukarbeidersker*) said, "We have always been told that our words had little or no importance, but now that we have our own trade union, we think this may help us gradually to do away with the thought of our own insignificance."[13]

Between 1889 and 1901 around twenty female trade unions were formed, mostly in and around Kristiania. They were quite often the result of encouragement from male workers within the same trade, but sometimes they arose through conflicts with male workers. After two vain attempts to organize female servants, a servants' trade union was established in 1898, though only for a short period.

In 1894 and 1895 associations for women were created as part of the local Labor Party groups in the two biggest towns, Kristiania and Bergen. These were party-supporting groups, which organized fund raising, bazaars, and other activities to aid the party. But they gradually developed into pressure groups within the party, voicing women's political preferences. Although always loyal to the party line, they criticized men within the party for neglecting problems of special importance to women and for keeping their wives away from political activity on the pretext that women's responsibility was to take care of the family. Martha Thynæs, who in 1906 became the leader of Arbeiderpartiets kvindeforbund (the Labor Party's Women's Association), stressed the importance of political awareness among working-class women, who were the main educators of coming generations. She was met with arguments of women's special biology and accused of splitting the working class according to sex.

In 1901 female trade unions and Labor Party women joined forces in the Labor Party's Women's Association. The goal was "to work for the social and political liberation of women, as well as to protect and further women's professional and economic interests in any way,"[14] a goal worthy of any part of the women's movement. Women's wish to strengthen their influence in the party coincided with the interests of the party leadership in recruiting women to the party, because women obtained limited suffrage at local elections the same year. The new association was welcomed. It grew from a membership of around 260 in 1901, when it was established, to 2,000 in 1914, expanding especially after 1909. That year saw the publication of the journal *Kvinden* (The Woman), later to become *Arbeiderkvinnen* (The Working-Class Woman), which widened the opportunities for contacts and discussions among working-class women.

In the beginning the Women's Association of the Labor Party was dominated by women workers, organized within female trade unions. They worked hard to create more female trade unions, but seemed at the same time to understand paid work as appealing mostly to unmarried women. The harsh working conditions offered to working-class women made paid work more of a degradation than a liberation, and for married women, who had to shoulder the double burden of work outside and in the home, paid work could be a threat to health. Such a situation was seen as a consequence of economic hardship within the family. Although the socialist women's association worked to create day-care institutions for children, these were perceived as a next-best solution. Nothing could replace mother at home.

As the *Faglige Landsorganisasjon* (National Trade Union League) grew in importance, it drew most of the female trade unions away from the Labor Party's Women's Association. Gradually the latter became dominated by women married to men within the Labor Party. Although work to strengthen female trade union participation and work for the vote continued, efforts were also geared towards such social policies as better schools, better housing, assistance to unmarried mothers, teaching of home economics, and, especially, protection of working women.

It is clear that working-class and middle-class women had many common goals. Each group pursued a double strategy of working for gender equality and of protecting and strengthening women's special responsibilities. What divided them was the belief in the ability of capitalist society to accommodate demands for gender equality. Working-class women saw capitalist society as the prime enemy of both their class-specific and their gender-specific goals. Middle-class women saw men of their own class as the main obstacle to change, and had no interest in altering the fundamental structures of society.

This divide proved hard to overcome. Attempts were made to attract working-class women to middle-class organizations, but cooperation across class lines was rare. Even the fight for the vote was mainly fought as two parallel, but separate wars.

The Fight for the Vote

As long as the male vote was not extended to all grown men, the demand for women's suffrage on the same conditions as for men—as put forward by the Women's Suffrage Association—meant strengthening middle-class influence by enfranchising middle-class but not working-class women. For working-class women the only possible claim was general suffrage regardless of sex. This was also the program of the Labor Party beginning in 1889. The Liberal Party, the best supporter of the bourgeois women's movement, however, was divided on women's suffrage. It gave preference to supporting general suffrage for men in the hope of winning working-class votes. Even the Women's Rights Association did not clearly support women's suffrage until 1906. Most conservatives only reluctantly accepted any widening of suffrage regulations.[15]

A turning point was reached when, in 1896, municipal suffrage was made almost general for men—only male servants were not enfranchised. This split the middle-class Women's Suffrage Association. Some of the members, headed by Anna Rogstad, decided to change tactics. They now demanded limited municipal suffrage for women, accepting the idea that female suffrage should be reached step by step, not by claiming immediate equality with men. Gina Krog, Frederikke Marie Qvam, and a group of other women objected, but lost against a small majority which approved the change in strategy. They then broke away and formed *Landskvinnestemmerettsforeningen* (the National Association for Women's Suffrage).

The fight for the vote owed a great deal of its success to a new organization, formed in 1896, *Norske Kvinners Sanitetsforening* (the Norwegian Women's Sanitary Association). It was meant to support national opposition to the political union with Sweden by educating nurses and preparing medical materials to be used in the case of a war between the two countries. The organization spread to all parts of the country and recruited from all social groups. It soon broadened its activities to health problems in general, especially the fight against tuberculosis. Quickly growing to become the biggest of all women's organizations, it gave its wholehearted support to women's suffrage and might well have been a decisive factor in the favorable outcomes in 1901 and 1907.[16]

The National Association for Women's Suffrage, headed by Frederikke Marie Qvam, who for some time was also leader of the Sanitary Association and president of the Women's Rights Association, quickly established local branches all over the country. It cooperated closely with the new Sanitary Association. By 1902 it had 1,566 members, and it concentrated on the struggle for general suffrage.[17]

The National Association for Women's Suffrage ran regular suffrage campaigns, and so did the Labor Party. The National Day, May 17, was used for suffrage demonstrations. In 1899 women of the Labor Party invited middle-class suffrage organizations to take part in a common suffrage demonstration. Unexpectedly, only the moderate Women's Suffrage Association accepted, demonstrating together with working-class women for three consecutive years. The National Suffrage Association declined, fearing it would gain an even more radical image than it already had, and thereby deter moderate women. Naturally, it did not make for cross-class understanding when Ragna Nielsen, well-known president of the Women's Rights Association, in 1898 publicly declared that she had changed her mind about women's suffrage. She now found that women had shown so much "stupidity and lack of interest" that they did not deserve the right to vote.

In 1901 limited municipal suffrage was won. This was the result of cease-less campaigning over the years on the part of the women's movement, but also of party bickering in Parliament. A majority of only three votes saved the proposal. Limited national suffrage was not obtained until 1907. The women's cause no doubt profited from the support given by the Sanitary As-sociation to national policies in the dispute with Sweden over the political union. A cunning signature campaign in support of the dissolution of the union in 1905 also greatly enhanced the image of women as politically sen-sible and responsible individuals. Thus, in this case, nationalism assisted women in the fight for political citizenship.[18]

By now it was only a matter of time before municipal and national suffrage were widened to encompass women on the same conditions as men. This happened in 1910 and 1913 respectively, in 1913 with a united vote in Parlia-ment. One of the great objectives of the women's movement was reached.

Although started by middle-class women, the claim for the vote was voiced also by working-class women as soon as they got organized. Arguments for the female vote ranged from strict claims for equality, based on natural rights, to a notion of femininity as something radically different from masculinity and therefore important for the well-being of the nation. Working-class women again and again stressed what they believed to be women's special ability to create peace and avert war as one of their most important arguments for the vote.[19] Even Gina Krog, staunch supporter of the strategy of gender equality, took to gender difference as an argument for women's suffrage. "The social question" could only be solved, she said in 1889, if women took part in decision-making "with their own feminine views."[20] A change of attitudes was to her, and to many middle-class women, more important than a change from capitalism to socialism.

THE NEW CENTURY—COMPETING LOYALTIES

As 1901 marked the beginning of the victory for one of the most important objectives of the women's movement, the new century also in many ways widened the class divide between women. The establishment of the Labor Party's Women's Association in 1901 was a signal to middle-class women that winning their working-class sisters for the middle-class organizations would not be an easy task. The Labor Party grew in importance, and beginning in 1906 it was represented in the Storting (Parliament). Middle-class women organized in conjunction with the nonsocialist parties. *Høyrekvinders Klubb* (the Conservative Women's Club) started up in 1909, and women in the Liberal Party followed suit two years later.

The decade preceding the First World War also saw national organizations of midwives (1908), of women teachers, and of nurses (both in 1912). All of these organizations recruited middle-class women.

Competition or Protection?

The question of special protection for women workers, especially prohibition of night work for women, was raised in 1901 and put before Parliament in 1909.[21] The proposal was put forward by the Radical Liberals and sponsored by the Labor Party. Conservatives and Moderate Liberals were against this interference with competition on the labor market. Earlier restrictions on women's work had not encountered much resistance, and night work being only a small part of all work, this new proposal was not seen as having much practical importance. Nevertheless, a vehement discussion now flared up, mainly between the organized working-class women and the liberal part of the women's movement. Arguing that special protection of women workers would weaken their chances on the labor market and showed little confidence in women's own judgment, the Women's Rights Association defended the principle of equality. The matter was discussed at the first meeting of the

Nordic Women's Rights Associations in 1902, where the same stance was adopted. In 1903 the Women's Rights Association organized a meeting attended by some eight hundred women workers. Female typographers and a group of *skeidersker*, that is, women who sorted out different ores, feared for their jobs and agreed with middle-class women.

But the Labor Party's Women's Association defended the proposal. They argued that it could be seen as one step towards a universal eight-hour day and, more important, that it would protect women against overwork and resulting bad health. In addition, it seems that the Labor Party wanted to distance itself from middle-class women's attempts to win over unorganized working-class women. At the same time, the question of special protection for women gave women within the labor movement an opportunity to strengthen their image as politically engaged socialists. Seen in this light, the conflict was part of a general competition for votes between Radical Liberals and the Labor Party. But to the women's movement it was one of many dilemmas involving a choice between the principle of equality and the principle of difference, between acting as competitors and protecting women who were especially vulnerable because of their maternal functions. In this situation, dividing lines did not clearly follow class lines. Radical Liberals, women and men, joined working-class women in supporting the proposal. But the outcome was a victory for the principle of equality: The proposal was rejected.

The question of special protection for women workers widened the gap between socialist and bourgeois participants in the women's movement. But it also showed that both bourgeois and socialist women were divided among themselves, and that a radical fraction of the middle-class women cooperated closely with some of the socialist women.

This was the case also in some other matters, probably most clearly in another long discussion, from 1901 to 1915, concerning Castberg's Children's Laws.

Sexual Morality—A New Version of an Old Theme

In 1902 Radical Liberals, headed by Johan Castberg, put forward a proposal for six laws, known as Castberg's Children's Laws. The proposal was written in close cooperation between Johan Castberg and his sister-in-law, Katti

Anker Møller, since 1901 deputy member of the board of the Women's Rights Association. The laws would require that municipalities grant support to unmarried mothers for a certain period, without counting such support as poor relief, and give children born out of wedlock the right to use their father's name and to inherit his estate.

Discussions running up to passage of the laws in 1915 concentrated almost exclusively on the question of name and inheritance. At the center was the problem of the double standard for sexual morality.[22] Opponents maintained that the laws would hurt the family, punish a man for mistakes he might have made before marriage, and even weaken a wife's economic situation in case of widowhood. Proponents, on the other hand, argued that the laws would, for all practical purposes, make marriage a fait accompli from the moment a child was conceived. They would therefore serve to combat the double standard and give motherhood some practical and economic support, not just empty words of praise.

Opinions were very divided within the middle-class women's movement, but the Women's Rights Association supported the proposal on the condition that separate property be enacted as the normal arrangement within marriage. This was seen as a measure to protect a wife against the claims put forward by a possible illegitimate child of her husband. But separate property would also, as had been argued already in the 1880s, allow women to obtain the vote on the same conditions as those limiting men until 1898.

Working-class women supported the laws. As a result there was cooperation between some Radical Liberal women, notably Katti Anker Møller, and the Labor Party's Women's Association, as during the debate of the question of night work for women. This constellation pointed to the future, when the same group of women would cooperate to promote family planning and fight to decriminalize abortion. But in 1914 this long haul had only just begun.

Around 1914 the women's movement comprised a wide spectrum of organizations, with a wide spectrum of priorities. What united them was the goal of changing gender relations. Some gave priority to upgrading and professionalizing housekeeping and childcare, others to equal rights with men wherever possible. If not always very clearly, both strategies experienced doubts about gender as a biologically determined category, and arguments rooted in "difference" as well as in "sameness" could be found on all sides. In fact, one and the same person sometimes stressed one approach, sometimes

the other. Surprisingly, it seems that socialist women and conservative bourgeois women were the staunchest supporters of upgrading the work of housewives and mothers. Another important observation may be that regardless of
class and political conviction, marriage for all members of the women's movement meant concentrating on the home and family. Equal wages and access
to the same professions and education as men were mainly seen as measures
to provide unmarried women with a decent living. The only exception to this
rule was a small number of married female teachers who started the fight for
a married woman's right to paid work outside the home.

ALLIES AND OPPONENTS

The earliest allies of the women's movement were the Radical Liberals.[23] The
questions of women's rights and of sexual morality divided the Liberal Party
and contributed, in 1888, to the split of that party into a liberal and moderate fraction. But the Radical Liberals were not fully trustworthy allies. In the
1890s they gave priority to the male vote in an effort to win over as many Labor votes as possible. In the eyes of those women who staunchly followed
the principle of equality, they also betrayed the cause by supporting the prohibition of nightwork for women.

A similar wavering support was to be found among socialists. Although
the Labor Party continued to press for women's vote, there is no doubt that
it too gave priority to the male vote. Male socialists generally were not very
interested in the women's movement, but socialist ideology, especially in its
international dimension, along with the wish to recruit members and votes
among women, made them support women in many cases.

The Conservative Party was mostly inimical to the women's movement.
Individual conservatives nevertheless at times supported issues of importance
to women, especially better education and job opportunities. In addition,
conservative men felt the burden of having to support unmarried daughters
and sisters, and welcomed better opportunities for unmarried women to earn
their own living. But the fear that, once these possibilities were opened,
women would desert the family, ruin marriages, and forget about children,
was stronger among conservatives than in other political camps.

Apart from political conviction, religion was also an indicator of friendship or opposition to the women's movement. Taken as a whole, it could be said that the church opposed any change in gender relations, resting its arguments firmly on biblical texts and on the strong belief that God had created women as men's helpmates, destining them for lives as wives and mothers. As one clergyman put it in the 1890s, to admit women to leading positions in society by accepting them in the clergy would be as unnatural as asking husbands to act as wives.[24] It was not a coincidence that in Norway the clergy was the very last profession to be opened to women—in 1956.

Another profession opposed as a rule to the women's movement was the medical profession. The medical faculty outright opposed admitting women in 1882, but the decision was overruled by Parliament. When women started receiving medical degrees, they were feared as wage lowerers and competitors, threatening the prestige of the profession. Interestingly, the strongest opposition came from obstetricians, who for many years kept women out of the job they mastered so well as midwives.[25]

But it should not be forgotten that enemies were also to be found outside of masculine arenas. Many women were also opposed to the ideas of the women's movement. Religious convictions and political inclinations also weighed with women. An analysis of women's stance on the question of female clergy at the turn of the century has revealed very little support for this idea even among quite liberal groups of women. Only the principle of equality and free competition seemed to persuade members of the women's movement to support this claim.[26]

Age, of course, was also important. The organized women's movement started with young middle-class women who decided to prepare themselves for university studies. Far into the twentieth century, they faced criticism from older women who argued that such activities would weaken their capacity to become good wives and mothers and should be abandoned the moment the decision to marry had been taken. An analysis of generational differences in the understanding of gender relations around the turn of the century has revealed that women born around the middle of the nineteenth century still defended hierarchical gender relations, within as well as outside marriage.[27] In the opinion of the elder generation, women derived their power from the influence they had over husbands and children, not from egalitarian arrangements. They severely criticized the younger generation's call for husbands who would accept them as equal partners in marriage and refrain from demanding obedience. They were appalled at the idea that husbands might accept wives who were not prepared to use all their energy in the home, who would not "sacrifice everything for love," and who questioned the notion that motherhood was the most important thing in life.[28]

But for many young women, too, the meaning of "the women's cause" was uncertain. Radical Liberal young women around the turn of the century also gave priority to marriage and motherhood. However, they did not accept marriage as a hierarchical arrangement, but expected it to build on love between two equal individuals. Marriage should allow the wife to continue to develop herself spiritually, not confine her to "the simple exigencies of the nursery."[29] The idea of spiritual equality, introduced by Camilla Collett in 1854, was still strong. Equality would mean the right to vote, even to stand for election, although not till 1922 to be nominated to a high government position. But it would not necessarily mean that women were prepared to become active politicians. And it would certainly not mean that women were prepared to take over the responsibility of provider for the family. That was a job most certainly still left for men.

Although formal barriers to women's activities outside the home were broken, strong mental and practical barriers continued to work. Perceptions of femininity and masculinity had changed in important ways since the 1880s, but continuities were still strong. The popularity of *Hjemmenes Vel* (the Association for the Welfare of the Homes) was an indication that the professional housewife was being born at exactly the moment when women began winning equality in the political and professional fields. The very structures that furthered the women's movement—lower marriage rates, lower birth rates, technological changes making household chores lighter, industrialization, urbanization, and democratization—at the same time also highlighted the importance of work done in the home. Mothers were needed to take care of all the new expectations created by better knowledge in the areas of hygiene, health care, and education of small children.

In the newly independent nation, many mothers saw themselves as the pillars of society, teaching the young the right values and transmitting national traditions through generations. They upheld the symbol of the nation as a home, protected by strong fathers and helpful mothers, where gendered sharing of responsibilities warranted stability.[30] Wives were needed as mental supports for husbands as well. As one of the leading women in Hjemmenes Vel put it: "When women stop acting as supports for their husbands, the nation is doomed and decay has started. This is what the history of nations has taught us."[31]

Gender-specific tasks and gender-specific responsibilities were valued also by proponents of the women's movement. When women were no longer barred by laws and regulations from achieving the same goals as men, they were able to accept femininity as a maternal calling. It took another wave of feminism, the 1970s women's movement, to change that ideal. But the perception of women as inferior to and subordinated to men had weakened substantially. Gender differences did not have to signify gender hierarchy. The perception of femininity had changed in important ways. Women had conquered public spaces, while at the same time strengthening their position as wives and mothers.

The understanding of masculinity was changing as well. No doubt, gender identities were relational and interdependent. Changes in the perception of femininity wrought parallel changes in masculinity. Although very little has been done to find out how men mastered the new challenges, small as they may seem to us at the dawn of a new century, we know that it was not always easy. A middle-class observer in the 1870s sharply criticized male peasants for leaving important economic decisions to their wives.[32] A man, according to middle-class ideals, should take charge of the family economy, not leave any such responsibility to women. The transition from an agrarian to an urban economy influenced the understanding of gender. Medical men in 1882 openly professed their fears of a feminization of their profession. Caricatures amply testify to the humiliations that were seen to accompany feminization of until then purely masculine arenas. The very idea of being reprimanded in public by members of the female sex might change a man to a gender hybrid, putting him into the most feminine of garments, the corset. The early supporter of the women's movement, Hagbart Berner, as late as in 1907 had to suffer being depicted as an old woman with knitting.[33]

Adding to the problems of changing masculine identity was the growth of nationalism. The need to protect the nation, if necessary with military force, made hundreds of "rifle rings" spring up all over the country. Shooting became a sign of masculinity, equaled probably only by the capacity to endure almost unthinkable trials of danger and harsh climate, as Fridtjof Nansen demonstrated when he crossed Greenland on skis in 1888. Nansen was greeted as a national hero on his return. Skiing had already in the 1860s been proclaimed a masculine sport, but it was now elevated to the national sport. Masculinity looked for other outlets as femininity crowded in on professional and political arenas.[34]

In this uncertain situation, men found comfort in their venerated position as providers. None, not even the staunchest supporters of the principle of gender equality, questioned a man's duty to provide for his wife and children. To fail here was the utmost humiliation. To see a married woman reduced to working for money, therefore, was a sign of failed masculinity on the part of her husband. Only a very tiny handful of female married teachers tried to challenge this idea before 1914.[35]

COUNTERCULTURE AND NETWORKS

The last few decades of the nineteenth century saw a growing protest against the strictly gender-divided society of the urban middle class. In agrarian and working-class life, women and men often worked side by side and took part in the same leisure activities. But in the urban middle classes, femininity was circumscribed by many taboos. Even at private social occasions such as dinner parties, women and men were quite often separated. As soon as the meal was finished, men withdrew to the smoking room to discuss politics, economics, and other matters. Women were not supposed to be capable of taking part in such discussions, and "were left to float around as best they could."[36]

When, in even small Norwegian towns, urban life developed a new and public sphere in the form of restaurants, theatres, concerts, and public meetings, upper- and middle-class women were welcomed only if accompanied by men. For a woman to enter a restaurant, even a fashionable one, without male company, not to speak of smoking cigarettes or drinking alcohol, was deemed very dubious behavior. However, a small group of middle-class women started breaking these taboos. They took part in public discussions and even practiced skiing and mountain hiking. The prominent feminist Gina Krog went as far as to take up mountain climbing. In the 1880s Eva Sars, a gifted singer and later the wife of Fridtjof Nansen, had to defend women's skiing against accusations of immorality. But gradually some sports, especially those which allowed women to move gracefully, such as skating and tennis, became accepted female activities. The journal of the Women's Rights Association greeted sports and outdoor activities as a means for women to strengthen their health and as an aid in their fight for equal rights.[37] Protests against fashions imprisoning women's bodies in corsets and high-heeled shoes resulted in somewhat vain attempts to introduce a loose and comfortable "reform dress," and a few women even ventured to cut their hair short, although they were criticized for "cutting off all their femininity and their most important adornment."[38]

No doubt, however, the gendered division of social life also offered women the opportunity to build female networks and form female friendships. The leading women within the women's movement formed small but close circles, mainly concentrated around Kristiania and the few bigger towns, such as Bergen, Trondheim, and Stavanger. They came from the middle and upper class, and many of them were connected through family ties. A number of them were married to men in influential positions—professors, politicians, newspaper and journal editors.[39] Some of the leaders had met as young girls when they started to prepare for university studies in the early 1880s. Their small association, Skuld, existed only for a very short time, but recruited the inner core of the Women's Rights Association of 1884 and of the Suffrage Association of 1885. A heavy overlapping of women in the boards of the central organizations also indicates a close network, at the same time demonstrating how few women at the time were willing and able to assume such onerous public tasks.

Family ties even worked across frontiers: to Denmark and to Sweden.[40] Unfortunately, little has so far been done to elucidate cooperation among the members of the women's movement in the Scandinavian countries. What is known is that, in spite of the national conflict, members of the Swedish and Norwegian women's movement cooperated in a sisterly spirit, except for a short period of crisis around 1905. For women of the labor parties, the conflict over the dissolution of the political union had no adverse effects on mutual support.[41]

International networks also reached beyond Scandinavia to the United Kingdom and to the USA, as indicated by the inspiration found in John Stuart Mill's work and in that of American suffragists. The journal of the Women's Rights Association, started in 1887, bore the symbol of the sunflower. The idea was taken from Kansas, USA, where the sunflower was a feminist symbol.[42]

In 1904 most of the bourgeois women's organizations grouped themselves within *Norske Kvinners Nasjonalråd* (the Norwegian Women's National

Council), forming the national branch of the International Council of Women.[43] The socialist women were invited to join, but declined. The Council also comprised a great number of other women's organizations, such as religious, missionary, and teetotaling organizations. It quickly became a respected organization, with conservative positions on some issues, such as family planning. Although not including women of the Labor Party, the Council was often seen to represent Norwegian women as such, and political authorities turned to it for expert advice on many questions concerning women.

CONCLUSION

Continuities in gender relations were strong. Not one of the organizations disputed the idea that women's first and foremost task was that of wife and mother, and that men's first duty was to provide for their families and protect the nation.

Nevertheless, changes were also pronounced. The acceptance of a gender hierarchy had weakened considerably. So had the concept of biologically determined differences as the basis for the construction of femininity and masculinity. Through the women's movement, women were conquering spaces in the public sphere without relinquishing their responsibilities in the private sphere.

Although the common characteristic of all parts of the women's movement was a desire to change gender relations, the different organizations had different views of how they wanted gender relations to change. Whereas the Association for the Welfare of the Homes focused on upgrading women's work as housewives and mothers, the suffrage organizations invoked gender equality in support of their demands for equal rights. Class and political adherence, as well as age and religious leaning, resulted in conflicting loyalties among women within the movement but did not conceal the common goal of changing gender relations.

Even if the number of women organized within the movement was never very great, the ideas and actions stemming from this activist core were discussed, protested, and supported in much wider circles. Political parties had to accept or reject such ideas and actions. Parliament discussed not only the vote but also a great number of other issues raised by members of the women's movement. Journals printed articles and discussions in one issue after the other. All of this testifies to the importance of the movement in forming modern society. No part of society remained untouched by initiatives emanating from the women's movement, just as the women's movement continually debated changes and continuities in the society of which it was an integral part.

CHAPTER 8

Gender and Feminism in Sweden: The Fredrika Bremer Association

ULLA MANNS

In 1921 the first Swedish parliamentary election in which women could participate was held. Through the new marriage law, which came into effect that year, married women were included in the democratic reform. Four women were elected—two from the Social Democrats, one from the Conservatives, and one from the Liberal Party. The women's movement had reached one of its major goals, political recognition and formal equality. In an international perspective the Swedish struggle for women's emancipation was considered successful, since the organized struggle for suffrage started in 1903 and the vote was won less than twenty years later. But the fight for equality existed both before and after the struggle for suffrage. Many of the early feminist demands were difficult to realize, and still are: changed gender relations, equality within sexual morals, equal working conditions, and equal pay.[1]

The Swedish women's movement achieved an organized form in late 1884 when *Fredrika-Bremer-förbundet* (FBF), the Fredrika Bremer Association, was founded. The FBF was the largest organization within the women's movement until the suffrage movement started in 1903, and the first with an aim to promote women's conditions at large. The organization gathered women and men mainly from the liberal, educated middle class. It was centered in Stockholm, but from the start it had local representation in several cities.[2] A women's rights organization had already existed, but it concentrated on a single issue, married women's property rights. *Föreningen för gift kvinnas eganderätt*, the Association for Married Women's Property Rights, was started in 1873 and became affiliated with the FBF in 1896. The local chapter of the In-

This chapter was originally written as a paper for a conference in 1995. I have limited my editorial revisions to include new research on the subject.

ternational Abolitionist Federation, which had existed in Sweden since 1878, also promoted certain women's rights, as did the international organization, but it was not explicitly a women's rights organization.

An unorganized women's movement had existed during the 1860s and 1870s. Its focal points were the Association for Married Women's Property Rights and the *Tidskrift för hemmet*, the *Home Journal.* The journal had been started in 1859 by the baroness Sophie Adlersparre (at the time under her maiden name Leijonhufvud). It gathered more or less the same group of persons who, under the leadership of Adlersparre, later initiated the FBF.[3] The *Home Journal* was immediately attached to the FBF, and from 1886 it was published under the name *Dagny* (a Nordic woman's name). In 1914 it took the name *Hertha*, after the famous emancipation novel written by Fredrika Bremer in 1856.

The FBF was founded with the aim to further women's emancipation. It intended to "promote the advancement of women morally, intellectually, socially, and economically," as the bylaws of 1884 stated.[4] Behind this rather moderate statement of purpose existed a more far-reaching aim to change power and gender relations. This is apparent both in discussions preceding the formation of the FBF and in the stance taken by the association in the ongoing debate about sexual matters, which was very intense during the 1880s. The FBF was founded in the spirit of Fredrika Bremer. Sophie Adlersparre quoted her at the constitutional meeting in December 1884: it was with the help of "true emancipation" that the new association would "combat a false emancipation."[5]

"True emancipation" became the motto of the FBF during the first wave of emancipation. In 1884 this motto was directed mainly against the philosophical naturalism often expressed in left-wing literary circles. In the debate about sexual matters naturalism had a large impact. In Sweden it contributed greatly to a general change in ideas of human nature, from a concept of humans as spiritual and cultural beings to one that emphasized their biological side. This change, founded in science, reinforced ideas about women as sexed beings. Naturalistic ideas in Sweden originated primarily from George Drysdale, Max Nordau, and Herbert Spencer.[6]

According to the FBF, false emancipation was primarily based on secularized ideas about human nature as governed by instinctive drives. Such ideas, it was said, would serve to keep women in a subordinate position. Naturalism would eroticize ideas about women and thereby make their conditions worse.

The "true emancipation" put forward by the FBF was based from the start on ideas about Christian love (love thy neighbor as thyself) and on an idealistic view of social progress. Everyone, irrespective of gender, was considered to have the same capacities and the same purpose in life—to develop into a full-fledged personality. According to the FBF, women's self-fulfillment was not hindered by nature, by an innate lack of certain faculties; as John Stuart Mill argued, attitudes and legal injustice were seen as the main obstacles. The defense of an idealistic conception of social and individual life was thus combined with a profound awareness of an existing gendered social order. But at the same time, the FBF deliberately put up a moderate and nonsocialist front. Its leaders emphasized the importance of reforms instead of revolution, of cooperation instead of confrontation, and of consensus instead of dispute. They did not hesitate to argue along the lines of feminism, even though arguments of women as morally superior to men rarely occurred.[7]

In many ways the FBF displayed the characteristics of what is usually described as liberal feminism. Its focus was on the improvement of legal rights, education, and self-support, and women were seen as beings with the same faculties of reason as men.[8] The concept of true womanhood was used, but usually in a vague way, almost as a model for human and Christian behavior. It is important to remember that the FBF in its early years had a clear awareness of gender as a power relationship. This was particularly obvious in debates concerning sexual morals and prostitution. It also recognized and criticized the ongoing process of gender construction. This led to a critique of the construction of "women" and of "men." Ideas and norms about gender had to be altered if real changes were to be accomplished. Cooperation with men was seen as very important—it was even stressed in the FBF by-laws—and in practice the FBF engaged many men, both as supporting members and as leading personalities. Of course the inclusion of men had practical advantages too. Many were prominent in parliament, in intellectual or academic circles, and in the mass media.[9]

To become organized was to act politically and collectively on questions concerning gender relations. It was to define a social problem that concerned a group not recognized as individuals and thus not as a collective. It was also to explicitly criticize an existing social order. This was expressed in various ways—in moderate claims as well as in explicitly angry and critical rhetoric, largely drawn from the writings of John Stuart Mill, Fredrika Bremer, and the Norwegian writer Henrik Ibsen. Women, the leadership of the

FBF claimed, had to be recognized as individuals, as actors, and as reasoning beings—contrary to the existing gender order which denied women capacities and traits such as reasoning power, individuality, and agency. Women's suffering within marriage and in the family was a widely discussed topic in the 1880s. The FBF, like Mill, did not hesitate to call attention to their subordination. It also criticized the denial of women's ability to reason in much the same way Mill did in *The Subjection of Women.*[10]

VISIONS AND GOALS

From the beginning the "true emancipation" of the FBF had two equally important goals: to end the subordination of individual women and to improve society in general. The latter goal originally included a vision of a new society based on a mixture of ideas from liberalism, Christian idealism, and feminism (here understanding "feminism" as a wish to end women's subordination). The new society was envisaged as one at a high cultural level and based on gender equality. It also seems to have been thought of as a social order less defined by gender. The members of this new society were to be full-fledged personalities, regardless of gender.

Sexuality was by no means neglected but was said to be of secondary importance both to the happiness of the individual and to social progress. The sexual drive was to be controlled and subordinated to mind and will, but not denied within marriage. Responsibility and fidelity in intimate relationships were to be the norm for women and men equally. According to the FBF, it would be impossible to ensure happiness for all if sexual drives governed life. Egoism would prevail and happiness be allowed only the chosen few (i.e., men). Christian love, caring, and responsibility required self-control, not liberal attitudes towards sexuality. The claim put forward by the FBF was already a norm for women and was to be made the norm for men as well. In this way an improvement of both private relations and social conditions was expected. There would be real emancipation and true happiness without human suffering. Liberty would be made compatible with equality.[11]

The vision expressed during the sexual debates was described in 1887 by the Danish feminist Elisabeth Grundtvig in a pamphlet which attracted large attention throughout the Nordic countries. Her ideas were similar to Sophie Adlersparre's and caused internal dispute when Adlersparre wanted

to give moral matters political priority, while the board of the FBF wanted
to promote practical work. Elisabeth Grundtvig described the feminist vision of the 1880s in the following words:

> If we envisage a society where desire coexists with love, where men and
> women live together in pure, happy marriages, helping one another in the
> work of daily life, a society where seduction, rape, prostitution, and all the
> misery that follows are barely known of, where no miserable homeless
> children exist—if we imagine this, all of us can surely say: this is
> happiness.[12]

Equality was the goal of both the women's movement and the radicals. However, the burning question was: according to which norm? Here the newly organized women's movement in the Nordic countries advocated a new sexual
order which would put an end to women's sexual and social subordination.

ACTIVITIES

The goals set by the FBF were to be achieved through activity on an extensive scale, mainly based on a liberal idea of self-help and on altered attitudes
towards gender.[13] The idea of self-help comprised practical matters but was
also seen as a means to increase awareness and self-confidence in women. In
addition, the FBF aimed at putting pressure on parliament to improve legal
and economic conditions for women, especially those who were unmarried.
A brief look at the wide range of activities initiated during a brief period dis-
plays the varying ways in which change was accomplished. These activities
were similar to those within many European women's rights organizations at
the time. What is striking in the case of the FBF, though, is the large scale
on which work was carried out within such a short time span.[14]

Through its journal, the FBF worked to promote changes in attitudes
concerning gender and women's social conditions. As mentioned above,
great attention was paid to moral aspects of sexuality and intimate relations
between women and men, and the FBF was one of the major participants in
the moral discussions of the 1880s in Sweden. It showed an awareness about
sexual matters in a context of power.

The FBF also promoted opportunities for formal education in order to
increase women's abilities to be self-sufficient and independent, economically as well as intellectually. It set up financial funds for education (which

still exist), established home study programs, and extended small loans for starting up enterprises. It opened employment bureaus for women, a health insurance office for teachers, and a pension fund for nurses. It soon became a petitioner of importance, especially in employment and educational matters. The FBF later (in the early years of the twentieth century) took a general stand against gendered labor legislation and advocated equal pay and equal working conditions in both industrial and white-collar work. It also acted as a consulting body when legal changes in matters such as working conditions, employment, and salaries were being discussed in parliament. In the early years of the twentieth century it was important in organizing working (mainly white-collar) women employed by the state.[15]

One of the first things the FBF did was to set up a bureau in Stockholm, which soon came to be a kind of semiofficial department of women's questions and was consulted by the government, mass media, and other women's organizations throughout the country. Both the journal and the bureau were used by several smaller organizations within or close to the women's movement for receiving and disseminating information and making contact with other reformers. At the bureau an advisory service was offered in legal and financial matters, employment, education, sanitary matters, etc. Through its journal and its bureau, the FBF played an important role as a link between different groups within the women's movement.[16]

The FBF tried to improve legal conditions for married women, concerning property rights, legal majority, access to divorce, and marriageable age. Women's interests in political and social matters were considered important from the very start. In 1887 the FBF produced special leaflets that were distributed to all women having the right to vote in municipal elections in Stockholm (unmarried and with a certain minimum income). The leaflets contained information about how to obtain documents necessary to register, how to vote, and when and where elections were held. This information was reissued several times and it seemed to increase women's participation in some of the elections in Stockholm. The work took place in cooperation with the Association for Married Women's Property Rights and later with the suffrage movement.[17] In 1899 the FBF officially demanded suffrage for women, and it was later active in the founding of the national suffrage movement.

The FBF also took an active interest in women's physical health. Dress reform (in Sweden mainly underwear, maternity clothes, sportswear, children's and baby clothing), sports, and physical activities for young women were on their program. The Dress Reform Association affiliated itself with the FBF in 1890. The FBF supported the work of female doctors, setting up special funds for female medical students and campaigning for sexual education.[18]

BEYOND GENDER

The immediate goals set by the FBF were deliberately kept moderate, but a broad range of activities, together with the theoretical discussions, reflects the eventual far-reaching goals of the FBF. As already mentioned, the FBF did not hesitate to discuss sexual conduct, the need for sexual education, and the physical and mental consequences of legal inequality in personal relations between women and men. Nor did the association hesitate to advocate a less gendered concept of human nature.

The FBF's vision of gender relations was gender transcendent in two respects. First, gender distinctions with regard to mental and moral capacities were to be dismantled. Second, the new concept of human nature also comprised men. The new kind of human being was a less gendered individual who was mature, active, and responsible in both private and social life. In such a person conventional gender features were integrated. These ideas stood in stark contrast to conventional ideas about gender and women's innate moral superiority. For both women and men, a one-sided development of gender was seen as a source of injustice, an obstacle to social progress, and an impediment to individual fulfillment.[19]

PRAGMATISM VS. IDEALISM

The moral debate in Sweden reached a climax during 1887–1888. The extent to which moral matters were to be given priority in the work for women's emancipation was discussed on the board of the FBF during this period. Sophie Adlersparre and friends regarded moral matters as an essential part of women's emancipation. They wanted to concentrate on achieving a major change in ethics concerning sexuality and gender. The majority of the board feared, however, that too much focus on moral matters would weaken the credibility of the new women's movement and thereby diminish the likelihood of attaining other reforms. The less controversial line was chosen, and the FBF took a large step towards a pragmatic view of women's emancipation. This pragmatism led to a more homogeneous and in some respects new idea of emancipation. Criticism of gender concepts decreased with the concentration upon practical reforms.

The two lines of thinking about emancipation within the FBF can be said to have coexisted relatively unproblematically from the start. There was a visionary idea of feminism, with far-reaching aims for altering gender relations, and a pragmatic idea of feminism, less critical toward complementary ideas of gender, that concentrated on improving women's conditions in the legal and economic spheres. When the theoretical consequences of these two lines collided at the end of the nineteenth century, pragmatism came to the fore. Because of its left-wing connotations and sexually liberal ideas the visionary form of maternalism did not attract the FBF either.[20] Challenges to the idea of gender were difficult to put into practice and, it seems, because of their religious base a bit out of date at the turn of the century. According to the majority of the board too much attention to sexual morals was also likely to jeopardize the work for other reforms. The board chose to promote practical reforms. With this change the gender-challenging project became less important. The influence of the founder Sophie Adlersparre also diminished.[21]

COMPLEMENTARITY AND SUFFRAGE

The individuals forming the new leadership of the FBF in the mid-1890s were mostly practical activists and social reformers, and to a lesser extent theorists or visionaries. With Agda Montelius (chairperson from 1903 to 1920), the FBF moved closer to newly organized social reform groups. The societal goal of women's emancipation was forcefully brought forward under her leadership. After the turn of the century, Swedish feminism on the whole can be said to have turned astonishingly nontheoretical. This was mainly due to the intense work for suffrage which dominated the entire Swedish women's movement for a period of almost twenty years, until 1919, when the vote was finally won.[22] Another important factor was that women had greater opportunities to influence social policy during the first two decades of the twentieth century.

The resistance against women's claims for suffrage was harsh, especially among conservative groups. Even though liberals dominated the national suffrage organization, the struggle for suffrage involved extensive collaboration between women's organizations of different social and political backgrounds. This required considerable diplomacy and a limitation of the struggle to the single question of suffrage. This cooperation had consequences for internal debates within the women's movement. Practical work, cooperation with related groups, and solidarity within the entire women's movement characterized Swedish feminism during the first decades of the twentieth century. The contrast with the debating and analyzing years of the 1880s and the 1890s is striking. Feminism definitely turned pragmatic. The resistance against women's suffrage from the political parties coincided paradoxically with an increasing recognition of the women's movement as a political force and as a legitimate actor in social policy.[23]

In 1896 the social reformer Ellen Key criticized the fundamentals of women's emancipation, and a heated debate about gender and emancipation took place within the women's movement. According to Ellen Key, the FBF was trying to promote a wrong-headed kind of emancipation, which neglected the biological differences between the sexes. The FBF, she said, was also too little concerned with social matters. Almost unconsciously, the FBF adjusted itself to rectify the main complaints made by Ellen Key, although it never accepted her secular world view and liberal ideas about sexuality. At the turn of the century the FBF gradually changed its thinking about emancipation to suit conventional ideas about gender. It also came closer to organized social reform work. The woman question thereby became more directly related to the social question, which did not necessarily focus on the subordinated position of women. Now the emphasis was on social change rather than on individual emancipation and changing gender relations. This is, of course, somewhat of a simplification. As the FBF shifted its attention to social reform, the struggle for equal pay and the fight against prohibition of women's night work increased.[24]

In 1903, the organized struggle for suffrage kicked off when *Landsföreningen för kvinnans politiska rösträtt* (LKPR), The National Association for Women's Suffrage, was founded. The FBF played a major, though not dominant, role within the LKPR, whose ideological leadership comprised a politically mixed group of feminists, dominated by liberals.[25] The pragmatism of the FBF grew stronger during the years of the suffrage campaigns, a period in which there was a backlash concerning women's working conditions. Ideas about gender complementarity were often put forward in debates concerning political power and social reform. It was hoped that suffrage would ensure social change in a maternalistic way and counteract legislation that, so the women's movement feared, would reduce women's possibilities of employment and equal pay.[26]

As a result of its growing pragmatism and its increasing ability to influence social policy, the FBF gradually began to accept a separate-sphere ideology. This was the mindset which much of the social reform work was built upon. Gender-transcending ideas still existed within the FBF, but in comparison with former years the ideological shift seems profound. The change is best described as a change in relation to an existing gender order.[27] Even though male norms and the gender hierarchy were increasingly criticized, gendered ideals about human nature came to be accepted. The FBF regarded a complementary concept of gender as a natural basis for the division of labor and of power. Furthermore, it increasingly supported a gendered division of labor as a means to gain political recognition. During the years of suffrage campaigns, gender complementarity arguments were dominant within both the FBF and the suffrage movement. These were often combined with conservative ideas about women's political obligations towards the state. Arguments about women's natural rights were seldom put forward in the struggle for suffrage. In the case of the FBF, this was mainly due to the socialist connotations of such arguments. Two similar ideas—the political obligations of female citizens and maternalism—had a strong appeal to the Swedish women's movement at large.[28]

During the first decade of the twentieth century visionary feminism was not absent within the FBF, but it did not hold an ideologically important place. It found expression primarily in the journal, where certain foreign feminists received strong support. Feminists such as Rosa Mayreder, Charlotte Perkins Gilman, and Olive Schreiner criticized a man-made world, pointed out the ongoing social construction of gender and, very similarly to the FBF in earlier years, proclaimed a less gendered idea of human nature. In particular, Rosa Mayreder's synthetic ideal of human nature was praised. The evolutionary feminism put forward by Gilman and Schreiner was not commented upon. The support given to these feminists came into sharp contrast with the maternalistic arguments put forward by the board of the FBF, especially in connection with suffrage and social work.[29] But, as mentioned before, the FBF was not attracted to the visionary form of maternalism proclaimed by Ellen Key.

Ideas of women's emancipation after the turn of the century differed widely from those of the 1880s. Surprisingly enough, this theoretical tension and ongoing change did not result in internal conflicts of any great significance. This was probably due to the fact that the idea of complementarity soon became established within the ideology of the FBF. A gender-transcending feminism did not threaten the more pragmatic and moderate ideas about emancipation which dominated during the suffrage years. It did create some conflict during the debates on sexual matters in the late 1880s, a conflict which Sophie Adlersparre and her allies lost. Again, in the late 1890s, conflict concerning gender and emancipation arose, caused by Ellen Key's criticism. The way in which this was received also caused some internal dispute. But pragmatism won again.[30]

During the suffrage years, complex questions concerning feminism, long-term goals, and gender were seldom discussed. This was the case not only within the FBF but within the entire Swedish women's and suffrage movement. After the turn of the century, the organizations concentrated mainly on social action and cooperation. During the almost twenty years that passed before the vote was finally won, a new generation of feminists came on the scene. This new generation, within the FBF and in other parts of the women's movement, was more identified with social reforms as a platform from which feminist demands were made. They seem to have had a more or less gendered vision of emancipation as a starting point.

GRADUAL CHANGE

When political parties were founded (Social Democrats in 1889, Liberals in 1900, Conservatives in 1904), women's participation within them became an inevitable, though complicated, question. Women with partisan interests founded separate women's organizations allied, to different extents, with their respective parties. Conservative women got organized in 1911, Liberals in 1914, Social Democrats in 1920, and rural women in 1921. Communist women did not form a separate organization but started a journal of their own, *Röda röster* (Red Voices), in 1919. Formal opportunities to act politically increased. In 1910 women with the right to vote in municipal elections could also be elected to office. Several women within the women's movement were set up as candidates. Municipal politics was seen as closely connected to the interests of the women's movement.[31]

The connections between social reform work and the women's movement were of great importance. Swedish feminism was close to *Centralförbundet för socialt arbete*, the National Association of Social Work (CSA), which was founded in 1903. This umbrella organization not only attracted a major part of the Swedish women's movement, it was by and large created and led by supporters of women's emancipation. Agda Montelius, from the FBF, was one of its founding members, and both the FBF and the local suffrage association in Stockholm were affiliated with the CSA. The CSA became an important pressure group concerned with social policy and included several members of parliament, from both the Liberal and Social Democratic groups.[32] The integration of women's emancipation, social reform work, and politics contributed considerably to the emergence of new ideas about emancipation. The transition to a conception of women and men as biologically different was important in this connection. In Sweden, as in many other western countries, Darwinism had a large impact on the political and cultural debate about gender.[33]

The most important change in the idea of emancipation concerned the concept of human nature. For the FBF this had great implications for the ultimate goal of emancipation. What kind of equal society was to be attained? A gendered society or a society above gender? The "true emancipation" of the FBF came about during the early twentieth century as an emancipation within an existing gender order. A feminism with an explicit critique of gendered conceptions of human nature had been of great importance to the original idea of emancipation. It had broad implications for the FBF during its years of formation but was soon held back by an increasing pragmatism. This pragmatism seems to have developed into a more homogeneous idea of emancipation: a striving for a better (and equal) society based on gender differences.

EPILOGUE

In 1921 the statutes of the FBF were changed. This took place when suffrage had finally been won (1919) and the suffrage movement dissolved. The FBF fought hard to recruit women from the suffrage movement throughout the country. Discussions within the FBF on how to attract them reveal the prominence of a readjusted idea of emancipation. In pamphlets written to attract new members, feminist ideas related to gender criticism or far-reaching goals are strikingly nonevident, as are angry demands to end remaining injustice.[34] In 1919 the FBF still declared that the goal was first and foremost to continue the work for emancipation. But the meaning of emancipation had changed. The FBF stated that it wanted to function mainly as a gathering place for women's common interests. Men were not mentioned any more in the new bylaws. The association was now to be seen as a place where women of all feminist persuasions could gather independently of party politics, but with the aim of preparing themselves for political work. Implicitly, emancipation was now put forward as equality within an existing gender order.

The case of the FBF was not unique in Sweden, nor internationally.[35] And Swedish feminism was by no means homogeneous—it comprised different ideas on how to bring about emancipation for women. Was it to include class, sexuality, Christian morality? Was it to be based on ideas about gender differences or not? On closer analysis, however, a striking degree of consensus within the women's movement is to be found concerning gender and power. The three major groups within Swedish feminism—the FBF, the Social Democratic women's movement, and the suffrage movement—all seem to have accepted a gendered social order after the turn of the century, even though other voices occasionally could be heard. In 1921, two major legal reforms concerning women came into effect—suffrage and majority for married women. A new era had begun.

PART IV

East Central and Eastern Europe

CHAPTER 9

The Emancipation of Women for the Benefit of the Nation: The Czech Women's Movement

JITKA MALEČKOVÁ

The history of Czech women could begin with the rule of the princess Libuše, elected for her wisdom and prophetic gifts, and with the "girls' war" of Czech Amazons, a variation on the well-known "women's revolt": after the death of Libuše, her companions, led by Vlasta, revolted against the establishment of men's rule and for many years successfully made war against men. The story could continue with the first female saints and the women followers of the Czech religious reformer Jan Hus, who in the fifteenth century did not hesitate to sacrifice their lives to defend their faith against Catholic (and foreign) enemies.

Indeed, representatives of the women's movement in the nineteenth century used these figures in order to legitimize women's rights. Female writers and poets elaborated upon the images of the mythical and historical heroines, and women's associations were named after the first Czech female saint, Ludmila, the princess Libuše, and the leader Vlasta, whom the promoters of women's emancipation did *not* emulate; instead of fighting against men, they chose moderate methods and cooperated with their progressive male compatriots.

The legends about the rule of Libuše and the girls' war mentioned in medieval chronicles were not rediscovered by feminists, but by the early Czech revivalists, and eventually they became a part of national mythology. Calling for women's assistance in the national movement, male intellectuals appreciated the merits of the Hussite women, the uniqueness of the female ruler Libuše, and the courage of Vlasta.

The research for this chapter was made possible by the Jean Monnet Fellowship at the European University Institute, Florence, Italy.

The connection between the women's movement and nationalism is emphasized mainly by foreign historians, although they differ in their evaluations. For Richard Evans, in his summary of the Czech women's movement, the nationalism of Czech women was an obstacle to their success.[1] Katherine David has presented a more persuasive image of the relationship between Czech feminism and nationalism at the turn of the century: She claims that she has "found no evidence that feminists traded away any radical demands in exchange for support from liberal nationalism."[2] Helena Volet-Jeanneret, in her study of the Czech women's movement in Prague between 1860 and 1895, found the specificity of the Czech case in the double struggle of Czech women—against social prejudices and the German culture—and in the role of philanthropy in the movement.[3]

Czech historians have provided interesting data on various aspects, personalities, and periods in connection with the efforts for emancipation, but until very recently no analysis and evaluation of the movement as a whole.[4] Worth mentioning especially are the works of Pavla Horská, which link women's activities to social, economic, and demographic conditions and pay attention to the German movement in the Czech Lands.[5] A good summary of the movement can be found in the entry on women's emancipation in an encyclopedia from 1908 written by the feminist Františka Plamínková; she characterized the struggle for political rights as a belated one.[6] In addition to this, a more detailed study of the early stages of the women's movement from 1914, interesting not only for its information value but also as a source, reflecting women's consciousness in the early twentieth century, is a book by Vlasta Kučerová. The author dates the emergence of the movement to the 1830s; the preceding "time of women's silence in the public" was interrupted only by the literary attempts of several female writers who were "feminists because they addressed their knowledge to women." The real women's movement began, according to her, with the feminist activity of a man, K. S. Amerling, in the 1840s.[7] Other historians give the title of the first Czech feminist to Božena Němcová, a female writer of the same period, or to Vojta Náprstek, a male founder of a women's association in the 1860s.[8] While according to David "one can speak of a true 'feminist' movement in Bohemia" from the 1890s,[9] Evans found "the first record of Czech feminism" in the Women's Club (which he wrongly dates to 1901).[10]

This chapter is not a polemic against the established histories of the Czech women's movement because, despite a number of partial studies, no widely accepted interpretation of the emancipation efforts of Czech women exists. I intend to pinpoint the specificities of the Czech women's movement and its continuity and changing emphases in various periods, and I include hypotheses which will be challenged by further research. This is not an overview of all women's activities and organizations, but rather an attempt to connect the characterization of the main trends of the periods with the views of some of the carriers of the development, which should demonstrate at least roughly the diversity of understanding about the woman question and of the processes of women's self-awareness.

The periodization is only tentative, emphasizing the main features of stages rather than specific dates as turning points. After the first expressions of women's awakening to national and public life, three periods are distinguished: the period of the first long-lasting women's organizations of mainly philanthropic and educational orientation, through which women started to realize not only their duties but also their rights; the spread and differentiation of the movement after the late 1880s and particularly in the 1890s when the woman question made its way to public discourse; and the time of politicization from 1905, with on the one hand a deepening diversification along political allegiances, and on the other hand a relative unanimity of various streams of the women's movement and some of the public about the relevance of suffrage.

DOUBLE AWAKENING

Czech civil society did not emerge through a revolution but, in a setting influenced by the Enlightenment and the reforms of the Habsburg rulers, took the form of a national movement. Despite the abolition of serfdom, declared religious tolerance, and advancing industrialization, the early nineteenth-century multinational empire was still an absolute monarchy, more centralized than ever before, and using German as a common language of its new bureaucratic administration. In this political and cultural context women started to get involved in public life, and their role in society began to be discussed.

In the first half of the nineteenth century and even later, a woman was viewed primarily as a mother. However, the second generation of Czech patriots, trying to create a Czech culture, expected women to be more than virtuous wives and mothers raising their sons as good citizens. Mothers were supposed to teach their children to speak Czech and to be proud of Czech culture and history. Therefore, women themselves needed better education and an understanding of national interests.

Some of the patriots considered the highest virtue of women to be their "Czechness," and a few went even further and accorded women, at least ideally, the role of "fellow-fighters" in the national movement. Trying to show how widespread and accomplished Czech culture was, and considering the contribution of women as a sign of a nation's maturity, they called for, supported, and glorified early literary works by women and themselves wrote poetry under female names. František Ladislav Čelakovský (1799–1852), a renowned poet who was behind the most successful mystification under a woman's name, was a friend of one of the first female poets, the nun Marie Antonie (1780–1831), whose works he revised.[11]

Male intellectuals encouraged women's participation in the life of the still-small patriotic circle. In the 1830s, young literati like Josef Kajetán Tyl (1808–1856) organized Czech amateur theater performances and salons, including women alongside men, and from 1840 also held Czech balls where patriotic poems addressed to and written by Czech women were circulated. The utopian socialist Karel Slavoj Amerling (1807–1884) included women in his patriotic educational enterprise "Budeč." He believed that a more serious form of education should serve to better prepare girls for family life, but above all as "human beings, and only then [as] women, girls, wives, mothers, and grandmothers."[12]

The national awakening marked the emerging awareness of women and their educational and literary efforts. The patriotic atmosphere was favorable to the activities of women, who, for their part, linked a concern for their female compatriots to an even stronger concern for the national community. Women entered cultural life with considerable self-confidence. They did not feel they had to justify why they, women, wrote, and even less so since they did not promote women's emancipation but rather traditional family values, though in a new context. They wrote for women, in Czech, and sometimes explicitly to celebrate the nation.

Magdalena Dobromila Rettigová (1785–1845) was the most outstanding example of the first generation of female writers. With deliberate effort, she learned to write in Czech and published a number of novels and a best-selling cookbook. While she taught girls in provincial towns cooking and housework, she also tried to acquaint them with literature, advising them to be "virtuous, faithful, and affable wives, sincere and careful mothers" and to inculcate their children with respect for father, God, and the Emperor—and "the Country as our common mother."[13]

The relationship between the public and the private was not always as simple as for the middle-class housewife Bohuslava Rajská (1817–1852). Rajská helped to organize classes for girls in the framework of Amerling's "Budeč" school in order to "educate patriotically thinking mothers and teachers for her wretched nation,"[14] and in 1844 established her own school for girls. Her promising yet brief public career ended when she married the recently widowed patriot Čelakovský, considering the marriage a patriotic duty.[15]

Rajská's decision to marry was influenced by Božena Němcová (1820–1862), the most famous Czech female writer of her time. Němcová was an exceptional woman, much before her time in terms of her articles on current political events and on social matters going far beyond charity. Unhappily married and poor, she strove in her private life for economic independence and personal freedom. Although she did not write especially for women, and her female characters were anything but emancipated, she questioned society's prejudices against women and publicly criticized the inadequacy of women's education. In several poems she exhorted women to educate their children as Czech patriots and even to fight for the country following the example of the mythical heroine Vlasta.[16]

The revolution of 1848 engendered a broader if temporary interest of women in politics and in their new forms of public activities. The first women's associations, *Spolek Slovanek* (Association of Slavic Women) and *Slovanská Dennice* (The Slavic Morning Star), were founded under the impact of current events, although they followed on the footsteps of previous efforts by the circle around Budeč and Rajská.[17]

During the June Uprising, women mainly from lower classes participated in the fights on the barricades: five of them were killed and ten were imprisoned. In addition to a few small-scale women's demonstrations evoked by local issues, women united to send petitions to Vienna concerning more general political matters. The second mission was preceded by a public meeting of Czech and German women who stressed that they were not struggling for emancipation, but wanted their voice, "as that of the citizens of the state," to be heard.[18]

While earlier women's efforts had aroused little public response, except for some complaints about female education being a distraction from their true destiny, their involvement in revolutionary events caused both enthusiastic admiration and alarmed criticism. A Prague newspaper reacted with articles against women's emancipation and political aspirations, describing a public meeting held by women as "a profaning of woman's nature."[19] This view was undoubtedly shared by many contemporary Czech men and women.

THE LADIES' FIRST STEPS

In the postrevolutionary decline of public life women gave little reason for criticism of their activities. *Spolek Sv. Ludmily* (Association of St. Ludmila) was founded in 1851 by German and Czech noble and upper-middle-class women, and along with the school attached to it was devoted to generally approved support for poor women. The philanthropic, educational, and self-help associations created by middle-class women in the following decades tried to prepare lower-class women for gainful employment and middle-class girls for housework, family life, and the female professions. Only one club explicitly aimed at promoting the awareness and self-confidence of women. These moderate activities nonetheless resulted in a gradual change in the movement's goals: in 1881, Eliška Krásnohorská claimed a woman's right for equal opportunity with men in education, and equal pay for work, and by 1890 her efforts had scored some success.

Women's organizations started to spread in the 1860s amidst the period of social revival, economic growth preceding the 1873 world crisis, and the Prussian-Austrian war of 1866 with its social consequences. The concept of citizenship gave new justification to the emancipation efforts of women, yet they were still forbidden to enter or found political clubs; universal male suffrage was not the main issue on the agenda either. Political discussions revolved around national rights and strategy towards Vienna, especially after the 1867 Ausgleich. Under the influence of the Old Czechs, the Czech deputies of the *Reichsrat* (Imperial Council) adopted the policy of passive resistance from 1863 to 1879. The Old Czechs' leadership of the Czech political scene was challenged by the emergence of the Young Czech Party in 1874, calling for more active steps, and in 1878 a new rival appeared in the Social Democratic Party. Besides the political and economic situation, the efforts of women were influenced by a revival of national cultural life with its emphasis on the Czech language and education.[20]

Although the first women's organizations followed a similar pattern of activity, at least two streams can be distinguished, neither of which was uniform. The more conservative stream limited itself to charity and philanthropy. Its most important and radical representative was undoubtedly Marie Riegrová (1833–1891), daughter of the outstanding Czech politician and historian František Palacký and wife of the Old Czechs' leader F. L. Rieger. When she became a member of the Association of St. Ludmila in 1864, Riegrová induced its complete reorientation according to her belief that it was necessary not only to cure but to prevent poverty, especially through education, enabling women to earn their livings. Alongside the patriotism characteristic of her family, Riegrová displayed an interst in scholarly philanthropy, and contributed to the foundation of girls' schools, orphanages, and nurseries. She was also comparatively successful in gaining support from the authorities in these efforts, due to her determination and her family background.[21]

The early charity and philanthropic organizations, with the participation of upper-class women alongside the middle-class bulk of the movement, were the only spheres where religion played some role. Although later associations in the countryside had a similar character, moral reform had never been the basis of the women's movement. Religion was a private matter and often a rather complex one. The majority of the Czech population were Catholics, but the Protestant past, with its national implications, influenced the attitudes towards the church. In the early twentieth century, the suffrage movement and the more moderate organizations in the countryside were often openly anticlerical.

While H. Volet-Jeanneret attributes Riegrová's philanthropic interests to the impact of Christian charity and particularly the teaching of the Enlightenment priest and scholar Bernard Bolzano, Pavla Horská suggests civil and political motivations, including support for the political activities of her husband.[22]

In any case, Riegrová explicitly distanced herself from any demands for women's emancipation as represented by the *Americký spolek dam* (American Ladies' Club). The "American" in the title referred to the inspiration which its founder Vojta Náprstek (1826–1894) had acquired during his voluntary exile in the United States following his participation in the 1848 revolution. On his return to Prague, Náprstek established an industrial museum and organized public lectures explaining the position and movement of American and British women, women's capability to perform most jobs, and the use of machines in order to save time which women in turn could use for self-education and for public benefit.

In 1865, in cooperation with the writer Karolína Světlá and a few other women who had been concerned with the woman question before, Náprstek founded the American Ladies' Club, which became a center of women's consciousness-raising and a basis of other activities.[23] In 1871, a group of women led by Světlá founded *Ženský výrobní spolek český* (Czech Women's Trade Association) in order to "improve the position of women dependent on their own work" (especially widows and orphans after the 1866 war). In the same year, the association opened a girls' school with commercial and industrial departments, and in 1874 courses for nurses were added.[24]

By this time gainful employment started to be more widespread, not only among the working classes but also among single women from middle-class families, which due to the changing economic, social, and demographic conditions could not provide a living for their unmarried female relatives any more.[25] Since the school reform in 1869, women were allowed to teach in state institutions, and teachers were the first female workers protected by the law. In 1874 they also founded the first women's professional association. With some pressure from the American Ladies' Club, women started to be admitted to administration; yet the profession of female teachers and clerks required celibacy.[26]

The second stream of the women's movement also focused on philanthropy and education. The writers Sofie Podlipská (1833–1897) and Věnceslava Lužická (1835–1920) emphasized family values, the role of women as mothers, their moral virtues, and their obligations towards the national community.[27] Both of them were active in philanthropy and tried to educate working-class women towards national awareness, and enable them to make a living in an honest way. In all of this they did not substantially differ from the group around Riegrová. At the same time, however, Lužická, Podlipská, and other members of the Trade Association and the Ladies' Club advocated the right of women for self-improvement, gainful employment, and involvement in various spheres of public life. "Should the woman constantly suppress the gifts of her spirit, should she use her abilities only for noncreative works in service of luxury . . . because she is not admitted to the sciences and to all spheres of the arts . . . ?" asked Sofie Podlipská in 1872.[28]

Podlipská's more famous sister Karolína Světlá (1830–1899) combined ardent work in the women's movement with a successful literary career. She was influenced by the views of her friend Božena Němcová as well as by foreign literature on the woman question. In 1871, in her speech on the establishment of the Trade Association, of which she became the first chairwoman, she subscribed to the views of J. S. Mill.[29] Despite her substantial contribution to women's emancipation, Světlá believed that women should sacrifice their feelings and wishes in the name of higher moral principles and in the interests of the community. She depicted nationally aware women with high moral standards, whose example and self-denial were capable of influencing and saving men. Rather exceptionally, in the 1866 novel *Rozcestí* (Crossroad), the heroine chose the career of a singer over marriage with the nobleman she loved.

A woman's right to a professional career and equal opportunity in education were at the heart of the activities of another patriotic writer, literary critic, and author of librettos to famous operas, Eliška Krásnohorská (1847–1926). Despite serious health problems, this daughter of a craftsman devoted considerable energy to women's emancipation. She was a secretary and, from 1891 to 1910, chairwoman of the Trade Association and the editor of the Association's journal *Ženské listy* (Women's Papers). With her often-criticized "manly" determination, she managed to establish the first girls' *gymnasium* (a secondary school preparing for university) in the Habsburg Empire, though the idea met with opposition among even educated classes. Several male professors denounced it rudely, and public support was unforthcoming even from F. L. Rieger and the Grégr brothers, who were known for their positive attitude towards women's education. At the same time, however, Karel Adámek presented and supported the question of women's secondary education in the Reichsrat in 1890, and was seconded by other deputies, such as Dr. Herold, Dr. Kaizl, Prof. Masaryk, and Count Dr. Kaunic.[30]

Krásnohorská appreciated the contribution of Czech men to the women's movement and considered the drift toward women's equality a Czech national feature. She emphasized the link between women's and Czech issues. The national struggle needed all forces; therefore women's goodwill should not be neglected and their abilities suppressed. Instead, women should be trained and allowed to enter all spheres of activity in the name of human rights and for the benefit of the nation. Although she believed that each success for the working-class movement meant a success for poor women and progress in the woman question, Krásnohorská understood the woman question primarily as a problem of middle-class women. The main goal was to secure for women the first natural right of all human beings: "the right to

develop one's highest abilities, choose a profession according to one's best capacity and belief, and serve the well-being of the community by fulfilling
those duties which one considers most sacred and valuable."[31]

GROWING UP TO EQUALITY

The 1890s are described as a period when the middle-class women's movement focused mainly on achieving full equality in education and access to
learned professions.[32] Indeed, the attempt to establish a girls' gymnasium and
further endeavors in connection with higher education involved much energy on the part of women, provoked a wide public response, and met with
considerable success. When the Minerva gymnasium was founded in 1890
and the first full-time female students were admitted to the philosophical and
medical faculties in 1897 and 1900 respectively, the struggle began to concentrate on other faculties, new gymnasia, and coeducation, in opposition to the
state-supported girls' lycea, which did not enable access to university.

Taking into consideration the movement as a whole, the period appears
to be characterized by an increasing interest in the woman question and involvement of women from a wider social and geographical spectrum, a
spread accompanied by a diversification of activities and views. Even Krásnohorská, who headed the educational efforts, led her *Ženské listy* beyond
support for education to other aspects of equality, including political
rights—and the journal was by no means the most progressive women's periodical of the turn of the century.

The level in general of the Czech women's movement in the 1890s was
displayed most clearly by the first Congress of "Czechoslavic" women, held
in Prague in 1897. Participants from Bohemia and Moravia (with a paper
from Slovakia) gave speeches on the history of Czech women's activities, on
women's duties to the family and nation, and on humanity and philanthropy. Other subjects were moral elevation, health care, and women's
rights—including a contribution on women's suffrage. The aims of female
teachers, clerks, servants, factory workers, and other professions were set
forth. To put its decisions into practice, the congress decided to found
Ústřední spolek žen českých (The Central Association of Czech Women) and
to publish a journal, *Ženský svět* (Woman's World).[33]

Despite the predominance of women from Prague, the congress evinced the expansion of women's organizations around the country. While in Prague philanthropy had shifted to the margins of the women's movement, the associations outside Prague were mostly devoted to philanthropy, often connected with educational, patriotic, or religious goals; at the same time, they facilitated women's participation in local social life.[34] A unique place among the widening activities of women was held by the women's chapters of the gymnastic organization *Sokol* (Falcon), which in the late nineteenth century spread in the countryside, contributing to the rise of women's self-awareness. Women learned how to develop their bodies and overcome the prejudices concerning its functions. They joined men in sport, leisure, and patriotic activities.[35]

The differentiation and radicalization of the women's movement at the turn of the century was reflected in the women's press. The first journal, *Ženské listy*, was growing closer to the Young Czech Party. Also the Central Association's *Ženský svět* was quite moderate. In the late nineteenth and early twentieth century, the selection of periodicals was enriched with an additional dozen, including a Social Democratic and two liberal journals published in Brno, journals close to the Progressive and National Socialist (and also Catholic) parties, not to mention several traditional nonpolitical periodicals.

The first university graduates and other Prague women who considered the Central Association too moderate and diplomatic founded in 1904 *Ženský klub český* (The Czech Women's Club), in order "to elevate the Czech woman to a desire for self-improvement and a full awareness of [her] human dignity, and to work for the equality of women with men."[36] The club was active in matters of communal or national interest, but concentrated on women's education and consciousness-raising, for example through public feminist lectures given for free by women and famous male scholars and politicians.[37]

The Moravian capital Brno more than seconded Prague. A girls' choir, *Vesna* (Spring), developed into an educational and self-help association. It was led by the teacher Eliška Machová (1858–1926), and was reminiscent of the Prague Trade Association. In 1898, a year after the foundation of the Central Association of Czech Women, the *Moravsko-slezská organisace ženská* (The Moravian-Silesian Women's Organization) united women's associations in Moravia. After the congress in 1902, a more radical stream promoting women's civil rights separated from the organization, headed by Zdeňka Wiedermannová (1868–1915), another teacher.[38] Brno also excelled as a center of the working-class and Social Democratic women's movement.

In the previous period, working-class women were primarily an object for philanthropy, while the first Social Democrats rejected the competition from women as cheap labor. Since large-scale employment of women in factories and in home industry quickly became a fact, the Social Democrats realized the potential of cooperation with women and encouraged women to enter their cultural and trade union associations and to establish their own.[39] Due to the persecution of socialists in Prague, the movement concentrated in Brno, where the first female working-class trade union was founded in 1888 and the Social Democratic women's journal *Ženský list* (Women's Paper) in 1892.[40] By the time the journal moved to Prague in 1901, the working-class women's movement had developed from educational and trade union associations to political aims, and had demonstrated a level of political awareness which aroused admiration from among the representatives of both the women's movement and other parties.[41]

Regardless of the different priorities, the working-class women's movement was for a long time a bedfellow rather than an opponent of the middle-class women's movement. The main rivals were the organizations of German women in the Czech Lands, ranging from women's branches of upper-class male clubs to women's working-class or religious and charity associations. Although Czech women never admitted it, it is unlikely that the foundation of the Trade Association in 1871 and of the Women's Club in 1904 were not influenced by the examples of the *Prager Frauen-Erwerb-Verein* (Prague Women's Trade Association) from 1869, and of the *Frauen-fortschritt* (Women's Progress), the most radical and influential German women's organization, created in 1894.[42]

The field in which Czech women openly competed with German women was education: they did not want merely to establish schools for girls, they wanted Czech schools as a counterbalance to German institutes, whose graduates were "lost" to the Czech cause. The aims of women corresponded to the efforts of Czech politicians, who had achieved some language concessions already in the 1880s—including the division of the Prague University into a Czech and German one. National conflicts increased in the 1890s, when the so-called Badeni's language statute in 1897 strengthened the status of the Czech language, resulting in nationalist clashes, a state of emergency in Prague, and finally the abolition of the statute.

Despite the national struggles and the fission of the Czech political scene, which was marked by the ascendance of the Young Czechs after the late

1880s, and despite the foundation of new political parties in the 1890s,[43] Czech society started to pay more attention to the woman question. Public discourse reflected women's efforts: "emancipationists" was a traditional label for the defenders of women's rights. When the term "feminism" became more widespread in the early twentieth century, it referred primarily to women's emancipation, sometimes with a negative connotation of extremism, though radical female activists often avoided the word. Less frequently, feminist meant feminine, pertaining to or specific to women. The word "suffragists" was mostly used in a negative and mocking sense, for foreign rather than Czech women.

The most outspoken opponents of women's emancipation were the Old Czechs and Christian parties. The Czech Christian-Social Party excluded from its 1897 program the issue of women's economic and political rights, and in 1899 the Catholics' congress emphasized that women could not be equal with men in this world.[44] The allies were more heterogeneous. The politicians who lectured in women's clubs included Masaryk, the National Socialists Klofáč and Choc, the agrarian Viškovský, the Social Democrat Winter, and even the Old Czech Mattuš. Václav Choc was also the first (1906) to call in the Reichsrat for universal suffrage for both sexes.[45]

The most important male supporter of women's rights was Tomáš Garrigue Masaryk (1850–1937), a professor at the Prague University, deputy of the Reichsrat, and later the first Czechoslovak president. Masaryk had influenced a whole generation of his students as well as future suffragists. His slogan, "Let woman be placed on an equal level with man culturally, legally, and politically," entered the program of the Czech Progressive Party in 1906. Masaryk acknowledged the impact on his views about women of his American wife Charlotte, who was active in the Czech women's movement. He saw the woman question as an important part of contemporary social and moral problems, criticized double standards and prostitution, and opposed the idea of women's intellectual inferiority, defending women's equality with men in all respects.[46]

While the mainstream women's movement was based on the principle of equality, some women, influenced by the movement but unable to identify with it, expressed their dilemmas and limitations in gender terms emphasizing the specificity of women. Thus the writer Růžena Svobodová (1868–1920) found the members of the Women's Club not "womanly" enough. After the death of her father, a well-to-do patriotic clerk, she soon gave up the effort for independence for the economic security of a wife, but she described women's doubts about marriage and sex and longing for personal freedom. In her novel *Zamotaná vlákna* (Entangled Fibers) from 1899, she depicted three types of woman: the first, reminiscent of Karolína Světlá's heroines, gave up her career to serve her family and the needy; the second, like Svobodová herself, chose marriage, but children brought only temporary compensation to her ambitions; the third type, single and independent, was modeled on Svobodová's friend Zdenka Braunerová and foreshadowed the next generation of feminists.[47]

Teréza Nováková (1853–1912), writer, author of ethnographic and literary studies and of an extensive piece on the role of women in Czech history, belonged to the mainstream women's movement. As the editor of *Ženský svět* she brought to the Czech milieu information on German and Anglo-Saxon feminism and on women's activities in the world. In 1903, Nováková wrote an article on women's suffrage in which she criticized women for sleeping through the opportunity to push through their demands, and political parties for their lack of interest in women's voting rights. Supporting women's suffrage, she exhausted all the major arguments used by feminists and political parties in the following period.[48]

MATURING INTO POLITICS

The decade following Nováková's complaint developed as if in an effort to prove her wrong: women did not oversleep, and female suffrage became not only the central goal of the women's movement but also an important issue in public discourse and party policy. As a result of massive demonstrations in 1905, a new election law for the Reichsrat was accepted which replaced the curial system with a universal voting right for men, and in 1907 the first elections based on this law were held. Women participated in the demonstration in November 1905, but when no speaker mentioned women's suffrage they held a separate meeting, and in December they founded *Výbor pro volební právo ženy* (Committee for Women's Voting Rights).[49]

Since women's political organizations were forbidden, the committee was a free association, working on the extreme limits of what was allowed. Its twelve members negotiated with political parties and organized public lectures and meetings. The leading personality of the committee was Františka

Plamínková (1875–1942). This Prague teacher represented the generation of women who had to make a choice between "only the life of a wife and mother, or only one's own profession which provided spiritual freedom and economic independence," and who publicly proclaimed themselves feminists, which meant an unfavorable social stigma.[50] Plamínková fought for the abolition of celibacy for female teachers, organized lectures on women's rights, and managed the nationalist campaign *svůj k svému* (to support Czech products), for which she was even taken to court. Her aim was to educate a "spiritually awakened and free" woman as a partner of a free man. According to her associates, it was also Plamínková who found a loophole in the legislation, enabling women to stand for elections to the Czech Diet.[51]

Unlike the laws for the Reichsrat and the Moravian Diet, which explicitly excluded women from both passive and active voting rights, the election procedure for the Czech Diet from 1861 enabled female taxpayers and representatives of some professions to vote and did not forbid their eligibility. The committee, therefore, nominated one of its members, Marie Tůmová, for the 1908 elections, and tried to persuade political parties to include female candidates. Social Democrats, supported by Masaryk's Czech Progressive Party, ran Karla Máchová, and three other parties agreed on a joint candidature of Božena Zelinková.

The danger that an election reform would soon take this last chance away from women intensified the committee's activity. While representatives of Social Democratic women insisted on universal suffrage for the Diet, the committee, in this case, put women's interests before national and democratic principles, favoring the feudal curial system, which enfranchised at least some women, over universal male suffrage. Even this view was justified in patriotic terms. The committee launched an all-national campaign for a female candidature as a protest against Vienna; an election that would show the unanimous determination of political parties and electors, women and progressive men, not to give up this national right.[52]

The situation was undoubtedly unusual. Several parties agreed to nominate only women, and kept their promise when it was likely that the candidate would really be elected: when in 1912 a deputy of the Diet died, Social Democrats ran Karla Máchová again, and the Young Czechs, supported by National Socialists and some Progressivists, nominated Božena Viková-Kunětická. The local organization of the Young Czech party in the constituency in question caused some embarrassment when it came with its own, male candidate. After he got on to the second round, however, he called on his supporters not to vote. Thus, a woman was really elected in 1912, and on a multiparty ticket.[53]

There were some shared motives behind the policy of various parties towards the female candidature and women's rights in general. Owing to the agitation of the representatives of the women's movement and some male politicians, female suffrage became an important subject in public discourse, and parties felt obliged to take a stand on it. Women began to be seen as a potential political force: some parties, despite legal prohibition, were opened up to women, or tried to secure women's votes and to make sure that women were not won by their political rivals.

Even in Catholic parties, which opposed women's political rights, voices were heard suggesting the need for a change if women were not to support the Social Democrats.[54] Liberal and socialist parties strove to get women out from under the influence of clericalism. The agrarians tried to confront clericalism in the countryside, and its youth organizations contributed to the rise of women's political consciousness.[55]

Another common motivation was that of patriotism. A female candidature was a legal tool for confrontation with Vienna. This could explain the policy of the Young Czechs, who otherwise did not support women's equality. Concurrently, the leading party of Czech bourgeois politics in the 1890s may have tried to countervail the decline in its popularity by an orientation toward female voters, as suggested by Social Democrats.[56] Women were supposed to strengthen the national movement since suffrage would enhance women's consciousness and responsibility. Even Social Democrats were not immune to the national question. When, after long debates, the Czech Social Democrats split in 1911 into the "centralists" and "separatists," women supported the latter, stressing the importance of national specificities given the present situation.[57]

The political equality of women and the presence of a female deputy were also viewed as an indication of the maturity of the Czech nation. Masaryk's Progressive Party explained its support for the Social Democratic candidate in the 1908 elections with the claim that "here, party interests step aside, while the great Czech interest and the question of our cultural maturity emerges so that . . . we can show to the whole world that as we were the first in central Europe to build a women's gymnasium, we also practice the ideal of women's equality and equity with men."[58]

The most consistent allies of the women's movement were the Social Democrats, National Socialists, and Progressivists, who included women's equality and suffrage in their programs and considered the woman question an important part of the current social problems, although they envisioned different solutions. Theories of sexual difference were not unknown to Czech opponents of women's emancipation, but the promoters of women's voting rights did not seem to take views on women's inferiority too seriously, and concentrated on refuting other objections. Difference was used to support women's rights. The often repeated claim that the potential of women would be beneficial to the community, especially in those problems (such as women's and children's work, alcoholism, prostitution, and marriage law) that only women could solve, was sustained by women's greater sensitivity and respect for human life derived from motherhood.

The reproach that women did not undergo military service was rebutted with a reference to childbirth and to the fact of their bearing and educating future soldiers. The most serious objection to women's enfranchisement, shared by liberals and radicals in various countries, was the fear of women's conservatism. Czech politicians and female suffragists did not underestimate this danger. They sometimes saw it as a necessary price for women's long exclusion from politics or used the example of the working class, which had also been considered "politically immature" and its enfranchisement a danger to political stability; yet the worries had turned out to be unjustified.[59]

The debates on female candidates and suffrage manifested a political diversification of women's voices. The Social Democratic women's journal *Ženský list* argued for women's suffrage on two grounds. If women were to fulfill their role of mothers, they needed better working and social conditions and legal protection, which they could achieve through voting rights and involvement in the Diet. Second, as oppressed human beings, women needed full political rights in order to fight for a new social order. The events around the election had also shown the difference between the socialist approach and the movement of "Ladies," and particularly the conservative, "mendacious and false" Young Czech party.[60]

Despite the fact that Social Democratic women separated from the middle-class women over the issue of suffrage, there was no antagonism between proletarian women and the women's movement as a whole. Even organizations speaking for "all women" were divided into more conservative and more radical ones. Concurrently, the Women's Club included the National

Socialist Františka Zeminová as well as the Social Democrat Karla Máchová (1853–1920), editor of *Ženský list*, who had joined with Plamínková and other feminists in preparing suffrage demonstrations, and with Charlotte Masaryk in charity work.[61]

The committee's candidate in the 1908 elections, the teacher Marie Tůmová (1867–1925), summarized in 1911 with three main claims the arguments for women's suffrage: it was necessary—both because women were equal human beings and because they had special qualities as mothers and educators; it was beneficial for the community—as manifested in the examples of Australia, New Zealand, and some American states; and it was possible—Czech women had proved themselves capable of fulfilling this "extra" duty. Here, Tůmová added an interesting argument. It was desirable that the care for the family and education of children ceased to be seen as a concern of the mother alone: it should be men's responsibility as well.[62]

While some politically active women like Zeminová were close to the views of the committee, others identified primarily as members of their parties. Thus a former teacher,[63] Pavla Buzková (1885–1949), explicitly stated that she wanted to be represented as an adherent of a political stream and rather by a man with similar political views than by an unprogressive woman. By "similar views," she meant the program of the Progressive Party which she entered in 1908, soon to become one of its executives. For Buzková, women's full equality was the basis of human society: without it the establishment could not follow justice in other respects and would fall into decline. Similarly, a nation could not survive without the support of equal women. The struggle for rights was not a fight of women against men, as some female representatives claimed, but the struggle of progress against reaction, especially against clericalism. Working-class women were more politically conscious and aware than middle-class women, whose organizations were often under the influence of clericalism. That was why women's political rights, which everybody theoretically acknowledged, had not been put into practice yet. Women could improve their situation if they joined political parties.[64]

Božena Viková-Kunětická (1863–1934) also supported the Young Czech party and criticized the women's movement and clericalism, but in a completely different context. Her real concern was national rather than political, and her anticlericalism was a part of her aversion to all organizational limitations to individual freedom, which included the women's movements as well as radical political movements, because there "the individual is a slave of an idea." In her election campaign she emphasized the all-national importance of women's equality, as opposed to the previous period when it had been only a concern of the feminists.[65]

Viková-Kunětická believed in women and especially in motherhood as "the only thing which purifies woman morally and socially, and elevates her culturally and as a human being." She reproached the feminist movement as potentially depriving women and the nation of children. Women's social and political equality was secondary: real emancipation lay first in a woman's inner, spiritual life, and second in her relationship to men. At the same time, Viková-Kunětická defended a woman's right to link work to motherhood, and even the right of women to have children and a relationship to men outside marriage, and demanded that this right be recognized by society.[66]

It may seem ironic that the first woman to be elected to the Diet was Viková-Kunětická. The choice was however characteristic of the situation. To accept the idea of a female deputy did not mean to accept radical feminism. Viková-Kunětická was also known as a "nationally conscious" writer. On the rare occasions when she agreed to participate in international women's congresses she criticized the national rather than women's oppression. This was not exceptional either.

The attitude of the Czech representatives towards the international women's movement had always been uncomfortable. The relationship with Austrian women's organizations was marked by national controversies which reflected the dissension between Czech society and Vienna, as well as women's efforts to enforce national interests even in the women's movement. Since they found little understanding for their language and cultural aspirations among German-speaking women, Czech representatives often refused to participate in all-Austrian women's activities. Czech women resented that they were represented in the international forum by the Austrian women's union and felt overlooked by the leaders of international organizations.[67] In 1908, at a congress in Amsterdam, Plamínková managed to achieve the acceptance of the Czech Committee for Women's Voting Rights as a direct member of the International Women's Suffrage Alliance.[68]

Thus, despite some disappointment on the part of political parties and the feminists in regard to the person of Viková-Kunětická, even they joined in the general enthusiasm, interpreting the election as a major victory of the women's movement and as a sign of the progressiveness of the Czech nation. Viková-Kunětická was never able to take up office because she did not receive authorization from the governor, and in July 1913 the Czech Diet was dissolved and never met again. Yet Czech women had only to wait five more years to acquire active voting rights and see women of various political and ideological viewpoints enter the parliament of the Czechoslovak Republic.

CONCLUSION

From the mid-nineteenth century up until 1914, the image of the Czech woman went through a substantial development within the framework of the women's movement as well as within society, following the impact of the movement and of the debates about the woman question: a development from woman as a mother who was there "for the others"—her family, the nation, the needy—into a human being with wishes of her own and rights for herself, and on to an equal who deserved a full share in public—namely political—life, for her own sake and for the benefit of the whole community. Owing to the lack of "Czech" nobility, and to a lesser extent other elites, the women's movement was a middle-class affair from its origins, unlike the movements in some other central and east European nations. A specific role was played throughout the period by female writers, and from the second stage, by teachers and representatives of the working-class women's movement.

Compared with women in other countries, Czech women gave more importance to education, particularly but not only in the early periods, and less to such matters as religious and moral reform, alcoholism, prostitution, and property rights. They came with their demands later than women in Great Britain or the United States and were more moderate in the means chosen to achieve their goals. On the other hand, once women's suffrage appeared on the agenda, it quickly became an all-society question and acquired considerably wide support.

Women's demands and the images prevailing in society were marked by foreign ideas, from the Enlightenment to socialism, by the personalities who had direct contact with more advanced societies, and by women's movements in other countries. At the same time, the movement drew upon the first endeavor made in the 1830s and 1840s, and a continuity can be traced from the emergence of women's gender awareness up to the suffrage struggles, especially in terms of what constitutes the specificity of the Czech movement: the prevailing subordination (or better connection) of women's aims to the interests of the whole nation, and the role of men in the women's movement, namely their active support of women, and women's deliberate collaboration with them. From its early beginnings, the Czech women's movement, emerging as a part of the national movement, shared a common "enemy" with the latter—Austrian rule and authorities, and Germanization. Thus, it was not directed against a Czech "male-dominated establishment" and Czech men. They were rather seen as co-sufferers and collaborators.

It can be claimed that women's efforts were supported by male politicians and intellectuals because the women's movement was comparatively moderate and mostly gave priority to national interests. Yet, it can also be claimed that the representatives of the women's movement did not have to reach for extreme methods because women did not encounter such violent opposition to their activities as occurred in some other countries, and patriotic discourse often linked the emancipation of the nation to that of women. Women defended national demands because they were sincere patriots and the national question was the most burning issue in Czech society.

In other words, the Czech women's movement fitted in well with the social life and discourse of Czech society. It emerged as a part of emancipation and liberal struggles, and in the circumstances of a small nation without independence, statements of publicly active personalities and later parties could hardly overlook the woman question. On the other hand, not to take into consideration the national question was nearly impossible, even for radical feminists, and to some extent even for socialists. The movement's nationalist attitude towards the German-Austrian and international women's organizations reflected the developments following 1848, when an agreement between the Czech and German inhabitants of the Czech Lands seemed less and less possible. The moderate character of the Czech women's movement also corresponded to mainstream Czech politics which, from the 1870s until the turn of the century, concentrated on slow compromises and gradual steps, with an emphasis on the use of the Czech language in administration and education.

Other tendencies, however, existed as well. Leaving aside the mass of indifferent population and the male and female opponents of women's emancipation, there were individuals who supported more radical claims, others for whom feminism was more important than nationalism, and others still, who viewed women's emancipation as part of an all-human progress or the putting into practice of a particular political ideology. These views, though only sketched out in this chapter, formed a part of the colorful quilt of the Czech women's movement and the discourse on the woman question.

Sisters or Foes: The Shifting Front Lines of the Hungarian Women's Movements, 1896–1918

JUDITH SZAPOR

A comparative approach to the European women's movements that intends to look beyond the thoroughly researched and documented western European movements must not omit the Hungarian case. Hungary's unique position, at once central and peripheral, guaranteed that it was affected by all major western trends of political, philosophical, and social thought—and also that these ideas always arrived late and suffered substantial transformations along the way. On the other hand, any comparative effort that includes the Hungarian women's movements can only be preliminary, owing to a striking lack of published documents and studies.

The history of women's movements is a sadly neglected field in Hungarian scholarship. Similarly, women's studies as a university teaching and research field is only at its beginnings. The documents of the Hungarian women's movements have not been published or reprinted, at least not since the First World War.

With a few notable exceptions, we lack studies focusing on women during the modernization period of Hungary or examining changes in women's work in various sectors of the economy, including the demographic and social effects of their changing role.[1] The few books on women's emancipation, published mainly in the 1960s and 1970s, focus exclusively on the legal aspects of women's access to political and educational rights and the professions, piling up statistical details in order to conclude that all was well in socialist Hungary.[2]

As of yet, no historians have taken on the study of women images at the turn of the century, despite the rich and varied sources that are available and the possible benefits of such studies for social and cultural history. Even the most developed field of Hungarian historiography, political history, ignores such basic questions as the stand of various political parties on the issue of women's suffrage. To take just one example: the major collective achievement of recent Hungarian historiography is the *History of Hungary* in ten volumes; it accomplished the feat of not once mentioning the words "feminism" or "women's movement" on any of the 1,422 pages of its seventh volume, which covers the period between 1890 and 1918.[3]

To demonstrate this striking gap in Hungarian historiography, I would like to cite a specific case of collective amnesia, concerning the Hungarian women's movements of the turn of the century. In the early 1980s, as a young historian, I became interested in the history of the turn-of-the-century Hungarian women's movements. The 1980s was a time of relative liberalization in the Hungarian academic world, which, coupled with the need of the Hungarian democratic opposition to find its legitimate tradition, brought a revival of interest in the Hungarian turn of the century. The political and cultural pluralism of the last decades of the Austro-Hungarian monarchy represented a democratic ideal to be recovered. (It was exactly the democratic and pluralistic quality of the turn of the century that had been found inconvenient and that was successfully repressed by both the conservative regime between the two wars and the Stalinist regime of the late 1940s and 1950s.)

Women's movements, including a full-fledged feminist movement, were an integral part of the rich and colorful political spectrum of turn-of-the-century Hungary. Nevertheless, while a good part of this pluralistic heritage was reintroduced and incorporated into contemporary Hungarian social and political thought, the feminist movement of that period has never received its due; the existence of feminism and feminists, although generally known and casually mentioned among scholars of the period, was never mentioned in print.

To list the various political, ideological, and professional factors that resulted in the above-described situation is beyond the aims of the present study. To put it simply, the political regimes in Hungary's modern history all had their reasons for finding feminism and the progressive women's movements uncomfortable to deal with. One could expect that an independent, democratic Hungary, going through a political, social, and academic renewal since 1989, would eagerly embrace feminism, both as a historical heritage and as a social movement. Apparently, that is not the case. Although some of the young historians and sociologists are eager to catch up with various streams of western feminist ideology and methodology, few of them see the continuity with Hungarian feminism as it existed in the nineteenth and twentieth centuries. Neither are they able to build on the existence of a strong feminist movement. In that sense, the title of a recent sociological study seems typical: "Why is There no Women's Movement in Hungary?"[4]

I.

The following overview of the Hungarian women's movements of the late nineteenth and early twentieth century is a first attempt to overcome a purely descriptive level of periodization and labeling and to evaluate women's movements in relation to their historical and social background. In doing so, I will necessarily refer to various social, political, and ideological events and terms of Hungarian history. When using labels, such as socialist, liberal, or bourgeois radical, to mention just a few, I always mean the local variety and try to provide a short explanation.

The lack of studies of women's movements results in a lack of commonly accepted periodization and labeling. The periodization I use in distinguishing the various phases in the women's movements follows more or less the one feminists of the early twentieth century themselves used.

In her foreword to a selection of documents of the early Hungarian women's movement, Rózsa Bédy-Schwimmer, the leader of modern Hungarian bourgeois feminism, established the starting point and the origins of early Hungarian women's movements in the late eighteenth century.[5] Her aim was to prove that the Hungarian women's movements, emerging by the late eighteenth century, were in step with similar movements in western Europe and that the claims for women's political and educational rights in the late eighteenth and early nineteenth century had stemmed from Hungary's constitutional and political system. The first point served as a reminder of better times, when Hungary followed closely the vanguard of European civilization. The second point addressed the debate of Rózsa Bédy-Schwimmer's own time and strengthened the conviction that modern feminism, just like early feminism, was organically embedded in Hungarian social and political development.

In a history of Hungarian women's emancipation, published in 1913, Andor Máday, a friend and supporter of the Hungarian bourgeois feminists, delineated the phases in the Hungarian women's movements of the previous one and a half centuries.[6] He identified the major phases as aspects of phases of Hungarian national history. The coincidence of certain historical milestones with decisive events in the history of the women's movement made the application of such parallels convenient, and also reinforced the notion that women's movements were an organic part of Hungarian national history. Subsequently accepted and used by the feminist press, this periodization established a genealogical line for modern Hungarian feminism, emphasizing the connection with the Enlightenment and the pioneers of women's education.

Owing to Hungary's belated modernization, women's rights movements in the western European sense did not begin to take root in Hungarian society until the end of the nineteenth century. Hungarian bourgeois feminists formed their independent political organization—meaning an agenda based solely on the fight for women's rights—in 1904. As political forces from Left to Right recognized the importance of women's issues, they either developed their own women's movement or incorporated the ones already in existence. A possible approach in labeling Hungarian women's movements would be to look at their organizational base and principles. We would need to locate Hungarian women's movements in relation to their social, regional, and organizational base and influence. In the absence of such studies, I can give only a rough outline, where one end of the scale would be occupied by the bourgeois feminists, representing a women's movement organized from below. Socialist women, trying to keep their grass-roots unions alive against their own party bureaucracy, would occupy the middle. Finally, conservative and philanthropic women's movements, organized entirely from above, would be on the other end. In this last case, we are especially in need of studies that would verify this judgment.

1. The earliest Hungarian spokespersons for women's emancipation, men and women alike, belonged to a generation of poets that came of age in the last two decades of the eighteenth century. Members of the educated nobility and influenced by the French Enlightenment, they simultaneously fought for the *droits de l'homme*, Hungarian national independence, and women's emancipation; this last goal meant mainly women's access to education.[7] It was the first but far from the last example of the transformation of ideas imported from the West and of the complex interplay between these

ideas and Hungarian political reality, in this case the urgent problem of national independence.

This first, embryonic period in the women's movement was followed by a second that lasted roughly from 1825 to 1867. Beginning in the so-called Age of Reform with its cautious attempts to transform the feudal system and including political upheavals such as the Hungarian bourgeois revolution and war of independence of 1848–49, it lasted until the end of Habsburg absolutism. The revolution of 1848 abolished feudal laws, including the rights noblewomen had enjoyed up to that time. During the revolution of 1848 and the following decades of absolutist government, Hungarian women shared the men's fight, and some even suffered martyrdom for the cause of national independence. This was also when the first efforts were made to create secondary educational institutions serving the needs of young girls from the nobility. Partisans of women's rights to education and to a broader public role temporarily sacrificed their cause in the fight for national independence. On the other hand, the heroic examples of women during Hungary's revolution and war of independence were to become oft-used arguments for women's rights in a later period.

Two philanthropic women's organizations established in this period set the example for many of the kind to come. The *Magyar Gazdasszonyok Országos Egyesülete* (roughly: National Association of Hungarian Proprietor Ladies) was founded in 1861 as an example of the patriotic spirit following 1848. Initiated by widows of the martyrs of the 1848 revolution and war of independence, the association ran an orphanage for daughters of the heroes of 1848, and served general charitable aims.

The *Pesti Izraelita Nőegylet* (Association of Israelite Women of Pest), founded in 1866, was the first among the philanthropic women's organizations organized by religion.

2. The year 1867, which marked the beginning of a new political era, the system of the Compromise in the Austro-Hungarian monarchy, also saw a more pronounced women's movement. For lack of an educated middle class, it came from the nobility—noblewomen being the only ones who had the opportunity to receive at least a private education. Not surprisingly, their efforts focused on access for women to educational institutions. Their association, founded in 1868 and called *Magyar Nőképző Egyesület* (Hungarian Association for the Instruction of Women), found little support among the

liberal fathers of the Compromise. The original demand of general access to secondary schools was denied and soon replaced by the modest demand to obtain the right to open a separate secondary school for girls.

By the early 1880s, special girls' schools and teachers' colleges for women produced the first group of women employed in white-collar occupations. Following 1867, Hungary's thorough modernization created an increasing demand for lower white-collar civil service and private industry workers. Some occupations, such as those of elementary school teacher, post office and bank clerk, court stenographer, and typist, became female par excellence and were consequently underpaid. Frequently depicted in period novels and plays, representatives of this new type of woman were subjected to abuse, humiliation, and discrimination.

This fast-growing group of female urban white-collar employees in turn served as the breeding ground for the first grass-roots women's rights organizations at the turn of the century. The *Mária-Dorothea Egyesület* (Maria-Dorothea Association), founded in 1885 to represent women schoolteachers, and the *Magyar Nőtisztviselők Egyesülete* (Hungarian Association of Women Clerks), founded in 1897, were the first women's organizations representing the economic interests and welfare of large female occupational groups. Simultaneously, a number of philanthropic women's organizations were founded—the *Országos Katolikus Nővédő Egyesület* (National Catholic Association for the Protection of Women) and the *Müvelt Nők Otthona Egyesület* (Association of the Home for Cultivated Women), among others—to assist the growing number of women in the work force. Owing to their ties to the local elites and the churches, philanthropic women's organizations were successful in extending their influence to working women, especially among the Christian middle class.

3. The period between 1896 and 1914 was the peak of the Hungarian women's movements and the only period when we can point to a well-defined and influential feminist movement among various streams of the women's movement. The beginning of the period is conveniently marked by a couple of significant events. A ministerial decree of December 1895 opened the faculties of medicine and arts of universities to women by 1896, and the same year brought the opening of the first girls' gymnasium.

The decree was but one in a series of laws and decrees created by Hungarian liberalism that were meant to complete the separation of church and state and the emancipation of the Jews and the Jewish religion. The opening of some university faculties for women was an important step. However, it guaranteed only limited access to the faculties, since gymnasia, granting final exams—the equivalent of the German *matura*—and thus entrance to universities, had been closed for girls. Until 1896, girls had been able to study toward the qualifying final exams and university entrance only as private students. Under these circumstances, the opening of a girls' gymnasium was an equally important step ensuring that a larger number of young girls could reach the university.

In the next few years, the Hungarian Association of Women Clerks grew into a comparatively large movement and produced a politically educated leadership, the first generation of feminist leaders. These women founded the *Magyar Feministák Egyesülete* (Hungarian Association of Feminists) in December 1904.[8] Over the next decade, under a shared leadership, the Association of Women Clerks and the feminists developed a collaboration where the association's mainly economic demands and activities were put into the feminists' political perspective. This double organization and its functioning was in many ways comparable to the cooperation between the Social Democratic Party and the unions, with the exception of the union's affiliation with socialist ideology.

It is interesting to note that the term "feminist" (*feminista* in Hungarian) was used proudly and without hesitation by the activists themselves. Needless to say, as the Hungarian women's movement assumed a more and more visible public role, the word "feminist" gained a negative connotation in conservative political opinion and press, just as it did in other countries. Nevertheless, Hungarian feminists never dissociated themselves from the word "feminist" or let it be taken over by their enemies.[9]

II.

From 1904 on, politics became the Hungarian feminists' battlefield and the vote for women their battle cry. According to their program, the right to vote was the key to all other rights. Presumably, it would bring about the realization of all other demands, such as access to education and the professions and the end of discrimination at the workplace.

As the Feminist Association grew in size and influence, feminism became the equivalent of the struggle for women's vote in the political discourse of the period. It would be tempting to attribute the central role of the suffrage to the influence of the British suffragists, especially in light of Hungarian feminists' frequent reference to them as their role models.[10] In fact, Hungary's entire political life revolved around this one issue during the decade preceding the First World War.

The Dual Monarchy was built upon a historical compromise between the two nation-states Austria and Hungary, and was based on the consent of the two historical parties of the Hungarian parliament. The intricacies of the constitution and Hungary's limited suffrage—enfranchising less than 6% of the male population—had successfully preserved the leadership of the traditional ruling elite. By the beginning of the twentieth century, this two-party system ceased to represent the political and social forces, and the Hungarian parliamentary system as such became anachronistic. Extraparliamentary movements and parties, representing the industrial and agrarian proletariat as well as the urban middle classes and intelligentsia, were clamoring for political representation.

Limited parliamentarism was just one of the innate contradictions of the system. The fast pace of industrialization—Hungary's growth rate was uninterrupted and one of the highest in Europe from the 1880s—left unsolved the problems of the agricultural sector. This sector was characterized by the existence of huge estates and the problem of an enormous, seasonally unemployed agricultural proletariat. The aristocracy and the gentry preserved their overwhelming influence in political life and in the civil service, at the expense of the middle classes and the non-Hungarian nationalities. The Catholic church kept many aspects of cultural life under its control, especially in the countryside. As for the middle class, its most dynamic entrepreneurial elements came almost exclusively from the ranks of assimilated Jews and Germans. The lack of an indigenous bourgeoisie led to a long-lasting and deep division in Hungarian social and cultural life.

By 1905–6, the cracks in the system of the Austro-Hungarian monarchy brought about the first overall political crisis since 1867. From then on until the war, the balancing act among the various destabilizing elements in the monarchy's system and between the parliamentary and extraparliamentary forces became increasingly difficult, and resulted in a state of permanent political crisis.

During the same period, the Social Democratic Party of Hungary evolved into a large mass party and—following the German example—made universal suffrage its main demand. Around the same time, a group of young liberal and socialist scholars gathered around a sociological journal, the *Huszadik Század* (Twentieth Century), and a debating society, the *Társadalomtudományi Társaság* (Society of Social Sciences). They represented only a tiny fraction of the bourgeoisie and consisted mostly of Jewish intellectuals, but made up for their limited numbers with the quality and scope of their intellectual and cultural influence. From 1905, their political efforts centered on the issue of universal suffrage.

Between 1906 and 1911, the agrarian proletariat was organized into a short-lived *Független Szocialista Párt* (Independent Socialist Party), also demanding universal suffrage. For short periods, these political parties, allied by the demand for universal suffrage as well as by other demands for democratic transformation, were able to join forces.[11] But they also tried to succeed through political concessions and deals, creating all sorts of unlikely alliances along the way.[12] With hindsight, it is obvious that they should not have resorted to behind-the-scenes intrigues. Political deal-making was an art form that Hungarian parliamentary politicians had been trained in for decades. Socialists, radicals, feminists, and the like, all burdened with principles, did not stand a chance. The only result of their temporary alliances with the parliamentary parties was the lost trust among the various streams of the Hungarian Left. It was recovered only after the war, during the short months of the bourgeois democratic revolution of 1918.

III.

1. Just where in this spectrum stood the feminists? At its founding, the Feminist Association represented the first generation of women who had completed secondary schools and, in some cases, even received postsecondary education. As teachers and white-collar office workers, they were independently employed. Their first leaders gained political acumen in the struggle against discrimination at the workplace and for access to broader secondary and university education.

A composite picture of the feminist leadership would show a highly educated woman—university or at least high school graduate, and fluent in German and French—born around the late 1870s in Budapest. Although she might be from the aristocracy and the gentry, typically she would be from the Jewish upper middle class. Of the dozen best-known feminist leaders, about half were married; of the two most prominent leaders, Rózsa Bédy-Schwimmer (1877–1948) and Vilma Glücklich (1872–1927), the first was married and the second single.[13] Regardless of their marital status, feminist leaders advocated a new type of woman whose life had its center in the professional and public sphere, rather than the family one.

2. As the feminists expanded in numbers and influence, not only in Budapest but in other Hungarian cities, their activities gradually became limited to the single issue of suffrage. In their struggle for women's political rights they used a wide range of arguments, borrowing elements from traditional nationalistic as well as socialist rhetoric. According to one of the popular arguments, the struggle between men and women for legal, political, educational, and professional rights was a genuine class struggle, even more so than the struggle between classes.[14] This seems to indicate the popularity of socialist ideas or at least socialist phraseology at the time.

Feminists used different arguments to make women's rights appealing for the conservative political elite. They alluded to the tradition of Hungarian feudal law that guaranteed some rights to noblewomen, as well as to Hungarian men's traditional gallantry. They often used the heroic examples of Hungarian noblewomen during the centuries of struggle for national independence.[15] Other arguments referred to the growing number of university-educated women and their achievements in private and public service, and to the growing proportion of women in the work force generally.[16] As more and more countries introduced various degrees of political rights for women, their positive influence on political and public life became part of the feminist argument as well.[17] Hungary's traditional politics and political language was based on common law, and its politicians were for the most part lawyers. Since women were not permitted to study law, the feminists relied on their male supporters' help in enriching their texts with the appropriate number of legal references.

The feminist slogan "No universal suffrage is universal without women" appeared on posters, newspaper ads, even postage stamps. Feminists applied the methods of their western counterparts: they orchestrated campaigns, organized rallies, signed petitions, tried to influence parliamentary parties and politicians, and published brochures and flyers. At one point, they collected the signatures of all women professionals and university graduates (thus providing an excellent source for future historians).[18] By the end of the first decade of the century, feminist demands had become increasingly visible, and their presence was an accepted fact of political life. At the same time, the original demand for universal suffrage went through slight transformations at every new turn of the political situation. In 1912, when the feminists accepted the limitation of suffrage by educational and property criteria, they suddenly found converts to the cause of women's rights among the conservatives. Their natural allies, the socialists and the bourgeois radicals, on the other hand, were gradually promoted to the role of main enemies.

3. In theory, the Social Democratic Party's program of 1903 demanded universal suffrage for men and women alike. In practice, however, the struggle for women's vote was not a priority for the socialist leaders. Nor did they encourage the organization of separate unions for women workers. Attempts from within the party to voice the separate interests of women workers, such as the founding of the newspaper *Munkásnő* (Woman Worker), were barely tolerated by the party and union leadership.[19]

In 1903, in one of the first efforts to organize women workers, the Association of Women Clerks and a few socialist women organized a series of lectures. The Social Democratic leaders, nervously guarding their charges against any "bourgeois influence," were not happy at all to see this arrangement. Besides, as the struggle for universal suffrage came to the forefront of their political agenda, the Social Democrats' stand on women's vote too went through a certain change. From 1906, the official line and the party's strategy emphasized the priority of universal suffrage for men. As the argument went, it would automatically bring about the vote for women.

The feminists also disagreed with the Social Democrats on the issue of social legislation. When the Hungarian parliament voted on the proposed ban of the night shift for women, the proposal's antiliberal opponents made use of the feminists' opposition to the proposal, without referring to their arguments. The feminists opposed the ban because they saw it as discriminatory and because it concerned only the relatively well paid factory workers, leaving all other women workers subject to exploitation.[20]

From the often vitriolic debates among feminists, socialists, and radicals a somewhat distorted picture emerges that emphasizes the differences between the feminists on the one hand and socialists and radicals on the other.

During the last few years before the war, extreme measures became quite common. These included sending spies or provocateurs to the other party's meetings or disturbing its demonstrations, not to mention the efforts to distort and discredit the others' political agenda.[21] At the same time, feminists, socialists, and radicals in many respects shared a common political culture. Through their participation in liberal-democratic institutions like the Freemason lodges, the open universities, the workers' courses, or the debates of the Society of Social Sciences, they were all part of a new, democratic Hungary.[22]

Besides, many socialists and radicals strayed from the party line and occasionally expressed an independent opinion on important issues. Powerful and popular socialist leaders supported women's suffrage even when the party's official line and tactics kept this goal on the back burner.[23] Likewise, the feminists had many avid supporters among the radicals, who, as a party, did not keep the women's vote on the agenda. The radicals cited the same argument as the Social Democrats, stating that to demand the women's vote was unrealistic and would have alienated their potential allies in the struggle for universal male suffrage.[24]

4. The growing international recognition of the Hungarian feminists was best demonstrated by the International Women Suffrage Alliance's VIIth Conference, organized by the Feminist Association in Budapest in 1913. As Hungarian feminists did not fail to point out, that event reflected their acceptance as a considerable political force.[25] But the feminists more lasting contributions were their pioneering initiatives concerning social work and public health or directing the public's attention to such social problems as illegitimacy, suicide, and prostitution.

These serious social ills, especially marked in Budapest, where rapid urbanization had been taking place, did not escape the attention of the socially more sensitive elements of the Catholic and Protestant churches. The last decade of the nineteenth and the first decade of the twentieth century witnessed a large increase in philanthropic women's organizations, trying to come to terms with these problems.

Hungarian philanthropic women's organizations still await their historian. We need further studies to establish their scope of influence and the role they may have played in the emancipation of women inaccessible for mainstream feminism. In the meantime, we can at least establish some preliminary trends: During the last decade of the old century, there had been a definite revival of the philanthropic organizations, with an attempt to extend their influence to working women, and they maintained a strong influence especially among Christian middle-class women. While the propaganda of the conservative press depicted the new type of independent, working woman as a mortal danger to family life and Christian morals, some of the newly founded conservative women's organizations gained supporters among the ranks of educated women. Although they exhibited a typically paternalist attitude, they provided temporary relief for the victims of urban social ills: the prostitutes, the orphans, the unemployed.[26]

True to their principles based on nineteenth-century liberalism and their faith in general progress and education, the feminists launched an ambitious program to publicly discuss and solve the important problems of the time: child welfare, the protection of mothers and newborns, illegitimacy, and the exploitation of and discrimination against women in the workplace. They regularly invited experts from Hungary and abroad and published the results of the discussions.

A focal point of these grave social problem was the so-called maid problem—social ills were most prevalent among the domestic servants—and the solution proposed by the feminists demonstrates the scope and the limits of their involvement in social reform. Since the generally accepted social norms prescribed the employment of at least one maid for every middle-class household, young, uneducated, single women from the countryside were attracted to the big cities in vast numbers.[27] Both socialist women and feminists—most of them in the double role of social reformer and employer—did their best to educate and organize these young women. While the socialists tried to unionize the domestic servants within the Social Democratic Party, bourgeois feminists proposed "central" or "communal" households as a possible solution to the maid problem.[28] The idea was originally suggested by Lily Braun and had been broadly discussed in German and Scandinavian feminist circles, and it found a rather large and unlikely following among the Hungarian middle-class bourgeois feminists. Incidentally, Budapest at the time had an outstandingly progressive mayor who employed many of the feminists in public service and was willing to implement some of their ideas. Plans for the building of communal apartments in Budapest, including elements of the central household, progressed well until they were interrupted by the outbreak of the war.[29]

IV.

At its peak, during the first two decades of the twentieth century, Hungarian feminism consisted of two clearly distinguishable strands. To the first belonged feminist movements and activists acting on the political level. That included accepting to some degree the established rules of political life, regardless of one's own agenda and principles. To the other group belonged feminists—males and females alike—who, despite their agreement with feminist principles, did not become involved in feminist organizations and politics; they can be called individual feminists.

Representatives of individual feminism in Hungary came mainly from two sources. The first was the growing group of university-educated women. Born around the early 1880s, thus slightly younger than the feminist leadership, they were the first generation of women professionals in Hungary. Medical doctors and pharmacists—a feminist petition counted 153 of them in 1916[30]—were followed in smaller numbers by librarians, historians, mathematicians, and chemists.

Almost all individual feminists came from the ascending upper bourgeoisie and a disproportionate number among them were Jewish. Statistics of university enrollment offer an explanation for this phenomenon. They reveal a marked overrepresentation of Jews among female university students at the faculties of arts, medicine, and pharmacy. Between 1896 and 1905, 48.6% of the women students at the University of Budapest were Jewish; in contrast, 29.5% of the men students were Jewish in 1895/6 and 34.1% in 1905.[31]

On the one hand, most of the women professionals agreed with the feminist agenda and supported the feminist cause by signing petitions, giving lectures in the Feminist Association, or writing articles in the Association's periodical, *A Nő és a Társadalom* (The Woman and Society). On the other hand, unlike the members of the Feminist Association, they were not politicians. This first generation of professional women tried to change the socially accepted image of the bourgeois woman not through politics but by way of their lifestyle. For a limited time and thanks to a number of fortunate circumstances, they seemed to succeed.

First of all, they found a nurturing environment in the circle of the progressive intellectuals. The debating societies, open universities, and Freemason meetings, along with the more informal salons and cafés, provided the training ground for the new type of female intellectuals. At the same time and within the limits of the socially accepted norms, the unwritten code of "good society," these institutions and activities contributed to a gradually changing relationship between men and women. The friendships and marriages that were established in this circle showed a remarkable degree of equality and an acceptance of women's professional and public life.[32]

Having the good fortune of a financially comfortable upper-middle-class background and an accepting, if limited social environment, these women seemed to have it all: family life, children, and an interesting career. Artistic activities, such as music, painting, photography, or dance, were admired. Purely intellectual endeavors, like opening experimental schools or studying psychoanalysis, as well as giving lectures or writing occasional pieces for journals, were celebrated. The choices, nevertheless, indicated both the limitations of the social norms that still applied and the fact that most of these women did not in fact need to make a living. With a few exceptions, these professional activities never grew into full-time careers. And it was generally expected that, in the long run, family life had priority over a professional career.[33]

Another distinctive group of individual feminists came from the ranks of the emerging modern poets and writers. Supported by a growing public for modern literature and art, Hungarian literary and artistic life flourished in the early 1900s. Centuries of Hungarian literature had produced only a handful of women poets, who almost exclusively came from the nobility. By the beginning of the twentieth century, more and more women found the courage to make a living from their literary work. Often forced to give up the appearance of a respectful bourgeois family life, they were the pioneers of a more bohemian lifestyle, previously unexplored by Hungarian women.

V.

Finally, we have to face the sensitive question: What can be said about the scope and influence of the Hungarian women's movements? In the absence of reliable studies concerning the socialist women's movements and any studies regarding the philanthropic women's movements, we cannot estimate their impact. As for the bourgeois feminists, we have at least some idea about the numbers involved. The Association claimed to have 700 members in the entire country in 1910.[34] Another source mentions 30,000 members in 1918, which seems too high, even if we take into account the growth in the 1910s and the mobilizing effect of revolutionary times.[35] There is no doubt that Hungarian bourgeois feminism grew into an influential political movement during the decade prior to the war. But we also know that in the same period the liberal, democratic, and socialist movements taken together reached and influenced only a very limited segment of the population. Also, they were limited mainly to Budapest and the largest cities.

The revolutionary period of 1918–19 brought the participation of feminists, and women in general, in political life in unprecedented numbers. The feminists had representatives in the elected National Councils. Their leader, Rózsa Bédy-Schwimmer, became ambassador to Switzerland in Count Károlyi's government and was thus the first woman with the rank of minister in Hungary's history. Nevertheless, the short weeks of democratic transformation resulted in the complete disintegration of the feminists as a political force. Disobeying their official policy of staying out of party politics, feminists joined parties from the Communists to the Legitimists, thus bringing to an end the illusion of women's solidarity transcending class and party divisions.

Hungary's conservative turn between the two wars and the marginalization of all the democratic political and social forces suggest an even more pessimistic conclusion as far as the impact of the women's movements is concerned. When Hungarian women finally received the right to vote in 1920, it was not the result of their own effort, but the dictate of the victors' peace conference. In the conservative and overly nationalistic atmosphere of the 1920s, democratic feminism was on the defensive and never reached the degree of influence and prestige it had enjoyed before the war.

As we have seen, the phases of the Hungarian women's movement closely correspond to the phases of the western "model." The peak of the feminist movement at the turn of the century was rooted in the relatively democratic and pluralistic political system and was inseparable from the influence of the international women's movement.

Following the First World War, the successive political systems imposed on Hungarian society were very different in their ideological base. Nevertheless, whether conservative or communist, these governments were strikingly similar in their paternalistic approach to social and gender issues. For reasons imbued in both the internal weakness of the Hungarian feminist movement and the political and social history of Hungary, feminism was unable to have a significant effect on gender relations or to play an important role in the political arena.

CHAPTER 11

The Polish Women's Movement to 1914

BOGNA LORENCE-KOT AND ADAM WINIARZ

The women's movement in Poland grew out of the end of traditional society, signaled by the Third Partition in 1795. That loss of political independence instituted tripartite colonization which, along with accompanying economic changes, so destabilized Polish society as to drive a wedge into all
existing definitions. This combination of events opened the way to discussion about women, their nature, and their function in society. But public
discussion about women, coupled with the fact that increasing numbers of
them were contravening their traditional role, did not result in redefinition
of Polish womanhood. Even though women expanded their social, political,
and economic role throughout the nineteenth century and more so in the
twentieth, Polish society continued and continues to view women primarily
as wives and mothers. Thus, whatever gains Polish women have made with
respect to their personal rights and freedoms in a world much changed since
1795, they continue to be squeezed into an old social formula.

Poles had a difficult time accepting their loss of independence, letting go
of their past identity, and adapting to unfree life in a rapidly changing environment. Refusal to acknowledge serious change for women may have been
the one area in which they could successfully cling to the past. As long as it
was on behalf of the nation, women's new public activism was not repudi-
ated, but neither was it fully acknowledged. Nor has it been to this day,
since Polish historians do not include women's contributions to national
cultural identity in their texts. Perhaps this is because Polish historians continue to focus on political and economic history, leaving social history—
which is where women are most likely to appear—as a thing apart. That segregation reinforces Polish determination to continue defining women
primarily as wives and mothers, and as such, women are outside the public

realm and therefore beyond the boundaries of what is deemed to be the nation's history. This is not to say that women's contributions to Polish society and the cause of independence are denied; when the question of women's activity is raised, it is acknowledged, but almost as an afterthought. Does this unwillingness to integrate all events into one seamless whole represent, with respect to women, a view that women's activism on behalf of society was and is no more than an extension of their familial obligation?[1]

Unwillingness to see women apart from families represents part of the complicated response of Poles to the task of entering the modern world. The West, which modernized first, had also kept women enmeshed in families, but once liberal ideology was in place, restricting women to the domestic sphere meant contravening the West's own creed, which sanctified the individual. Components of new western ideology twice gained some foothold in Poland, but were soon distorted or erased by the internal unreadiness of Polish society and the external circumstances of foreign control. In the eighteenth century, Enlightenment ideas promoted a wider social role for noblewomen who sought personal autonomy and public participation. But the external circumstances of the First Partition of 1772 soon made allies of traditionalists and reformers who redefined, in an updated version, women primarily as mothers. The Partition precipitated a reform movement that sought to safeguard the nation by rearing future generations in a spirit of intense national loyalty, a formula in which women as mothers played a leading role. That call to mothers, to work on behalf of the nation, eliminated any chance for Polish women to enter the public realm on the basis of individual self-expression. The next opportunity for women came with the Polish version of positivism which, following the failure of the 1863 Uprising, urged improvement of society instead of armed insurrection. As part of their effort to transcend nationalism and politics in favor of material progress, Warsaw positivists enshrined women's right to education along with the doctrine of hard work.[2] However, once more internal unreadiness and external politics combined to reinforce what R. F. Leslie sees as the continuing tendency throughout the period of partition for Polish propertied classes to make common cause with the occupiers in trying to stave off radicalism. Economic improvement was highly desired, but its expansion drew hitherto silent worker and peasant masses into the public arena, and this raised new social dilemmas for those who wanted to maintain control in a traditional manner. As Leslie points out:

Agrarian discontent and restiveness of the working classes revealed that the Poland of the future might arise from more fundamental forces than those which the educated classes by themselves could generate. The impending social conflict began to seem more threatening than the nostalgia of the szlachta (nobility) for the idealized concept of the past.[3]

This issue cannot be pursued here, yet it must be noted because in referring to the increasing democratization of Polish social ideas Leslie is raising, indirectly, the issue of citizenship. The definition of citizen—limited in the eighteenth century to nobleman—was gradually expanded until it came to include the lower classes and women. Previous nonentities became assets in the struggle for independence. But, of course, they also represented a threat to the old social order.

The breakdown of women's traditional role had already begun in Poland in the mid-eighteenth century, and the movement expanded during the nineteenth century. A woman's movement emerged in the 1880s, forming a complex mix of a tiny minority which sought personal rights and opportunities, a larger number which sought access to education and paid work for practical and ideological reasons, and a yet larger number which broke with tradition for patriotic reasons. Current scholarship is beginning to untangle these strands but has not advanced sufficiently to either theorize or periodize the process. Fortunately, the Historical Institute at the University of Warsaw is sponsoring volumes on women's history which will, in the aggregate, serve as a basis for interpretation, and a handful of scholars outside of Poland are adding their pieces.[4] This essay offers a provisional periodization which groups all innovative women's activities together without attempting to distinguish the underlying motifs.

FIRST PHASE

The growth of women's activism during the nineteenth century came in three waves, the first of which began around 1840 and ended in 1849, when police repression halted women's conspiratorial activities centered in Warsaw, then part of the Russian-controlled Kingdom of Poland. After the failure of the 1830–1831 Uprising a group of women subsequently named Enthusiasts became politically active, probably prompted by a combination of ideology and practical necessity. Their ideological motive emerged from the

European debate about emancipation as expressed by the social movements of Fourier and Saint-Simon, the novels of George Sand, and French feminist writings which had begun appearing in 1832. The practical stimulus arose from the massive emigration of defeated men who had participated in the uprising—about nine thousand in all, including many leaders of the Left. About two-thirds were of noble background, officers outnumbering common soldiers.[5] Women whose lives had previously been buffered by men were left to fend for themselves and, in many instances, for others who now became their dependents. According to Narcyza Żmichowska, the most prominent Enthusiast, women sought emancipation because of the "absence of noble and educated men who would lead their sisters, wives, and daughters on a path to intellectual and moral improvement."[6]

In the early 1840s Enthusiasts grouped around the *Przegląd Pedagogiczny* (Pedagogical Review), edited by Edward Dembowski, and announced their program for emancipation. They sought truth and goodness, independent action, economic self-sufficiency, access to higher education, and social and legal freedom.[7]

Widespread public discussion about women's rights followed proclamation of the Enthusiast agenda. Centered in Russian-occupied Warsaw, the Enthusiasts garnered many supporters as well as opponents. Their best-known woman sympathizer was the politically moderate Eleonora Ziemiecka, who was highly educated, interested in Hegel, and editor of the philosophical and literary monthly *Pielgrzym* (Pilgrim) as well as *Myśli o wychowaniu kobiet* (Thoughts about the Education of Women).[8] Among male supporters were two subsequent editors of the *Przegląd Naukowy* (Pedagogical Review), Edward Dembowski and Hipolyt Skimborowicz. The latter's wife, Anna, belonged to the inner Enthusiast circle. Both men came from landowning families.

Popular magazines such as *Pierwiosnek* (Primrose) and *Biblioteka Warszawska* (Warsaw Library) opposed women's emancipation. *Pierwiosnek* abounded with anonymous women who glorified the contemporary male role, but the best-known defender of tradition was Sabina Grzegorzewska, who wrote for the *Biblioteka Warszawska*. She said that the woman who seeks to enlarge her activities beyond the domestic sphere and intrudes upon public matters is "an unpleasant and dangerous anomaly to her sex. For men are born to the plow, the sword, and the compass . . . while women have only one occupation, which is family life. . . . This is the law of nature."[9]

Lionesses, a group of women whose extravagant public behavior perverted and ridiculed the serious Enthusiast agenda, helped fuel public derision of both idealistic and ersatz departures from norms. Loss of independence did not disabuse Polish society of its traditional values. It probably reaffirmed them, which meant that most Poles were not interested in differentiating among groups who challenged the ideological status quo. Stanisław Bogusławski, whose contributions to the development of Polish theater are too numerous to mention, conflated Enthusiasts and Lionesses in his play *Lwy i lwice* (Lions and Lionesses) as did August Wilkoński in *Emancypacja Sabiny ze stanowiska absolutnego* (An Absolutist Perspective on Sabina's Emancipation).[10]

Enthusiasts participated, as did innumerable other Polish women, in nationalistically conspiratorial organizations such as *Towarzystwo Demokratyczne Polskie* (Polish Democratic Society), *Stowarzyszenie Ludu Polskiego* (Polish People's Association), and *Związek Plebejuszy* (Plebeian Association). By 1848, as conspiracy was heating into action, Enthusiasts started working with Warsaw artisan groups, but czarist secret police uncovered their activities and arrested many, including Żmichowska and the Skimborowicz couple. Żmichowska was released from prison in February 1852 but remained under police supervision, in Lublin, for three years.[11]

The women's movement in Poland, as initiated by the Enthusiasts, never broke ranks with the political quest for national independence, which raises the question of whether there would have been a women's movement had Poland been free.

Wounds sustained during the 1848 upheavals were hardly healed when new political events drew Polish women into the national struggle. In 1860 and 1861 numerous women, of all social strata, participated in provocatively ostentatious commemorations of national anniversaries in Warsaw and other Kingdom of Poland towns. After Russians killed five Poles in Warsaw on February 25, 1861, women initiated national mourning on Warsaw streets by demonstratively abandoning crinolines and ornaments in favor of black dresses trimmed with white ribbons and black hats with draping crepe. Women's input as service providers and as warriors during the unsuccessful 1863 Uprising remains unstudied since existing literature does not begin to document the scope of women's participation, nor does it reveal the compensatory functions women assumed in the first difficult years following the uprising.[12] Women who avoided imprisonment or exile were again forced to replace absent males as heads of household. Some voluntarily followed their husbands into Siberian exile while several hundred were imprisoned or also deported. In that respect czarist authorities accorded Polish women equal rights with men.

SECOND PHASE

At the end of the 1860s Warsaw positivists took up the cause of women's emancipation as part of their new prescription for Polish society.[13] They suggested that Poles stop armed struggle for independence and put their energy into improving their society. According to Norman Davies,

> After the January Rising of 1863, Conciliation became the dominant trend
> in Polish politics for almost half a century. . . . Predictably enough, the
> most fervent advocates of Conciliation were drawn from the ranks of
> disillusioned insurrectionists—from men and women who had followed
> the revolutionary road in their youth and who had seen its limitations with
> their own eyes.[14]

Warsaw positivism appeared as a new social and philosophical current that promised to resolve the difficult political and economic issues facing Poles after the failure of the Uprising. It sought material progress through "universal education, technological progress, and, above all, intense work."[15] It appeared to be gender- and class-free, transcending politics. It urged Poles to return to basics under the slogan of "organic work" and sanctioned women's emancipation by supporting their autonomy through work. Karol Swidziński's poem "Naprzód Pracą" (Forward through Work) defined the positivist credo by emphasizing work before battle, science before art, and careful thought before rash action.[16] Heated exchanges among Warsaw positivists on the subject of women were preceded by a general European discussion among publicists, pedagogues, social activists, and literary figures arguing for women's equal economic rights. Discussion was most lively in England and France because in Germany action had already replaced debate. Within that sequence Polish polemics lagged behind European polemics—not surprising considering that the course of Polish events never did fit the European rhythm.

For Polish women the paramount issue was economic, and they agitated for entry to professions and access to education. Warsaw again served as the center for the debate on women, as new publications, Polish and translated, fueled discussion. John Stuart Mill's *Subjection of Women* came out in 1870 and was followed the next year by Eliza Orzeszkowa's *Kilka słów o kobiecie* (A Few Words about Woman). In 1873 Orzeszkowa published *O kobiecie* (About Woman) and Edward Prądzyński published *O prawach kobiet* (About the Rights of Women), in which he opposed full equality because of his belief that male authority was sacrosanct.[17] Nonetheless, he did want women to become educated and work for pay.

Publishers of family journals shared Prądzyński's prescription for women, but with variations. The most radical of them, *Kółko Domowe* (Family Circle), proclaimed women's rights to all education, professional work, and participation in public life. The journal *Rodzina* (Family) was more conservative and argued that women could not reconcile their family obligations with activity outside the home, that women could never equal men intellectually, and that women's aspirations to match men's minds only testified to their vanity and desire to shine in public.[18] Contributors to family magazines used a sliding scale about women and work that hinged on their status but was absolute with respect to unattached women. They expected upper-class women to stay home and raise a national elite whose example would radiate out to other families, while women lower down the social scale were encouraged and expected to work as part of their familial and social obligations.[19]

In the discussion about women there was no shortage of hostile views during the 1860s and 1870s. Antoni Nowosielski, one of the most determined opponents of the women's movement, predicted that their emancipation would cause the disintegration of families and public morality. For him, the whole thing smacked of socialism and other radical sociopolitical tendencies.[20] He was seconded by Roman Bierzyński, author of the famous *Somatologie de la femme*, which was full of paradoxical proclamations about women that relentlessly trivialized and ridiculed their aspirations.[21] He claimed that "the legion of emancipated women consists of divorcées, widows, old maids, childless women and those separated from their husbands."[22] In Prussian- controlled Poland similar hostility came from Stanisław Bronikowski of Poznan, who asserted in *Emancypacja i równouprawnienie* (Emancipation and Equal Rights) that Polish women did not need emancipation, which was, after all, the unhealthy product of the antitraditionalist United States of America.[23] He posited the pious woman as the ideal counterpart to the emancipated one. His views captured the inherent Catholicism of Polish culture under Prussian partition, which, not surprisingly, served as the obvious and only glue holding Poles together against Prussian efforts to depolonize them. How many, like Bronikowski, opposed women's emancipation from the fear of diffusing energy intended for national goals? Such fears were groundless, since Polish women gave their first energy to the nation.[24]

Criticism notwithstanding, the women's movement gained momentum, especially in the Russian-held Kingdom of Poland, where it was driven by women's economic plight following emancipation of the serfs. A similar momentum drove it under Austrian control following the great Viennese crash of 1873.[25] In both occupied areas, disintegration of the traditional economy forced women out of rural family households and drove them to towns in search of survival. Orzeszkowa published her famous *Marta* in 1873 to portray the fate of women unprepared for autonomous existence. Her novel served as a clarion call for hundreds of déclassé women from landowning families. *Marta* propelled young women, even those of assured existence, to study and, in turn, travel to universities, especially in Switzerland and France. Anna Tomaszewicz-Dobrska, the first Polish woman physician to graduate from the University of Zurich, opened her Warsaw office in 1878 to mixed feelings from male colleagues, but she was soon followed by other Polish women physicians as well as pharmacists, dentists, telephone operators, and clerks. Women also opened and ran day-care centers, and other female schools and businesses, demonstrating that they were as capable as men.[26] Most of the white-collar women came from previously landowning families.

Why didn't Polish women of the 1860s and 1870s act collectively? It could be said that women lacked organizational experience and the tight-knit community necessary to facilitate organizational work. Women also already had their hands full seeking social and professional rights, and contending with resistance from their own families and social milieus, all in addition to fighting the good national fight against Prussians, Austrians, and Russians. Once Swiss and French women gained access to higher education, professional access followed naturally, but in Poland—particularly under the Russians, who feared organizational activity—women could not expect acceptance or smooth transitions.

THIRD PHASE

Despite such obstacles, women did organize during the 1880s in all partitioned areas.[27] Kingdom and Lithuanian Women's Circles, inspired by the émigré Polish League in 1886, expanded their patriotic agenda by absorbing women's issues. The circles included elite women from all partitions and radiated out to Polish groupings in Petersburg, Moscow, Kiev, and Odessa as well as to émigrés in France and Switzerland. The circles included many radical women and Orzeszkowa along with Maria Konopnicka, the poet, as their patronesses.[28] Most members had landowning roots and were evolving into the intelligentsia. The circles sponsored secret schooling for children and pedagogical courses for adults; their commitment to such cultural activities as reading and publishing Polish works revitalized and expanded the women's cause during the 1880s. This happened despite the lack of social support or encouragement from the Catholic church and other important institutions, all of whom resorted to a familiar use of irony and ridicule. But that tone changed eventually, as did their manner of argumentation, as the movement expanded and gained more powerful women. In time, critics became less aggressive and more balanced.

By the end of the 1880s the women's movement had a program and connections to western Europe. Paulina Kuczalska-Reinschmit (1859–1921), who was of landowning background and was referred to as the "commander-in-chief of the women's movement in Poland," had formed the program.[29] Well educated, she was an ideological democrat and feminist, as well as a zealous patriot who kept reminding foreigners of her nation's suffering. She guided the Polish movement into the international arena through contact with women in France, England, Germany, Bohemia, and Russia. In 1889, along with Maria Szelig, she took part in the International Women's Congress in Paris. On returning to Poland she organized a covert branch of the *Alliance Universelle des Femmes* under the name *Unia*, which subsequently became a section of something called the *Delegation*, affiliated with the Museum in Przemyśl. By 1891 that entity was transformed into the *Koło Pracy Kobiet* (Circle of Working Women) and was officially registered with the czarist authorities.[30] Unia's program sought access to higher education, professional employment, and equal rights with men. At the same time, Unia announced a wide array of educational activities in the form of lectures implemented by Jadwiga Bojanowska, the closest and most loyal of Kuczalska's co-workers.

The magazine *Bluszcz* (Ivy) documented the women's movement. It was founded and edited, between 1865 and 1896, by Maria Ilnicka (1825–1897), daughter of a colonel in the Polish armed forces, wife of an 1863 insurgent exiled to Siberia, and herself a provisioner to the insurrectionists.[31] She supported women's equality with men only to the extent that it provided women with the broadest of skills for the purpose of running households. She used the magazine to inform others about the legal and political gains of western European women, focusing on English women. Antoni Krzyżanowski, an Anglophile who urged Polish feminists to imitate their English counterparts, was a frequent contributor to Ilnicka's magazine. He was eager to stress the respectable conventionality of English feminism, saying that

> in fifty years since emancipation became a part of the English public forum, women have not lost a single iota of their female aura: they continue as good wives, exemplary mothers, and devoted citizenesses. In fact, it is the amplification of those qualities in women which has gained such widespread admiration for English family values. English women are popularly associated with calmness, sincerity, poetry, and the dutiful fulfillment of their obligations, much in contrast to the disheveled shrillness and false pretenses of French women.[32]

Bluszcz was read mostly by landowning women. After Ilnicka's departure in 1896, the magazine pushed for a bolder model of women's emancipation by emphasizing social and political issues. It gave a detailed account of the 1896 International Congress of Women in Berlin and the subsequent one held in Paris in 1900, by describing motions and providing profiles of prominent western European feminists.

Between 1890 and 1914 the women's movement prospered best in Galicia, under Austrian rule, and developed least under the Prussians. Galician women started their official drive for the vote in 1890 under the leadership of Kazimiera Bujwidowa, Maria Turzyma, and Justyna Tylicka-Budzińska in Cracow, and Maria Dulebianka, Maria Konopnicka, and Stefania Węchslerowa in Lvov.[33] Women sought reform of family laws and revision of ethical norms concerning premarital continence and fidelity.[34] Iza Moszczeńska and Kazimiera Bujwidowa, wife of Odo Bujwid (the leading Polish bacteriologist and pioneer in prophylactic medicine), condemned the double standard and received public support for their position.[35] But even in this context of discussion about companionate marriages based on full trust between spouses, there was no shortage of critics who blasted the women's agenda. Father Kapłanski in *Przeciw emancypacji kobiet czyli supremacji kobiet nad męszczyz-nami* (Against the Emancipation of Women, which is Simply about Women's Supremacy over Men) claimed that

> under the guise of equal rights women are seeking supremacy over men. If that happens, our nation will be faced with a disaster greater than the partitions, for if this unhealthy principle spreads among our women, if they seek to rule under the guise of equal rights, their antipathy toward men will increase, and men will lose the respect and adoration they have toward women out of fear of having emancipated wives. Fear will stop them from marrying, childlessness and licentiousness will prevail, and male depravation will result in the decline of families, the debasement of society, and loss of the nation. For those reasons the emancipation of women is the mortal enemy of every nation.[36]

The women's movement in Prussian Poland was weak because all social resources, including women, were harnessed to the defense of Polishness, under continuous attack by Prussian authorities. The battle of nationalities even played out in the German feminist K. Schirmacher, whose hostility to everything Polish included Polish feminism, in contravention of the internationalist spirit of the European women's movement. Her defense of Germany's eastern borders against purported Polish claims was probably animated by the same spirit that infused the patriotic position of Polish women. In 1910, the Posen *Verein für Fraueninteresse* refused permission for her lecture on its premises, but she had no trouble finding accommodation in Bydgoszcz, Sopot, and Gdańsk.[37]

Arranging conferences under conspiratorial conditions in a politically segmented society was extremely difficult. Yet they did occur, and the first was organized by the Working Women's Circles in Warsaw in 1891 with 198 participants.[38] Officially the conference was to address economic matters, but participants managed discussion of national education, secret schooling, and social welfare.

The second conference was held in Austrian-controlled Lvov in 1894 and was organized by the Circles of Crown and Lithuanian Women. It was proposed for a date that coincided with the centenary of the Kościuszko Uprising. The organizers probably chose that date in an attempt to commemorate this last attempt to forestall the Third Partition of Poland. Fearful Austrian authorities forbade the meeting. Delegates therefore traveled ahead to "branch" conferences on purported medical, literary, and pedagogical topics. At the pedagogical forum women demanded access to education, particularly to universities.[39]

Over three hundred women from all partitions attended the third conference at Zakopane, which was opened on July 7, 1899. The major speaker, writer Wanda Marren-Morzowska, pointed out that women sought autonomy in a justly organized society—not battle with men.[40] This statement of purpose closely resembled the position of socialist women, whose development during the 1880s and up to 1905 paralleled that of the moderate right wing of the women's movement. Since the various branches did not rival each other, many women worked simultaneously for more than one; their collaboration provoked no suspicion or negative connotation since common goals transcended sectarianism. Cooperation proved so fruitful, in fact, that by the twentieth century Polish women had developed a broad social program and ways to popularize it. They published their program in 1903 as a series of articles by diverse women. Contributors included prominent Galician women, members of the Polish Social Democratic Party, members of the Kingdom of Poland Socialist Party, and nonparty radicals. *Glos kobiet w kwestii kobiecej* (Voices of Women on the Woman Question), as it was titled, demanded equal pay for equal work, access to all forms of education, and access to new professions. Initially the program had been more radical, but it was tempered for publication out of concern for shocking the public. The following year, a new Warsaw publication, *Kobieta współczesna* (Contemporary Woman), showed little concern for public sensitivity and boastfully listed women's accomplishments.[41]

The socialist branch of the women's movement was a latecomer and cut into the nationalistic tone of the moderate and conservative branches. Filipina Plaskowicka (1847–1881), yet one more déclassé landowning woman, first connected the women's movement to socialism and later served as a model for the numerous women who helped organize the first Polish Social Revolutionary Party, called Proletariat. Płaskowiecka also organized propaganda circles, the Rural Women's Circles, the Workers' Circles in Warsaw, and assistance to socialist political prisoners. Arrested by czarist police in 1878, she was eventually sent to Siberia but died en route.[42] The women organizers of the Proletariat Party were also of landowning, gentry background, metamorphosing into the Warsaw intelligentsia and wealthy bourgeoisie. Well educated and politically alert, their first proclamation, in 1882, demanded equal rights for women in every social area.

In the first phase of the party's existence, women propagandized, organized, agitated, and assisted prisoners.[43] Several women played an important role in the party's second phase, 1884–1886;[44] most famous was the activist Maria Bohuszewiczówna (1865–1887), because following the 1884 arrest of the party's leader, Ludwik Waryński, who was also of landowning background, and the subsequent arrests of Stanisłav Kunicki and Maria Jankowska, she took over leadership at the tender age of nineteen. She organized various circles, addressed workers' meetings, collected money, and supported the party press from her own funds. She corresponded with prisoners in the Warsaw Citadel and published as well as distributed socialist brochures. Official Russian correspondence of that era regarding activities of the Proletariat referred to her as a leading socialist. She was arrested along with fifty-five other socialists, and after incarceration at the Citadel was sent to Siberia, where she died in 1887. She was the great-granddaughter of the famous army officer and statesman, Tadeusz Kościuszko.[45]

Nineteenth-century socialists, who are not to be confused with the apparatchiks of socialist realism, valued and supported the women's struggle. They particularly admired women who sought learning and economic independence. In fact, they applauded such women, as is evidenced by the author of an article in the socialist *Przedświt* (Daybreak):

> It is amazing how much ridicule and derision befalls women who instead of darting their eyes all over and focusing on dancing and balls where they hope to cement their future . . . spend their days in painstaking study and their nights in supporting their comrades in the struggle to win the right to work.[46]

The 1905–1907 period of revolution radicalized women's own demands and those they made on behalf of the nation, as the October 1905 General Polish Women's Conference in Cracow demonstrated. The political thaw allowed conspiratorial organizations such as *Koło Kobiet Korony i Litwy* (Crown and Lithuanian Circles), *Kobiece Koło Oświaty* (Women's Circle for Rural Education), and *Uniwersytet Latajacy* (Flying University) to surface. In addition, hearing of the League for Women's Equal Rights in Russia, Polish activists organized. *Polskie Stowarzyszenie Równouprawnienia Kobiet* (Polish Association for Women's Equal Rights), which was registered in April 1907, when the new law of association took full effect. The association, headed by Paulina Kuczalska-Reinschmit, was soon split by differences of opinion, particularly about protection for women's work. Deepening differences led the older activists to drop out and form *Związek Równouprawniena Kobiet* (Union for Women's Equal Rights), again headed by Kuczalska-Reinschmit. Further splintering came as positions polarized with respect to the aims and tactics of the women's movement, so that in 1908 seven more women, with Cecylia Walewska in the lead, formed an independent women's section alongside the association, known as *Kultura*. Kuczalska-Reinschmit suggested federation of all three groups so that they could collaborate on such important issues as changing the civil code and the regulation of prostitution.[47]

In the first decade of the twentieth century, the nationalist wing of the women's movement gained momentum under the aegis of National Democracy. In 1909 the Committee of the National Association of Polish Women in Kalisz organized an exhibit of women's work that proved to be a national happening, with aristocratic, landowning, and peasant women exhibiting their handwork. On the exhibit's opening day the *Gazeta Kaliska* published a poem by Zofia Kęczkowska which called on Polish women to assert their equal rights with men.[48] In lectures on the woman question Anna Chmielewska spoke about women's tasks, while Irena Rzepecka, from Poznan, focused on social work and equal rights.[49]

On the eve of World War I, the rural women's movement emerged from under the landowners' tutelage. This youngest branch took its first independent organizational and programmatic steps, making itself known through *Zarzewie* (Hotbed), a journal run by Irena Kosmowska, who was just beginning her political career.[50] Young village people from agricultural schools clustered around the publication. Better educated than previous generations of peasants, they began examining the meaning and function of women in families and in rural communities, but change did not follow swiftly.

The Polish women's movement developed in a society that had lost its independence and was on the cusp of economic modernization. Political trauma and disruptive economic change did not engender a new ideology that could accommodate the practical needs of Polish women dislodged from a traditional way of life (this dislocation affected women above the working class and peasant levels). Upper-class women floundered within new economic realities, while most of society continued to imagine them in their old social role—despite such glaring displacements as the wholesale emigration of gentrymen following the 1830 Uprising and the massive loss of men in battle and to Siberia following the Uprising of 1863. The fact that women had no husbands at all or ones who could not support them provoked no general social discussion about how to assist them or how to transform defunct views of women into ones that reflected living realities. Not until the Warsaw positivists, who like the women activists were only a small percentage of Polish society, was there a serious attempt to think about alternatives to continuing insurrections—to think about society in its totality and outside the framework of battle or conspiracy.

Norman Davies describes the fundamental change in Polish thinking following the Uprising of 1863: There was a widely felt revulsion toward conspiratorial politics. Efforts were made to dispel the mystique of nationality fostered by romantics and messianists and to normalize Polish life by focusing on what could be accomplished in daily reality. Literature now strove "to replace the one-sided obsession with the Polish cause by a full range of genres and interests, as exhibited in the cultural life of other European nations. It was as much concerned with the Fine Arts as with national politics."[51] The change also appears to have, perhaps unwittingly, freed women to greater pursuit of their own agendas, or at least agendas that, because they were social and not political in nature, ultimately served women's specific interests better than had the energy spent in providing support services to men in battle.

The women's movement in Poland began in a society that lingered in its feudal past, had no sizable and vocal middle class, and was preoccupied with regaining its independence. Women heeded that cause, although a few here and there also voiced a women's agenda. Charting the development of the movement in Poland also means observing the formation of a Polish middle class in its intelligentsia, professional, and business personas. The Polish middle class arose from the same roots as the women activists—landowning gentry now become déclassé.

This overview of the women's movement in Poland is preliminary to further work. A detailed account of the movement at every stage and in every part of occupied Poland is in the making. Following that, will standard works on Polish history include women?

CHAPTER 12

Feminism and Equality in an Authoritarian State: The Politics of Women's Liberation in Late Imperial Russia

LINDA EDMONDSON

Over the past twenty years some of the most cherished assumptions made about nineteenth-century women's movements in Europe—and the European cultures of the wider world—have been subjected to critical scrutiny. This critique has encompassed the most fundamental questions in historical interpretation (of class, economic development, ethnicity, colonialism, relations between state and society, religion, tradition, and so on). None has been more unsettling, however, than the critique, from within present-day feminist scholarship, of the ideals of equality, individual rights, and representative democracy. It has been argued that a discourse of women's emancipation based on the principles of liberal individualism—the dominant political tradition in Britain and North America during the nineteenth and twentieth centuries—is flawed not only because it disregards other political traditions within Europe and outside, nor because it ignores the inequalities of class and ethnicity that undermine the political rhetoric of equal rights, but more fundamentally still because it is a man-made discourse that necessarily excludes and subordinates women. In this argument the very tradition through which nineteenth-century activists for women's rights traced their own aspirations to equality—Enlightenment rationalism and egalitarian theories of citizenship deriving from the American and French revolutions—has been redefined as the source of a new form of women's oppression.[1] Indeed, Carole Pateman has sought to demonstrate that there is nothing accidental in the exclusion of women from liberal political thought. The

This essay was written as part of a research project, "Gender and Citizenship in Russia, 1860–1920: Issues of Equality and Difference" (R000236013), funded by the Economic and Social Research Council in Britain, at the Centre for Russian and East European Studies, University of Birmingham, 1995–98.

original political right, she claims, is "conjugal right," the right of a man "to have sexual access to a woman's body."[2]

The critique of reformist feminism has been particularly effective in light of women's continuing inequality throughout the twentieth century and the failure of women's enfranchisement to make more than the shallowest dent in male domination of political power. As the suffrage movement's prediction that politics would be transformed turned out to be woefully optimistic, and as second-wave feminism failed equally to change the nature and conduct of politics, it has been tempting to ask whether the suffragists were barking up the wrong tree all the time. This questioning of the value of the suffrage movement, and of the value of studying it, has been given additional weight by the widening scope and changing priorities in women's and gender history (social and economic history, sexuality, the body, culture, representations) against which conventional histories of feminist politics appear rather old fashioned. At the same time, however, this widened scope has allowed the diversity of the nineteenth- and early twentieth-century women's movement to be recognized and described.

This essay is intended as a contribution to the understanding of feminism and movements for women's rights before the First World War, and to the current debate over the aims, purposes, and even the very concept of women's emancipation. By focusing on a society where liberal individualism was definitely not the dominant discourse, but where for that very reason liberal ideas—and particularly the concept of personal autonomy—acquired an allure, I hope to shed some light on the complex relationship between the politics of women's emancipation and the process of political change in an authoritarian and powerful state. While recent critiques of egalitarian feminism and equal rights theory have been effective and persuasive, nevertheless they tend to ignore the absolute necessity, for women and men, of political theories based on rights and individual freedom in societies lacking a tradition of constitutional rule, such as Russia both before and after 1917.[3]

Before proceeding further, I should make some observations about the term "feminism," which strictly speaking is an anachronism when used of the women's movement in the mid-nineteenth century. Karen Offen has pertinently shown that activists in the movement tended to avoid it until the end of the century and beyond.[4] In Russia the word had pejorative connotations not only for the women's movement but also for its revolutionary opponents, not to mention the official censors. All the same, the word is invaluable, perhaps even more for Russia than, say, for Britain, where political feminists at least could call themselves suffragists. In Russia up to the 1905 Revolution, feminists clumsily described themselves as "activists of the women's movement" (*deiatel'nitsy zhenskogo dvizheniia*); thereafter they might claim to be "equal-righters" (*ravnopravki*), taking their name from the movement's most active and most uncompromising feminist organization, formed during 1905.[5] If only for convenience, the term "feminism" is the one I shall use here.[6]

There are several reasons feminism has been a pejorative term to women in Russia (as in east-central Europe overall), and these do not stem solely from the disillusioning experience of "sexual equality" under communism. Apart from a widespread and often justifiable anxiety that ideas from the West, however progressive and well-intentioned, have been enthusiastically exported without any regard for the existing cultures of the recipients, there are other factors which are less specific to the current situation. These need to be borne in mind, as they are highly relevant to the history of the Russian women's movement. Most pervasive is an inherited ambivalence within Russian culture towards western ideas, culture, and institutions. Not only was intellectual life in the nineteenth and early twentieth centuries haunted by a continuing dispute between "westernizers" and "slavophiles"; even among the westernizers there was no unanimity as to what the West actually signified. Closely related to this was a constant search for the true identity of Russia, along with an intensifying—and state-sponsored—nationalism, as intense as anywhere in Europe in the same period. The extent to which the preoccupation with Russia's national identity influenced both the women's movement specifically and gender relations overall is only beginning to be explored.

For obvious reasons, much of the work on women and gender in Russia since 1991 has been concerned with the immediate present—the impact of the so-called "transition from communism" on women, the family, and gender relations. The impact of the collapse of the Soviet Union on the study of history, however, has also been profound. For the first time since the 1920s serious historical research into the lives of women, freed from the imposed categories of the "official" line, has become not only possible but essential too.[7] For many feminist historians the most critical task has been to recover the personal histories of their mothers' and grandmothers' generations, using oral as well as archival material. For obvious demographic reasons this task has been an urgent one—by the end of the twentieth century it was almost impossible to find witnesses who had grown up before the 1917 Revolution.[8]

Within the mainstream academic profession in Russia, research on women has been directed more towards their participation in Russian cultural life, especially in literature, than towards political, economic, and social issues in Russian women's history.[9] While it is true that some of the most original research in the West has also been focused on a recovery of women as writers and artists, I think the reasons may be somewhat different, linked to the current diversity of gender studies in the West.[10] In Russia, apart from reflecting the historical profession's overall indifference to women's history, the bias derives from a widespread revulsion in post-Soviet society against women's involvement in the "masculine" sphere of public life, above all, politics. It has been widely assumed that a woman's contribution to Russia's national culture will be expressed in the more naturally "feminine" world of the arts, and (far more importantly) through the family, in her time-honored and civilizing role of nurturer and keeper of the hearth. In Russia there has been a greater tendency even than in the West to categorize women's writing as a separate and—with few exceptions, notably the "canonized" Akhmatova—inferior genre.[11]

To lose an ideology which claimed to have explained the development of women's emancipation in Russia—and to lose it so abruptly, over only six years—must obviously have serious consequences for historians of Russian women in the West as well as at home. The entire subject had been conceived in the context of the continuing existence of the Soviet system, which in the 1970s and early 1980s seemed, for good or bad, destined to endure indefinitely. While it would be ridiculous and self-defeating to propose that all the history written before 1991 should be jettisoned, nonetheless many of its assumptions must be reexamined, to be confirmed, modified, or rejected.

One example is the periodization of the Russian women's movement. All histories of Russia's political opposition focus on Alexander II's Great Reforms as the time when opposition politics first developed from being the exclusive property of tiny social and intellectual elites (often working in exile or refuge abroad) into a precariously legal and publishable activity. The late 1850s and 1860s are understood to be the moment when politics first became a public concern, the moment when the woman question suddenly became fashionable and the women's movement began to take shape. The history of that movement can be (and generally has been) contained within the turbulent half-century that followed, an era that witnessed the long overdue emancipation of the peasants from serfdom and the concomitant crisis of the gentry; rapid industrialization and urbanization which (although it left the empire in 1917 still an overwhelmingly agrarian society) had immense repercussions for the economy and politics of Russia; the development of radical political movements, including terrorism; the assassination of the czar in 1881, followed by an intense political reaction; the strengthening of Russian nationalism and the upsurge of nationalist movements among the many non-Russian subject populations in a continually expanding empire; a growing social and political crisis that finally exploded in the 1905 Revolution; the intensifying antagonisms in international relations, leading to the catastrophe of the First World War and the fall of the monarchy in February 1917.

There are three reasons this conventional interpretation may now seem a little too neat. First, recent research by specialists in women's literature has put in doubt the claim that the women's movement suddenly erupted in the 1850s and 1860s.[12] It is now possible to demonstrate that although the phenomenon of women organizing on their own behalf (a reasonable definition of a movement) did indeed first appear in the late 1850s, women had already created a cultural identity for themselves as writers by the 1820s, and had been published in the established journals of the time.[13] This is particularly relevant to our understanding of the origins and development of the women's movement in Russia, because of the emphasis that the first publicists in the 1850s placed on the dangers to society of female ignorance and the urgent need for the education of women. This rhetoric was very powerful (and not misplaced, considering that only a minute percentage of women could read, let alone pursue an intellectual career), but it depended on a deliberate forgetting, or underestimation, of a previous generation of highly educated and creative women. This generation was admittedly tiny, and small even in relation to the number of men engaged in literature at that time, but in terms of influence, far from negligible.[14]

It is significant that the major protagonists in the debates on the woman question in the 1850s and 1860s were men, liberals and radicals. Also, unlike most of the early women writers, they came mainly from rather humble origins and were openly antagonistic towards a previous generation of politically radical men (such as Alexander Herzen) whose family backgrounds were gentry and nobility. What one might crudely term "class and status politics" was a strong element in the polemical writings of the generation of the 1860s; for all their eloquent statements about sexual equality, one is often left with the sense that their concern for women's emancipation (however genuinely felt) served to mask a quite different preoccupation with their own status in the world. With some writers, notably Chernyshevskii (the author of *What Is To Be Done?*), this is particularly clear; there is little evidence in anything he wrote that he was capable of seeing women as real people not so different from himself and his male friends.[15]

The second reason for feeling a little uncomfortable with the accepted periodization of the women's movement is that it corresponds so closely to the obligatory interpretation in Soviet historiography, according to which the "people of the sixties" created the essential progressive intellectual and moral environment for the later development of "scientific" Marxism and its triumphant realization after 1917. Events in Russia between 1855 and the Revolution thus became the servant of revolutionary teleology. The scheme that many historians (including myself) adopted in studying the various aspects of women's liberation fitted in with this chronology, which was dominated by a view of Russian history divided permanently by 1917. Self-evidently this suited the perspective of the Soviet world-view (and equally that of its dedicated opponents in the West). When the dramatic collapse of the Soviet Union revealed the permanence of the Revolution's achievement to be an illusion, however, the shape of Russian history both before and after 1917 lost the clarity and certainty it had acquired from the Revolution.

The third problem with periodization concerns the women's movement specifically; that is, when did it come to an end? To answer this one has to be certain precisely how to define it, whether one can include in it the political activities of women who openly rejected the women's movement because they saw it as too narrow and failing to address Russia's urgent social crisis, and whether one can possibly talk about the Bolshevik program for women's liberation in the 1920s (directed by *Zhenotdel,* the women's section of the Communist Party) as the culmination or natural conclusion of the movement.[16] These are difficult issues to resolve.

It has traditionally been argued that the Russian women's movement was composed of two incompatible elements: the moderate, reforming activists in the self-styled women's movement (women who might possibly have accepted the sobriquet feminist if the word had been in common currency in the mid-nineteenth century); and their radical opponents, who both claimed and practiced sexual equality, but saw women's subordination to men as only one aspect of an exploitative and patriarchal system. Radicals attacked the women's movement for allegedly diverting attention from the real needs of Russia, dissipating the energy required to overthrow the existing regime. This antagonism appeared the moment the woman question was first posed. Although it was of course present in the politics of women's movements all over Europe, its particular significance in Russia lay in the fact that legitimate political life was so poorly developed as to be unable to support a stable, moderating center, and that consequently the extremes of Left and Right acquired a decisive influence. Thus in an assessment of the women's movement it would be impossible to exclude the central importance of female radicalism, from the 1860s right up to 1917. Yet at the same time I find myself in some doubt whether women who so scornfully dismissed the aims and motives of the women's movement can then be included as its radical wing.

On the other hand, the suggestion has been made that this mutual antagonism has itself been exaggerated in an ideological war between Marxists and liberals which raged in the last years of the old regime and which after 1917 became fossilized as dogma in Soviet historiography. There is plentiful evidence of personal links and cooperation between radicals and feminists during the 1860s and 1870s; further research may well reveal similar contact even in the more highly polemical environment of the early twentieth century.[17] For the present, therefore, it remains difficult to know exactly how to define the women's movement and whom to include in its ranks.

The related question of whether to consider the postrevolutionary Zhenotdel to be part of the women's movement is also debatable, but I would hesitate to include it for one overriding reason. Zhenotdel as an organization existed as an official section of the ruling party in a one-party state, attempting to carry out a government program intended to liberate women from feudal and capitalist oppression and to mobilize them in support of the still insecure regime. This is not to suggest that the women who worked in it were responding to an agenda from above, as they would certainly have been if the organization had been set up in the 1930s. The section was run by women who had been active in the bitter struggle within social democracy before 1917 to get their own party to support work among proletarian women; for them the creation of Zhenotdel was a triumph. As a number of western historians have vividly described, the battle to get working-class women's needs—and their potential as a revolutionary force—acknowledged by an almost entirely male-focused party was at times as intense as the reformist feminists' attempts to influence the czarist government's policies.[18] In this sense, it would be true to talk of a dissident women's movement within social democracy before 1917.

To a certain degree the relationship between Zhenotdel and its political masters was not dissimilar, particularly after Lenin's illness forced him to withdraw from active involvement in government and as Stalin strengthened his authority over the new regime. At the same time, however, a social movement surely cannot merit the title without a considerable degree of independence in its policies and activities, and this Zhenotdel ultimately did not possess. From this perspective, I would be inclined to argue that the women's movement as a relatively autonomous force was closed down by the October Revolution, and that socialist feminists (as we would call them now) such as Alexandra Kollontai, Inessa Armand, and many lesser-known Social Democrats became briefly the new legislators of Russia, attempting to implement the party's program on sexual equality and family welfare. Given that Zhenotdel existed for only a few years and its work was never considered to be central by those outside it, one might be tempted rather cynically to argue that the Bolsheviks had appropriated the symbols of women's liberation in their remarkable program of legislation, organization, and propaganda during the 1920s. After 1930, when Zhenotdel was abolished, only the propaganda remained.

Having posed all these problems (which others may not see as such), I shall seem to backtrack by concluding that the conventional periodization will probably be sustained by future historians, taking due account of research on the early nineteenth-century women writers as well as the changing significance of 1917. For one thing, it would be quite misleading to see the period from 1855 to 1917 as only a construct of Soviet historiography. Contemporaries themselves—those who witnessed or participated in the women's movement—were the first to claim 1855 (the opening of Alexander II's reign) as a watershed in Russian history. They were very conscious of the uniqueness of the moment and, often, very conscious of their own role in molding the destiny of their nation. While one has to regard contemporary interpretations with at least as much critical detachment as one brings to historians' accounts, their perceptions of their own world must be taken seriously.

In light of what I have just argued, it may seem strange to use the 1880s as the opening point for a discussion of the Russian women's movement. On first reflection it would seem that in periodization (as in so much else) the Russian experience stood apart from that of many western European nations. This was a decade when the earlier energy of feminism and female radicalism came close to being stifled by the political reaction engulfing Russia after Alexander II's assassination in March 1881. At the end of the 1860s and throughout the 1870s the women's movement had been celebrated abroad for its daring and (especially considering Russia's reputation for cultural backwardness) its remarkable success. In 1869, for example, John Stuart Mill had addressed a letter to the initiators of the innovative higher education lectures for women, praising them for achieving what the rest of Europe was still struggling for.[19] This sense of achievement, along with the optimism that inspired the movement during the best years of the Great Reforms, was already on the wane by the late 1870s, when the government found itself confronted by a terrorist organization (in which women were prominent) determined to kill the czar, and it became increasingly risky even for liberals opposed to terrorism to voice their criticisms of government actions. The women's movement never recovered its early effervescence, except briefly during the 1905 Revolution and for an even briefer period just after the February Revolution of 1917.

Despite the fact that 1881 marked a low point in the women's movement, the 1880s may nevertheless be a very illuminating moment to begin a study of it. The restrictions, repression, and despair of those years were far more characteristic of Russia's political culture than the relative openness and hopefulness of the early years of Alexander II's reign.[20] Without doubt, the 1860s were the most exciting and intellectually stimulating period in the history of the woman question in Russia, but they can easily dominate that history and give a false picture of late czarist Russia as an increasingly open society in which sexual egalitarianism and respect for the autonomous individual were becoming well established. Moreover, the last two decades of the century are interesting in other respects.

One is the fact that during the 1880s the movement began to consolidate its achievement in gaining access to higher education for women. It was only in 1878, after almost two decades of persistent campaigning and very limited gains, that the first officially sponsored full-time higher courses for women were authorized in St. Petersburg. These were the equivalent of university education, though without any of the privileges that male students enjoyed when they graduated.[21] In 1880, women who had been trained as doctors in Russia, but allowed to practice only as "learned midwives," were at last given the title "woman doctor," partly in recognition of their services during the recent Russo-Turkish war. The assassination of Alexander II put all this at risk; medical courses were suspended for a decade and a half, and only the St. Petersburg higher courses, out of all those that had sprung up in university cities, survived the onslaught against the liberals in the government and the universities—that is, against the men who had provided indispensable support to the campaign for higher education. This being so, it may seem rather perverse to talk about "consolidation." However, for all the difficulties, it was during this decade that higher education for women ceased to be a matter of furious controversy and the principle became gradually accepted. The very restrictions imposed on the running of the higher courses served the useful function of turning a daring new enterprise into a fairly safe bureaucratic institution—intensely frustrating for many of the young women who studied there, but more suited to hard political times.

Another development that had a profound effect on the women's movement over the last two decades of the century was the rapid industrialization and growth of the major cities. Peasant women were migrating from the countryside to find work in the factories and, in greater numbers, in domestic service; more immediately relevant to the women's movement, whose main supporters were from gentry and middle-class backgrounds, was the steady expansion in the number of jobs available in white-collar occupations, from clerical work to teaching. This, of course, helped to ensure the future of the higher courses, which provided the graduates to fill the new positions.[22] As the industrial economy developed, employment opportunities for women with an education continued to increase. By the early twentieth century, primary education was not only expanding, it was becoming a female-dominated profession. Women's increasing prominence in public education, however, did not necessarily bring with it enhanced status. Many restrictions were imposed on their autonomy (most notoriously the marriage ban on women teachers in St. Petersburg),[23] while in rural schools, where middle-class women were quite frequently employed in preference to peasant men with equal qualifications (because women were expected to be politically docile), women teachers often suffered social isolation, as well as the vocal resentment of peasant communities, who saw them as middle-class intruders.

The newly sprawling cities not only brought work for women arriving from the villages and for educated middle-class women, they also exacerbated a host of social, medical, and administrative problems: overcrowded and insanitary housing, hazardous working conditions in factories and workshops, the exploitation of an expanding class of domestic servants and shop assistants, occupations which were steadily becoming feminized.[24] Urban expansion proceeded without planning controls, and city administrations had insufficient resources to deal effectively with existing social problems made worse by uncontrolled expansion: homelessness, contagious and chronic diseases, prostitution, illegitimacy, alcoholism, and many others.

From its earliest years the women's movement had tried to address these issues in the form of philanthropy, insofar as it was allowed to by a government very wary of initiatives that were independently sponsored and not directed by a ministerial department.[25] In the latter part of the century, both the government and the professions (now steadily acquiring a corporate identity which brought them into conflict with the state bureaucracy) began to take an official interest in welfare issues, convinced that unless solved these would make the populace more susceptible to both the lure of revolutionary propaganda and, even more alarming, the threat of physical degeneracy, undermining public order and ultimately endangering the survival of the Russian nation. One of the consequences of these preoccupations for the women's movement was the opening of more opportunities for training in new and existing professions. Even before the 1920s, when women moved rapidly into the less prestigious levels of medical practice, medicine was becoming an acceptable occupation for female graduates; a number of leading feminists were doctors. Women were employed by rural and municipal councils, not only as teachers, doctors, and medical assistants, but also in less obviously caring professions such as statistics or agronomy.[26]

Cultural priorities were also changing; the change was expressed in literature, the arts, philosophy, and journalistic debate. The fierce egalitarianism and rationalism of the "men of the sixties" now seemed rather old hat, their naive faith in progress severely knocked by the failure of both the Great Reforms and 1870s populism, and by the force of the political reaction during the 1880s. The self-assured agnosticism and contempt for superstition and church ritual (many of the radical men of the 1860s had been educated in a seminary and were the sons of priests) gave way to a strong religious revival, not necessarily a return to the Orthodox Church, but a preoccupation with spiritual values and inner wisdom. Discussion of the woman question moved away from the simple solutions of education, work, and egalitarian relations between the sexes, and showed an increasing concern with the undercurrents of sexual politics—the complexities of sexual desire and the difficulties of creating intimate relations between men and women, a new "scientific" search for the true nature of gender difference, and the revived cult of the "eternal feminine."[27]

This shift should not be exaggerated, however. The same period also saw the institutionalization and increasing prestige of science, a process which embraced many of the now middle-aged scientists who had participated in the radicalism of the 1860s. Moreover, the ascetic and rationalist ethic of those early radicals was very evident in many of the revolutionaries thirty or forty years later.[28] Marxists claimed to work on scientific principles and greatly esteemed the "generation of the sixties" for its clear-headed opposition to obscurantist religion and the cult of the irrational. And though discussion of the woman question had become more complex in society at large, the declared aims of the women's movement did not alter significantly. Changing intellectual and cultural fashions did not lessen feminists' concern to widen the scope of women's autonomy and "self-activity" (*samodeiatel'nost'*) and increase their employment opportunities. Even in the sphere of education, which remained the greatest achievement of the women's movement before 1905, the gains were not secure, nor yet sufficiently extensive for the issue to cease to be important.

Towards the end of the century the women's movement cautiously began to develop a new interest, which reflected the increasingly open concern for political change in Russia and the decreasing ability of the government to prevent it, hard though it tried. During the 1890s radical political groups, which had been shattered by a decade of government reaction, began to recover some confidence. The sterile polemics of the 1880s between populists and Marxists slowly and painfully gave way to a new concern with propaganda among the urban working class, in most cases quickly brought to a halt by the secret police. By the earliest years of the twentieth century, however, revolutionary political parties were taking shape—the Russian Social Democratic Workers' Party, founded in 1898 and then dramatically split into

Bolsheviks and Mensheviks at the Second Party Congress in 1903, and the Socialist Revolutionary Party, founded in 1902 and following in the populist tradition. Both parties adopted "minimum" programs guaranteeing constitutional rights, including universal suffrage without distinction of sex, religion, or nationality. At the same time, liberals were also grouping—first into a broad alliance, the Union of Liberation, and then, during the 1905 Revolution, into a liberal political party, the Constitutional-Democratic Party. More moderate liberals refused to participate in an organization which engaged in open confrontation with the government and which by the end of 1905 had adopted a radical agrarian program and universal suffrage, and they subsequently formed smaller centrist fractions. It was only in these frenetic months, when political activity in Russia became open, if not strictly legal, that feminists were at last able to turn to the very issue that has tended to be considered (however erroneously) the essence of the women's movement internationally before the First World War. Russian feminists began to demand votes for women.[29]

The revival of the movement during the 1890s and, especially, in the early 1900s clearly owed a great deal to the rising assertiveness of opposition groups overall; it was an integral part of that opposition and was affected to much the same degree as other groups by changing political conditions. It is less clear how far developments in the women's movement internationally provided a stimulus to action—not because the effect of foreign ideas and personal contacts was insignificant (quite the reverse), but because of the complex interplay of external influences and domestic politics in Russia during the second half of the nineteenth century. Russian feminists were very concerned to maintain contact with feminists in the West and did so throughout the life of the women's movement, from its beginnings in the mid-1850s to 1917 (and even beyond, where that was still possible).[30] They corresponded with individuals in the West, who sometimes became close friends, and they attempted to create institutional links, most notably with the International Council of Women (ICW) and the International Woman Suffrage Alliance (IWSA). But these links were of necessity unofficial and, lacking bureaucratic sanction, were subject to interference whenever the Ministry of Internal Affairs might choose. Even quite moderate liberal feminists, a number of them well-connected socially, were unsuccessful in their repeated attempts to establish a Russian National Council of Women, which could be affiliated to the ICW.[31]

The difficulty of deciding the extent of feminist influence from abroad is well illustrated by the story of the 1893 World Columbian Exposition in Chicago, and Russian women's reaction to it. Leaders of the women's movement in the United States were keen to use the occasion to mount an international exhibition of women's achievements and to host the first quinquennial meeting of the recently formed International Council of Women. The invitation met an enthusiastic response among women in St. Petersburg, who saw it as an opportunity to develop links with western women, advertise the existence of the Russian movement, and stimulate interest at home in the type of general association that already existed in America and Germany but had not yet been made acceptable to the authorities in Russia. An exhibit was prepared for Chicago and the first moves were made to establish a women's association in St. Petersburg.[32] After many trials and tribulations with the Ministry of Internal Affairs, the association was eventually authorized in 1895 as the Russian Women's Mutual-Philanthropic Society (*Russkoe zhenskoe vzaimno-blagotvoritel'noe obshchestvo*), a name unwished for by the organizers and reeking of bureaucratic control, but which nonetheless accurately reflected its permitted scope. Anything resembling political campaigning would have been out of the question at that period, but even in its educational activities, which were officially sanctioned, it had little freedom of maneuver.[33] Hampered by these restrictions, it had no chance of becoming the sort of popular middle-class association that its founders envisaged. The fact that it survived, however, is a testimony to the persistence of the women's movement leaders and an indication of the remarkable, if halting, development of a civil society in late czarist Russia.

How far did the Chicago Exposition and the foundation of the International Council of Women influence the revival of the Russian women's movement? It is clear that the American invitation to participate made a strong impact on leading figures in the Russian movement (it is impossible to gauge its impact on others) but that their ability to respond was dependent on the renewal of public activism in Russia, without which the call to organize would have gone unanswered. Late czarist Russia, even in the worst years of repression, was not hermetically sealed against foreign ideas and considerable numbers of women, already enjoying access to foreign periodicals and travel abroad, were well informed about the growth of an international women's movement, if able to do very little. As it was, the political environment in Russia was changing in the early 1890s, making it possible for the first time for Russian feminists to consider responding to an initiative from abroad. The increasing complexity of international organizations, whether government-sponsored, nongovernmental or antigovernment (notably the Socialist International before 1914), may also have stimulated the growth of public activism in Russia; while technology—the transformation of printing, the invention of the telegraph and later the telephone, the expanding railway network, the greater comfort and safety of sea travel—made possible an intensity of international communication that earlier social activists could only dream of.[34]

Similar questions might also be asked about the eruption of the women's suffrage issue at the end of 1904. Events within Russia itself would be sufficient to explain the unprecedented feminist campaign for political rights. The country had been plunged into political and social crisis by a bungled war with Japan, which had brought to the boil a cauldron of simmering discontent in all strata of a highly stratified society. At the core of the political conflict between the czar's government and an increasingly confident liberal opposition was the demand for a constitution, which would establish a representative legislature and a wide (if not universal) franchise. The issue of a constitution was not confined to the professional classes who were the mainstay of liberalism; the discourse of rights was expressed in working-class and peasant protest, in demands for autonomy for the subject nations of the empire, in calls for religious toleration for non-Orthodox communities, in student protest, and even in revolts among schoolchildren.[35] Moreover, the two main revolutionary parties (the Social Democrats and the Socialist Revolutionaries) had made civil and political rights one of the focal points of their propaganda.

It would have been astonishing if feminists, in such an environment, had not thrown off their fear of prosecution to join the liberation movement in a campaign for equality. It was almost as if they had been waiting for a signal to politicize the women's movement. By the end of 1904, after the assassination of a hated minister of internal affairs and the subsequent intensification of public protest, calls for full political rights for women were beginning to be heard and the first moves being made to organize a union to campaign for them. It took only the fiasco of the Bloody Sunday massacre of St. Petersburg workers and their families in January 1905 for feminists—like the liberation movement generally—to throw off the last restraints. Within a few months Russia's first feminist political union had been founded and, after a few protests from other unions, accepted into the main coalition of left-liberal political action in 1905, the Union of Unions.[36] Its program included unconditional universal suffrage without distinction of sex, religion, or nationality, and this became the focus of its campaigning during 1905 and 1906, first to convince the liberal opposition to support it (with overall success) and then to persuade the government to adopt it in law (with no success at all).

The Union of Equal Rights was the most dynamic organization in the history of the Russian women's movement, and by far the most outspoken during 1905 and 1906. But the politicization of the women's movement was not limited to the left-liberal opposition. The more moderate Russian Women's Mutual Philanthropic Society (hitherto hamstrung by bureaucratic restrictions) also called for women's suffrage during 1905, sending a mass of petitions and declarations to officials and leading political figures. It also made the first moves to hold a national congress of women, which (after many setbacks) was finally held in December 1908.[37]

While there is no doubt that the politicization of Russian feminism in 1905 owed more to events at home than to any influence from outside, all the same there are some striking coincidences. Looking at the issue of suffrage in Russia from a British or American perspective, it seems obvious that the Russian movement lagged far behind the West. This was doubtless true: there was no parliamentary system of any sort before 1906 and discussion of political rights was not permitted, in the women's movement or anywhere else. At the same time, however, suffrage had not been a major issue in the international women's movement until the foundation of the International Woman Suffrage Alliance in 1904; the suffrage campaign in Britain was in the doldrums until the very end of the nineteenth century; women in Prussia and a number of other German states were not permitted to engage in politics until 1908. Russia's notorious "backwardness," therefore, though real in many respects, was not absolute.

One of the distinguishing features of the politics of women's liberation in Russia, which set it apart from the Anglo-American experience (but not from the German or Austrian), is the influence of radicalism on opposition politics, and particularly the influence of Marxism. The Russian Social Democratic Workers' Party was tiny compared with the German Social Democrats, not only because it operated illegally, even after the inauguration of the State Duma in 1906, but also because the industrial proletariat (though growing rapidly) remained a very small minority of Russia's working population as late as 1917. But social democracy's influence on Russian politics was out of all proportion to its size—and not only in the light of its history after 1917. Its relationship to the nonrevolutionary women's movement in the last fifteen years of the czarist regime was generally antagonistic, although there is evidence that individuals on both sides were able to work together on occasion, as populists and feminists had done a generation earlier and continued to do. This antagonism between Social Democrats and feminists was especially fierce on the issue of women's suffrage: Social Democrats accused the bourgeois feminists of pursuing the narrow goal of female emancipation, which they claimed would benefit only middle- and upper-class women and betray the interests of the working class. Feminists accused the Social Democrats of sacrificing the needs of women on the altar of class struggle.

Participation in politics in Russia was not primarily a question of gender, or even class or nationality, but instead a matter of principle which was never conclusively settled before the Revolution. In theory Russia was an autocratic state; in practice the government was forced to concede some of its authority, first in local government (from the 1860s) and then, in 1906, in a nationally elected legislature. Neither the local assemblies nor the State Duma, however, were free from government supervision and interference, and authority remained with the czar and his ministers. This fact determined much of the feminists' campaigning on the issue of women's political and civil rights. Although a separatist feminist minority criticized the majority's decision to work within the general (that is, male-dominated) liberation movement against autocracy, there was never any realistic possibility of doing otherwise.[38] In this sense one might see the women's movement facing the same problem within its ranks that it faced in its relationship with its Social Democratic antagonists—in both cases, the problem was how to reconcile the particular concerns of women with the perceived demands of society's liberation. Almost invariably the specific needs of women were subordinated to the needs of the political moment.[39]

This insistent and continuing problem was a constant theme in the history of the Russian women's movement. The political conflict between bourgeois feminists and Marxist women (and before that, between feminists and nihilists in the 1860s and feminists and populist revolutionaries in the 1870s) has also dominated our perception of the movement up to now. It is a vivid illustration of the extent to which the historical horizon was occupied by the inflated vessel of Soviet ideology, which emphasized every instance of conflict and denied the possibility of compromise with liberals and reformers. While it would be a mistake to ignore these schisms, to focus on them to the exclusion of other, equally significant phenomena is to distort the history of the Russian women's movement and obscure its diversity.

One aspect of this history that has been largely ignored is the problem of describing and analyzing a movement that developed in a multinational empire dominated in every meaning of the word by Russia. It is true that most historians have had no linguistic access to the other cultures of the empire, except through the Russian language or their own. It is also not unreasonable to focus a study of feminism in the empire on one particular region or ethnic group, especially if it was the politically dominant element. However, the neglect of the nationalities also reflects the extreme sensitivity of the national question in the czarist empire, and in the Soviet Union too.[40]

Another question of national identity that is critical in assessing the Russian women's movement is Russia's interrelationship with the West and Russians' perception of what "the West" actually was and is (and whether it even exists). The West has featured so prominently in Russian discourses, as an ideal, as a bogey, as a point of comparison. It has been intrinsic to all consideration of Russianness, of the Russian national destiny. In the writing of women's history it has tended to lie beneath the surface, although it becomes more explicit in any discussion of the validity of feminism (as I noted earlier), as it does also in debates over the weakness of liberalism, the necessity of revolution, the relevance of political and civil rights, and even the very nature of the Russian woman.[41]

Finally (although there may be many other questions that need asking) there is the problem of gender and political power, the extent to which those men and women who argued for sexual equality envisaged women acquiring political rights and possessing political authority. Because of the severe restrictions on the activities and concerns of the Russian women's movement before 1900, the issue of political power was debated only in generalities and clichés, although it underlay every discussion of female emancipation. This meant that a controversy that feminists had to address in Britain or America from the earliest years of the women's movement was allowed to slip away unrecognized in Russia until the beginning of the twentieth century, when political rights came on the agenda at last. The Soviet experience of political participation was always an artificial one—the form of democracy existed, but not the reality. In that system, women were guaranteed a fixed proportion of elected seats, but at no time in seventy-five years came close to holding political power. The questions that now seem relevant for historical investigation are those that look beneath the rhetoric of political rights, as adopted by Social Democrats, Socialist Revolutionaries, and a substantial minority (or maybe small majority) of liberals early in the twentieth century, not so much to examine the sincerity of the rhetoric, but rather to ask how political equality was defined. Was it simply "the vote," or was it the equal participation of women in government? And how many of those who advocated the latter envisaged women's involvement in the political process fundamentally altering its nature? In other words, were women to be incorporated into an existing system made by men, or did their participation necessitate a redefinition of politics?

These are just a few of the questions that need to be addressed in future study of the Russian women's movement. There are many more that I have barely mentioned in this chapter, in particular the social history of women, a flourishing area of research whose insights have a great deal to tell us about Russian feminism.[42] Studying Russian women's history is often an isolating experience—it lies on the periphery of mainstream women's history, separated not only by a difficult language, but by Russia's own peripheral status in the western world, an isolation partly self-imposed over several centuries and partly caused by our own cultures' insularity. Yet the history of the Russian women's movement reveals many similarities to and points of contact with women's movements in other countries. While it is important to identify the elements in that history that are unique to Russia and explicable only in its cultural context, we can also hope that greater opportunities for collaboration between historians will lead in the future to a far more balanced and subtle understanding of the Russian experience, both before 1917 and in the Soviet period.

PART V

Southern Europe

CHAPTER 13

The Rise of the Women's Movement in Nineteenth-Century Spain

MARY NASH

Carmen de Burgos (1879–1932), schoolteacher, writer, and feminist, claimed that the first public act of Spanish feminists took place in 1921, when a manifesto demanding civil and political rights for women was handed out in the streets and presented at Parliament and the Senate.[1] Later, writing in 1927, de Burgos classified Spanish feminism in three types: Christian feminism; revolutionary feminism, which looked to socialism as the means to achieving women's emancipation; and independent feminism, a strand with which she identified. The latter advocated sexual equality, political franchise, an end to legal discrimination against women, equity in jobs and wages, and the establishment of a divorce law.

De Burgos's opinion on the feminist movement raises a number of issues to be explored in a discussion of the development of first-wave feminism in Spain in a comparative European perspective. While she associated feminism with the public defense of women's specific public and civil rights, this essay points to the existence of multiple definitions and genealogies of feminism that do not necessarily comply to de Burgos's notion of feminism in the terms of suffragism, political enfranchisement, or political rights. Moreover, her definition raises the need to reconsider what is understood as a women's movement. Is it to be defined by public acts, by collective action, by individual activism, by political statements, or by women's experience?

The categorization by this early feminist also implies that Spanish feminism began as a movement in the early 1920s, thus questioning standard European chronology that places the development of the women's movement from the 1880s to 1914. The establishment of a general periodization in the framework of Europe raises the issue of its validity in the context of the women's movement in different countries and regions. Rereading feminism through differential patterns of growth of the women's movement in Europe may, in fact, lead to the creation of different sets of periodization and reveal more plural definitions of feminism.[2] This essay argues that conventional chronological divisions for the development of the women's movement in Europe, such as the 1880s to the First World War as a specific divide, do not neatly fit into a chronology of the growth of the women's movement in Spain.

The difficulties arising from the macro application of established canons in the interpretation of international feminism have been discussed in other studies.[3] Applying general conceptual frameworks in specific historical contexts can be dangerous. Attempts at elaborating a universal approach to the definition and characterization of feminism can create blinders that impede the identification of a women's movement that does not fit into preconceived explanatory models of feminism. Moreover, set definitions of feminism tend to imply that there are "proper" paths to women's emancipation and "correct" modes in the historical development of feminism. This, in turn, can lead to interpretative schemes that regard those manifestations of feminism that do not fit neatly into established canons as backward, underdeveloped, or discordant with "correct" patterns of feminism.

Definitions of feminism must be elaborated in the dual context of national and international historiography. Indeed, the hegemony of standard interpretative schemes of international historiography has produced a certain degree of distortion within national historiography.[4] Moreover, since studies on women's movements within countries are not always translated or given adequate circulation, they can go unnoticed in international historiography. The wider recognition of similarities rather than differences in national and regional women's movements can also reinforce more uniform models that do not unveil the specificity of the historical manifestations of feminism. At the same time, the lack of comparative perspectives in national historiography entails an impoverishment of analytical tools. Comparative approaches are essential, but as historians we must also be attentive to nuances of different experience and the need to generate an open dialogue that enables us to refine and enrich our analytical tools.

This essay discusses some aspects of the women's movement in late nineteenth- and early twentieth-century Spain. Its goal is to sketch some of the achievements of the nineteenth-century women's movement, to present a mosaic of itineraries rather than a detailed study. My understanding of the paths of the early women's movement in Spain is based on the notion of experience and women's social and political development as an apprenticeship in collective responses. Experience integrates socioeconomic reality and diverse cultural, political, and gender perceptions. It structures collective mentality and inspires resistance strategies, choices, and ways of conceiving emancipation.[5] The diverse expressions of gender, social class, national identity, and political culture played a crucial role in Spanish women's experience of emancipation. They can also account for the plural strategies of female resistance and the decisions women took in developing a social movement. This essay thus raises the issue of the specificity and diversity of the historical development of feminism in Spain but, also, the need to take account of traits it shared with other European women's movements.

THE GENESIS OF THE WOMEN'S MOVEMENT

In Spain in the late nineteenth century there did not yet exist a general social movement that can be identified as feminist. Until the early twentieth century there were only isolated instances of demands for women's rights by individual writers, teachers, thinkers, political reformers, and women activists, none of whom carried the debate on women's emancipation to the level of a wide social and political practice. It is my understanding that, as a social movement capable of developing a common identity and purpose and collective strategies for action, feminism did not develop in Spain until the early years of the twentieth century. However, the discourse of feminism, sets of ideas on women's emancipation, and individual feminist codes and practices form part of the complex genealogy of Spanish feminism in the nineteenth century.

From Duoda in the fifteenth century to the Enlightenment thinkers, there is a genealogy of individual Spanish writers devoted to "la querelle des femmes."[6] Early in the eighteenth century, Benito Jerónimo Feijoo defended the intellectual equality between men and women in his *Teatro crítico universal.*[7] By the end of the century the Aragonese Enlightenment writer Josefa Amar y Borbón published one of the first foundational texts of Spanish feminism. Her *Memorial literario, Discurso en defensa del talento de las mujeres y de su aptitud para el gobierno y otros cargos en que se emplean los hombres* (1786) and *Discurso sobre la educación física y moral de las mujeres* (ca. 1790) denounced the situation of women's inferiority in Spanish society.[8] Following the lines of Spanish Enlightenment discourse, her arguments were based on the notion of equality between men and women. Like many Enlightenment feminists, she claimed women's access to education as a crucial tool for cultural transformation and female emancipation, while at the same time recognizing gender differences. She had complete trust in the regenerational capacity of education and in women's intellectual capacity. The current state of studies makes it impossible to establish if there is any connection between these well-known eighteenth-century works and nineteenth-century Spanish feminism. However, it is quite clear that education became the core agenda in first-wave feminism, while "regeneration," a key concept in modern Spanish political and social history, was also a crucial tenet in the development of feminism in Spain.

To understand the development of the women's movement in Spain, one must look at the political background of state building. State politics shaped many strands of Spanish feminism while state building and regional national identities were crucial in articulating women's responses and strategies for emancipation. Political change shaped women's issues and stances according to a chronology that differed from that of other European countries, although the comparison with Italy is particularly relevant here.

Nineteenth-century Spain is characterized by sharp discontinuities in the liberal revolution and by an ongoing struggle to modernize the state and consolidate liberalism. The chronology of events fits to some extent into the political scheme of European political changes, but there is also a pattern specific to Spain: the initial establishment of the constitutional regime in 1812; the return of absolutism and its final demise by 1837; the failure of progressive liberalism during the *Bienio Progresista* (1854–1856); the failure of the *Sexenio Democrático* (Democratic Revolution, 1868–1874); the Restoration of the Bourbon Monarchy (1875); the colonial "disaster," with the final loss of the Spanish colonies in 1898; the dictatorship of Miguel Primo de Rivera (1923–1929); the Democratic Republic (1931–1936); and the Civil War (1936–1939).

When the first Spanish liberal Constitution was drafted in Cadiz in 1812, there was no debate on citizenship and women's rights. The lack of interest in the gender dimension of citizenship is not surprising. The context of the ongoing War of Independence against Napoleon and the traditional hostility to France led to a general rejection of any French political influence in the liberal Constitution of Cadiz. Moreover, the predominance of traditional sociocultural values meant that the innovative new constitutional changes eliminating the absolutist regime did not contemplate women as citizens.[9] Women were also expressly prohibited from attending public forums, although, disguised as men, some attended the parliamentary sessions.[10] Despite this defiance, current studies so far have not unearthed any discussion by women claiming political rights. In the early nineteenth century, even while acknowledging the principle of male/female equality, progressive liberals quite clearly advocated the norms of domesticity and women's confinement to the home.[11]

In the 1840s the explosion of literature by romantics such as Carolina Coronado or Gertrudis Gómez de Avellaneda gave voice to female subjectivity. These women writers clearly expressed their experience of oppression, as the following verse by Carolina Coronado proclaims: "Libertad! ¿pues no es un sarcasmo/el que nos hacen sangriento/con repetir ese grito/delante de nuestros hierros?"[12] In 1845 this romantic poet identified women's confinement to the home as imprisonment and challenged established restrictions to women's role in society.[13]

By midcentury international influences together with political and social advancement within Spain inspired further development of women's voices and a clearer expression of feminism. Early evidence of a discerning feminist consciousness can be attributed to the influence of the French social utopian Charles Fourier, whose followers in Cadiz were one of the first groups to express openly a feminist perspective. A small number of women poets and writers collaborated in the publishing of the Fourierist journal *El Pensil de Iberia* (The Garden of Iberia) in the 1850s.[14] This journal, which published lyrical poetry, philosophical essays, and social criticism from a democratic perspective, spread Fourier's thought throughout Spain and paid considerable attention to women. The Cadiz Fourierists advocated equality between the sexes, an end to male supremacy, and the development of new foundations for gender relations based on Fourier's idea of "attractive passion." They also denounced the exploitation of working women and advocated social harmony. Censorship and political repression impeded the continuing publication of the journal. Despite the fury it aroused among established authorities, particularly the Church, this strand of pioneer feminist thought appears to have remained isolated from a larger audience of women. The women involved with the Fourierists were later associated with spiritists, freethinking groups, and Freemasonry, which, toward the end of the nineteenth century, became a significant forum for the development of feminism.[15]

During the mid-nineteenth century the change to a more progressive liberal government in the two-year period of the Bienio Progresista (1854–1856) led to further, although isolated, demands for women. Women played an important role as instigators and participants in social protests during this period of significant social and political change.[16] Steep increases in food prices and high unemployment led to numerous social protests and collective action. Many riots took place in central Spain; shops, factories, and houses were burnt in social disturbances. Rallying to the cries of "Freedom!" and "Bread!" women were significant actors in these protests. Their nurturing role in the family led to public involvement in social action centering on such issues as food supplies and fair prices. However, claims for specific women's rights were not formulated by these women activists. During this period working women were also dynamic in the Catalan labor movement, where they were a core workforce in the textile industries. Children's nurseries were included in the series of demands presented by Catalan workers to the central government in the course of social and labor conflicts.[17] On a more political level there is also some evidence of women mobilizing around specific female rights in this period. An unidentified program demanding suffrage for women of "integrity," participation in the "destiny of the nation," administration of property, the extinction of celibacy, the promotion of conjugal union, and the establishment of criminal regulations against "coquettes" appeared in the newspaper *La Unión Liberal* in September 1854.[18] However, as current research stands, there does not appear to be any connection among these isolated instances of female mobilization, collective action, and feminist demands.[19]

Another moment of significant political change was the Sexenio Democrático, when a modernizing, democratic political scenario provided greater interest in women's issues. The outcome of political unrest and the exile of Queen Isabelle II, this period of democracy spread liberal, bourgeois revolution and implemented liberal and democratic reforms.[20] This brief and fragile democratic experience also included the first switch from a monarchy to a republic in Spain with the establishment of the First Republic (1873–1874). The six years of radical political changes and social transformation heralded important advances in such areas of liberal democracy as freedom of speech, freedom of religion, and education. The provisional revolutionary government established universal male suffrage for the first time in Spain in October 1868, when all males over 25 were enfranchised. However, whatever improvements there were in the social condition of women cannot be attributed to policies geared to eliminate discrimination against them. Rather they were a result of the general revision of existing legislation. Thus, the introduction of civil as opposed to religious marriage resulted from dominant anticlerical feelings and the desire to separate church and state, not a reconsideration of married women's subordinate status. The articles of the new law on civil matrimony retained the clauses relating to female dependency, wives' obedience to husbands, and their obligation to obtain their husbands' permission for such crucial activities as the administration of their own personal belongings, legal transactions, and the publication of scientific or literary works. The liberal democratic governments were unsympathetic to women's demands, while the defenders of universal male suffrage failed to address the issue of female enfranchisement.[21]

Yet in the absence of women politicians, political reforms led some significant male politicians to inaugurate public discussion on what was conventionally known as the woman question. Francisco Pi y Margall, a noted federal republican and democrat, later elected president of the Federal Republic, in June 1873, addressed the issue of women in a lecture called *La misión de la mujer en la sociedad*, published in 1869.[22] He was a fervent advocate of the ethical and cultural renovation of Spain and within that framework admitted the civilizing and educational authority of women within the family. Women were defined as mother educators with a significant role in civilizing Spanish society. Civilization was, in fact, a key tenet in the gradual admission of women's rights. The notion that women were a vital civilizing influence in society was crucial to the gradual legitimation of feminism. However, influenced by Proudhon, like many progressive politicians of the day, Pi y Margall rejected women's right to waged work and their political emancipation.[23] He claimed that women working in factories could not attend correctly to their duties in the home and did not fulfill their educational duties to their children:

> Women . . . today leave the home for the workshop, and abandon their children to the care of others or even to themselves. Their love gets colder, their modesty diminishes, and the new generations whom they are called to educate grow up in isolation without any guidance or limits.[24]

This progressive politician admitted, however, that the political program of the federal republicans had few references to women except for the agenda to exclude them from subterranean work in the mines and to keep them from workshops and factories. Although he eventually recognized the need to develop reforms that would further women's emancipation, he did not elaborate on them.[25]

However, just as the principles of liberal democracy reached beyond the Pyrenees, so, too, did the ideas of liberal feminism. Rafael Maria de Labra, in his lecture "La mujer y la legislación castellana" applauded the petitions for female enfranchisement formulated by John Stuart Mill in Great Britain and proposed a similar electoral reform based on women's suffrage.[26] He contended that the law must not be conditioned by gender and that reforming the legal status of women was crucial for the progressive modernization of Spanish society. For many defenses of female emancipation, modernization was another key concept in the legitimation of feminism and was a significant vehicle to formulate the defense of women's rights. An exception among political reformers of the day, de Labra's voice was lost and concern for women's political enfranchisement was not placed on the political agenda in the nineteenth century, not even by most progressive politicians.

STATE BUILDING, POLITICAL CULTURE, AND
GENDER IDENTITY

In 1874 the coup d'etat of General Manuel Pavía put an end to the progressive politics of democratic revolution and to the political instability, social conflict, and civil war that had characterized the six years of the Sexenio Democrático. A year later the monarchy and Bourbon dynasty was restored. The Restoration initiated a long stage of political stability in Spain that lasted until the military coup of General Miguel Primo de Rivera in 1923. It is my contention that the experience of politics and gender culture throughout this period shaped the responses of Spanish women and their definition of feminism.[27]

The political system of the Restoration has been described as "oligarchical liberalism."[28] It was based on a formal liberal constitution under which corrupt political practices developed that changed the nature of the constitutional system. The practice of patronage (*caciquismo*), fraudulent elections, royal government appointments, and the maintenance of a minority elite power group reunited throne and church and operated to guarantee existing social structures and to impede access to power by progressive political forces.[29] Despite the reintroduction of universal male suffrage in 1890, the Restoration generated a political culture that discouraged most social groups from identifying with political struggles as a means to achieve their social advancement. More significantly, on the level of popular political culture, the experience of political malpractice disseminated the notion that political progress was not necessarily linked with political rights, thus creating disaffection with democratic values. The political fracturing of the Spanish state and its inability to achieve political cohesion through established political structures also influenced the choices women made in defining their strategies for emancipation. As I have argued elsewhere, the prevalent political culture led Spanish feminists to search for emancipation strategies that were not necessarily linked with political rights.[30] Indeed, political feminism and suffragism were of little relevance to the orientation of the women's movement in Spain in the period under consideration.[31]

The experience of predominant gender culture—domesticity, gender identity linked with motherhood, and female legal subordination—also conclusively shaped women's view of their paths to emancipation and their choice of strategies. The Constitution of 1876, sanctioning the alliance between throne and church, revoked previous legislation and reestablished legal norms in consonance with canonic law and patriarchal prerogatives, reinforcing traditional gender norms and roles. Still openly influenced by the Napoleonic Code, the Civil and Penal Code clearly established women's subordination. Married women were particularly constrained by existing legislation. For instance, Article 57 of the Civil Code (1889) established that "the husband must protect his wife and she must obey her husband." The husband was the administrator of the goods and chattels of the couple as well as the representative of his wife, who needed his permission to participate in any public act such as lawsuits, purchases, and sales (except those for normal family consumption) or any kind of contract (Articles 58–62). Women dedicated to business, shopkeeping, or commerce were totally dependent on the goodwill of their husbands, as their permission could be arbitrarily revoked at any time. Furthermore, women did not control their wages, which by law were administered by their husbands.[32]

According to the law any transgression of marital authority could be punished severely. Disobedience and verbal insults were sufficient motive to have a woman imprisoned, whereas a man was punished only if he openly ill-treated his wife (Penal Code, Article 603). The double moral standard was legally entrenched, as can be seen by the unequal gender treatment of crimes of passion and adultery. According to the Penal Code, the punishment of a husband who caught his wife in adultery and killed either her or the adulterer or caused them serious injury was banishment to a minimum radius of 25 kilometers from his legal address for a period that could vary from six months and a day to six years. If minor injuries were caused, the husband was exempt from punishment. For women who committed such crimes, the punishment was significantly more severe, as crimes of passion that resulted in the death of the husband were considered parricides and were punishable by life imprisonment (Penal Code, Article 238). Adultery also had different gender readings: an adulterous woman was subject to a prison sentence of two to six years, while a husband's infidelity was not even considered adultery unless he "had a concubine in the conjugal house or elsewhere" and furthermore had caused "public scandal" (Penal Code, Articles 448 and 452). According to gender norms of conduct reinforced by law, the double sexual standard was considered legitimate; only when the social institution of the family or public decorum was threatened by male behavior was it deemed necessary to restrain and punish the man. On the contrary, any woman, however discreet, who transgressed the gender sexual code was guilty of questioning male supremacy and a husband's right to control his wife's body and therefore considered a profound threat to the maintenance of the patriarchal family. Such deviant behavior was considered so threatening that it was explicitly punished by law. Through its legal system the state thus reinforced gender models of masculinity and femininity while establishing "honor" as one of the key concepts in the definition of male gender identity. Control of women's bodies together with parental and marital authority characterized the legal system that guaranteed the continuity of a highly stratified, patriarchal family. Legal endorsement of such discriminatory treatment of married women continued until the democratic legislative reforms introduced in the Second Republic during the 1930s.

Together with political culture, the major influence shaping Spanish women's choices and their definition of feminism was their gender identity. Acceptance of differential gender roles and the politics of maternalism led many women to legitimate their claims for rights on the basis of gender difference rather than equality.[33] Until the 1920s the women's movement embraced social rather than political feminism, focusing on demands within civil society and claiming rights primarily in the fields of education and paid work.

Gender discourse based on the ideology of domesticity, reinforced by church norms, regulated gender roles and appropriate female behavior. Gender cultural norms disseminated in the discourse of domesticity were a very forceful mechanism of informal social control that was even more powerful than the law in defining gender codes of conduct and women's role in society. The symbolical violence inherent in gender discourse also explains the uses of consent, the prevalence of correct gender conduct, and the choices women made concerning their strategies for emancipation.[34] Domesticity was the foundation of traditional gender discourse in Spain. Motherhood figured as the maximum horizon for women's self-fulfillment and social destiny. The models of the *Angel del Hogar* (Angel of the Hearth) and the *Perfecta Casada* (The Perfect Married Lady) generated the notion that women's ambitions had to be exclusively limited to good mothering and housewifery within the strict boundaries of home and family. Women's cultural identity thus derived from their biological distinction as mothers. The influence of gender cultural norms and women's experience of domesticity shaped Spanish women's formulation of feminism through the lens of gender difference.

THE FEMINIST AWAKENING

Despite severe restrictions and a strict implementation of gender roles in Spanish society, a number of individual women developed a feminist consciousness, and by voicing women's needs, they established an agenda for women's emancipation. Lawyer, prison reformer, philanthropist, and writer Concepción Arenal (1820–1893) from Galicia was one of the most outstanding feminists in the nineteenth century. Although not representative of most Spanish women, Arenal's views can give us a clue to the system of ideas against which Spanish women had to measure their behavior and to the meanings of their challenges or compliance. A convinced reformist liberal, Arenal espoused the moral reform of society and a radical change in individual mentality. She was a leading defender of women's rights, and her writings can be considered the foundational texts of modern Spanish feminism. A follower of liberal Enlightenment philosophy, she defined herself as a

"friend of progress" and espoused science, education, and culture as the ve-
hicles of material and moral progress, equality, and civilization. A radical humanist, she defended social reform, philanthropy, and ecumenical Chris-
tianism against the traditional tenets of Neocatholicism.[35] Social justice,
freedom, education as a social right, rationalism, and humanism characterized her agenda. Hers was one of the first clear voices raised in defense of
Spanish women and in establishing a feminist agenda. She was also an exceptional female figure in nineteenth-century Spanish society as she crossed
the boundaries of anonymity to become a woman of acknowledged public
recognition, and became an internationally known figure in the fields of
criminality and penitentiary reform.

Arenal had a clear notion of women's intellectual capacity. In an article
published in 1869 called "La mujer del porvenir" (Women of the Future), she
challenged prevalent scientific notions of women's innate physiological,
moral, and intellectual inferiority.[36] In an open debate on Gall's findings in
Physiologie du cerveau, a study based on craniology that was very popular in
Spain and one of the scientific foundations of the notion of women's inferiority, Arenal rejected his arguments and maintained that intelligence depend
on the quality and not the size of the brain. She contended that natural causes
were not the root of women's inferior cultural achievements, as female intellectual inferiority was not organic but cultural. In the 1880s the debate on
women's intellectual capacity continued. Then the women's journal *La Muger,*
published in Barcelona in 1882 under the motto "*La muger* will defend
women's rights," openly rejected the misogynous perspective of the theories of
Joaquin Galdieri and other scientists who maintained similar arguments on
women's natural inferiority. Therese de Coudray, director of the journal, rejected such claims as false and unscientific and contended that they were the
basis to justify women's social relegation in society.[37] The attention dedicated
to scientific debates defining gender roles, norms, and identities in this period
points to a significant turn, similar to that in other European countries, from
religious to scientific foundations of gender discourse.

EDUCATION AND WOMEN'S EMANCIPATION

In a comparative European framework, one of the key issues that marks
Spanish feminism is the problem of literacy and access to education. In the

course of the nineteenth century the advances in public instruction in other European countries such as France and Great Britain had led to a gradual leveling of differences in illiteracy between the sexes.[38] In Spain the overall quality of education was appalling, and female education notably worse. The deficiencies in the school system and the failure of educational reform resulted in extremely high illiteracy rates among the whole population, and gender differentials were clear, since female illiteracy rates were substantially and consistently higher than those of males. In 1860, 86 percent of the female population was illiterate; by the turn of the century this rate had been reduced to 71 percent, in contrast to the much lower male illiteracy rate of 56 percent. During the first decades of the twentieth century, there was a slow decrease in overall illiteracy, and by 1930, illiteracy figures had dropped to 48 percent female and 37 percent male: the level of illiteracy was still significantly high, affecting almost half the female population of Spain.[39]

According to Concepción Arenal differential gender access to education was the major cause of women's cultural inferiority. In line with Enlightenment thinkers and later twentieth-century feminists, Arenal placed education at the center of her feminist agenda. Writing at the close of the nineteenth century, she pointed out that "in the girls' schools (that is, when there are any) most of the time is spent on needlework, and only exceptionally does the schoolmistress know how to read with some sense, write correctly, and do the most elementary arithmetic."[40] Lack of access to education continued to reinforce traditional constraints on female cultural opportunities. The educational experience of Spanish women was a decisive factor in the historical development of their feminist agenda, which as late as the Civil War continued to define education for adult women as a priority goal.[41]

Arenal perceived education as a social question and saw it as a crucial means to achieve social progress. She clearly showed that it was in the overall interest of men and society in general for women to acquire an education. Moreover, she claimed that women had higher moral and humanistic values and that it was thus necessary for society to benefit from them.[42] The emergence of the concern for female education can also be attributed to the modernization of Spanish society and a growing awareness of the need for better educated mothers to carry out their task of socializing and educating their offspring. Mother educators in civic culture were a key factor in the development of modernity and progressive liberalism. Spanish liberalism identified education as the crucial area of the woman question. In fact, the major benefits for women in the period of the Sexenio Democrático derived from progress made in the field of education. Under the aegis of the reformist, progressive, anticlerical educational movement known as *Krausismo*, women's education was addressed as the most crucial dimension of women's issues. Progressive Krausismo has been identified by historians as one of the most significant strands of the Spanish liberal revolution.[43] It proposed a utopian pedagogics based on a rationalist, secular education that renovated approaches to education. It also encompassed female education in its overall reform. More radical in its initial years, this educational reform movement, later promoted by the Institución Libre de Enseñanza, founded in 1875, was a significant step toward modernizing and renovating the educational system. In its attempt to break with the traditional hegemony of the Roman Catholic Church in the field of education, it advocated progressive, secular, rationalist modern principles in education. The Krausistas and later the Institución Libre de Enseñanza played a crucial role in the development of education and liberal values in Spain in the late nineteenth century.

The Krausistas introduced Spain to the feminist debate by placing respect for the individual, tolerance, and education as the foundation for social transformation. Their view of education was a decided advance for female education, which, at the time, was primarily devoted to needlework, piety, deportment, and social behavior.[44] Nonetheless, it must also be said that Krausismo failed to present an overall critique of women's situation in Spanish society and did not represent an egalitarian view of education.[45] The Krausistas' conception of women's education was based on the traditional ideology of domesticity, oriented toward the improvement of women and a certain widening of their cultural horizons with a view to their achieving a better performance in their traditionally assigned roles of nurturance as wives and mothers. Fernando de Castro, then rector of the University of Madrid and one of the promoters of the *Conferencias Dominicales*, the Sunday Lectures dedicated to the education of women, made the goal of a differential educational gender model for women quite clear in his inaugural lesson:

> A woman is, in effect, a help to a man in the education of his children and when, as an industrious homemaker, she carries out the government of the interior of the home; she is also [a help] consoling and attending her husband in his old age and sickness; with her virtues, her grace, and

beauty, she is a powerful stimulation for his thought and work, as she inspires and foments his enthusiasm on the difficult and harsh path of life.[46]

Women were thus to be educated to fulfill their gender destiny in society as educated spouses, mothers, and nurturers. Women's education was targeted as a goal to achieve a civilizing influence in society, to educate "the only pure, honest, and pious" group left in the country,[47] and to promote a new gender model of an educated, cultured woman as the best way to achieve efficient household management and domesticity. Differential pedagogy and not an egalitarian educational focus was the core to a politically progressive but highly gendered educational reform movement which nonetheless played a decisive role in the improvement of women's education.

Some feminists challenged this differential educational model for women and the fact that by the end of the nineteenth century women were still being educated for "domestic utility."[48] In 1892, the writer, novelist, and feminist Emilia Pardo Bazán, with exceptional clearsightedness, vigorously denounced the utilization of women and the gender focus of female education: "The present-day education of women, in truth, cannot be called *education* as such," she caustically proclaimed. "Rather must it be called *taming*, as its proposed objective is obedience, passivity, and submission."[49] Pardo Bazán denounced the infantilism of Spanish women, who were confined to a state of frivolity and lack of ideals through the deprivation of education and culture which led them to a situation of inferiority and dependence contrived by men. The dissenting voice of this major writer claimed that women were victims of male politics and thus not responsible for their social condition.[50]

Less radical in feminist outlook, pedagogue Suceso Luengo de la Figuera was very active in the development of education for women in southern Spain at the turn of the century. She claimed that education could not be an exclusive male patrimony.[51] Highly influenced by the so-called Disaster of 1898, when Spain lost the last of its colonies—Cuba, Puerto Rico, Guam, and the Philippines—Luengo de la Figuera was very active within the regeneration groups that saw social pedagogy as the means to redeem and modernize Spain. In her view, women were central to this regenerational drive as mother educators in the civic culture. She clearly accepted women's traditional gender role as mothers but saw that educated mothers were needed in order to raise cultural levels in society:

The lack of culture in a mother, and specially, pedagogical ignorance, is of fatal consequence for her child, and thus for society, which may have educated, erudite, wise beings, but without the virtues and generous energy that as a supreme goal in life can only be inspired by the soul of an intelligent and enlightened mother.[52]

Women's emancipation was constantly linked with their right to education, which was perceived as the key to social progress and therefore beneficial for society as a whole. Educated mothers were seen as key tools to achieving the regeneration and civilization of Spanish society. The women's journal *La Muger* defended this social view of women's education as a general civilizing force. However, it also clearly saw education as a significant tool in the "dignification" of women and the improvement of their social status. Feminists rejected prevalent stereotypes of women as feeble, inconsistent by nature, and incapable of an independent moral existence outside male tutelage. However, they also functioned within the parameters of a gender compliance that saw education as a reinforcement of women's gender role as mothers, defined as women's "sacred mission" in life.

FEMINIST EXPECTATIONS AND THE EMPOWERMENT OF WOMEN

A small number of feminists challenged the constraints of predominant gender codes by claiming a role for women well beyond the private sphere of home and family. Writing in 1893 in the *Boletín de la Institución Libre de Enseñanza*, Berta Wilhelmi openly defended women's rights to culture, education, science, and professional employment: "If women, in their own right, claim the right to all professions, to participate in the conquests of science, to cooperate in social problems, we believe that they demand what is just: they claim the rehabilitation of half of humanity."[53] Some nineteenth-century feminists, such as Concepción Arenal and Emilia Pardo Bazán, came to demand the recognition of women as individuals who were not exclusively defined by their gender function as mothers and wives. In 1881 Concepción Arenal published *La mujer de su casa* (The Housewife), where she challenged the prevalent gender discourse that identified women as mothers and spouses only. Neither the Angel del Hogar nor the Perfecta Casada could be the basis for Arenal's definition of the housewife.[54] In line with her individualist liberal approach, Arenal perceived women primarily as persons undetermined by their gender roles. She advocated both in her writings and in her everyday life that women had to aim to be more than wives and mothers. "It is a grave error and one of the most harmful," she argued in her report presented at the Pedagogical Congress in 1892, "to inculcate women with the idea that their sole mission is that of being a wife and mother: it is the equivalent of telling them that by themselves they cannot be anything, and of annihilating their moral and intellectual *self* by training them with depressing absurdities for the great struggle of life." She went on to urge that women "must first affirm their personality, independent of their state, and persuade themselves that, single, married, or widowed, they have duties to carry out, rights to vindicate, a job to do. . . . Life is something serious, and if they take it as a game they will be unremittingly treated as a toy."[55] Arenal urged the public recognition of the dignity of women and saw education as the tool to developing their self-esteem. The empowerment of women as individuals was crucial in Arenal's definition of feminism. She argued the centrality of women in life and society and espoused the cultural and social promotion of women not just as mothers and spouses but as individuals. In her view women had first to achieve perfection as persons, and then they would be better mothers:

> When they are more perfect persons, they will be better mothers, because the perfection of the mother, like the father, cannot consist in the partial application of certain human elements, but the total of all that constitutes women and men, as intelligent and affectionate beings.[56]

The contradiction between the attempt by men to "belittle and put down women" while at the same time venerating the figure of the mother[57] was another target for attack by Arenal, as were traditional religious views on women's exclusive restriction to the home. However, Arenal did not openly challenge gender roles. She claimed new employment and cultural openings for single women, but in consonance with their "natural sweetness."[58] Suceso Luengo de la Figuera also challenged the empty role of the affluent, frivolous, lazy, and traditional bourgeois women in Andalusia and suggested to them new educational and cultural outlets. However, like Concepción Arenal, she saw women's basic social role in matrimony, within the family. Still profoundly influenced by traditional gender discourse, most nineteenth-century feminists accepted differential gender roles and even a distinct feminine nature. Yet at the same time they challenged women's subservience to these roles as individuals. Their view of women's emancipation realized the paradox of sentimental dependence and moral independence. As Arenal clearly stated in her definition of an agenda for women's emancipation:

> For women we want the dependence of affection, not that which nature has established by making her weaker, more long-suffering, and more impressionable; but we refuse dependence based on unjust laws, on immoral or absurd customs, or the misery of those who have no means to make an indispensable living; we want the independence of dignity, the moral independence of a rational and responsible being; for we are persuaded that women's happiness is not in independence but in affection, in loving and being loved, pleasing her husband, brother, and child.[59]

Emancipation for nineteenth-century feminists in Spain did not imply challenging maternalism and women's domestic role.

Education was fundamental to women's definition of strategies for emancipation. However, some voices were raised in defense of legal reform, particularly regarding the elimination of discrimination against married women. Priority was given to improving the civil status of women and eliminating obstacles to paid employment and professions for single women. As early as 1869 Concepción Arenal had pointed out the incoherence in the legal system that made "the most virtuous and enlightened woman by law inferior to the most vicious and ignorant man."[60] By the early twentieth century, legal reform, particularly regarding women's marital status, was being demanded by women writers such as Concepción Gimenez de Flaquer and Carmen de Burgos. However, although claims were made for legal equality, particularly for an improvement in the status of married women, women did not promote the enactment of legislation to provide female suffrage. In 1891 Pardo Bazán translated John Stuart Mill's *On the Subjection of Women*; the book was published as *La esclavitud femenina* (Female Slavery) in the collection *La Biblioteca de la Mujer* (The Women's Library).[61] Bázan had indignantly pointed out in 1890 that many of the cultural and political advances achieved in the nineteenth century had increased the distance between the sexes: "Freedom to teach, freedom to worship, the right to hold meetings, suffrage, and parliamentarism have been used [by men] so that half of society gains in strength and activities at the expense of the female half."[62] The achievement of political rights for women did not figure on the agenda of nineteenth-century women feminists. Pardo Bazán's mistrust of politics reflects the general political culture of the time and the experience of politics that led to disaffection with democracy and political rights.[63] The journal *La Muger* warned quite clearly that women's participation in politics was not among its goals of women's emancipation.[64] Nineteenth-century Spanish feminists were not suffragist, and their resistance strategies did not include the struggle for female enfranchisement. Undoubtedly influenced by their experience of political culture in Spain, Spanish women did not demand political rights. As Adolfo Posada, a male advocate of feminism, wrote in 1899, "The concession of the vote to women, even in local elections, is so far from predominant public opinion on women's political capacity that it is not even an issue in Spain."[65]

Women also formulated claims for emancipation based on civil rights and empowerment through the achievement of dignity and self-esteem. Literary feminists defended women's right to express themselves even when that meant transgressing gender norms of female silence or speaking out in public on topics that were not traditionally open to discussion by women. Galician poet Rosalía de Castro (1837–1885) voiced the problems of transgression and female identity when women writers accepted their subjectivity and expressed their individuality in a society that condemned them to silence:

> D'aquelas que cantan as pombas y as frores
> todos din que teñen alma de muller
> pois eu que n'as canto, Virxe d'a Paloma,
> ¡Ay! ¿de qué'a terei?
>
> *(Women who sing of doves and flowers,*
> *everyone says they have the soul of a woman,*
> *but I who do not sing of them, Virgin of the Dove,*
> *Oh! what is mine [my soul]?)*[66]

The women's journal *La Muger* survived through only nine numbers (1882–1883) and its increasingly conservative approach points not only to economic difficulties but to the hostility existing in Spanish society to women's collective initiatives in defense of their rights. Therese de Coudray, the director of *La Muger*, called for women's collective emancipation, writing "Nobody better than ourselves can desire our own emancipation. We are women, we know the physical and moral state of our sex, and we understand that there is no greater level of emancipation than that which admits our capacity to consider ourselves collectively."[67] However, there were few statements that evoked women as a collective, and even towards the end of the century, though individual voices discussing emancipation were isolated, women's emancipation continued to be framed in terms of the individual.[68]

Until the turn of the century, women's emancipation and rights were the concepts used to identify women's issues. However, in 1899 the term feminism became more generalized in Spanish society in journals and the press. The major impulse in the generalization of the term can be attributed to the publication of the book *Feminismo* by Adolfo Posada, jurist, university professor, defender of women's rights—the Spanish equivalent of John Stuart Mill. Dedicated to former pupils of the Institución Libre de Enseñanza, Posada's book was based on a series of articles previously published in *La España Moderna*. This book, with the authority of a male academic, legitimized the claims of feminism much more effectively than existing female voices. By 1915 feminism was being discussed in such distinguished official institutions as the Barcelona Academy of Jurisprudence and Legislation.[69] By then, too, the term feminism had become socialized and was adopted by a number of women, for instance, used openly by Catalan women to define their movement for emancipation.[70] By the early twentieth century in the new social and political context of modernization, Catalan and Basque nationalism,[71] labor and social movements, and changes in economic and demographic patterns, women shaped new and plural definitions of feminism and organized collectively to achieve emancipation. Like their nineteenth-century foremothers, twentieth-century feminists had choices and goals that were shaped by the boundaries of their political, social, and cultural experience as women.

CHAPTER 14

National and Gender Identity in Turn-of-the-Century Greece

ELENI VARIKAS

The emergence, in the late eighteenth century, of national consciousness among the Greek populations of the Ottoman Empire was marked by the development, diffusion, and reelaboration of French Enlightenment ideas. It was in the name of liberty, equality, and self-determination that the Society of Friends prepared the ground for the 1821 Revolution. In reinterpreting these ideas, patriotic propaganda developed around a fundamental opposition between the "obscurantism" and "barbarity" of the Ottoman rule and the ideals of liberty, civilization, and progress represented by the Greek people, whose glorious ancestors had invented democracy. The opposition was reinforced by a discourse of romantic philhellenism that popularized the Greek cause within international public opinion, or, according to the favorite expression of the time, within "the civilized world."

Stressing the superiority of national identity, this process of differentiation opened new possibilities for a redefinition of gender identities. Though the ancient distinction separating a Greek from a barbarian had never entailed women, early revolutionaries such as Rhigas Ferraios, the author of the Balkan Charta, had outlined the possibility of a citizenship based on equality between the sexes, including training in arms and education for both men and women. For Rhigas, education was not just a right but a "duty for all without exception."[1] Formulated in a universal language, appeals of the first revolutionary governments to the people declared that the fatherland was in urgent need of "virtuous and cultivated human beings" and urged parents to send "their beloved children—boys and girls" to school.[2] The Parthenon School for females, established in 1825–1826, was organized according to the principle of "self-government" in order to "prepare students for the duties of a good citizen." According to its founder, Nikitopoulos, a school was a nation in miniature; its organization should resemble the political system of a nation, so that the pupil gets used, at an early age, to govern and be governed according to the law.

However, the idea that women's participation in the nation implied training in citizenship was by no means shared by the majority of the Greek insurgents. Despite the considerable participation of women in the Revolution, traditional gender hierarchies were not fundamentally changed. While there were prominent women commanders such as Lascarina Bouboulina and Mado Mavroyenous, who figured importantly in romantic literature and iconography, haunted the national legends, and fascinated the imagination of European philhellenists, most of the women fighters fought under the strict control of the male heads of their households and were excluded from any decision-making. This was probably why their exclusion from citizenship, after the proclamation of independence, met with little resistance. When Mado Mavroyenous, having spent her huge fortune for the Revolution, asked to be integrated, with the rest of the officers, in the new national army, she was offered a widow's pension or an invalid's indemnity: "as if my services to the fatherland were of another nature than that of the others, as if the nation in its appeals and decrees had ever made any distinction between men and women serving in the military field."[3]

The domestic and international context in which national identity was constructed after the proclamation of independence (1827) increasingly favored a clear-cut differentiation of the nation's expectations of men's and women's capacities and roles. The absolute dependence of the country on the three "protecting powers," England, France, and Russia, the imposition of a Bavarian king and court, and the brutality of cultural and institutional westernization resulted in a deep crisis of identity which weighed heavily on the new gender relations.

The need for differentiation from the Orient was felt all the more as interest in the Greek cause faded away and as the gap between the modest, oriental reality of the small independent nation and the romantic anticipations of the resurrection of ancient Greece became visible. Even the Greeks from the diaspora who came to settle in Athens could hardly hide their disappointment at the sight of this small, semidestroyed village and its oriental inhabitants who seemed so far from corresponding to the civilizing mission assigned to them. It is not a coincidence that the first theories on the "definitive extinction of the glorious race of Greeks" appeared during the decade following the formation of an independent Greek nation. Their initiator, the German historian J. P. Falmerayer, had formerly described modern Greeks as "the descendants of precisely the same men who had struggled in Plataia and Salamina for the liberty of humankind,"[4] but he was now arguing that modern Greeks were mere "albanized" tribes without a single drop of pure Greek blood, and therefore could not claim any continuity with ancient Greeks.[5] For all his "scholarly" biological, linguistic, and cultural argumentation, Falmerayer could not hide his disillusionment with modern Greece's "inability to become Westernized."[6]

Challenging one of the rare sources of national pride during the first decades of independence, Falmerayer's theories constituted a deep trauma whose long-standing effects may easily be traced even in the present nationalist delirium over the Macedonia question. In fact, Falmerayer's case was based on a misinterpretation. Far from being an advocate of Pan-Slavism, as his Greek opponents would have it, Falmerayer stressed modern Greeks' inability to westernize only to prove their incapacity to contain the "Slav danger." This misinterpretation was favored by the fact that actually only a handful of German-speaking Greeks ever read his book (which was not translated until 1989). Yet it was largely in reaction to his presumed "Greek-hating Pan-Slavism" that national ideology was (and is being) constructed in modern Greece. This implied a systematic repression of everything that, in the official culture, recalled the recent "oriental" past, everything that could compromise the idea that Greeks were part of the "civilized" West. But nationalist ideology also implied a hurt distrust of the "bloody Francs" (Europeans), a necessary, if contradictory, ingredient of westernization.

The humiliation of dependence, the disillusionment of people who saw their long struggle end up in this tiny state governed by the Bavarians, and the systematic depreciation of popular culture engendered bitter reactions against the brutal invasion of western culture imposed both by the court and the Greek bourgeoisie of the diaspora, anxious to initiate these awkward citizens into European "decency."[7] In this context, the strengthening of traditional gender values offered a palliative for the humiliated national pride and, at the same time, a privileged realm of resistance to the invasion of foreign standards of behavior. Amid the impossibility of successfully contesting the dominating policies of the court or the foreign embassies, one could denounce instead the invasion of European dances that permitted "anybody to hold our women in his arms," as a popular hero of the Revolution complained.[8] Throughout the century, the discourse of resistance to the cultural hegemony of the West was largely based on references to sexual morals. The defense of Greek women's virtue offered one of the rare realms of social consensus and national cohesion.[9] Moreover, this discourse constructed a set of gendered images asserting the manly superiority of local morals as opposed to the degeneracy of western ones: shaving, using cosmetics, or wearing the western waistcoat became signs of effeminacy, provoking mirthful boos from the street crowds against foreign visitors and local bourgeois men.

National identity was thus constructed through a complex and often contradictory process of differentiation which situated gender at the center of national self-definition and its (in)stability: differentiation from the "Turk," the barbarian par excellence, to whom the Greek opposed "his" rootedness in western civilization; differentiation from the licentious and effeminate "Franc" (the European), to whom the Greek opposed "his" healthy national traditions; differentiation between feminine and masculine through the association of the former with the negative aspects both of the West (immodesty, luxury, moral levity) and of the Orient (ignorance, backwardness, irrationalism) and association of the latter with the positive aspects of both western and national traditions.

The crucial importance of the national question in the development of nineteenth-century Greek society made such differentiations central to gender identities. These antitheses largely shaped women's negative image and subordinate position in the new society while at the same time opening new educational and professional possibilities, especially for women of the urban petite bourgeoisie and professional middle classes.[10] The revival of nationalism at the end of the nineteenth century widened such possibilities. The crisis and imminent disintegration of the Ottoman Empire reactivated the national Great Idea, whose expression was summed up in the ancestral dream of taking back Constantinople. To the irredentist aspirations of liberating the Greek populations still under Ottoman rule were added the expansionist projects of the bourgeoisie aiming at the creation of a Greater Greece through the annexation of the areas around the Aegean Sea. The Greeks were invested with the great civilizing mission of diffusing western cultural values, the assumed continuation of classical Greek civilization, throughout the Orient. This perspective opposed Greeks to the other Balkan peoples (Bulgarians, Albanians, Serbs) who were contesting the territorial possessions of the "Great Sick Man of Europe."

In this context, the symbolic status and social position of women became important stakes. Women were not only the potential producers of soldiers but also the depositaries of an oral tradition "uncontaminated by external influences." Most of all they were the untarnishable source of the true national language, the language of the people, the mother tongue. As the language question gained importance and became intimately linked to the national question, women were situated at the center of national(ist) strategies. "The only truth is the hatred each Greek vows to the Turk and the love for his fatherland and for the language in which his mother talked to him when he was a child," declared Jean Psychari, the leading figure of the language-reform movement (demoticist), one of the most influential figures of the turn of the century. For "what the army does with the national frontiers, the language can do for the spiritual frontiers."[11] Indeed, the language spoken by the populations of the contested territories of Macedonia and Thracia would obviously weigh heavily on the final attribution of these areas. Instruction of mothers in the Greek language would enable them to transmit this language to their children. Furthermore, women's education could provide the newly established Greek schools of the Ottoman Empire with abundant and cheap labor. Thus, from the last quarter of the nineteenth century, hundreds of young female teachers (often 15 or 16 years old) were sent to the most remote parts of Macedonia, Thracia, and Asia Minor to diffuse the "Greek lights" among populations often unwilling to receive those "lights," let alone "relearn" their presumed mother tongue. Torn by opposing nationalisms, these people considered this crusade of hellenization a major threat to their own strategies.[12]

It was in this context that the first feminist collective in Greece was formed by women of the urban petite bourgeoisie and professional middle classes, mainly school teachers. The first wave of Greek feminists developed around a well-read (5000 copies) weekly, the *Ladies' Newspaper*. For twenty years (1887–1907) this publication fought for equal educational and professional opportunities, civil rights, and, to a lesser extent, political rights. But most of all, the *Ladies' Newspaper* fought to develop women's confidence in the possibility of self-emancipation and to persuade a part of (male) public opinion that gender equality was a necessary condition for the fulfillment of national destinies. This elaboration of a positive gender identity implied a critical distance from and revision of national(ist) ideology, while at the same time reactivating or reproducing some of the major assumptions and oppositions on which this ideology was based. Nationalism provided feminists with arguments in favor of women's emancipation but also with a model for the construction of collective identity that marked both the critical potential and limitations of early Greek feminism.

"One of the tasks of the *Ladies' Newspaper* is to turn whole libraries upside down in search of historical arguments in favor of our sex."[13] The privileged status of history in the feminist discourse largely confirmed this statement, published in the sixth-anniversary issue of the *Ladies' Newspaper*. This generation of Greek feminists lived in the midst of passionate disputes over the interpretation of the past, and they did not underestimate the powerful legitimating function of history. "Though our sex has played a major part in national history," they argued, "historical tradition has only included men's action."[14]

Giving back to women the place they occupied in the struggle for national liberation constituted an early concern of the journal. References to the heroic feats of the women of Souli, to the leading military services of Bouboulina and Mado Mavroyenous, and to the crucial role played, in the development of militant philhellenism, by the Greek *salonnières* of Italy verified the tradition in which women were active makers of history. At the same time, the journal underlined the injustice of a patriarchal order which had excluded half of the Greek nation from the right to self-determination.

The reconstitution of a women's collective memory concerned not just the recent past of national revolution but all of human history, where examples could be found of women's contributions. Greek and Roman antiquity, Byzantium, the western Middle Ages, and the French Revolution were turned into new fields of confrontation with patriarchy and its male-centered tradition. Out of this confrontation emerged the first team of "specialists" in women's history, including Callirhoi Parren, the leading figure of turn-of-the-century feminism herself. Greek women's was an epic history, largely inspired in its methods and assumptions by contemporary historical approaches that stressed the continuity of the race as well as by an unselfconscious tendency to trespass the borderline between history and mythology. Substituting "women's exploits" for "men's exploits," women's historiography encompassed diverse mythical and historical figures, from the Virgin Mary to the queens of Byzantium, from Sappho to Boer women, all of whom challenged the claim that men were the sole makers of history and civilization.

Besides this history of "outstanding women," there was also a critical re-reading of the past, based on the assumption that gender antagonisms and male domination were factors which necessarily determined interpretations of historical facts and informed the creation of myths. This approach attained some moments of remarkable originality. Examples are the interpretations of Greek tragedy and mythology written by the famous educator Sapho Leon-dias at the end of her life. Unlike most of her contemporaries, Leondias thought myths were not mere descriptions of historical facts reported by oral tradition. They were to be read as creations of the social imagination, significant of intentions, desires, or fears of the times in which they appeared. For instance, the myth of the birth of the Greek goddess Athena did not necessarily "prove" the exceptional character of women's wisdom in ancient Greece, as the dominant tradition would have it. Rather it suggested the patriarchal character of ancient Greek society, which could not accept Wisdom being represented by an ordinary woman. According to Leondias, this explained the creation of a motherless Athena and the disappearance of her real mother, the wise Metis, reported by earlier traditions:

> This might account for the invention of a Zeus cruelly devouring his first wife Metis, the real mother of Athena; the goddess of Wisdom and Courage could then spring from the male head of the king of gods. And how many mortal husbands in that period would not, if they could, devour their own wives, those in particular who were wiser than themselves, as was the case with this first mythic Metis?[15]

The feminist reevaluation of the past did not merely redress the male-centered perceptions of women in history. It put forward alternative human values whose historical bearers were women. The cult of male violence was systematically criticized and the value of war heroism constantly relativized. According to Callirhoi Parren, "woman is not born to exercise the bloody activity of war, imposed by the avidity of the powerful." But, she added, "each time this is necessary, women of the temper of Bouboulina are ready to arise."[16] It is significant, though, that what was celebrated in the person of Bouboulina was not so much her military courage but her intervention, after the conquest of Tripolis, in favor of the women and children of Hoursit Pasha's harem. After a long and extremely murderous siege of Tripolis, in which Bouboulina lost her beloved son, the Greek army triumphantly entered the city and gave itself over to savage reprisals against the Turkish population. "Defying the revengeful wrath of Greek and Albanian soldiers, who considered [the enemy's women] their rightful prey," Bouboulina stood up alone "with drawn sword" and managed to save "her unfortunate sisters."[17] This episode, quoted only by women historians, is significant of the critical dynamics of feminist reevaluation of national history and the break it introduced in the homogeneous representation of Greeks fighting for freedom against Turkish barbarians.

The constitution of a female collective memory allowed the creation of a distinct social category with its own contribution to civilization, its own struggles, and its own historical interests. History provided a locus for the denunciation of male domination and the celebration of resistance. It showed the diverse and therefore alterable character of the relation between the sexes, and it located the causes of gender oppression not in the natural inferiority of women but in the evolution of the woman question. Far from being inscribed in nature, women's inferior status was the product of patriarchal power which had deformed the natural order. Woman was a creature deformed by men's laws and traditions, to the detriment of her happiness and of men's as well.

Drawing on the ideology of natural rights as it had shaped the revolutionary discourse against Ottoman tyranny, Callirhoi Parren used its oppositions to reread the past from the perspective of gender antagonism. The mighty, she said, had abused their power, and the weak had started looking for means of reducing their suffering and combating the oppression and cruelty of their tyrannical masters. This was the start of the struggle between the sexes, a struggle all the more desperate and merciless since the weapons were unequal and the enemies joined to each other with powerful bonds. History was thus turned into a battlefield and gender antagonism into a universal key to its interpretation. Yet if "male egotism and domination marked the history of all peoples," didn't that mean that patriarchy was a historical inevitability? In a period when historical determinism was a dominant intellectual trend and when historical race theories were increasingly summoned up to legitimate the great idea of the nation and its historical mission, Greek feminists became increasingly engaged in finding a "solid foundation on which the New Woman [could] establish the edifice of her regeneration and, through her, the regeneration of humankind."[18] This quest took up a theme developed by early nineteenth-century Greek nationalism and reactivated in the context of late nineteenth- and early twentieth-century irredentism: the appeal to the historical existence of a paradise lost which legitimated the possibility of its resurrection.[19]

Indeed, from the 1890s on, there were abundant references in the feminist press to a golden age which had supposedly preceded patriarchy. This notion was increasingly used in the debates of the public sphere as an argument against the inescapability of gender asymmetry. If a social order without gender oppression had existed in the remote past, didn't that prove that inequality between the sexes could be abolished once more in the future? Greek feminists were familiar with the abundant literature on the matriarchy. Studies such as Bachofen's *Das Mutterrecht* (1861), Letourneau's *L'évolution du mariage et de la famille* (1888), or MacLennan's *Studies in Ancient History*, quoted by Callirhoi Parren,[20] were known to the Greek cultivated public, especially the intellectual circles, to which a large number of feminists belonged. Regardless of the historical validity of such theories, what is of interest are the ways in which they were used to elaborate a feminist vision of history, or rather of human evolution.

What fascinated Parren and the other feminists, more than the idea of a reign of women, was the idea of a reign of female values. For them, transition from polyandry to the "matriarchal family" was "the first step of humanity towards civilization, the first step which differentiated the human being from the brute."[21] And this step was taken by woman, "in whom emerged for the first time the feeling of . . . maternal love" that pushed her "to defend her infant from the savage instincts of man."[22]

> Paternity did not yet exist, the polyandry rendering impossible the search for the father. The mother, however, this great creator and reformer of the world, caressed and kissed the creature she bore in her arms. . . . And little by little she communicated to it the exquisite feeling of love.[23]

Matriarchy offered a historical foundation to the civilizing potential of maternal love and female qualities; it designated women as a collective subject and made of their first opposition against male "savage instincts" a founding act of civilization. Inverting the traditional meaning of original sin, this view testified to the existence of an era when women still had all their human dignity. Through the myth of an original state of nature, a state of equity and innocence, Eve was transformed from the first temptress into the first victim.[24] Of course the image of nature as a generous *magna mater* was already included in the logic of natural law,—at least its optimistic versions. After all, as Ernst Bloch has pointed out, "what the optimists of nature put forward is neither bestial nature nor nature as a perfect mathematical law but rather nature matriarchal."[25] What was new, however, was the development of a vision which evaluated history "according to an idolatry of sex difference."[26]

An illustration of this vision is the insistence on certain themes of Greek mythology. In a series of articles published in December 1900, the editor of the *Ladies' Newspaper* developed an analysis of the myth related to the contest between Poseidon and Athena over the protection of Attica and the naming of Athens. It was the women of Athens, she argued, who voted in favor of the goddess of wisdom and who, being a majority, assured her victory. "Dreaming of a peaceful life,"[27] they preferred Athena's promises of wisdom, peace, and prosperity to Poseidon's promises of power and glory. Infuriated, the god of the sea inundated the plain of Attica with sea water. To calm his furor, "women had to be punished: they were deprived of the right to vote; they lost the status of free citizens and the right to transmit their name to their children."[28] This myth, "one of the most fascinating and the most relevant to our way of thinking,"[29] was used by Parren as an allegory of the historical defeat of women:

> Several centuries went by. The sacred tree of peace had been forgotten. . . . The city of Athena was bathed in the blood of its children. In this place, where gods had established their thrones, one could see only ruins. Athena the peaceful goddess was transformed into a bloodthirsty warrior participating in human sacrifice. Women were sent back home and condemned to their looms for having dared to vote for a peaceful future. . . . And little by little, they were carried away by the fury of human sacrifice and gradually forgot their vocation. Instead of giving their children, together with life, a craving for happiness, they were preparing them for death.[30]

The transformation of the dispute between Athena and Poseidon into a confrontation between feminine and masculine principles in history was typical of the effort to elaborate a female cultural tradition, a tradition which defined women's opposition to male values as a redemptive power. Athena was no longer the hybrid goddess who, according to the dominant tradition, had sprung, perfectly armed, from her father's head. She was Πολιος (protector of the city) and Εργανη (industrious), the symbol of wisdom, peace, and prosperity—the attributes she had inherited from Metis, her devoured mother. Her transformation to Αθηνα Προμαχος (fighting on the first line) had marked the defeat of her feminine attributes, her submission to the warlike masculine values that had made her forget her peaceful vocation. And this defeat, which was at the same time the defeat of civilization and humanity, was precisely the result of women's loss of political rights and the triumph of "human sacrifice over happiness."

The dispute of Athena and Poseidon situated women at the center of the national heritage while at the same time challenging the unified representation of such a heritage. In a historical moment when the resurgence of the national question in the Balkans reactivated the memories of past glories and victories over the "barbarians"; when Greek women's duty to bear future soldiers capable of liberating their unredeemed brothers of the Ottoman Empire appeared as an undisputed urgency; when the major national poet (and close friend of Callirhoi Parren), Costis Palamas, celebrated the courage of Spartan mothers ready to "throw their beloved children in the abyss of war,"[31] Parren's critical opposition to women's transformation into "cannon fodder machines" was not a slight heresy. Her articles provoked an outcry among the Athenian intellectuals. "Women are biased; instead of debating with objectivity, they become advocates of their sex," accused the distinguished novelist Antonios Matesis from the tribune of Parnassos, the most prestigious cultural association of Athens.[32] At the same time the editorialist of an important daily newspaper, *Estia*, set out to refute the positions of the *Ladies' Newspaper* on feminine qualities by putting forward the savage cruelty of the Amazons who killed their own sons.[33] "We never implied that women have always been angels and men bloodthirsty monsters," replied Callirhoi Parren in the *Ladies' Newspaper*.

As for the Amazons—if they ever existed—their reign must have been situated around the end of the matriarchal era when men might have attempted to change the regime. It is possible that the most courageous women took arms to defend their rights and privileges in danger. . . .

Anyway, there is only one conclusion that may be drawn from this tradition: women declined and were submitted to slavery when . . . they
took arms to shed blood . . . , when instead of preaching the Bible of
love and solidarity between the peoples, as the emancipated women do
now, they were seduced by the quest for tyrannical power and started
imitating men.[34]

While the interpretation of the past offered a positive vision of women as
a group, it also entailed a revaluation of the present and a legitimation of future struggles. Feminist celebration of the maternal right did not give way,
as was the case with Bachofen, to nostalgic evocations of a past gone forever.
In the *Ladies' Newspaper* nostalgia for the past was turned into utopian aspi-
ration for a future without violence and oppression, a future which would
somehow repair and resurrect the past. What made this attainable for Greek
feminists was their unwavering faith in the ineluctable triumph of progress
and reason. For them the course of progress did not imply the end of the
qualitative values of the remote past but, on the contrary, constituted the
supreme promise of their realization in the future. In a controversy with the
eminent jurist A. Petalas, who claimed women's emancipation would develop criminality, the *Newspaper* replied:

But how could it be that the triumph of a truth might have harmful
consequences for society? . . . Progress, the development of humankind
according to the laws of nature and morality, develops together with the
good. . . . Truth, according to the eternal moral laws, is virtue. How could
they possibly harm society?[35]

This unshakable faith in the development of humankind according to the
laws of nature and morality provided feminists an argument of weight in favor of women's emancipation:

How can one expect our fatherland to progress and develop in the hands
of political leaders whose spirit bears the stamp of oriental domination?
These are men who are marked by the egotism inherited from the barbarian conquerors and who consider women—including their mothers
and sisters—to be mere *odalisques*.[36]

Arguments of this kind made women's emancipation a prerequisite for
progress and development of the fatherland. At the same time, the oriental

metaphors invading the feminist discourse, the images of "harems," "sera-glios," and "blinds" that had to be torn down, took up the opposition "ob-scurantism–Orient–Turks" versus "progress–Western world–Greeks" and ex-tended it to the field of gender antagonism. In doing so, feminists effected a radical reversal in the dominant hierarchy of values associated with this op-position: men, in their quality of oppressors, were now on the side of barbar-ity and backwardness, and women, as a collective subject fighting for free-dom, represented progress and civilization. This vision was often extended to the whole world. Celebrating the Chicago International Conference of Women of 1900, the *Ladies' Newspaper* described the participants as "a part of the huge female army which is transforming the face of the modern world . . . ," an *avant-garde* "who *announced* to the community of women, still *unaware* of their power, what they could accomplish not only for women but for all humankind."[37]

The identification of women's emancipation with emancipation of hu-mankind was deeply rooted in a perception of time which embraced past, present, and future in a single messianic movement. This bears a striking re-semblance to Walter Benjamin's "messianic time," which characterizes the historical viewpoint of the defeated:[38]

> There is only one element *today* capable of stopping the impetuous stream
> of social decline: woman's renaissance. Woman, who until *yesterday* . . .
> was erring in the obscurity of ignorance, who ignored her great human
> mission . . . stands against the impetuous course of egotism and personal
> interest. . . . Woman is the rear guard which providence has been keeping
> in the background, passive and humiliated, to make her emerge from
> obscurity in the midst of social decadence.[39]

This soteriological claim, which accompanies the *Ladies' Newspaper* throughout the twenty years of its publication, is according to Max Weber a major characteristic of the self-esteem of underprivileged social groups, pre-cisely those who feel an earnest need for salvation:

> The hunger for a worthiness that has not fallen to their lot, they and the
> world being what it is, produces this conception from which is derived
> the idea of providence, a significance in the eyes of some divine authority
> possessing a scale of values different from the one operating in the world
> of man.[40]

The religiosity of salvation goes back to the Judeo-Christian heritage and its promise that "the last shall be the first."[41] In the case of the *Ladies' Newspaper*, however, these references appear in an otherwise nonreligious discourse, which frequently attacks the misogyny of the fathers of the church and does not hesitate to call upon science to disqualify the biblical version of original sin.[42] But this approach is not necessarily incompatible with a religiosity specific to ideologies of the chosen people, as found in various nonreligious national or class movements.[43] Indeed, the only religious references one can find in the *Newspaper* are those which assert the providential role "the humble, the sick, the victims of injustice, fishermen, and women" are called to play "in the triumph of truth and justice."[44]

It is noteworthy that such an eschatology of salvation presents women as both the subjects and the means of salvation. The "triumph of truth and justice" is at the same time the triumph of women's emancipation and the victory of civilization over barbarity. This ambiguity is according to Weber a major trend in the self-representation of pariah peoples, for it permits a double restitution of the oppressed group's dignity: not only will women be liberated from their humiliating position, since they are called to salvation, but they will bring about the salvation of all humankind.[45] This offers the unprivileged—women in our case—a means to replace "what they cannot claim to be by the worth of that which they will one day become, to which they will be called in some future life, here or hereafter."[46] In other words, the present situation of women, their despised otherness, and their centuries-long oppression are turned into signs of redemption, into privileges (Weber uses the term negative privileges), into guarantees of their promotion to the status of historical subjects. Indeed, their long exclusion from power is interpreted as a radical lack of responsibility for the present evils of society:

> Since the beginning of Greece, the archaic or colonial Greece, the free Greece and the enslaved, it is man who has been maintaining the government, hegemony, tyranny, and absolute power. It is man and not woman. Therefore, if social affairs are badly run, it is the governing and not the governed who bear the responsibility.[47]

To underline women's fundamental lack of responsibility for the evils of society was a way of asserting their responsibility to redress those evils. According to the *Ladies' Newspaper*, this responsibility was both historical and moral: unlike men, who had proved their utter inability to assure a harmonious society, women represented "a force never used for the profit of society."[48] Furthermore, having been kept in the margins of power, they were "not polluted by individual ambition and interest."[49] As the oldest victims of injustice, they were the best situated to detect all kinds of unjust social relations.[50] Claiming this critical distance, this Archimedean point which Weber attributed to "pariah intellectualism,"[51] Greek feminists asserted that women could "represent the interests of all humankind" and therefore form "a community in which women and men would feel at last the warmth of relations based on solidarity, equality, and love."[52]

If differentiation is necessary for the subjective construction of any identity, the forms it takes and the terms in which it is articulated are neither fortuitous nor given in advance. Early Greek feminism appeared in a context which both favored women's inclusion in the nation and imposed severe limitations on the demand for self-determination and the expression of their interests as an oppressed group. The feminists of the *Ladies' Newspaper* situated themselves within nationalist discourse probably because they shared with men its aspirations and basic assumptions. Many of them had participated in the national crusade of schoolteachers sent to the remotest parts of the Ottoman Empire to diffuse the mother tongue and its civilizing gifts. Some of them had done so in spite of the constant threats of rape and death that confronted schoolteachers of opposing nationalities (Greek, Serb, Bulgarian).

Situated within the logic of nationalism, feminists gained an unexpected audience and became for more than two decades an important component of the public sphere. At a time when other currents of opposition (socialist, anarchist) could hardly survive more than a few months or years, the *Ladies' Newspaper* attained a stable readership of 5,000 and a wide network of correspondents throughout Greece and the communities of the diaspora. Drawing on the arguments of nationalism, feminists used its modes of legitimation to develop a sense of gender belonging and a common project formulated in terms that could be understood, if not accepted, by a public opinion utterly hostile to any substantial transformation of gender relations. They were thus able to ground the relevance of women's public action in national interests and form alliances to open new educational and professional opportunities for women. Reinterpretation of the historical and mythological heritage provided them with a privileged and legitimate domain in which gender antagonisms could be worked out and women could become agents of social transformation. Indeed, it is not a coincidence that the most virulent attacks on patriarchy and male power appeared in the course of the critical revaluation of the past. Parren's articles in the *Ladies' Newspaper* had a surprisingly enthusiastic reception from readers, which indicates a large-scale thirst for dignity that could partly account for the success of the paper. At a time when a substantial mobilization for women's self-emancipation appeared so improbable, these arguments contributed to the development of messianic faith in the possibility of change.

But messianism is not only a vision of revolt; it can also be a vision of endurance, a reaction of those for whom real action is forbidden.[53] The ambiguity of pariah messianism, in which the chosen people may be sometimes the subject and sometimes the instrument of salvation, weighs particularly heavily on women. For, more than any group, women are called to save the others, including their own oppressors. The soteriological claim may thus function either as a utopian prospect in the name of which the present is rejected or as an *a posteriori* justification of an imposed role.

The model on which Greek feminism drew for the construction of a gender identity was related to an ideology that instrumentalized women. To the extent that feminists grounded the legitimacy of their action on the premises of this ideology, to the extent that they used its oppositions to define women as a collective subject of transformation, they were permanently confronted by serious dilemmas. The ambivalent vision they had of motherhood, at once a choice and a duty for Greek women, offers a typical example of the dilemmas which pervaded feminist strategy. The difficulty of reconciling nationalist assumptions with feminism culminated in their problematic conceptualization of women as an oppressed social group and collective agent of social change. Indeed, while feminists were ready to act in solidarity with Chinese women, with the Russian *narodniki*, and even with the first women strikers of their own country, this sisterhood stopped brutally at the frontiers of the "Orient." There was no mention of Egyptian or Turkish women who, at that very period, started organizing for gender equality. One has the impression that these women only existed to serve as metaphors in the discourse of their Greek "sisters," muted symbols of subjection not just to patriarchal order but to some essential oriental barbarity.

These tensions pervaded the *Ladies' Newspaper* throughout the long period of its publication and ultimately resulted in the collapse of the feminist collective during the First World War. While the majority of its members ac-

tively supported Greek participation in the war, and sometimes the imperialist projects of the Greek government, the *Newspaper's* editor, Callirhoi Parren, was exiled in 1917 for her pacifist convictions—an unintended tribute
to someone who had struggled for women to be recognized as historical and
political subjects. Parren was the first female victim of political deportation,
introduced in 1915, which was to prove a powerful means of neutralizing
those who challenged the homogeneity of the nation.

PART VI

Comparative Views

British and American Feminism: Personal, Intellectual, and Practical Connections

CHRISTINE BOLT

The current scholarly interest in comparative studies of feminism[1] partly stems from the fact that enough work has been done on national women's movements to make extended comparisons possible. Such studies help to pinpoint the distinctive features of the movements that are compared. And they are particularly suitable where feminism is concerned, since activists have always seen the oppression of women as transcending national boundaries, just as antifeminists have presented the condition of women as biologically determined and so basically the same the world over. There is, of course, a danger that comparative work will ignore the great diversity within the national feminist movements and make their struggles tidier than they have been. Given the twentieth-century preoccupation with feminist ideology, it also may be tempting to set an egalitarian Anglo-American feminism against a European variety ready to celebrate female difference.[2] But these are risks worth taking.

This comparison will be between England and the United States, two countries where the experiences of women are often equated but where the differences that emerge are, I have argued elsewhere,[3] highly significant. It is my belief that unless these differences are fully grasped, it is impossible to understand the marked contrast between the English and American women's movements that existed in the later twentieth century.[4] Consequently, national distinctions will be my focus in this essay. I shall, however, begin with a reminder of the most obvious similarities between English and American feminism. Organized women's movements emerged first in Britain and the United States, at a time when transatlantic kinship, cultural, and economic ties were very strong. The two movements were dominated by middle-class women who had served an apprenticeship in benevolence and reform, developed a comparable range of arguments and objectives, and were obliged to grapple with many of the same problems and opportunities. Among these were the advance of democracy, industrialization, and urbanization; the evolution of liberalism; the emergence of socialism, applied sociology, social Darwinism, and sexology; and the eruption of world war.

Even before the development of feminist movements, shared religious and humanitarian goals had brought British and American Quakers and non-conformists into close contact. Women in the British and American peace and temperance movements had collaborated, and the antislavery movement had afforded even greater opportunities for the transatlantic exchange of information, advice, encouragement, and visits.[5] Given the rigors of travel at the time, such visits were generally sufficiently lengthy for genuine friendships to develop, and for visitors to talk to a range of groups and get a feel for the host society.

The contacts that subsequently developed between feminists in the United States and Britain were similar in nature, and arose naturally out of these larger, often family-based reform networks. They both contributed to and were affected by the changing nature of the Anglo-American relationship, with British radicals of all kinds initially drawing inspiration from American labor conditions, educational provisions, relatively democratic politics, and egalitarian ethos; and American reformers during the Progressive Era looking to see what they could learn from well-established British efforts to tackle the problems created by industrial and urban change.[6] British and American feminists from the various branches of their national movements visited each other's countries for specific events, to lecture and to network. While living away from home or on vacation, they might also work in each other's campaigns.

The 1857–1858 sojourn in the United States of the pioneering English feminist, Barbara Leigh Smith (Bodichon), allowed her to compare the conditions and leaders of American and British women, and to consider the connection between different kinds of human subjection at a crucial stage of her life.[7] In much the same way, Elizabeth Cady Stanton had been radicalized by her experience of the 1840 World Anti-Slavery Convention, during her wedding trip to Europe.[8] Emma Paterson's career as an organizer of British working women owed much to her observation of American female trade unions in the course of a honeymoon stay in New York,[9] and the preparation of her daughters for careers by the English suffragist Louisa Martindale involved a world tour which included visits to key American social reformers and re-form institutions. The preparation paid off, and by 1901 Hilda Martindale was launched on her successful career as a factory inspector.[10] Mary Beard, the American feminist and historian, was turned towards suffragism and the problems of working-class women by her friendship in the 1890s with Em-meline Pankhurst.[11] And the temperance leaders Lady Henry Somerset and Frances Willard exchanged protracted visits, with Willard coming to regard Somerset as her "English daughter" and the two allies fruitfully comparing ideas about politics and organization.[12]

American feminists like Elizabeth Blackwell, Susan Anthony, Sarah Re-mond, Ida Wells, Vida Scudder, Jane Addams, Carrie Catt, Elizabeth Robins, Charlotte Perkins Gilman and Margaret Sanger all found themselves wel-comed into British reform circles and learned from them,[13] and Mrs. Stanton, while staying in Britain with her daughter, Harriet Stanton Blatch, during the 1880s and early 1890s, was able to make an unusual impact on the radical suf-frage circle connected with the Bright family.[14] When militant British suffra-gettes needed a friendly hearing and a boost to their funds in the early twen-tieth century, they thought it natural to cross the Atlantic.[15] Such contacts were reinforced following the creation of international feminist organizations: the World's Women's Christian Temperance Union (WCTU) in 1884, the In-ternational Council of Women in 1888, the International Women's Suffrage Association in 1904, and the Women's International League for Peace and Freedom in 1915. Given the importance of these Anglo-American exchanges, Millicent Garrett Fawcett's refusal to travel to the United States was an un-derstandable source of irritation to the leaders of its suffrage movement.[16]

Links between the two countries were further strengthened by the fact that British feminist journals reported American conventions, publications, pre-occupations, campaigns, leaders, and achievements, while the corresponding American journals and the American *History of Woman Suffrage* returned the favor. Moreover, activists were given a sense of solidarity by awareness of their shared indebtedness to certain influential feminist texts.[17] The writings of Mary Wollstonecraft, Frances Wright, John Stuart Mill, and Charlotte Per-kins Gilman, for example, had an acknowledged impact on both sides of the Atlantic. It is, incidentally, worth saying at this point that the publications and activists I am familiar with also paid tribute to continental European in-fluences and role models; British and American feminists eagerly visited the continent and worked with European activists in the international organizations of women.[18] Among the heroines for whom these historically minded feminists scoured the past, no figure was more revered than Joan of Arc. Among the commanding authors with whom they engaged, few were more provoking than Auguste Comte or more admired than Madame de Staël. After all, feminism was an international movement whose adherents shared basic objectives and ideological emphases, notwithstanding the movement's many national variants, especially with regard to periodization, links with nationalist struggles, religious connections, and attitudes towards modernization. Nonetheless, British and American feminists saw themselves as having a special influence and relationship. Accordingly, when Mrs. Stanton's feminist son, Theodore, published a collection of essays in 1884 called *The Woman Question in Europe*, he aimed it at the public of England and America, and admitted that

> England has the first place and the lion's share of the volume. But, as it is in Great Britain of all Europe that, on the whole, the most marked progress has been made, especially in the direction of political rights, the "summum bonum" of the age, the largest space and the post of honor justly belong to the Mother Country.[19]

Common roots and shared difficulties did not, however, diminish American and British feminists' sense of their own distinctiveness. For women as well as for men, the Anglo-American relationship involved rivalry as well as friendship; tapped into normally veiled but significant feelings of national superiority. Americans and Britons had formed views of each other in the wake of the American Revolution that did not entirely change as their two countries grew more alike, politically and economically.

In an essay of this length, I can only give a few examples of the chauvinism that galvanized women activists on each side of the Atlantic. It emerged, most famously, when American feminist-abolitionists attended the 1840 World Anti-Slavery Convention and complained frankly of the timidity of their British sisters.[20] One of their number, Elizabeth Cady Stanton, later criticized British reserve, snobbery, class prejudice, segregation of the sexes, and centralized political system, believing that American reform conventions were better and that British feminists were ill advised in their support for partial suffrage.[21] The Anglophile Frances Willard was, when in her own land, clear about "the advancement that characterizes the [women's temperance] movement in this country" and was not matched abroad; while Lady

Somerset, though invigorated by the "simplicity, generosity and faith in impossible things" among Americans, noted they had the faults of a young country and so were "aggressive, vulgar, crude."[22] American activists resisted the importation of British militancy in the last stages of the suffrage campaign, in part because they were convinced that American conditions made it unnecessary.[23] Yet British feminists could see obstacles to progress in America's elaborate procedures for amending the Constitution and in its enfranchisement of young male voters with little standing in the community.[24]

A writer like Henry James might believe that it took "an old civilization to set a novelist in motion";[25] but his compatriots tended to think that it took a new one to energize reformers and were offended by Britain's open inequalities. British observers, for their part, could find comfort in the conviction that American freedom had its pitfalls, Britain's established culture its advantages. Thus the pro-American English feminist Frances Power Cobbe warned that just because American women were less circumscribed than the British by "long-established custom," they should be even more careful to be on their "guard to keep the great onward movement of our sex within the bounds of the strictest discipline."[26] Equally, it was obvious to British feminists that their transatlantic sisters were, in the nineteenth century, likely to have been inspired more by British than by American authors, George Eliot and Elizabeth Barrett Browning being particular favorites. As Ann Douglas has pointed out, when *Uncle Tom's Cabin* took Europe by storm in 1852, Harriet Beecher Stowe was the first American woman novelist to reach international eminence;[27] and some two decades later, the *Englishwoman's Review* was still remarking that America had "as yet produced no national literature."[28]

The recent history of British and American feminism has, of course, been shaped by legacies other than the sense of pioneer activists in each country that they had unique advantages and represented the cutting edge of reform. In the rest of my essay, I want to look at three of the most significant differences between early American and British feminists that continue to have significance: namely, those related to organization, politics, and ideology. And naturally these differences were produced not simply by the women's movements' independent agency but also by the larger societies in which they operated. Most obviously, American campaigners have been shaped by the vastness of their country and its regional variety, frontier experience, federal political system, interventionist courts, powerful and pragmatic parties, religious disestablishment and diversity, polyglot population, and domestic racial tensions. Conversely, Britain's reformers have been affected by their country's unitary political system, class consciousness, strongly established institutions (including political parties), small size, relatively homogeneous population, and pride of race, most vigorously projected through the empire.

ORGANIZATION

Although feminists on each side of the Atlantic emerged from a Protestant religious tradition and reform connections, against a background of political and economic change, the link between abolitionism and feminism was less important in Britain than it was in the United States. Clare Midgley's work has made it clear that while British antislavery women became more assertive in the 1850s, as feminism gained ground, they did not customarily combine feminism and abolitionism. It was only once their primary antislavery objectives appeared to be gained that a considerable number went on to feminist campaigning, notably against the Contagious Diseases Acts and in the first suffrage associations. Middle-class British women abolitionists seem to have been more satisfied with their social position, in a class-conscious society, than American women, in a more fluid one, were with theirs.[29] Slavery was, additionally, a distant evil for British activists, and if the slavery of sex was frequently asserted by Victorian feminists, it was not proclaimed with the urgency summoned by their American counterparts.

There are two other reasons abolitionism in Britain had a more limited role in moving women towards organized and separatist feminism than it did in the United States. First, as Seymour Drescher argues, antislavery enjoyed approval throughout the political order in Britain, where it was one of the first modern social movements; for all the political and economic risks that it posed, it was emphatically not the radical, outsider cause that it came to be in the United States from the 1830s.[30] Accordingly, antislavery endeavors held out to British women a respectable means of entry into the nation's political culture.[31] This may, in turn, explain why British female abolitionists, despite their extensive links with Garrisonian, feminist-influenced abolitionists, held so firmly to their own preference for respecting customary gender roles and keeping contentious issues apart.

The second point to note is that though women were initially recruited to separate auxiliaries in both the British and American antislavery movements, by the 1850s, when the British women had gained the numbers and influence to secure participation in gatherings with men, they regarded such participation as a radical development. In the context of British reform it was; after all, working-class men and women were also separately organized in the period from the 1850s to the 1880s. Hence, when British women eventually took up feminist causes, they would have considered continued collaboration with men of their own class as a progressive as well as a natural move. American feminist-abolitionists may have been anxious to shake off auxiliary status and work with men in an unpopular cause, but even before the Civil War, America's reformist women tended towards separatist organizations. When, during the 1860s, many of America's feminist-abolitionists parted company with their former antislavery colleagues over who should be included in the post–Civil War constitutional amendments,[32] they were coming into line with that separatist tradition. British women abolitionists experienced no such jolting challenge to their solidarity with men.

Feminist separatism had been fostered in the United States by a wide range of factors: the national commitment to limited government; the early achievement of white male suffrage, a development which elevated the importance of remaining sexual and racial disadvantages; the large number of women college graduates; and the absence of a strong party of the left that promoted social welfare issues.[33] We should not therefore exaggerate the organizational differences between the British and American women's movements. Each involved cooperation with men (for instance in social purity and suffrage), and each produced women's only associations (such as the temperance bodies and the cross-class groups largely devoted to economic issues). Moreover, in Britain and America alike, from the 1870s to the First World War, feminist and other voluntary organizations, buoyed up by their belief in woman's moral mission, were committed to reform on a broad front and constructed effective and elaborate links with other reformers and diverse political interests. But the fact remains that there was a persistent tendency among feminists in Britain to value collaboration with men, pragmatism, and single-issue campaigning, which may account for their failure substantially to radicalize the male-dominated British temperance movement or to produce women's-club and settlement-house movements which rivaled those of the United States.

Another contrast between American and British feminists is the slower involvement of the latter in the separatist international associations that came to depend so heavily on European and American women. British women led by Josephine Butler did, of course, take the lead in internationalizing the social-purity movement during the 1870s, setting up the British, Continental, and General Federation for the Abolition of Government Regulation of Prostitution. But the prosperity that allowed American feminism to recruit so many women into groups which extracted membership dues was an asset in pursuing universal sisterhood abroad. And those who did so were influenced by their nation's faith in its exceptional destiny; by the cosmopolitanism of early American reform; by American women's strong sense of Christian mission; by the boost their organization and self-awareness were given during the Civil War; and by the confidence that sprang from living in the first country to sustain an organized women's movement. American women launched the World WCTU in 1883, to tackle drink and drug abuse worldwide, and "enlist our British cousins to the utmost as . . . active friends" of that enterprise.[34] American activists were behind the foundation of the International Council of Women in 1888, aiming to intensify women's "love of liberty"; to give them a "sense of the power of combination"; to correct the tendency towards "an exaggerated impression of one's work as compared with that of others"; and to "put the wisdom and experience of each at the service of all."[35] They then led the drive to create an International Woman Suffrage Alliance, and Carrie Chapman Catt was its leader from 1904 to 1923.[36] With the advent of World War I and the slow involvement of the United States in the conflict, American activists were conscious of their important role in funding IWSA, offering cheerful news of undisrupted suffrage activities, and keeping national animosities from destroying internationalism.[37]

It is necessary now to ask whether Anglo-American organizational differences had significant consequences. The mobilization of American women in separatist associations was undoubtedly striking, and they secured a direct influence on federal government policy via the Children's Bureau (1912) and Women's Bureau (1920): bodies that had no parallel among the organizations established by British feminists. The strength of the American separatist tradition may have contributed to the more substantial organizational framework of American feminism in the later twentieth century, especially at the national level. Equally, the greater opportunities women enjoyed from the first in American higher education may help to explain why feminism and women's studies have found a stronger base in American colleges than they have in British academic communities since the 1960s. On the other hand, it is hard to show that the first American feminists were generally more effective in obtaining legislation than British activists. Indeed American women and their allies had notably less success in securing national welfare laws than did British women, often in collaboration with men in the Labour movement.[38]

Clearly the earlier abandonment of laissez-faire principles by British politicians, Britain's unitary political system, and acceptance of class legislation may have made it easier to win measures at the national level with regard to working conditions or social purity; but these advantages should not be exaggerated. British women had to struggle for married women's property-law reform, changes to the divorce law and the suffrage, while the power to experiment at the state level in America, combined with more assertive courts, led to earlier (albeit patchy) progress on these issues in the United States. Feminists in the two countries achieved gains not just because of the organizational forms they adopted or the broader political structures in which they had to operate. Both factors were important, yet so too were such additional issues as political affiliation and style, and ideology. In each of these areas, as in organizational matters, British and American feminists were driven by a belief in the wisdom of their own national stance; by a conviction that successful reform involved agitators in going with, not against, the national grain.

POLITICAL AFFILIATION AND STYLE

Reformers in many different periods of history have seen the wisdom of steering clear of partisan politics, just as they have acknowledged the advantage of seeking backing from minority parties eager for allies and less wedded to the status quo than more powerful political groupings. In the United States, this ambivalence about parties was strengthened by their equation in the young republic with the factions thought to have corrupted the British constitution. The American Constitution did not refer to parties, and when they did emerge, their coalition nature and caution about embracing divisive ideologies prompted many reformers to despise them, and to pursue their objectives with reference to a higher law than that of man. Once parties became more legitimate, powerful, and programmatic, in the 1850s and 1860s, and the limited achievements of moral suasion became apparent, male and female reformers alike were obliged to reconsider their stance towards electoral politics and party involvement. Such a shift naturally increased women's desire for the vote, a desire which had been growing even before the Civil War.[39] Nonetheless, bipartisanship remained an attractive stance for women who wanted to demonstrate that they took a distinctive approach to politics, so that their entry into the public sphere would not merely duplicate the opinions and attitudes of men. The experience of finding the Republicans unwilling to support women's suffrage during Reconstruction, because it was "the Negro's hour," also disillusioned activists who had once seen them as their best political hope. The rebuff was a sharp indication of the danger of relying on a single political party.[40]

Middle-class women in Britain had been politicized and drawn towards electoral politics somewhat sooner than their counterparts in the United States, through Chartism and the Anti–Corn Law League. Their participation was justified because they were the mothers, wives, and daughters of the men involved. It was legitimatized on the grounds that "muscular force has given place to moral energy," and that causes connected with "humanity and justice" appropriately activated women, regardless of the "frigid rules of artificial society."[41] By the 1860s, pioneer British feminists had been reminded of the importance of political activism and of their own political impotence by campaigns to revise the married women's property law, to obtain the vote during the agitation for the 1867 Reform Bill, and to secure the repeal of the Contagious Diseases Acts. As had been the case in the United States, their hopes for a political breakthrough were disappointed. But the disappointment of British activists was not as sharp as that of American feminists who had collaborated with abolitionists for decades and therefore had some reason to hope that their ambitions might be realized jointly in the upheaval that accompanies war. Hence if American women tended for years after the war to accept the need for political engagement but to work through the class-based, businesslike reform bureaucracies that it had brought into being,[42] British feminists never lost their early faith in the goodwill of Liberal politicians. Unfortunately, the party of progress had certain deficiencies, being regularly disrupted by radical sniping and by clashes between libertarians and humanitarians within its ranks, as well as tending to take its reformer supporters for granted until World War I.[43]

The attachment of British women to the Liberals was increased from the 1880s by the needs of both major parties for unpaid workers, after the Corrupt Practices Act (1883) had limited electioneering expenditures. The Tories'

Primrose League (1883) and the Women's Liberal Federation (1886) involved women in a range of political chores, giving them organizing skills and greater confidence but bringing about no rewarding commitment to female suffrage in the male hierarchy of either party. The generally mixed-sex branches of the Primrose League may have inhibited women members from pushing feminist issues, though the mass of Conservative women were in any event disinclined to promote them. However, the Tories proved very effective at mobilizing female supporters, making good use of upper-class women long accustomed to political involvement through their families. The League thereby laid the foundations for Conservative recruiting success among women voters during the interwar years of the twentieth century. Conversely, the Women's Liberal Federation, though agreeing to promote "just legislation for women," was hindered by smaller resources than the Tories and growing divisions among its members over the legitimacy of agitating on the suffrage question. In addition, by the close of 1888, the desire of some of the Liberal women's groups to affiliate to the main women's suffrage societies was a source of contention within British suffrage circles.[44]

The Liberal leadership clearly appreciated the work of the Federation but—like its Conservative counterpart—expected party women to put the party agenda first. So, too, did the leaders of the Labour party, and their determination to woo Labour women from bourgeois feminist allies and distractions became particularly marked once women had the parliamentary suffrage.[45] Of course there were some gains from the British strategy of seeking both politicization and formal involvement in partisan politics. Activists were clearly proud of that involvement,[46] and it assisted the passage of legislation beneficial to women and children. Their recruitment by Conservatives and Liberals also helped women to take full advantage of the various local government openings that had been developing since the 1870s.[47] Meanwhile, American feminists continued to be politicized by reform and to support third parties like the Populists, Socialists, and Progressives, which offered unusual opportunities for women.[48] It was accepted, as Susan Anthony put it, that if women were to be heard, they must make themselves "a power, irresistible in numbers and strength, moral, intellectual and financial, in all the formative gatherings of the parties they would influence."[49]

As had happened in Britain, American women became more inclined to abandon bipartisanship in the early twentieth century, when they had gained much political experience and the Victorian women's culture, which stressed women's differences from men, was coming under attack. Nonetheless, that culture was strongly entrenched in American women's separatist associations, and feminists' lack of integration into the structures of the two main political parties made it hard for them to compete with the economic, ethnic, and other interests that dominated Republican and Democratic councils. In consequence, the suffragists of the Congressional Union (1913; renamed National Woman's Party from 1917) might have been able to campaign against the party in power with less heart-searching than the Liberal British suffragists, who moved away from their party connections before World War I. But it must be acknowledged that the drawbacks to bipartisanship were at least as great as those attached to partisanship. Indeed, in trying to keep out of party politics, feminists moved uncomfortably close to the antisuffragist view that women's place was above and not in the political world. It was only in the 1930s and 1940s that American women achieved full representation on Democratic and Republican committees, and only in the 1980s that American feminism became "partisan in nature."[50]

Contrasting attitudes to political parties between feminists in Britain and the United States in turn help to explain some of the differences in political style that are detectable in the two countries. These should not, incidentally, be exaggerated. Some early British feminists might congratulate themselves on their "practical moderation and rather humdrum common sense," which had "prevented a good deal of what strikes one as rather comic" about the women's movement "in other countries."[51] Equally Elizabeth Stanton, when in Britain for part of the 1880s and 1890s, might be conscious of the greater radicalism of American suffragists.[52] Yet each movement had its radicals and moderates, each movement was slow to deploy such controversial tactics as tax resistance, and each movement was dominated by women who would have endorsed the 1902 judgment of the American suffragist Catharine Waugh McCulloch that "When good behavior is made a test of eligibility to vote, no organization of women will suffer in comparison with men's organizations[;] and among the dignified well behaved organizations, the associations of suffrage women will lead all the rest."[53] British and American women alike might have produced regular quarrels and schisms over tactics, but they did their best to present the public face of feminism with womanly dignity, compliments, music, flowers, and all the appealing visual imagery that they could muster. Their efforts were helped by the strength of female friendships and the customary feminist emphasis upon women's collective experience.[54]

The eruption of diverse militant tactics in the last phase of British suffragism thus merits the attention it has received. Militancy may have its roots in nineteenth-century Anglo-American radicalism and may have entered American suffragism during World War I, when it had been abandoned by British campaigners. It remains, however, more significant in Britain than in the United States and, while there are many reasons for this,[55] one of them is the initial involvement of a number of British suffragettes with the Labour movement, whose protest tactics they had adapted even as they despaired of gaining practical benefit from the party's commitment to adult suffrage. Despite the growing strength of socialism in America before 1914,[56] the important political connections of feminists in such states as New York, and their growing sensitivity to the needs of the working class,[57] American suffragism in the twentieth century was introduced to militancy by British suffragettes and suffrage campaigns. And Mrs. Catt, the leader of the biggest American suffrage organization, who in the 1920s felt able to praise Mrs. Pankhurst as the John Brown of the suffrage struggle,[58] remained committed at home and abroad to "toleration, compromise and forbearance" as the best weapons in the feminist armory.[59]

IDEOLOGY

As the work of Levine, Dyhouse, Kent, and other commentators makes plain,[60] the women's movements of the nineteenth and early twentieth centuries, though concerned with political and legal equality and influenced by other reform efforts, ranged very widely and cherished their distinctiveness. Much of their originality lay in the realm of ideas: especially in the assertion of a connection between the allegedly separate public and private spheres; and in the attempt to show what united women, while simultaneously asserting their rights and variety as individuals. In the process, they analyzed women's position in education, the churches, marriage and the home, the economy, and the political arena, recognizing feminine strengths and weaknesses and daring to debate sexual questions and women's friendships with each other. Since nonfeminists measured women in relation to men, feminists often focused on what set women apart. They certainly gave some thought to the "new man" that might inhabit the better world they were making, but his qualities were generally less fascinating to feminists than those of the "new woman." Given the determination with which the changing ideals of middle-class masculinity were promulgated in Victorian Britain and America, the activists' focus was prudent as well as predictable. Unfortunately, stress upon women's special characteristics and destiny could take feminists perilously close to one of the chief planks of antifeminism, even as an emphasis upon equal rights could lay feminists open to the charge of selfishness in family-minded societies.

The current interest in disagreements between feminists who seek equality or "sameness" between the sexes, and those who stress women's difference from men, can be explained in several ways. In the first place, these disagreements have existed from the nineteenth century to the present, and divisions within any movement can weaken its effectiveness and encourage opponents. Second, their durability makes them a major challenge to the theorists of feminism. And third, such theorists are now more numerous than they have been before, because of the strength of women's studies in the academic world, notably in the United States. If the first American women social scientists helped to undermine "the Victorian conception of sexual polarity" and break down opposition to women as college students, their work also challenged the intellectual foundation of female reformism, and women were unable to consolidate their position as faculty members once universities became a more secure part of the social establishment in the 1920s and Depression struck in the 1930s.[61] But by the 1960s and 1970s, colleges and universities were again responsive to dissenters of all kinds, and the subsequent deployment by academic feminists of the findings of poststructuralism has given a further fillip to the debate about feminist ideas, within and beyond the United States.

No doubt reflecting some of the pragmatism that Victorian feminists were so proud of, I would just question at this point how productive the disputes over feminist theory have been since the late 1980s. Naturally ideological debate is vital, since without it there would be no women's movement, or any other social movement. Furthermore, all ideologies are subject to change and questioning, and at times of transition—like the period between 1900 and 1914 or the 1920s—the failure to redefine feminism in a way that had general appeal encouraged its exponents to separate into single-issue and class-based groups. Yet the fuss surrounding the recent series of blockbusters[62] that have criticized feminist thinking should make us concerned lest the theories of the movement overshadow its practical endeavors and actually erode the acceptance of feminist ideas that seemed so secure only a few years ago.[63] The different-or-equal divide especially is not confined to the women's movement and is not an issue that ever can be settled: feminists must surely accept that both emphases have their value and move on.[64]

Leaving that cautionary note to one side, I would stress that I see a range of feminisms existing more or less comfortably in the nineteenth and even the early twentieth centuries on each side of the Atlantic. Neither the American nor the British women's movement, I would contend, shifts *simply* from one kind of feminism to another:[65] from equal-rights arguments shaped by utopian socialism and Enlightenment individualism to social feminism reliant upon functional arguments, with the passage from one century to the next and from one generation to the next. Because of the power of women's separatist organizations in the United States, the strength of women in the churches, and the value placed on their willingness to carry out traditional duties in a developing society where they were often scarce, the empowering aspect of women's domestic role was urged with particular force by American feminists. And because of the American reluctance to acknowledge class as an organizing factor in political parties or a proper basis for legislation, women activists were slower to establish cross-class feminist associations than were their British sisters, in whose country the social and political significance of class was proudly proclaimed.

In the international organizations where they played such an important part, and notably in explaining their opposition to war, American feminists frequently employed the same emphasis upon women's nurturing qualities. The ICW, for instance, pledged itself to promote "the highest good of the family and of the nation,"[66] but such a focus was to be found among social feminists and radical feminists, among British and American activists.[67] It was, of course, common for individual feminists—like other reformers—to use more than one kind of argument: to maintain that only with legal and political equality could women obtain legislation geared to their special interests; or that women entering fields once dominated by men would bring unique qualities to them, rather than becoming identical to the opposite sex. Only when the question of protective labor laws arises does the division between equal-rights and maternalist or social feminists become polarizing.

The debate over such laws arose first in Britain because of its earlier acquaintance with the problems of industrialization and its earlier abandonment of strict laissez-faire principles in government. And it was given a distinctive slant among British feminists once Labour women grew in numbers and strength, ultimately symbolizing the economic and political division between the two during the interwar years of the twentieth century.[68] On both sides of the Atlantic, however, the debate was damaging; and if it largely affected opposing groups of middle-class feminists in the United States by the 1920s,[69] the wrangle was still more bitter there because of the parallel effort to obtain an Equal Rights Amendment and the realization that the welfare measures it was thought to jeopardize were (with the exception of mothers' pensions) not yet the equal of those that had been secured in Europe. The influence exerted by American women in international women's associations made it inevitable that the equality/difference dispute also entered that arena, yet we should not give it undue attention. As Rupp has pointed out, the members of these associations disagreed about how far to push feminist goals and how far to subordinate their "individual national identities."[70] They nonetheless persisted in their attempts to give meaning to the concept of universal sisterhood.

British and American feminists in the nineteenth and early twentieth centuries assumed that sisterhood was universal in a way that would be unthinkable today. Although they denounced the injustice of women being represented politically by men, they assumed that the active minority of women could speak on behalf of the rest of their sex. In the American context this meant largely ignoring class until the later nineteenth century, from which point middle-class women reached out to working women in bodies like the consumers' leagues and settlement houses. But race could not be ignored, producing an uneasy relationship between black and white female reformers before the Civil War, in the wartime Equal Rights Association, and in the later club and suffrage movements. White women might stress their concern, as mothers, with the future of the race, but the race in question was generally assumed to be white. When interest in race issues grew among white activists from the late nineteenth century, they found it all too easy to accept the separate organization of black women, making the attitudes of the larger society their excuse and taking heart from the fact that black women seemed willing to ally with reformist men of their own race.

Leaving aside questions of alternative options and blame here, we should note that black women activists were not deterred by poverty, separatism, or white prejudices. They proved willing to work alongside white women where they could, for example in the Association for the Advancement of Women

(1873–1897), and they enjoyed some advantages over their white sisters in terms of ideology. The analogy between chattel slavery and the slavery of sex may have diverted attention away from black slaves, male or female, but black feminists were not constrained by the cult of true womanhood, which was held up as an ideal for white women. Accordingly, they found it a more straightforward matter to urge the merits of both motherhood and paid jobs, their distinctiveness as well as their entitlement to equal rights.[71] Whereas female temperance workers, educational reformers, and suffragists sometimes worried about collaborating with other groups of activists to achieve shared goals, black feminists took advantage of the resources of black male reformers when it seemed appropriate, since racial self-help and sexual self-help were hard to separate. From the first, they were aware of the need to relate "multiple interrelated oppressions,"[72] and their awareness has contributed to the current high level of support for the ideas of the feminist movement among black women in the United States, albeit this is not normally accompanied by support for "mainstream feminist organizations."[73]

Yet while it may be possible to characterize black feminism in terms of its "visionary pragmatism," one should concede that the leading black activists of our period were frequently separated by class from their black sisters and faced some of the problems in bridging the gulf that were experienced by middle-class white feminists.[74] They also transcended the divide between difference and equality partly because their objectives were, perforce, not always tested in the political arena, and partly because they avoided making this divide the kind of issue it has become in modern feminist circles and was beginning to be among white feminists in the early twentieth century.

Race did not have the same significance for British feminists, living in a country whose nonwhite population was tiny, though class was openly acknowledged as a complicating factor. But even in Britain, class did not divide the movement until the early twentieth century and the emergence of a viable socialist feminism. In Ray Strachey's judgment, from about 1911 "the gulf between the [bourgeois] feminists and the leaders of the labour women widened. Each, indeed, approved of the aims of the other, and shared the same ultimate ideal; but their paths towards it diverged."[75] The significance of class and the important contribution of socialist feminists to British women's history should not, however, be allowed to obscure the salience of race for Victorian and Edwardian feminists. Like their American sisters, they saw themselves as members of the favored Anglo-Saxon race, and often looked to the British Empire for opportunities that American feminists could not replicate, despite their nation's brief flurry with conventional imperialism and the growing involvement of American women in missionary work. While such British activists can be criticized for their ethnocentrism and imperialism, we have moved beyond the simplistic association of white women in the Empire with the hardening of caste lines and reduction of humanizing sexual ties between white men and native women.[76] It is now clear that the women of the Empire, like the men, played a variety of roles and entertained a variety of views. And both in the colonies and from Britain, a number of female activists undertook a "civilizing" mission towards indigenous women which was not entirely self-serving, leading in India, for instance, to pressures for enlarged organizational opportunities, better education, and female suffrage.[77] The complicated story of these British women may not have been recovered by the time that black feminism became a force in Britain in the 1970s. But it has undoubtedly become known since feminist theorists have responded to the attack on their narrow focus, and feminist historians have moved to address the question of race.[78]

Women's Emancipation Movements in Europe in the Long Nineteenth Century: Conclusions

SYLVIA PALETSCHEK AND BIANKA PIETROW-ENNKER

I. HISTORY AS AN ARGUMENT

Each successive present unfolds a new perspective of the past. Like all historiography, the historiography of women's emancipation movements is marked by contemporary political conditions and the current zeitgeist. The dominant gender relations and the contemporary form of the feminist movement also leave their stamp. Both the methodology within the scholarly community and the national historiographic tradition influence how the history of the women's emancipation movement will be researched.

After the turn of the twentieth century representatives of the first wave of the women's movement were the first to attempt a history of their movement. These included Ray Strachey in England, Helene Lange and Gertrud Bäumer in Germany, and Johanna Naber in the Netherlands.[1] In 1930, at the International Congress of Historical Sciences, the Polish historian Lucie Charewiczowa called for the writing of a history of the feminist movement. She noted that the movement was constantly growing and that working back through the movement's history might help overcome the prejudices which confronted it.[2] The first archives and libraries were set up at this time to preserve documents of the history of the women's movement.[3] These early studies made from within the ranks of the women's movement show, according to Jane Rendall, "the diversity of the ways in which each woman reconstructed her own history and her cultural and political traditions."[4]

For the women's emancipation movements of the nineteenth century, history was important for self-confirmation and the creation of legitimacy. This is shown repeatedly in the chapters in this book. Thus, Charlotte Carmichael Stopes, an English activist for women's rights, traced "the spirit of British womanhood" back to the battle of Queen Boadicea against the Romans.[5] The manifold undertakings of the French feminist culture included the publication of an illustrated feminist almanac in 1906. In this almanac all male and female saints were replaced by the saints of feminism, i.e., by men and women who had fought for women's emancipation. Other plans included the publication of a feminist encyclopedia and the collection of documents about the French feminist movement: "History and memory were considered essential to integrating women into the public sphere. . . . Instituting *lieux de mémoires* by erecting monuments . . . was also a way in which this fundamentally political feminist culture sought to express itself."[6]

A newspaper published by the Greek women's movement at the turn of the century demonstrated "the privileged status of history in the feminist discourse."[7] It emphasized the powerful legitimizing function of history: "Though our sex has played a major part in national history, historical tradition has only included men's action." Greek female fighters for independence in the 1820s, *salonnières*, mythical and religious female figures, and prominent women of different nations and historical periods were used for the "reconstitution of a women's collective memory."[8] The leader of the Greek women's movement at the turn of the century, Callirhoi Parren, was also one of the first experts on women's history. Special value was placed on the feminist reinterpretation of the ancient Greek tragedies. Czech women's rights protagonists delved into Czech history and mythology in order to justify female emancipation, using such figures as Princess Libuše, the Czech Amazons, the Czech saint Ludmila, and the female Hussites as part of their argumentative strategy.[9]

With the decline or standstill of the women's emancipation movement after the 1930s/1940s, these early efforts to create a women's tradition were interrupted or forgotten.[10] Contributing to this was the fact that it was men who had formed the remembrance culture of European society and who had developed historical scholarship in the nineteenth century. Male fields of action, achievements, experiences, and values continue to dominate our cultural memory.[11] There were, and are, only a few institutions which have permanently focused on the remembrance of women's historical deeds and the circumstances of their lives, providing continuity and permanently establishing them in the collective memory.

Sustained work on the history of women's emancipation movements began again in the western European countries with the resurgence of the fem-

inist movement during the 1970s. Since then there have been numerous relevant studies. Case studies on specific questions or time periods are the dominant topics of research; as some of the authors in our volume stress, a unify-
ing synthesis is often still lacking in research. There are significant differences
in what has been achieved: the history of the feminist movement has been
more broadly researched in western, central, and northern Europe than in
eastern, southeastern, and southern Europe. Research on the history of western women's emancipation movements has been more strongly influenced by
current issues within today's feminist movements. The perspective of the
work on women's emancipation movements in central and eastern Europe
was first influenced by the East-West conflict and then by the political
changes after 1989. In part this led to a change of paradigms; it also marked
the beginning of broader-based research on women's emancipation movements in these countries.

Mineke Bosch's chapter on the historiography of the Dutch women's
emancipation movement excellently illustrates how writing on the history of
western women's movements has developed since the 1970s. Because of the
strong Marxist-socialist influence on feminism in the 1970s, the initial works
were primarily concerned with the social democratic position on women's issues or dealt with the antagonism between the bourgeois women's movement and the working-class movement. Structural causes of the repression
of women were investigated by bringing the differences between the private
and public spheres and the influence of capitalism into play. The focus was
on economic and political demands and activities.

A similar development is evident in the research of the 1970s and early
1980s on German, British, and French women's movements. In the case of
Germany, the proletarian women's movement was researched first. "Investigative priorities followed political orientation or sympathies. . . . Only
with the more recent and detailed studies, which deliberately went beyond
dominant concepts of political science, did the focus shift to women's self-
esteem."[12] With respect to research in France, the feminist movement was
first taken up in the 1960s in work on the history of the working-class movement but, nevertheless, was pejoratively labeled "bourgeois." Only since the
1970s has it been perceived as an independent topic.[13]

Early works stemming from the "old" women's movements were either ignored or received rather critically. An example is a book published in 1948 to
preserve the memory of the Dutch women's movement from 1789 to 1948.

The new historians of women's history in the Netherlands held "mixed feelings towards this classic."[14] It was criticized as being too descriptive and lacking definitions of feminism and the women's movement.[15]

It was characteristic of the works published between the 1970s and the mid-1980s to label as traditionalist those elements of the women's movements which did not pursue an equal-rights feminism but instead based their argumentation on difference. "This conclusion, in its focus on what unites and what divides 'them' from 'us,' reflected the general characteristic of identification in most early women's history. The attempts to pursue a more theoretical or 'scientific' approach succeeded at the same time in relativizing the 'equal rights paradigm' by attracting attention to the importance of difference arguments in the history of first-wave feminism."[16]

The concept of "women's culture" which has been adopted since about the mid-1980s likewise reflects the contemporary feminist discussion but now includes issues related to cultural history. This depoliticized women's history. Identity, self-perception, and communication became the main issues. Thanks to a strong interest in returning to primary sources and a wish to avoid political bias, new findings were made. The distinction between "difference feminism" and "equal-rights feminism" was defused, and the difference arguments were rehabilitated. The influential feminist debate about equality and difference, which was carried on in the 1990s, had the same effect. Mineke Bosch points out, however, that these studies are open to the accusation that "instead of historicizing feminism" they were "again set into the mode of identification and molded history to the contemporary desire to deconstruct equality versus difference."[17]

In her chapter, Christine Bolt traces the reasons why, well into the 1990s, there was such an interest in the ideologies and emancipation strategies of the first wave of feminist movements. She writes:

> The current interest in disagreements between feminists who seek equality or "sameness" between the sexes, and those who stress women's difference from men, can be explained in several ways. In the first place, these disagreements have existed from the nineteenth century to the present, and divisions within any movement can weaken its effectiveness and encourage opponents. Second, their durability makes them a major challenge to the theorists of feminism. And third, such theorists are now more numerous than they have been before, because of the strength of women's studies in the academic world, notably in the United States.[18]

Karen Offen's essay "Defining Feminism," which developed the concepts of relational and individualist feminism,[19] was very influential in the discussion of the concept of feminism which took place at the end of the 1980s and the first half of the 1990s. Both its acceptance and critique[20] were very productive, although, as Karen Offen writes in her chapter, it was often misunderstood. For heuristic purposes she identified two lines of argument within the women's emancipation movements of the nineteenth century: relational and individualist. The strategists of relational feminism demanded rights for women based on their special efforts for others, i.e., the family and society, and stressed the differences between women and men. The proponents of individualist feminism demanded women's rights and individual self-realization based on natural law and general human rights. They tended to see specific gender differences as secondary or denied them altogether.[21]

As Karen Offen stresses in her chapter here, she tried to use this heuristic concept to transcend the currently accepted line of argument that the Anglo-American women's movement was characterized by equal-rights feminism and that the continental European one stressed women's difference. Instead, Offen wanted to show that a strict distinction between equality and difference arguments was meaningless for nineteenth-century women's emancipation movements. Both lines of argument were used by the Anglo-American and continental European movements. The contemporary phrase "equality in difference" makes this clear.

Other chapters in this book confirm that these lines of argument were used independently of political orientation. Therefore, labeling one or the other as radical or conservative is meaningless. Relational and individualist arguments were used strategically and flexibly. As research has shown, both arguments have to be seen within their contemporary political, social, and cultural framework.

Since the 1990s, with the adoption of a poststructuralist critique of identity, an emancipatory subject-oriented women's history has developed based on discourse analysis and the deconstruction of women's and gender history. Accompanying this was the need to integrate women's history into the greater whole of general history. The new methodological challenge was to look at traditional themes of political history from a gender perspective.[22] This approach has been very productive for women's history and has also shed new light on feminist movements.[23] Nevertheless, knowledge has remained very fragmented; "in a way 'the subject is lost': there are . . . no book-length studies of first-wave feminism, or aspects of it."[24]

The history of the historiography of the Hungarian and the Russian women's emancipation movements can be used to illustrate the developments in the former east-bloc countries. These examples show how political conditions and their change put the women's movements into a new perspective. Judith Szapor shows the interrelationship between the political events in Hungary and the historical treatment of the Hungarian women's movement. The Hungarian movement was "part of the rich and colorful political spectrum of turn-of-the century Hungary."[25] For the conservative regime between the two world wars as well as for the Stalinist regime of the late 1940s and 1950s, however, the developments at the turn of the century were an irritation. "Nevertheless, while a good part of this pluralistic heritage was reintroduced and incorporated into contemporary Hungarian social and political thought, the feminist movement of that period has never received its due." Szapor writes of "a specific case of collective amnesia, concerning the Hungarian women's movement of the turn of the century."[26] It has only been since the political changes in the 1980s that a new interest in the political and cultural pluralism at the turn of the century has been reawakened in Hungary, which has also helped to gradually refocus attention on the Hungarian women's movement.

The Russian case provides an example of how the demise of the communist system affected the interpretation of the women's movement. "When the dramatic collapse of the Soviet Union revealed the permanence of the Revolution's achievement to be an illusion, . . . the shape of Russian history both before and after 1917 lost the clarity and certainty it had acquired from the Revolution."[27] The formerly accepted pattern of explanation, along with the associated division into periods, now seems questionable because "it corresponds so closely to the obligatory interpretation in Soviet historiography, according to which the 'people of the sixties' created the essential progressive intellectual and moral environment for the later development of 'scientific' Marxism and its triumphant realization after 1917."[28] The differences between Marxism and liberalism which had become a dogma within Soviet historiography, and which rubbed off onto the history of the women's movement, are now being questioned. "There is plentiful evidence of personal links and cooperation between radicals and feminists during the 1860s and 1870s . . . For the present, therefore, it remains difficult to know exactly how to define the women's movement and whom to include in its ranks."[29] Which direction future Russian research will take is, according to Linda Edmondson, unclear. "There are several reasons feminism has been a pejorative term to women in Russia (as in east-central Europe overall), and these do not stem solely from the disillusioning experience of 'sexual equality' under communism." Explanatory reasons also include "anxiety that ideas from the West, however progressive and well-intentioned, have been enthusiastically exported without any regard for the existing cultures of the recipients."[30]

A look at the history of historiography shows how the questions have changed and how varied the paths of research have been in different parts of Europe. Although there are similarities, there is no homogeneous European perspective.

II. THE PERIODIZATION OF THE WOMEN'S EMANCIPATION MOVEMENT IN EUROPE

The different stages of the women's emancipation movements in Europe took place in overlapping time periods rather than as a uniform pattern of development. As Mary Nash observes with reference to the Spanish women's movements, "the establishment of a general periodization in the framework of Europe raises the issue of its validity in the context of the women's movement in different countries and regions. Rereading feminism through differential patterns of growth of the women's movement in Europe may, in fact, lead to the creation of different sets of periodization and reveal more plural definitions of feminism."[31] To provide an overview of the European women's emancipation movements, we have taken the central developments for specific time periods and sketched the status of the women's movement in the respective European countries. These four time periods are designated: 1. the years between the Enlightenment and the end of the French Revolution; 2. the first half of the nineteenth century; 3. the 1850s/1860s through the 1880s; 4. the 1890s to World War I.

The chapters of this book show that the European women's emancipation movements in the long nineteenth century can be divided into four different phases. The beginning was marked by individual male and female forerunners who stimulated the debate about the role of women and gender relations. The first networking took place through publications, circles, groups of friends, or salons; collective organizations did not yet exist. An early phase of the move-ment began when the first organizational attempts were undertaken in the form of associations and groups, although these were often not of a lasting na-ture. The real phase of organization began with the continued existence, con-solidation, and development of feminist organizations. The peak phase en-compassed further differentiation and finally had a mass basis and broad public impact. These different phases of the movement took place at different times within European states or regions.

1. From about 1700 to 1810: Precursors during the Enlightenment and the Janus-Faced Legacy of the French Revolution

As Karen Offen shows in her chapter, the Enlightenment demands for wom-en's education and women's right to participate in public affairs were a Eu-rope-wide phenomenon.[32] The role of women in society was an integral part of the Enlightenment discourse in the eighteenth century.

The discussion about women during the Enlightenment was based on the commonly held idea that although there were different tasks for men and women within society, women should participate in the "tasks of hu-manity." Topics were put forward at the time that would be developed fur-ther during the nineteenth century. Of central importance were women's ed-ucation and legal equality under civil law, particularly with respect to married women. In the political discussion the women's issue coincided with other relevant issues such as slavery, Jewish emancipation, bourgeois emancipation, and nationalism. From all of this it becomes clear that de-mands for women's emancipation were not a product of the nineteenth cen-tury, of industrialization, or of political revolutions.

The French Revolution played a key role throughout Europe for the later development of the women's emancipation movements in the nineteenth century. During the French Revolution, middle-class and lower-middle-class males gained access to the political sphere. Women, however, remained ex-cluded from the general franchise, which ensured their exclusion from pub-lic politics. Education and social work were all that remained as specific fe-male spheres of participation. However, tracts about women's issues, such as Olympe de Gouge's "Déclaration des droits de la femme et de la citoyenne" and the writings of Condorcet, circulated throughout Europe. Emancipation from male guardianship and women's political participation became thinkable. The ideas spread across national borders, even if they could not yet be realized.

During the French Revolution the first political women's clubs were founded, although they were later banned. The victory of the counterrevolution and the passing of the Napoleonic Code in 1804 cemented the legal dominance of men over women in marriage, which spread throughout Europe with the Napoleonic Wars. The unprecedented intensity of the attack on male dominance which had taken place during the French Revolution was countered during the reactionary period with the need to control women more firmly than before. It was within this highly politicized context, according to Karen Offen, that the specific forms of women's emancipation developed in the nineteenth century. Explicit political demands were not the first order of business because as a consequence of the failure of the Revolution and the victory of the counterrevolution such political goals could not have been achieved. Instead, demands turned towards reforming the educational system and improving the legal and economic position of women.

2. From 1810 to 1850/1860: Nationalism, Literary Feminism, and the Early Women's Emancipation Movement

Three developments in the first half of the nineteenth century were important for the future of the women's emancipation movement. First, women began to mobilize in support of nationalism in parts of central, eastern, and southeastern Europe. Second, literary feminism spread throughout almost all of Europe, reaching its peak between the 1830s and 1860s. Third, between about 1830 and 1850, an early phase of the movement, with close ties to social, political, and religious reform movements, developed in England, France, and Germany.

At the beginning of the nineteenth century, women's emancipation movements and their precursive discourse began to develop within national networks of communication and within the emerging nation-states. Although there continued to be international exchanges of ideas, writings, and personal contacts, the national networks were dominant.

In the first half of the nineteenth century, women began to mobilize as a result of national wars of independence, the emergent national movements, and the revolutions of 1848/1849. This applied especially to those nations in central, eastern, and southeastern Europe which formed part of multinational states or were under foreign rule: the German states under Napoleonic occupation, divided Poland, Hungary, and Bohemia in the Habsburg Empire, and Greece, which since the 1820s had begun the process of freeing itself from Ottoman rule.

The involvement of women in the national movements and the inclusion of gender in nationalist rhetoric were originally not aimed at emancipation. However, within the course of the national struggle for independence, women learned to participate in public affairs. Men discovered women as the upholders of a national culture and as the future educators of a nationally independent people. Women's associations were founded to support freedom fighters, and some women even participated in battles for independence.[33] Women became politicized within the nationalist movements and they tied their expectations of public and political participation to the nation.

The second development contributing to the women's movement in the early nineteenth century was literary feminism. Particularly between the 1830s and 1860s, and sometimes later, literary feminism had an enormous impact all over Europe. A publicly effective discussion of the role of women and gender relations took place in key novels. In the 1830s and 1840s, in Denmark, Spain, Germany, Bohemia, and Poland, highly regarded novels and educational magazines denounced the poor education and employment opportunities for women. Beginning in the 1850s, works by Camilla Collett and Amalie Skram were very influential in Scandinavia. The height of this literary feminism was embodied by Nikolai Chernyshevskii's popular novel *What Is To Be Done?*, which was published in Russia in the 1860s. Even after the zenith of literary feminism had passed, publications continued to fuel the debate about women's issues. In the 1880s plays by Henrik Ibsen were influential in the Scandinavian countries and beyond, and in the 1890s the Dutch author Cécile Goekoop-de Jong van Beek en Donk took up central themes of the women's movements.

In Britain, France, and the German Federation of States an early phase of the women's emancipation movement took root between 1830 and 1850. There was close cooperation with early socialism, the antislavery movement, and the religious nonconformist movement. In the early French socialist movement, during the 1830s, followers of Fourier and Saint-Simon regarded improvements in the condition of women as a precondition for a just and harmonious society. Changes in patterns of ownership and gender relations were central to their utopian model of society. Female followers of Fourier and Saint-Simon founded women's magazines in the 1830s and 1840s. During the French revolution of 1848 they were involved in political activities and women's associations. In Britain the women's issue was discussed in the early Owenite socialist movement. Many women were members of the movement, but their number declined after 1840. Thereafter, English women organized more actively in religious antislavery and temperance movements.

The relationship between religious dissent and women's emancipation is apparent in the early phase of the French and German movements. In Britain and the United States, women from the nonconformist sects of the Quakers and the Unitarians were disproportionately represented in the women's, antislavery, and temperance movements. In the early German women's movement of the 1840s, male and female religious dissidents made up the core activists. The women's associations which they founded also included some feminist goals.

The early phase of women's movements was accelerated in parts of continental Europe by the social awakening during the 1840s and the 1848/49 revolutions. The easing of censorship laws made it possible in Germany and France to publish women's magazines with political and feminist leanings. During the revolutions, political women's associations were founded in France, Germany, and parts of the Habsburg Empire that supported the revolutions and in some cases made political demands for women, though the revolutions did not trigger demands for women's emancipation. Like the French Revolution of 1789, they temporarily created an area in which women could become active; women were caught up in the basic process of politicization and became publicly involved. Indeed, by excluding women from parliamentary politics and from political associations, the 1848/49 revolutions solidified gender roles and the distribution of power,[34] and this exclusion led in the long run to feminist politicization.

In France and the German Federation of States these early women's emancipation movements were disbanded during the reactionary phase which followed the failure of the revolutions. The period of reaction after 1850 with its curtailment of the right to assembly had devastating effects in central and eastern Europe. Many women who had been active in political or women's movements had to flee from the counterrevolution. These included Hungarian, German, and French female revolutionaries who fled usually to Britain or the United States. Their persecution after 1848 was a setback, substantially weakening the development of the women's movement in continental Europe. As Ute Gerhard writes, referring to the German women's movement, this was not a continuous process of development: "It [was] a history of repeated setbacks, halts, and painful and courageous new beginnings."[35]

The women's emancipation movement which developed on a broad scale in the second half of the nineteenth century thus had a number of important stepping stones: the European Enlightenment discourse, the revolutionary experience of 1789, the political conditions in the ensuing reactionary periods, the mobilization of women in the cause of nationalism and revolution, literary feminism, and the first organizational attempts in association with contemporary social, political, religious, and moral movements. These experiences provided necessary skills for future action.

3. From 1850/1860 to 1890: Continued Organization in Western, Central, and Northern Europe; the Early Phase and Forerunners in Eastern and Southern Europe

The earliest sustained organization in the women's emancipation movement began in England. Demands for women's emancipation had been incorporated in the social movements of the 1830s and 1840s; the first women's organizations appeared in the mid-1850s. The first concern of these organizations was to improve the legal status of women and create new employment opportunities. The early inception of this movement in England can be explained by the stability of the parliamentary system and the solid foundation of liberalism. The rest of Europe, in contrast, was experiencing a postrevolutionary reactionary phase. In England women were able to carry on within an existing tradition of political involvement because the antislavery movement and religious-moral movements had not been disbanded, as was the case for the opposition movements on the continent. Feminist activities on a broader scale began in Britain in the mid-1860s. The first demands for suffrage were articulated and the first suffragette organizations were formed, whereas there were no such developments in other western and central European countries at the time.

During the 1860s, the organized women's emancipation movement began in a group of countries in western and central Europe which included Germany, France, and Bohemia. In the 1870s and 1880s, the Netherlands and the Scandinavian countries joined the ranks with their own organizations. During these years women fought first for better education and employment opportunities and for improvements in civil rights. The demand for suffrage came during the 1880s. At the same time, the influence of the social-purity movement spread abroad from Britain. During the campaign to prevent the regulation of prostitution the double standard of sexual morals was discussed. Temperance also became an issue. The campaign against alcohol was of special concern: alcoholism directly impinged on women's lives with devastating effect in lost household money and spousal violence.

Diverse women's magazines played an important role in the organizational process of the women's emancipation movement. Sometimes they followed the founding of an association, for example in Germany, where the magazine *Neue Bahnen* was created after the General German Women's Association was founded in 1865. Or they preceded the organization, as in France, with *Le droit de femmes*, which had been published since 1869. These magazines were instrumental in connecting diverse activities, served as forums of exchange, and helped expand the circle of male and female activists.

Up until 1880 the women's movement made very slow progress in Russia, Poland, Hungary, Greece, and Spain, so that there was no continuous organization to speak of in eastern, southeastern, and southwestern Europe. There were efforts in Russia, Poland, and Hungary to improve women's education, and women's charitable organizations also existed. Some of these were led by women, and their goals were not merely social but also included feminist activities.[36] In Greece Callirhoi Parren began publishing the *Journal des Dames* in 1887, in which women's issues were discussed. Briefly during the 1880s, a journal dedicated to women's issues appeared in Spain, but it was not continually effective. Some Spanish women, such as Concepción Arenal, were personally involved in women's emancipation. The Russian and Spanish examples show how restrictive political conditions, combined in some cases with an agrarian-feudal social structure, served to hinder the development of women's emancipation.

A certain measure of political repression prevailed also in central Europe, Germany, and the Habsburg Empire, where, for example, the Law of Associations of 1850 forbade women's participation in political associations. In

Germany antisocialist laws were passed which remained in force until 1890. In spite of these limitations, however, there was general freedom of thought, speech, and the right of assembly. Although no other country had a democracy similar to that of the Third Republic in France, which had been set up in 1871, most of the other countries, with the exception of Russia, did have a constitutional monarchy with a parliament. This shows that in order for a women's movement to be sustained, specific political and social parameters are necessary.

4. From 1890 to 1914: The Height of the Movement in Western, Northern, and Central Europe; Continuous Organization in Eastern and Southeastern Europe; Beginnings in Southwestern Europe

In most European countries the women's emancipation movement reached its peak in the two decades around the turn of the century. Where movements had been organized and consolidated between 1860 and 1890, an upsurge with subsequent mass participation occurred. In her study of the Netherlands Mineke Bosch speaks of the "roaring nineties" with the emergence of a lively social, political, and cultural life. In France at the turn of the century feminist topics received a great deal of public attention. According to Florence Rochefort, "feminism actually became something of a fashion, at least in Paris."[37] Jane Rendall writes that the term "feminism" can be applied for the first time to the British movement for the period between 1900 and the First World War because of the number of activists, the variety of strategies, and the dramatic campaign of the suffragettes.[38]

The height of the movement in western, central, and northern Europe was a period of diversification. Membership in women's organizations increased, broadening the movement's impact to include more conservative women. Social democratic, socialist, or proletarian women's movements appeared in Germany and Bohemia during the 1890s, and in Britain, Hungary, Norway, and Russia after the turn of the century. Women's unions emerged, filling a gap between women's professional organizations and the social democratic efforts on behalf of women—and with the creation of the social democratic women's movement political conflict became manifest; class lines did not stop at the door of the women's movement.

In most countries there was a national consolidation of existing organizations between 1890 and 1910. This was inspired by the example of the

American women's movement and by international congresses of women's associations, which had been taking place since the late 1880s. National coalitions were initiated under the influence of international exchanges and contacts. Owing to the wide spectrum of women's associations, which included conservative and religious groups, the national umbrella organizations formulated rather moderate goals.

In the countries of western, central, and northern Europe, therefore, the women's emancipation movement around 1900 was a mass movement with much diversification. Following the first demands for women's suffrage in Britain in the 1860s, and in continental Europe after the 1880s, most women's movements began a broad campaign for suffrage after the turn of the century. This was accompanied by new forms of action. Instead of merely petitioning, women took to the streets. Mass demonstrations took place, leaflets were circulated, and occasional acts of civil disobedience were carried out.

In the countries of eastern and southeastern Europe in the 1890s the women's emancipation movement came into a phase of continuous organization. The years between 1896 and 1914 can be seen as the peak in Hungary, "the only period when we can point to a well-defined and influential feminist movement among various streams of the women's movement."[39] In Russia, in particular around the time of the 1905 Revolution, there was an explosion of feminist activity. After the turn of the century publications and public involvement increased in Spain and Greece.

With the exception of a small group of feminist pacifists, feminist solidarity broke down in Europe during the First World War. The women's movements in individual countries placed themselves at the service of the national interest, hoping by this to gain recognition of their civil and political rights, and when numerous countries in Europe granted the franchise to women, many of the leaders took an active role in party politics and became members of parliament.[40]

III. SUPPORTERS OF THE WOMEN'S EMANCIPATION
MOVEMENT

Generally the women's emancipation movement was supported by women of the urban middle class. In central and eastern Europe a large percentage of noblewomen were involved, as a middle class had yet to develop in these areas. This is a good example of how social structures influenced the structure of the women's movement.[41] Feminists were usually embedded in a network of friends and relatives who, in turn, put them into contact with other social and political movements of the times: liberalism, social reform, religious nonconformism, and the antislavery and temperance movements. This network among the opposition had a large influence on the development of the women's emancipation movement.

The British women's movement shows this especially well. Feminists of both sexes often came from the dynamic local intellectual and middle-class elite. These "dynasties of radical reforming families within major British cities"[42] were concerned with a variety of demands for reform at both the local and the national levels. From the 1840s on, women from the working class began to pull back from political activities as the working place outside the home became more radically politicized, the image of the male as the family breadwinner was reinforced, and the labor union movement turned into a movement for skilled labor only. When women from the working class later became active in the women's movement, this often took place within religious associations. The religious roots of the British women's movement are particularly obvious. Feminist activists often came from nonconformist religious groups such as the Quakers or the Unitarians. Quaker and Unitarian families were an influential part of the dynamic elite within the cities who were active in the causes of antislavery and women's suffrage, or in international peace and temperance movements.

The findings of a study based on a sample of 40 leaders of the German women's movement showed that middle-class women dominated (approx. 85% middle class, approx. 10% from lower social classes, 5% noblewomen). The number of teachers was particularly striking. About half of the women were married, and among the single women a surprising number had lived in long-term female relationships. The women were relatively young, usually joining between the ages of 20 and 40. Women's circles and women's networks played an important role in recruitment and in stabilizing the movement: "Below the traditional forms of political and social organization there was an informal network of women's relations and friendships that had an important influence on political theory and practice."[43]

Jewish women and freethinkers, i.e., religious nonconformists, were overproportionately represented among the leading German feminists. This was also the case in France. Leaders of both sexes often came from Protestant, Jewish, or freethinking minorities. Immigrants from Poland, Britain, Russia, Switzerland, and Germany were noticeably numerous. The importance in France of friendships and family relationships is reflected by the fact that male supporters of feminism were often related to, married to, or a friend of a female activist.[44]

Noblewomen dominated the women's emancipation movements in Russia, Poland, and Hungary. These women often came from the socially declassed elite and were trying to obtain a place for themselves in the newly emerging intellectual class. Because there was no educated middle class in Hungary, the women's education movement of the late 1860s was initiated by noblewomen, "noblewomen being the only ones who had the opportunity to receive at least a private education."[45] In Hungary from the 1880s, the first generation of women with higher education began to enter the education professions and the new clerical positions. The first feminist leader and founder of the Hungarian Association of Feminists in 1904 came from the Association of Women Clerks. From the turn of the century in Hungary women from the middle class began to be more strongly represented; assimilated Jews and Germans and other non-Hungarian minorities constituted this dynamic middle class. The feminists at the turn of the century were usually highly educated, often came from the Jewish middle class or the nobility, and often spoke fluent German and French.

To sum up, there was a greater tendency to question the traditional role of women among those who had a critical attitude towards religion, belonged to a religious or ethnic minority, had close ties to people actively involved in social reform and opposition movements, had a certain level of education, or had a broader perspective as an immigrant or foreigner.

Men composed a significant minority group in the women's emancipation movements, and, remarkably, there was a considerably larger number of men involved in the early phase of the movement than in later phases. In some cases, such as in France and Norway, men were decisively involved in the founding phase of the first organizations. Between the 1830s and the 1880s, individual well-known liberal politicians, social reformers, early socialists, and leaders of religious protest movements were involved in the issue of women's rights. Many joined the women's movements convinced that real social change could only be achieved by changing the situation of women. Often they became involved in the feminist cause through their friends, wives, sisters, or mothers. In most countries the active role of men declined, at the latest during the height of the movement. This was the case in France after the turn of the century: "The avant-garde, which had been sexually mixed, evolved into a movement composed of women. Men were not excluded, but they were no longer accepted as leaders, and some new groups were made up exclusively of women."[46]

IV. ACTIVITIES AND GOALS

Women's emancipation organizations were committed to: 1. debate on the rights and duties of women and on gender relations; 2. improvement of women's education; 3. better employment opportunities for women; 4. civil and political rights for women; 5. the social-purity movement, i.e., the fight against the double standard in sexual morality and the regulation of prostitution; and 6. social and charitable work.

It is possible here to give only a condensed overview of these areas of involvement and the goals of European women's emancipation movements. To arrive at deeper insights it is necessary to make specific comparisons. Only in this way can one ascertain which national differences existed between the movements with respect to their priorities. The movements pursued a broad range of goals. However, the division of labor between the sexes in the family was generally not yet called into question. What Ida Blom writes in her conclusion applies to other movements besides the Norwegian one: "Continuities in gender relations were strong. Not one of the organizations disputed the idea that women's first and foremost task was that of wife and mother, and that men's first duty was to provide for their families and protect the nation."[47]

1. The Debate about the Status of Women

The debate about the status of women and about gender relations accompanied women's emancipation movements from the Enlightenment until the twentieth century. This discussion was fostered by tracts and novels, books, newspaper articles, and the various journals of the women's emancipation movements, which become even more numerous after the 1860s.

Gender relations were discussed in circles and salons, among networks of friends, and in religious, political, and social associations since the beginning of the nineteenth century. The debate was intensified by the emergence of an organized women's emancipation movement as of the 1860s. From the last quarter of the nineteenth century, the number of national and international gatherings of feminists, conferences, and exhibitions continually expanded in Europe. All of this contributed to the discussion of the women's question and even occasionally impinged on parliaments and political parties. After the turn of the century mass demonstrations for women's suffrage with leaflets and dramatic individual actions brought the debate on women's rights to the general public.

2. Women's Education

The demand to improve women's education was already part of the Enlightenment discourse. It was based both on general human rights and on the right of women to education as individuals. There was also a hope that the advancement of women's education would lead to improvements in society and the nation. The argument that women needed to earn a living began to play a more central role. Demands for improvements in education were to continue throughout the entire nineteenth century, although these initially only concerned women from the higher social classes. In the second half of the nineteenth century higher education for girls and the admission of women to universities was demanded. Improvements in the education of women were expected not just to end the subordination of women and make it possible to employ women in higher positions but also to extend the range of occupations open to women. Women aspired to open up academic occupations, which had hitherto been reserved exclusively for men. In some countries this resulted in violent attacks and resistance, particularly on the part of male graduates who feared female competition and a concomitant change of gender roles.

For women from lower social classes there were efforts to improve vocational training. Feminists founded schools for girls, women's vocational schools, and training classes for female servants. At the same time through the increase in educational facilities for women the number of qualified jobs for women in education and training expanded.

It is interesting to observe at what point better educational opportunities were opened to women in the different European countries and whether in each case private or state institutions were involved. The state education of girls was accepted relatively early in central and eastern Europe. In Russia, for example, higher secondary state schools for girls existed as early as 1858, and between 1859 and 1863 women were admitted to the University of St. Petersburg as guest students. Since women's emancipation had been discussed in the 1860s as part of the liberation of society from serfdom and since modernization also brought an increased demand for a skilled workforce in its train, the state yielded to the mounting social pressure. From 1872 the higher education of women was gradually institutionalized. The Russian achievements in the area of academic education for women were commented on favorably, notably by John Stuart Mill, not least because of the oft quoted Russian backwardness.

In the Habsburg Empire the first private secondary school for girls was opened in Prague in 1890. In the same year Czech delegates took up the demand for state higher education of girls, and in 1897 and 1900, respectively, women students were admitted to the philosophical and medical faculties of the universities. Systematic studies are still needed on the opening of educational institutions and the importance of the individual educational types for women and girls in the different European countries.

3. Women's Employment

Demands for the improvement of women's employment opportunities arose in the 1830s and became more emphatic beginning in the 1860s. The goal was to make women economically independent, no longer tied to marriage and the family for their upkeep. New areas of occupation, a thorough vocational training, the removal of legal restrictions on their employment, and the question of protective legislation for women workers were at the forefront of the discussion. At the same time the demand for gainful employment of women was closely connected to the question of their education and legal position. Important issues included the admission of college-educated women to the civil service, the right of married women to decide whether they wished to work, and their right to dispose of their own earnings.

In the last two decades of the nineteenth century, the organization of women in unions or women's professional associations, which championed the legal and economic improvement of their clientele, came to the fore. Professional organizations such the German Association of Female Teachers and the Professional Association of Women Clerks in Hungary were a catalyst for the women's emancipation movements. The employment of women was supported by the national umbrella organizations of the various movements. In the Netherlands, a National Committee for the Legal Regulation of Women's Labor was founded to push for the legal and social protection of women affected by economic modernization. National exhibitions dealing with women's work were accompanied by activities promoting the economic independence of women.

4. Demands for Civil and Political Rights

Demands to improve the legal standing of women, particularly in matrimonial and family law, arose at the beginning of the nineteenth century and remained strong thereafter. A systematic compilation and comparison of the different laws pertaining to women and the legal demands of the women's movements in the various European countries still remains to be done; the demands depended on the specific political culture and were of varying importance within the different movements. In Britain, for example, after the 1850s feminists struggled to enforce changes in the property rights of married women. Because the right to vote was dependent on property, these efforts were linked to the demands for women's suffrage. Although suffrage before the middle of the nineteenth centry became an issue only in isolated cases— during the French Revolution, for instance, and during the revolution of 1848—in the 1860s the demand for women's suffrage began to become more widespread in Britain, and at the beginning of the twentieth century the British suffrage movement became more radical. Disappointment about the lack of results in their decades-long struggle for suffrage led the suffragettes to begin a campaign of civil disobedience modeled on the Irish independence movement. It rapidly escalated, attracting a great deal of attention throughout Europe.

The arguments for women's suffrage differed. They were in part arguments which had been framed during the debate on universal or limited male suffrage and were then expanded. In England certain prominent proponents of women's rights, such as Lydia Becker, based their arguments on the traditional notion that the head of a household who could show himself to be in possession of sufficient property was entitled to vote—and that this right should therefore be extended to include women of property. A different position, which was advocated by John Stuart Mill and Barbara Bodichon, among others, proceeded from the assumption of the equality of the sexes under natural law, which implied full citizenship and therefore the right to vote for both men and women. The right to vote was considered a prerequisite for the exercise of social responsibilities. Women would only be able to train their public spirit when they were full citizens and able to serve the nation through their full participation in public life. A third position, advocated by the Women's Franchise League, founded in 1889, was based on the idea that full citizenship was derived from the performance of productive and reproductive work. Proponents of this position took the emergence of working-class movements into account and demanded the vote for women based on their productivity.

By the 1880s and 1890s, women's emancipation movements in western, northern, and central Europe took up the cause of women's suffrage, as did the eastern and southeastern European women's movements after the turn of the century—by then, the vote for women had come to stand for women's emancipation in general. Feminists believed that once they were able to make their influence felt on political parties and parliaments through their votes, they would be able to carry out reforms in all of the central areas in which women were disadvantaged. In almost all countries the period of the greatest struggles to achieve the vote for women was between the turn of the century and the First World War.

In nonsovereign states the women's suffrage movement was often closely linked to national movements. In Bohemia at the turn of the century Czech liberals and left-wing parties supported the demand for the full citizenship of women in the name of a general national emancipation. When men in Bohemia received full suffrage in 1905, the proponents of women's suffrage founded a committee for women's voting rights. In 1908, supported by the nationalist parties, the committee put forward a woman candidate based on the old curial electoral laws, in 1912 the first woman delegate took her seat in the Bohemian Diet. By reverting to the old feudal curial voting system and electing a woman, the Czech nationalist movement and women's movement challenged Austrian rule. This led to a further elevation of the Czech women's movement as a pillar in the national struggle for independence. The social democratic women's movement, however, disassociated itself from this campaign in the name of universal suffrage.

In Norway the women's emancipation movement linked its demand for suffrage to its nationalist involvement working towards the dissolution of the union with Sweden in 1905. A central role was played by the Norske Kvinners Sanitetsforening (Norwegian Women's Sanitary Association), which supported the movement for independence and prepared women all over the country for their role in a possible war with Sweden. In addition to training nurses the association turned its attention to general questions of health and hygiene and supported women's suffrage. The Norwegian Women's Rights Association, the Norwegian Women's Suffrage Association, and the Norske Kvinners Sanitetsforening were connected in the person of Marie Qvam, who was head of all three associations. The successful efforts of Norwegian women in national activities led to their being given the vote—albeit a limited suffrage—as early as 1907.

Systematic comparative analyses are also lacking for women's suffrage. Such an analysis would need to elucidate which type of suffrage (limited or universal suffrage, at the municipal, local, or national level) was demanded at what period and in which countries and when this was finally achieved. An inquiry into the social function of the struggle for political equality of women is also necessary.[48]

5. Moral Reform, Temperance, and Social-Purity Movements

In England the movement for social purity began to organize itself with Josephine Butler's fight to repeal the acts regulating prostitution and the founding in 1869 of the Ladies' National Association for the Repeal of the Contagious Diseases Acts. In Sweden and Norway there were several successive waves of debate on sexual morality from the 1870s on. In the Netherlands and in Sweden women's emancipation movements began to have a broad public impact as promoters of moral reform and regeneration. The Nederlandsche Vrouwenbond ter Verhooging van het Zedelijk Bewustzijn (Dutch Women's League to Elevate Moral Conscience), founded in 1884, saw its responsibility in fighting prostitution and the trade in women. In 1876 a branch of the International Abolitionist Federation was organized in

Sweden. Swedish feminists founded the Fredrika-Bremer-förbundet (FBF) in 1884, which took up central issues of the women's emancipation movement while particularly stressing the importance of moral renewal and the reform of society.

In other European countries the movement for moral reform did not become more widespread until the turn of the century. It began earlier in Protestant countries, where it also had a greater prominence. The movement for moral reform criticized state controls which degraded prostitutes and discriminated against them. It fought the double sexual standard, campaigned for better legal rights for unmarried mothers and their illegitimate children, and brought up the issue of women's rights to sexual self-determination. These attacks struck at central concepts of gender relations, and in their treatment of sexual relations they touched on subjects which had hitherto been taboo.

6. Social and Charitable Work

Women's charitable societies had already existed in the early nineteenth century, and charity work by women, first of the upper and later of the middle classes, was held in esteem. Charitable work for the amelioration of social conditions led women to involvement in emancipation movements. It often, though not necessarily always, also functioned to bridge the gap to feminist activities, for women began after a time to demand the right to participate in public decisions. Through their charitable work women gained political competence. Their growing preoccupation with the hardship of others led them to realize that redress could only come about with improved education of women and an accompanying change in their legal and political position. This was what brought many women into the emancipation movements.

V. STRATEGIES AND CONFLICTING LOYALTIES

It is not possible to distinguish rigorously between relational and individualist feminism or between equality and difference feminism for any of the movements treated here. Both lines of reasoning were used, usually at the same time.[49] However, it appears that in the struggle for women's suffrage at the turn of the century a preference developed for arguments based on the postulated difference between the sexes. Contributing to this was the spread of the women's movement through the integration of different social and religious societies. Equal-rights feminism based on human rights and the right to individual self-determination was more prevalent in the early stages of the movement and during times in which gender relations were discussed, but concrete activities by feminists were rare and the social basis of the women's emancipation movement was still slender.

The use of difference or equal-rights arguments cannot be linked directly with any particular factions within the women's emancipation movements. However, as Christine Bolt has shown in her analysis of the British and the American women's movements, there was a polarization with respect to the question of labor legislation. "Only when the question of protective labor laws arises, does the division between equal-rights and maternalist or social feminists become polarizing."[50] In general, different factions developed because of differences in their tactical course of action and not so much because of different lines of argumentation. In France, for example, one section of the women's emancipation movement, which had to consider its republican links, only hesitantly supported women's suffrage and advocated only moderate measures. Another section preferred a course of action which would attract large publicity and did not shrink from creating scandals.

Different trends and conflicting loyalties within the women's emancipation movements usually developed during boom periods where the number of supporters was increasing, one generation was succeeded by the next, and a social democratic women's movement began to emerge. In the German women's movement, for example, a moderate and a radical wing developed at the turn of the century. Although both factions pursued the concept of "spiritual motherhood" and supported improved education and employment opportunities for women, many of the younger generation of feminists tended to be stronger supporters of the right to individual self-determination, sexual and legal reform, and women's suffrage.

The relationship between the women's movement and the labor movement was characterized throughout Europe by the fundamental problem that in all socialist parties the women's question was subordinated to general problems of class conflict. The parties included women's suffrage in their general demands for freedom and equality but it was clearly secondary in their programs, and they were not prepared to place any additional emphasis on the special interests of women in their political struggle or to promote their organization.

Conflicts between middle-class and social democratic women's movements emerged in particular in the question of limited or universal women's suffrage and in questions of social policy. If, as in France, the social democratic women's movement was weak, then few appreciable conflicts arose in collaborations between middle-class and social democratic feminists. If, as was the case with the Czech and the Polish women's movements, there was a common enemy in the shape of German-Habsburg domination or Russian rule, then different forms of tactical collaboration ensued. In countries where there was a strong social democratic women's movement conflicting loyalties emerged after the turn of the century. In Norway, for example, this was the case with respect to protective labor legislation for women workers and sexual reform. In Hungary relations with women socialists became strained after the middle-class women's emancipation movement voted for a limited franchise for women on the basis of an educational and property census in 1912. In the German women's movement the conflicts between middle-class and social democratic women's movements were intensified by the Anti-Socialist Laws and the relatively strong class divisions in German society. When a national umbrella organization of German women's associations was founded in 1894, it refused, in order to retain the membership of conservative and Christian women's associations, to admit social democrats. The social democratic women for their part refused to join for political and ideological reasons. However, there was more crossing of borders between feminism and socialism than the long-established image of the "hostile sisters" would lead us to suppose. Historiography has also exaggerated the rift between the two wings of the women's movement for political reasons.

In her discussion of the British feminist movements Jane Rendall remarks that "feminist political cultures were fractured, split by differences, allowing fragmentation and choices." This also applies to the other women's movements in Europe. Conflicting loyalties resulted from the dividing lines of class, religion, nationality, and race which split all women's groups. Divergent feminist identities were possible and also manifested themselves symbolically. As the French example shows, Madeleine Pelletier, wearing men's clothes, worked alongside the "feminists in lace," as the women journalists of the journal La Fronde were nicknamed.

The conflict between feminist identity and national identity showed itself in the different enemies which the different women's movements perceived. The lack of full national sovereignty meant that Czech and Polish feminists were ambivalent about the Austrian and German women's movements, as were Greek feminists about the Turkish women's movement. A comparison between Britain and America testifies to the divergent forms the feminist groups took, influenced as they were by different social and political circumstances. In the United States race conflicts had a much greater impact than class conflicts on the movement. Black feminists were more likely to work together with black male activists. For British feminists race did not have the same importance, "though class was openly acknowledged as a complicating factor."[51]

Nevertheless, according to Christine Bolt, the existing differences between women did not play a dominating role in the consciousness of nineteenth-century feminists: "British and American feminists in the nineteenth and early twentieth centuries assumed that sisterhood was universal in a way that would be unthinkable today. Although they denounced the injustice of women being represented politically by men, they assumed that the active minority of women could speak on behalf of the rest of their sex."[52]

VI. SOCIAL CHANGE AND THE WOMEN'S EMANCIPATION MOVEMENT

The various women's emancipation movements developed along different paths owing to differences in underlying social conditions. Before summarizing these relationships it is necessary to look briefly at the particularities of the various national movements described in this volume.

A special feature of the British women's emancipation movement is its early demand for women's suffrage and women's property rights. This was due in a large part to the importance of the vote in British politics. A further particularity is that there was no sharp break after 1848 in the traditions of the women's movement, in contrast to developments in continental Europe where the impact of subsequent reactionary politics was deeply felt. In Britain there was thus a continuity in organizational and political experience. A third particularity is the extreme militancy of the suffragettes after

1900, which can be explained by disappointment resulting from the lack of results in the struggle for women's suffrage. At this time the movement was very strong, and it took an example from the militant tactics which had been employed in the Irish struggle for independence.

The most conspicuous characteristic of the French emancipation movement is pointed out by Florence Rochefort: "What was particularly French about French feminism were its ties to the Republic."[53] It is also striking that by 1900 a wide range of cultural areas for women had developed, including a feminist theater. A special feature of the French women's movement seems to be its fragmentation. Numerous associations existed for very limited purposes and often with so few members that the leaders of such associations were mockingly described as "generals without an army."

What is particularly impressive about the German women's movement is the breadth of its organization and its numerical strength at the turn of the century. Another particularity was the sharp conflicts between the different kinds of women's associations: middle-class and socialist, moderate and radical, religious and nondenominational. There were several reasons for these conflicts, including the breadth and diversity of the movement and the stark differences of class and religion in Germany. In addition, German political parties represented ideologies rather than interests. This led to sharp conflicts between groups with different world views and emancipation strategies. German feminists thus appear to have incorporated the special features of the German political tradition. It may be, however, that these sharp lines of conflict have been overemphasized by historians.

What is particularly noteworthy about the Dutch women's movement is the influence of a literary discourse coupled with the extensive promotion of the historical study of the movement. Also important were efforts to put the movement on an international footing, for example in the struggle for women's suffrage.

The striking feature of the Swedish women's movement is its intensive and early preoccupation with morality and sexuality. The concept of "true emancipation" linked the emancipation of women to the postulate of Christian love and social progress, had strongly visionary traits, and was directed against philosophical naturalism and the concept of human nature as solely governed by instincts. Both the Swedish and the Norwegian women's movements were influenced by the Danish women's movement which had emerged at the beginning of the 1870s. Among the Danish, Swedish, and Norwegian women's movements there were close literary and personal exchanges.

An unusual feature of the Norwegian women's movement was its early success in achieving women's suffrage, in 1907. This can be explained by the support which it gave to national policies and its contribution towards the dissolution of the union with Sweden. The social structures in Norway also played their part. Norway had long been primarily agrarian with only a small middle class. In this thinly populated country where manpower was in short supply and resources had to be used effectively it would not have been possible to dispense with the economic, political, and cultural contributions of women.

A specific feature of women's movements within the Habsburg Empire, such as in tripartite Poland, was their close ties to the different patriotic national movements and the great importance attached to women's education. Symptomatic for the Czech women's movement was that it developed in part as a national opposition to the Austrian women's movement and to Austrian rule. In Hungary there were links between the women's movement and the nationalist movements as well as close ties to the liberal-democratic avant-garde at the turn of the century.

What is striking about the Russian women's emancipation movement is its connection to the liberation movement and its adoption of radical demands in the area of education. Due to the very brief time of reform and the necessity of working under conditions of almost constant political repression, the borders between the feminist women's movement and the revolutionary movement were fluid.

The Spanish women's emancipation movement was shaped by the repressive system which predominated for most of the nineteenth century with only brief liberal democratic intervals. This led to the withdrawal from politics by Spanish society, an abstinence which also affected the Spanish women's movement. Another repressive element was the Catholic church, which had virtually unlimited power and which allied itself with the forces of political reaction. These restrictive political circumstances, coupled with the agrarian structures, explain the late development of an organized women's movement in Spain.

What was particularly noteworthy about the Greek women's movement was the strength of its journalism, its close connections to the Greek national independence movement against Turkish rule, and its efforts to create

a specific female tradition. Its numerical weakness was due largely to the socioeconomic backwardness of the country and the long years of national
suppression.

The women's emancipation movement in Europe was the result of and at
the same time the driving force behind cultural, political, and socioeconomic processes of modernization. The following social conditions made
the development of women's emancipation movements possible:

First, it is important to look at the philosophical roots. In the Enlightenment there was for the first time a broad intellectual basis for examining inequalities resulting from the existing gender order. Here are the beginnings of
the philosophical and literary feminism which flourished in individual European states at different times with the help of both men and women. In some
cases, such as in Russia or Spain, feminist literature was the primer; in other
countries, like the Netherlands and Norway, literary feminism expanded
public awareness of already existing women's emancipation movements.

After the French Revolution demands for liberty and equality based on
the concept of natural human rights spread through Europe. Such demands
were understood as having universal application, but it required the involvement of women like Olympe de Gouges to apply the Declaration of
Human Rights to the rights of women. Since this time women attempting
to change gender relationships and to emancipate themselves from various
forms of male domination have repeatedly referred to these arguments. The
prevailing gender relationships were considered social constructs and therefore subject to potential change. It was not just the Enlightenment and natural law which made the concept of women's emancipation conceivable and
legitimate. Other theories such as early socialism, Marxism, utilitarianism,
and positivism which developed in the course of the nineteenth century
emphasized the importance of women's emancipation for the general good.

Second, we must look at political conditions. The political constitution
of each nation determined the opportunities for the development of
women's emancipation movements. The assurance of such constitutional
rights as the right of assembly, freedom of speech, freedom of religion, and
freedom of political activity favored the advent of women's emancipation
movements. Restrictive and reactionary political systems, the extremes of
which were to be found in Spain and in Russia, delayed or hindered development. Political movements of men which supported the demands of

women's emancipation were usually underpinned by the new social classes and tended to be affiliated with liberalism or socialism. The movements' adversaries were the old political and clerical elites together with conservative men and women who opposed the integration of women into public life and were prepared to allow women's involvement only in traditional charitable forms of activity.

In states or societies which were predominantly Protestant (such as England or Sweden) there was a close correlation in the early stages of the movements between women's emancipation and religious and moral reform. In predominantly Catholic countries (France and Spain) and in Orthodox Russia the early women's emancipation movements were more strongly anticlerical. As the women's emancipation movements turned into mass movements, they also became more open to religion. During the height of the movement the established church and traditional religious forms were no longer necessarily in conflict with women's emancipation.

When women's emancipation movements initially emerged, they were usually closely connected to political and social opposition movements. In liberation movements and revolutions in which men and women jointly exerted themselves for basic rights, national independence, and a constitutional charter, the position of women was also on the agenda. Some men, although not the majority, were prepared to accept women as companions with equal rights. Women availed themselves of the additional scope for action which materialized during periods of social upheaval. There arose new forms of feminist involvement in the form of societies, journals, and alternative lifestyles.

In those countries in which revolutionary uprisings and social upheavals were replaced by periods of reaction and repression the success or defeat of democratic movements also influenced the further development of the women's emancipation movement (for example in France, Poland, and the German states until about 1860). If reaction won the day, women suffered doubly. The politically exposed feminists were persecuted as enemies of the state, and improvements in the position of women were circumscribed or rescinded by reactionary legislation. If the political opposition was victorious, it soon became apparent that the freedom fighters who now determined the national policies were not prepared to share political power with women. In part this was due to the fear that the majority of women, should they become eligible to vote, would vote conservative. In part this reneging was in order to court conservative male voters who might otherwise have been put off by the adoption of feminist goals. In the long term it was possible for women to gain some share of political power only after they had founded their own associations, formed coalitions, and mobilized public opinion for their interests.

In states which were not fully sovereign (such as Bohemia, Poland, and Norway) women were integrated in the struggle for national independence by the particular value accorded to maternity and women's work for the family. The suppression of national sovereignty threatened the national culture as manifested in language, religion, customs, and traditions. If the nation had ceased to exist, as was the case in Poland, then the family became the nucleus of the nation. Women regarded themselves initially as the helpmates of men, but their national and social involvement led to a new sense of self-worth and to demands for a voice in public affairs. Feminist demands tended to be moderate so as not to endanger the patriotic consensus. The overriding goal remained national independence and sovereignty.

Third, the women's movement was linked to socioeconomic change, i.e., the dissolution of the old social order and the growth of industrialization. The social consequences were migration, urbanization, and the erosion of traditional family bonds. With the spread of capitalist production processes a middle class and an industrial working class emerged. Socioeconomic change affected the position of women from all social classes. Activated by religious, charitable, and political motives, they initiated social and educational reform movements. Under widely different political conditions and for a wide range of different reasons the women's emancipation movements fought for improved education and employment opportunities.

Women's emancipation movements developed early in those countries where socioeconomic change was already advanced, and soon had a mass following. The emergent industrial and civil society resulted in a closer interaction among all classes. In the last decade of the nineteenth century women's associations with widely different goals increasingly united on national and international levels. This consolidation was the result of intensified communication which encouraged the exchange of ideas and accelerated developments in the different national women's movements.

With regard to the success of European women's movements it is possible to note in summary that they played an essential role in the process of social and cultural modernization: by undermining gender hierarchies they brought about changes in gender relations. The gradual democratization in this area opened up new fields of activity for "the second half of humanity" in education, employment, and public affairs. The ideal of civil society was given sub-stance by the multitude of autonomous activities directed towards emanci-pation. In this sense, even if it was not able to flourish in all European coun-tries, the women's movement must be seen as one of the great social movements of the nineteenth century, and an echo can be heard in all of the countries presented here.

Reference Matter

Notes

Chapter 1

1. Up until now little work has been done on women's emancipation movements from a synthetic point of view. Pioneer works are Richard Evans, *The Feminists. Women's Emancipation Movements in Europe, America and Australia, 1840–1920* (London: Croom Helm, 1977); Jane Rendall, *The Origins of Modern Feminism: Women in Britain, France, and the United States, 1780–1860* (New York: Schocken Books, 1984); important sources were examined and synthesized by Susan Groag Bell, Karen Offen, eds., *Women, the Family, and Freedom: The Debate in Documents, 1750–1950.* 2 vols. (Stanford: Stanford University Press, 1983); a stimulating reader is Tayo Andreasen et al., eds., *Moving On. New Perspectives on the Women's Movement* (Aarhus: Aarhus University Press, 1991); now as a new standard work see Karen Offen, *European Feminisms 1700–1950. A Political History* (Stanford: Stanford University Press 2000); on the women's emancipation movement in the first half of the nineteenth century see Bonnie S. Anderson, *Joyous Greetings! The First International Women's Movement* (New York: Oxford University Press, 2000). Soon to be published is an anthology by Ute Gerhard on the history of the feminist movement in the twentieth century. A useful bibliography of new main works on the history of European women's movements is to be found in Offen, *European Feminisms*, pp. 509–20; further titles are listed in Karen Offen, "Liberty, Equality, and Justice for Women: The Theory and Practice of Feminism in Nineteenth-Century Europe," in Renate Bridenthal, Claudia Koonz, eds., *Becoming Visible: Women in European History*, 2nd ed. (Boston: Houghton-Mifflin, 1987); Karen Offen, Ruth Roach Pierson, Jane Rendall, eds., *Writing Women's History: International Perspectives* (London: Macmillan, 1991). For a selection of recent work on the feminist movement as well as specific aspects of the women's movement from a comparative perspective see Tjitske Akkerman, Siep Stuurman, eds., *Perspectives on Feminist Political Thought in European History, from the Middle Ages to the Present* (London: Routledge, 1998); Gisela Bock, Pat Thane, eds., *Maternity*

and Gender Policies: Women and the Rise of the European Welfare States, 1880s–1950s (London: Routledge, 1991); Mineke Bosch, Annemarie Kloosterman, eds., *Politics and Friendship: Letters from the International Woman Suffrage Alliance, 1902–1942* (Columbus: Ohio State University Press, 1990); Caroline Daley, Melanie Nolan, eds., *Suffrage and Beyond. International Feminist Perspectives* (New York: New York University Press, 1994); Anne-Marie Käppeli, "Feminist Scenes," in Genevieve Fraisse, Michelle Perrot, eds., *A History of Women in the West.* vol. 4: *Emerging Feminism from Revolution to World War* (Cambridge: The Belknap Press of Harvard University Press, 1993), pp. 482–514; Marlene LeGates, *Making Waves: A History of Feminism in Western Society* (Toronto: Copp Clark/Addison Wesley, 1996); Gerda Lerner, *The Creation of Feminist Consciousness: From the Middle Ages to 1870* (New York: Oxford University Press, 1993); Margret H. McFadden, *Golden Cables of Sympathy: The Transatlantic Sources of Nineteenth-Century Feminism* (Lexington: University of Kentucky Press, 1999); Sheila Rowbotham, *Women in Movement. Feminism and Social Action* (New York: Routledge, 1992); Leila J. Rupp, *Worlds of Women: International Women's Organizations, 1888–1945* (Princeton: Princeton University Press, 1998); Barbara Ryan, *Feminism and the Women's Movement. Dynamics of Change in Social Movement, Ideology and Activism* (New York: Routledge, 1992); Ulla Wikander, Alice Kessler-Harris, Jane Lewis, eds., *Protecting Women: Labor Legislation in Europe, the United States, and Australia, 1880–1920* (Urbana: University of Illinois Press, 1995). For literature about the national women's emancipation movements please refer to the sources in the following chapters.

2. Up until now the history of women's emancipation movements prior to the First World War has been better researched than that of the period between the wars. More recent research may be able to correct the notion that women's movements disintegrated once the right to vote had been achieved.

3. Representative titles from the literature on the women's movements which were not treated here are: Harriet Anderson, *Utopian Feminism: Women's Movements in Fin-de-Siècle Vienna* (New Haven: Yale University Press, 1992); Carol Coulter, *The Hidden Tradition. Feminism, Women and Nationalism in Ireland* (Cork: Cork University Press, 1992); Annarita Buttafuoco, *Cronache femminile: Temi e momenti della stampa emancipazionista in Italia dall'unità al fascismo* (Siena: Università degli studi di Siena, 1988); Fiorenza Taricone, *L'associazionismo femminile in Italia dall'unità al fascismo* (Milan: Edizioni Unicopli, 1996); Denise de Weerdt, *En de vrouwen? Vrouw, Vrouwenbeweging en feminisme in Belgie, 1830–1960* (Ghent: Maserellfonds, 1980); Eliane Gubin, ed., "Cent ans du féminisme en Belgique," in *Revue du Groupe interdisciplinaire d'Études sur les femmes,* No. 1, 1993; Joao Gomes Esteves, *A Liga Republicana das Mulheres Portuguesas: Uma organizacao politica e feminista, 1909–1919* (Lisbon 1991); Beatrix Mesmer, *Ausgeklammert, eingeklammert. Frauen und Frauenorganisationen in der Schweiz des 19. Jahrhunderts*

(Basel: Helbig & Lichtenhahn, 1988); Sibylle Hardmeier, *Frühe Frauenstimmrechts-bewegung in der Schweiz (1890–1930). Argumente, Strategien, Netzwerk und Gegen-bewegung* (Zürich: Chronos, 1997); Neda Bozinovic, *Zensko Pitanje u Srbiji u XIX–XX Veku* (Belgrade: Dvadeset cetvrta, 1996); Claudia Schöning-Kalender, Ayla Neusel, Mechthild M. Jansen, eds., *Feminismus, Islam, Nation. Frauenbewe-gungen im Maghreb, in Zentralasien und in der Türkei* (Frankfurt: Campus, 1997). Further literature in Offen, *European Feminisms*, pp. 509–20.

4. The early creation of nation-states such as we are familiar with from the U.S.A., France, and Britain does not apply to the majority of European states and nations. Beginning in the 1820s, Greece gradually separated itself as a nation-state from the supranational Ottoman Empire in a process which continued through-out the nineteenth century. Italy achieved national unity in 1861. Until the found-ing of the German Empire in 1871, Germany consisted of numerous individual sovereign states. Until 1905 Norway was bound to Sweden in a personal union. The building of nation-states in the southern part of eastern Europe began after the First World War with the decline of the Habsburg Monarchy and the Ot-toman Empire. However, within these multinational states national movements had already existed since the beginning of the nineteenth century, generating vio-lent political tensions.

5. Ida Blom, Karen Hagemann, Catherine Hall, eds., *Gendered Nations: Na-tionalism and Gender Order in the Long Nineteenth Century* (Oxford: Berg, 1999).

6. Thus Richard Evans: "The term 'feminism' is defined in this book in its usual meaning as 'the doctrine of equal rights for women, based on the theory of the equality of the sexes.' It first came into English usage in this sense in the 1890s from the French, replacing the term 'womanism' . . . For most of the period cov-ered by this book, the term 'feminism' is thus, strictly speaking, anachronistic, though it is still preferable to 'womanism' on grounds of common usage; it is also, I believe, superior to 'women's movement', a term which came to be extended to almost every aspect of women's organised activities, on grounds of clarity and pre-cision." Evans, *Feminists*, p. 39.

7. Tayo Andreasen, Anette Borchorst, Drude Dahlerup, Eva Lous, Hanne Rimmen Nielsen, "Introduction," in Andreasen et al., eds., *Moving On*, p. 9; on the question of definition cf. ibid. pp. 8–12.

8. Cf. Offen's article in this collection, p. 29. For her complete reflections on the choice of terminology see Offen, *European Feminisms*, pp. 19–21.

9. Karen Offen expresses this point precisely: "Feminism has been a controver-sial term since its introduction into European discourse in the 1880s and 1890s. Is it still too dangerous today to define, embrace, and utilize it? If we don't claim it, we leave it to others to use against us." (Offen's article in this collection, p. 23).

10. Andreasen et al., eds., *Moving On*, p. 9.

11. Karen Offen, "On the French Origin of the Words Feminism and Feminist," in *Feminist Issues*, Vol. 8, 1988, pp. 45–51.

12. A study of the history of the term "feminism" describing its different meanings and usage in European women's emancipation movements in the twentieth century would be very useful.

13. Rendall, p. 34 in this volume.

14. Nash, pp. 243–44 in this volume.

15. Cf. Mineke Bosch's thoughts about the possibilities of comparison in her article on the women's movement in the Netherlands.

16. Originally articles on morals and suffrage from a comparative perspective were planned for this anthology. Unfortunately, they could not be submitted. Therefore, the only articles here from a comparative perspective are by Christine Bolt, who compares the American and British women's movements, and by Karen Offen, who compares women's demands for emancipation at their inception and the first women's movements from 1789–1860. These articles show the direction which further systematic research should take.

Chapter 2

1. Space does not permit a discussion of several studies that offer more limited comparisons: Donald Meyer's *Sex and Power: The Rise of Women in America, Russia, Sweden, and Italy* (Middletown, Conn.: Wesleyan University Press, 1987); Naomi Black's study, *Social Feminism* (Ithaca, N.Y.: Cornell University Press, 1989), which compares three post–World War I movements (U.S., English, French); or Anne-Marie Käppeli's "Feminist Scenes," in Georges Duby, Michelle Perrot, eds., *History of Women*, vol. 4 (French ed., 1991; English ed., 1993), which offers a wide-ranging and useful survey for the nineteenth century, but in the absence of any discussion of the serious political obstacles that organized feminism in Europe had to surmount. Nor have I opted to discuss the short section, "Traditions Rejected: A History of Feminism in Europe," in Bonnie S. Anderson, Judith P. Zinsser, eds., *A History of Their Own: Women in Europe from Prehistory to the Present*, vol. 2 (New York: Harper & Row, 1988). Gerda Lerner's *The Creation of Feminist Consciousness: From the Middle Ages to Eighteen-seventy* (New York: Oxford University Press, 1992) provides only cursory treatment of feminism in eighteenth- and nineteenth-century Europe.

2. Richard J. Evans, *The Feminists: Women's Emancipation Movements in Europe, America and Australasia, 1840–1920* (London: Croom-Helm; New York: Barnes & Noble, 1977). Evans subsequently published an important collection of related articles, *Comrades and Sisters: Feminism, Socialism and Pacifism in Europe 1870–1945* (Sussex: Wheatsheaf Books, and New York: St. Martin's Press, 1987), which will not be discussed here.

3. See Evans's conclusion, *The Feminists*, pp. 232–45.

4. Ute Gerhard, "A Hidden and Complex Heritage: Reflections on the History of Germany's Women's Movements," *Women's Studies International Forum*, vol. 5, no. 6 (1982), p. 565.

5. Susan Groag Bell and Karen M. Offen, eds., *Women, the Family, and Freedom: The Debate in Documents, 1750–1950*, 2 vols. (Stanford, Calif.: Stanford University Press, 1983).

6. This strategy was a response to the heavily U.S.-based content of two documentary collections that appeared in the early 1970s: Miriam Schneir, ed., *Feminism: The Essential Historical Writings* (New York: Random House, 1972) and Alice Rossi, ed., *The Feminist Papers* (New York: Columbia University Press, 1972). Our collection was initially designed to supplement Susan Groag Bell's collection, *Women: From the Greeks to the French Revolution* (Belmont, Calif.: Wadsworth, 1973; now published in a second edition by Stanford University Press).

7. Many of the arguments in *Women, the Family, and Freedom* were recapitulated and refined in my essay "Liberty, Equality, and Justice for Women: The Theory and Practice of Feminism in Nineteenth-Century Europe," published in the second revised edition of Renate Bridenthal, Claudia Koonz, eds., *Becoming Visible: Women in European History* (Boston: Houghton Mifflin Company, 1987), pp. 335–73.

8. *Women's Studies International Forum*, vol. 5, no. 6 (1982); republished in book format as *Reassessments of "First Wave" Feminism* (Oxford: Pergamon Press, 1983).

9. Jane Rendall, *The Origins of Modern Feminism: Women in Britain, France and the United States, 1780–1860* (New York: Schocken Books, 1984, and London: Macmillan, 1985).

10. See Rendall's "Introduction," in *Origins*, p. 1.

11. I worked out the notion of relational feminism in the following articles: "Ernest Legouvé and the Doctrine of 'Equality in Difference' for Women: A Case Study of Male Feminism in Nineteenth-Century French Thought," *Journal of Modern History*, vol. 58 (1986), no. 2: 452–84; "Liberty, Equality, and Justice for Women" (see note 7 above); and "Defining Feminism: A Comparative Historical Perspective," *Signs: Journal of Women in Culture and Society*, vol. 14, no. 1 (1988): 119–57.

12. Rendall, "Introduction," in *Origins*, p. 2.

13. See Jane Rendall's article in this collection. See also Jane Rendall, "Citizenship, Culture and Civilisation: The Languages of British Suffragists, 1866–1874," in Caroline Daley, Melanie Nolan, eds., *Suffrage and Beyond: International Feminist Perspectives* (Auckland: Auckland University Press, New York: New York University Press, and London: Pluto Press, 1994); and Rendall, ed., *Equal or Different: Women's Politics, 1800–1914* (Oxford: Basil Blackwell, 1987), which includes her article, "'A Moral Engine'? Feminism, Liberalism and the *English Woman's Journal*."

14. See Brita Rang, "'Jus fasque esse in rempublicam litterariam foeminas adscribi': Gelehrt(inn)en-Enzyklopädien des 17. und 18. Jahrhunderts," *Paedagogica Historica*, vol. 28, no. 3 (1992): 511–49; and Gianna Pomata, "History, Particular and Universal: On Reading Some Recent Women's History Textbooks," *Feminist Studies*, vol. 19, no. 1 (1993). See also Susanna Bucci, "La produzione letteraria dedicata alle donne illustri: pubblico e autori nel clima polemico del dibattito sui diritti del sesso femminile," in Fiorenza Taricone and Susanna Bucci, *La condizione della donna nel XVII et XVIII secolo* (Rome: Carucci, 1983), pp. 137–219.

15. See esp. Joan de Jean, *Tender Geographies: Women and the Origins of the Novel in France* (New York: Columbia University Press, 1991).

16. See Elizabeth Goldsmith and Dena Goodman, eds., *Going Public: Women and Publishing in Early Modern France* (Ithaca, N.Y.: Cornell University Press, 1996).

17. See Karen Offen, *European Feminisms, 1700–1950: A Political History* (Stanford: Stanford University Press, 2000), esp. chap. 2, "Reclaiming the Enlightenment for Feminism."

18. Rendall, *Origins*, p. 320.

19. See Constance Jordan, *Renaissance Feminism: Literary Texts and Political Models* (Ithaca, N.Y.: Cornell University Press, 1990); and Londa S. Schiebinger, *The Mind Has No Sex? Women in the Origins of Modern Science* (Cambridge, Mass.: Harvard University Press, 1989).

20. For further discussion of the texts mentioned in the rest of this paragraph, see Offen, *European Feminisms*, chap. 2, "Reclaiming the Enlightenment for Feminism."

21. Recent examples of such international collaboration include: Gisela Bock and Pat Thane, eds., *Maternity and Gender Policies: Women and the Rise of the European Welfare States, 1880s–1950s* (London: Routledge, 1991); and Ulla Wikander, Alice Kessler-Harris, and Jane Lewis, eds., *Protecting Women: Labor Legislation in Europe, the United States, and Australia, 1880–1920* (Urbana: University of Illinois Press, 1995).

22. The only scholar to date to address in a substantive manner the complexities of "backlash" arguments in the immediate postrevolutionary period is the French philosopher-historian Geneviève Fraisse, in *Reason's Muse: Sexual Difference and the Birth of Democracy* (Chicago: University of Chicago Press, 1994). This work was originally published in French as *Muse de la Raison* (Paris: Alinea, 1989).

23. I am in complete agreement on this point with Amanda Vickery. See her "Historiographical Review: Golden Age to Separate Spheres? A Review of the Categories and Chronology of English Women's History," *The Historical Journal*, vol. 36, no. 2 (1993): 383–414.

24. This radical demand was articulated in 1789 in an anonymous text entitled

"Requête des dames à l'Assemblée Nationale" (1789), reprinted in *Les Femmes dans la Révolution française, 1789–1794,* presented by Albert Soboul, vol. 1 (Paris: ED-HIS, 1982).

25. The words of P. B. von W. and "Rosa Califronia (contessa romana)" are translated in *European Feminisms,* chap. 3, "Challenging Masculine Aristocracy."

26. See Fraisse, *Reason's Muse* on this debate over literacy.

27. On the difficulties of historical memory for nineteenth-century French feminists and their attempts to reclaim the revolution, see Karen Offen, "Women's Memory, Women's History, Women's Political Action: The French Revolution in Retrospect, 1789–1889–1989," *Journal of Women's History,* vol. 1, no. 3 (1990): 211–30.

28. See Christine Planté, *La Petite Soeur de Balzac: Essai sur la femme auteur* (Paris: Seuil, 1989); and Susan Kirkpatrick, *Las Romanticas: Women Writers and Subjectivity in Spain, 1835–1850* (Berkeley and Los Angeles: University of California Press, 1989).

29. Madame de Staël, *De la littérature* (Paris, 2nd ed., 1800), as translated in *An Extraordinary Woman: Selected Writings of Germaine de Staël,* trans. and introd. by Vivian Folkenflik (New York: Columbia University Press, 1988), pp. 201, 205.

30. Rendall, *Origins,* pp. 291, 298–9.

31. I have tried to clarify this problem in "Women, Citizenship, and Suffrage with a French Twist, 1789–1993," in Daley, Nolan, eds., *Suffrage and Beyond,* pp. 151–70.

32. See Florence Rochefort's essay, this volume. See also Laurence Klejman and Florence Rochefort, *L'égalité en marche: Le Féminisme sous la Troisième République* (Paris: des femmes and Presses de la Fondation Nationale des Sciences Politiques, 1989).

33. The Prussian Decree on Associations is translated in Bell, Offen, eds., *Women, the Family, and Freedom,* vol. 1, doc. 86, pp. 286–7.

34. Tayo Andreasen, Anette Borchorst, Drude Dahlerup, Eva Lous, Hanne Rimmen Nielsen, ed., *Moving On: New Perspectives on the Women's Movement* (1992), Acta Julandica LXVII:1, Humanities Series 66 (Aarhus: Aarhus University Press, 1991).

35. Ibid., introduction, p. 8.

36. See Karen Offen, "On the French Origin of the Words 'Feminism' and 'Feminist,'" *Feminist Issues,* vol. 8, no. 2 (1988).

37. Offen, "Defining Feminism."

38. For a discussion of male feminism, see Offen, "Ernest Legouvé," cited in note 11.

39. Rendall is referring primarily to Davidoff and Hall's *Family Fortunes;* however, the text *Connecting Spheres: Women in the Western World, 1500 to the Present,*

ed. Marilyn J. Boxer and Jean H. Quataert (New York: Oxford University Press, 1987) should also be mentioned here as a highly successful attempt to arrive at a holistic interpretation that takes political considerations into account.

40. See especially the critiques of Landes's interpretation by Keith Baker, "Defining the Public Sphere in Eighteenth-Century France: Variations on a Theme by Habermas," Craig Calhoun, ed., *Habermas and the Public Sphere* (Cambridge, Mass.: MIT Press, 1992); and Dena Goodman, "Public Sphere and Private Life: Toward a Synthesis of Current Historiographical Approaches to the Old Regime," *History and Theory*, vol. 31 (1992), no. 1: 1–20.

41. The concern with "democracy" that informs the otherwise invigorating works of Christine Faure, Michèle Riot-Sarcey, and Anne Phillips thus seems somewhat anachronistic. See Rendall, "Citizenship, Culture and Civilisation."

42. The problems inherent in juxtaposing equality with difference have been ably identified by the U.S. historians of nineteenth-century France, Claire Goldberg Moses and Joan W. Scott. See also my article, "Reflections on National Specificities in Continental European Feminisms," *University College, Galway Women's Studies Centre Review*, vol. 3 (1995), pp. 53–61.

43. See, among other examples (listed in order of publication): Sandra Stanley Holton, *Feminism and Democracy: Women's Suffrage and Reform Politics in Britain, 1900–1918* (Cambridge, Eng.: Cambridge University Press, 1986); Ann Taylor Allen, *Feminism and Motherhood in Germany, 1800–1914* (New Brunswick, N.J.: Rutgers University Press, 1991); Eliane Gubin, ed., "Cent ans de féminismes," special issue of *Sextant: Revue du Groupe interdisciplinaire d'études sur les femmes*, no. 1 (1993); Anne Cova, *Droits des femmes et protection de la maternité en France 1892–1939*, 4 vols. (Florence: Doctoral thesis, European University Institute, Department of History and Civilisation, 1994).

44. Rendall, "Citizenship, Culture and Civilisation."

45. Kari Melby, "Women's Ideology: Difference, Equality or a New Femininity. Women Teachers and Nurses in Norway 1912–1940," in Tayo Andreasen et al., eds., *Moving On*, pp. 138–54.

46. See, for example, the following works (listed in order of publication): Bogna Lorence-Kot, "Klementyna Tanska Hoffmanowa, Cultural Nationalism and a New Formula for Polish Womanhood," *History of European Ideas*, vol. 8, no. 4–5 (1987): 435–50; Martha Bohachevsky-Chomiak, *Feminists Despite Themselves: Women in Ukrainian Community Life, 1884–1939* (Edmonton: Canadian Institute of Ukrainian Studies, University of Alberta, 1988); Katherine David, "Czech Feminists and Nationalism in the Late Habsburg Monarchy: 'The First in Austria,'" *Journal of Women's History*, vol. 3, no. 2 (1991): 26–45; Norma L. Rudinsky, *Incipient Feminists: Women Writers in the Slovak National Revival* (Columbus, Ohio: Slavica Publishers, 1991); see also the article by Judith Szapor in this vol-

ume. For Greece, see Eleni Varikas, "La Révolte des Dames: Genése d'une conscience féministe dans la Grèce du 19 siècle (1833–1908)," Ph.D. diss., University
of Paris 7, 1986 (since published in Greek [Athens]), and her article in this volume. For Russia, see Bianka Pietrow-Ennker, *Rußlands "neue Menschen". Die En-*
twicklung der Frauenbewegung von den Anfängen bis zur Oktoberrevolution (Frank-
furt/ Main: Campus, 1999). For Hungary, see Susan Zimmermann, *Die Bessere*
Hälfte? Frauenbewegung und Frauenbestrebungen im Ungarn der Habsburger
Monarchie 1848 bis 1918 (Budapest: Napvilag Kiado; Vienna: Promedia, 1999).

47. See Bonnie Smith, "Gender and the Practices of Scientific History: The
Seminar and Archival Research in the Nineteenth Century," *American Historical*
Review, vol. 100, no. 4 (1995): 1150–76.

Chapter 3

1. Charlotte Carmichael Stopes, *British Freewomen: Their Historical Privileges*
(London: Swan Sonnenschein, 1894).

2. Judith Walkowitz, *City of Dreadful Danger: Narratives of Sexual Danger in*
Late-Victorian London (London: Virago, 1992), p. 165; Lina Eckenstein, *Woman*
under Monasticism: Chapters on Saint-Lore and Convent Life between A.D. 500 and
A.D. 1500 (Cambridge: Cambridge University Press, 1896). See also, on Eckenstein, Lucy Bland, *Banishing the Beast: English Feminism and Sexual Morality*
1885–1914 (Harmondsworth: Penguin, 1995), pp. 169–77.

3. Ray Strachey, *The Cause: A Short History of the Women's Movement in Great*
Britain (reprinted London: Virago, 1978 [1928], with preface by Barbara Strachey),
pp. 11–12; on Strachey, see Kathryn Dodd, "Cultural Politics and Women's Historical Writing: The Case of Ray Strachey's *The Cause*," *Women's Studies International*
Forum, vol. 13, no. 1/2 (1990): 127–37; Brian Harrison, *Prudent Revolutionaries:*
Portraits of British Feminists between the Wars (Oxford: Oxford University Press,
1987), chap. 6.

4. Kathryn Kish Sklar, "'Women Who Speak for an Entire Nation': American
and British Women at the World Anti-Slavery Convention, London, 1840," in
Jean Fagan Yellin and John C. Van Horne, eds., *The Abolitionist Sisterhood: Wom-*
en's Political Culture in Antebellum America (Ithaca, N.Y.: Cornell University Press,
1994), pp. 301–33, here 315. Sklar identifies three levels of that culture before the
1860s in Britain and the United States: group activity beyond the limits of the
family; gender-conscious group activity; and group activity intended to advance
women's rights and interests.

5. Claire Goldberg Moses, "Debating the Present, Writing the Past: 'Feminism'
in French History and Historiography," *Radical History Review*, vol. 52 (Winter
1994): 79–94.

6. In 1869, women ratepayers were given the borough vote, though in 1872 this was limited to unmarried women only. From 1870 ratepaying women could vote and all women could stand for the new school boards. From 1875, eligible women could stand for poor law boards. From 1894 eligible women could stand for parish and district councils and for London vestries. Only in 1907 could they be elected to city and county councils. Patricia Hollis, "Women in Council: Separate Spheres, Public Space," in Jane Rendall, ed., *Equal or Different: Women's Politics 1800–1914* (Oxford: Basil Blackwell, 1987), pp. 192–213.

7. For general perspectives on nineteenth-century feminism, see Philippa Levine, *Victorian Feminism 1850–1900* (London: Hutchinson, 1987), and Philippa Levine, "'The Humanising Influences of Five o'Clock Tea': Victorian Feminist Periodicals," *Victorian Studies*, vol. 33, no. 2 (1990): 293–306.

8. Olive Banks, *Becoming a Feminist: The Social Origins of "First Wave" Feminism* (Brighton: Wheatsheaf, 1986).

9. Philippa Levine, *Feminist Lives in Victorian England: Private Roles and Public Commitment* (Oxford: Basil Blackwell, 1990).

10. Ibid., p. 8.

11. Judith Walkowitz, "Male Vice and Female Virtue: Feminism and the Politics of Prostitution in Nineteenth Century Britain," in Ann Snitow, Christine Stansell, and Sharon Thompson, eds., *Powers of Desire: The Politics of Sexuality* (New York: Monthly Review Press, 1983), p. 422, quoted in Levine, *Feminist Lives in Victorian England*, p. 81.

12. Levine, *Feminist Lives in Victorian England*, p. 176.

13. Barbara Caine, *Victorian Feminists* (Oxford: Oxford University Press, 1992). Barbara Caine's *English Feminism 1780–1980* (Oxford: Oxford University Press, 1997) was published too late to be considered in the writing of this article, but chapters 1–3 address the issues considered here.

14. See, on this debate, Caine, *Victorian Feminists*, chap. 1; Karen Offen, "Defining Feminism: A Comparative Historical Approach," *Signs*, vol. 14, no. 1 (1988): 119–57; Nancy Cott and Ellen DuBois, "Comments on Karen Offen's Article, 'Defining Feminism: A Comparative Historical Approach,'" *Signs*, vol. 15, no. 1 (1989): 196–209.

15. Sklar, "'Women Who Speak for an Entire Nation'", p. 302.

16. Alice Kessler-Harris, *A Woman's Wage: Historical Meanings and Social Consequences* (Lexington: University of Kentucky Press, 1990), p. 97.

17. Janaki Nair, "On the Question of Agency in Feminist Historiography," *Gender and History*, vol. 6, no. 1 (1994): 82–100, here p. 100.

18. The term "Anglo-British" is taken from Colin Kidd, *Subverting Scotland's Past: Scottish Whig Historians and the Creation of an Anglo-British Identity, 1689–c. 1830* (Cambridge: Cambridge University Press, 1993).

19. Neal Blewett, "The Franchise in the United Kingdom, 1885–1918," *Past and Present*, vol. 32 (Dec. 1965): 27–56; H. C. G. Matthew, Ross I. McKibbin, J. Kay, "The Franchise Factor in the Rise of the Labour Party," *English Historical Review*, vol. 91, no. 361 (1976): 723–52.

20. José Harris, *Private Lives, Public Spirit: Britain 1870–1914* (Harmondsworth: Penguin, 1993), p. 186.

21. Ibid., p. 6.

22. See Jane Rendall, "Citizenship, Culture and Civilisation," in Caroline Daley and Melanie Nolan, eds., *Suffrage and Beyond: International Feminist Perspectives* (Auckland: University of Auckland Press, 1994), pp. 127–50, especially pp. 131–3.

23. On Mill, see Stefan Collini, *Public Moralists: Political Thought and Intellectual Life in Britain* (Oxford: Clarendon Press, 1991), chap. 4; John M. Robson, *The Improvement of Mankind: The Social and Political Thought of John Stuart Mill* (Toronto: University of Toronto Press, 1968).

24. Louisa Shore, "The Emancipation of Women," *Westminster Review*, vol. 102 old series, vol. 46 new series (July 1874), reprinted as *The Citizenship of Women, Socially Considered* (London: Savill, n.d.) and reprinted in Jane Lewis, ed., *Before the Vote Was Won: Arguments For and Against Women's Suffrage 1864–1896* (London: Routledge, 1987), pp. 184–222, here 218.

25. Sandra Stanley Holton, "To Educate Women into Rebellion: Elizabeth Cady Stanton and the Creation of a Transatlantic Network of Radical Suffragists," *American Historical Review*, vol. 99, no. 4 (Dec. 1994): 1112–1136.

26. June Hannam, *Isabella Ford* (Oxford: Basil Blackwell, 1989), pp. 101–5.

27. The issue is discussed in M. J. D. Roberts, "Feminism and the State in Later Victorian England," *Historical Journal*, vol. 38, no. 1 (1995): 85–110; Levine, *Feminist Lives in Victorian England*, pp. 48–54.

28. Levine, *Feminist Lives in Victorian England*, pp. 48–50. Levine also examines the occupational backgrounds of the husbands of her sample: 9% of women in the sample had married men in political careers and 5% academic; 4% and 5% had married into the law and business respectively.

29. Brian Harrison, "A Genealogy of Reform in Modern Britain," in Christine Bolt, Seymour Drescher, eds., *Anti-Slavery, Religion and Reform: Essays in Memory of Roger Anstey* (Folkestone: Dawson, 1980), pp. 119–48.

30. Paula Bartley, "'Seeking and Saving': the Reform of Prostitutes and the Prevention of Prostitution in Birmingham," unpublished Ph.D. diss., University of Wolverhampton, 1995.

31. "I have been thrown into such low spirits by being very much laughed at, at Gladstone's party the other night as my poor little Committee somehow found its way into the London papers." She had recently founded a women's suffrage committee in the small Gloucestershire village of Stroud. Lady Amberley to Helen

Taylor, 16th February 1871, f. 39, Mill-Taylor Papers vol. 19, British Library of Political and Economic Sciences, London School of Economics.

32. Lady Frances Balfour, *Ne Obliviscaris: Dinna Forget*, 2 vols. (London: Hodder and Stoughton, 1930), vol. 2, p. 127, quoted in Leah Leneman, *A Guid Cause: The Women's Suffrage Movement in Scotland* (Aberdeen: Aberdeen University Press, 1991), p. 33.

33. Those who do, however, include Phoebe Marks (later Hertha Ayrton), from an immigrant working-class Polish-Jewish family; Isa Craig, a hosier's daughter who married an iron merchant; Sarah Dickenson, whose husband and father were both enamelers. Levine, *Feminist Lives in Victorian England*, p. 50.

34. Dorothy Thompson, "Women and Nineteenth Century Radical Politics: A Lost Dimension," in Juliet Mitchell, Ann Oakley, eds., *The Rights and Wrongs of Women* (Harmondsworth: Penguin, 1976).

35. *The Autobiography of Mary Smith, Schoolmistress and Nonconformist: A Fragment of a Life, with Letters from Jane Welsh Carlyle and Thomas Carlyle* (London: Bemrose, 1892).

36. I owe this reference to Helen Rogers, "Poetesses and Politicians: Gender, Knowledge and Power, 1830–1870," unpublished Ph.D. diss., University of York, 1994, p. 322.

37. Jill Liddington and Jill Norris, *One Hand Tied Behind Us: The Rise of the Women's Suffrage Movement* (London: Virago, 1978), chap. 5.

38. Karen Hunt, *Equivocal Feminists: The Social Democratic Federation and the Woman Question 1884–1911* (Cambridge: Cambridge University Press, 1996).

39. Levine, *Feminist Lives in Victorian England*, p. 38.

40. See especially Clare Midgley, *Women against Slavery: The British Campaigns, 1780–1870* (London: Routledge, 1992); Louis Billington and Rosamond Billington, "'A Burning Zeal for Righteousness?' Women in the British Anti-Slavery Movement 1820–1860," in Jane Rendall, ed., *Equal or Different*, pp. 82–111; Clare Taylor, *Women of the Anti-Slavery Movement: The Weston Sisters* (Basingstoke: Macmillan, 1995), pp. 82–111.

41. Harrison, "A Genealogy of Reform in Modern Britain"; Alex Tyrrell, "'Woman's Mission' and Pressure Group Politics in Britain (1825–1860)," *Bulletin of the John Rylands Library*, vol. 63, no. 1 (1980): 194–230.

42. For instance, Leonore Davidoff and Catherine Hall, *Family Fortunes: Men and Women of the English Middle Class, 1780–1870* (London: Hutchinson, 1987); Jane Rendall, *Women in Britain, France and the United States, 1780–1860* (Basingstoke: Macmillan, 1985), chap. 3; Francis K. Prochaska, *Women and Philanthropy in Nineteenth-Century England* (Oxford: Oxford University Press, 1980).

43. Levine, *Feminist Lives in Victorian England*, pp. 31–3 and 184 n. 52. Levine

also finds three representatives of Judaism in her sample: Lady Goldsmid, Phoebe Marks, and the Bradford feminist Fanny Hertz.

44. Figures are drawn from Alan D. Gilbert, *Religion and Society in Industrial England: Church, Chapel and Social Change 1740–1914* (London: Longman, 1976), pp. 40–1.

45. Elizabeth Isichei, *Victorian Quakers* (Oxford: Oxford University Press, 1970); John Seed, "The Role of Unitarianism in the Formation of Liberal Culture 1775–1851: A Social History," unpublished Ph.D. diss., University of Hull, 1981; Ruth Watts, "Knowledge is Power—Unitarians, Gender and Education in the Eighteenth and Early Nineteenth Centuries," *Gender and Education*, vol. 1, no. 1 (1989): 35–50. Since this paper was written, Kathryn Gleadle's *The Early Feminists: Radical Unitarians and the Emergence of the Women's Rights Movement, 1831–1851* (Basingstoke and New York: Macmillan and St. Martin's Press, 1995) has added greatly to our knowledge of radical Unitarianism in the first half of the nineteenth century.

46. Jane Rendall, "'A Moral Engine?' Feminism, Liberalism and the *English Woman's Journal*," in Rendall, ed., *Equal or Different*, pp. 112–38; Josephine Kamm, *Hope Deferred: Girls' Education in English History* (London: Methuen, 1965), pp. 175–6.

47. Holton, "To Educate Women into Rebellion"; idem, "From Anti-Slavery to Suffrage Militancy: The Bright Circle, Elizabeth Cady Stanton and the Women's Movement," in Daley and Nolan, eds., *Suffrage and Beyond*, pp. 213–33; idem, *Suffrage Days: Stories from the Women's Suffrage Movement in Britain, 1865–1918* (London: Routledge, 1996).

48. Rev. Thomas Guthrie, "The Rights of Women," *Englishwoman's Review*, vol. 3 (April 1867): 159–61; Lecture by the Rev. Ward Beecher on the suffrage [from the *New York Daily Tribune*, February 14, 1867], in *Englishwoman's Review*, vol. 3 (Apr. 1867): 180–91 ; Rev. T. G. Crippen, "The Testimony of Holy Scripture Concerning the Social Status of Women," *Englishwoman's Review*, vol. 3 n. s. (July 1870): 127–63.

49. Sandra Stanley Holton, "Free Love and Victorian Feminism: the Divers Matrimonials of Elizabeth Wolstenholme and Ben Elmy," *Victorian Studies*, vol. 36 (Winter 1994): 199–222.

50. Edward Royle, *Radicals, Secularists and Republicans: Popular Freethought in Britain, 1866–1915* (Manchester: Manchester University Press, 1980), pp. 246–47.

51. See Diana Burfield, "Theosophy and Feminism: Some Explorations in Nineteenth-Century Biography," in Pat Holden, ed., *Women's Religious Experience* (London: Croom Helm, 1983), pp. 27–56.

52. See especially Esther Breitenbach and Eleanor Gordon, *Out of Bounds: Women in Scottish Society 1800–1945* (Edinburgh: Edinburgh University Press, 1992); Leah Leneman, *A Guid Cause: The Women's Suffrage Movement in Scotland*

(Aberdeen: Aberdeen University Press, 1991); Eleanor Gordon, *Women and the Labour Movement in Scotland 1850–1914* (Oxford: Clarendon Press, 1991). On Wales, see Angela John, *Our Mothers' Land: Essays in Welsh Women's History 1830–1930* (Cardiff: University of Wales Press, 1991).

53. Leneman, *A Guid Cause*, pp. 18–24; Elspeth King, "The Scottish Women's Suffrage Movement," in Breitenbach and Gordon, eds., *Out of Bounds*, pp. 121–50.

54. Callum G. Brown and Jayne D. Stephenson's pioneering essay, "'Sprouting Wings': Women and Religion in Scotland c. 1890–1950," in Breitenbach and Gordon, eds., *Out of Bounds*, pp. 95–120, does not address the issue of the religious background of Scottish feminists.

55. See: Margaret Ward, *Unmanageable Revolutionaries: Women and Irish Nationalism* (London: Pluto Press, 1983); Rosemary Cullen Owens, *Smashing Times: A History of the Irish Women's Suffrage Movement 1889–1922* (Dublin: Attic Press, 1984); Cliona Murphy, *The Women's Suffrage Movement and Irish Society in the Early Twentieth Century* (New York: Harvester Wheatsheaf, 1989); Mary Cullen, "Women's History in Ireland," in Karen Offen, Ruth Roach Pierson, and Jane Rendall, eds., *Writing Women's History: International Perspectives* (Basingstoke: Macmillan, 1991), pp. 429–42.

56. Denise Riley, *"Am I That Name ?" Feminism and the Category of Women in History* (Basingstoke: Macmillan, 1989); Patrick Joyce, *Democratic Subjects: The Self and the Social in Nineteenth-century England* (Cambridge: Cambridge University Press, 1994); Benedict Anderson, *Imagined Communities: Reflections on the Origin and Spread of Nationalism* (London: Verso, 1983).

57. Patricia Hollis, "Women in Council," in Rendall, ed., *Equal or Different*, pp. 208–9; idem, *Ladies Elect: Women in English Local Government, 1865–1914* (Oxford: Clarendon Press, 1987); review of *Ladies Elect* by Susan Pennybacker, *Gender and History*, vol. 1, no. 2 (1989): 238–40.

58. Mary Smith, "Ethelflaed Queen of Mercia," in *Progress, and Other Poems* (London: John Russell Smith, 1873).

59. Lydia Becker, "The Rights and Duties of Women in Local Government," reprinted in Lewis, ed., *Before the Vote Was Won*, pp. 347–353.

60. *Women's Suffrage Journal*, vol. 25 (1 March 1872): 30, and vol. 33 (1 Nov. 1872): 142; John W. Burrow, "'The Village Community' and the Uses of History in Late Nineteenth-Century England," in Neil McKendrick, ed., *Historical Perspectives: Studies in English Thought and Society in Honour of J. H. Plumb* (London: Europa, 1974); Eugenio Biagini, *Liberty, Retrenchment and Reform: Popular Liberalism in the Age of Gladstone* (Cambridge: Cambridge University Press, 1992), pp. 319–28.

61. On Stopes, see Ruth Hall, *Marie Stopes: A Biography* (London: Virago, 1977), pp. 15–16.

62. Anne Summers, *Angels and Citizens: British Women as Military Nurses 1854–1914* (London: Routledge, 1988), chap. 5, "Philanthropy and the Battlefield, 1854–1878."

63. Ibid., p. 153.

64. Antoinette Burton, "The White Woman's Burden: British Feminists and 'The Indian Woman,' 1865–1915," in Nupur Chaudhuri and Margaret Strobel, eds., *Western Women and Imperialism. Complicity and Resistance* (Bloomington: Indiana University Press, 1992), pp. 137–57; idem, *Burdens of History: British Feminists, Indian Women, and Imperial Culture, 1865–1915* (Chapel Hill: University of North Carolina Press, 1994), pp. 141–55; Vron Ware, *Beyond the Pale: White Women, Racism and History* (Oxford: Polity, 1992), pp. 147–64.

65. David Rubinstein, *A Different World for Women. The Life of Millicent Garret Fawcett* (Hemel Hempstead: Harvester Wheatsheaf, 1991), p. 116.

66. Antoinette Burton, "Rules of Thumb: British History and 'Imperial Culture' in Nineteenth- and Twentieth-Century Britain," *Women's History Review*, vol. 3, no. 4 (1994): 483–500.

67. See, for instance, the encounters described in Raewyn Dalziel, "Presenting the Enfranchisement of New Zealand Women Abroad," in Daley and Norton, eds., *Suffrage and Beyond*.

68. Bland, *Banishing the Beast*, pp. 159–61.

69. Nair, "On the Question of Agency," p. 100.

Chapter 4

1. On the problem of internationalism in women's history, see Mineke Bosch, Marjan Schwegman, "The Future of Women's History: A Dutch Perspective," *Gender and History*, 3 (1991): 129–46.

2. Karen Offen, "Defining Feminism: A Comparative Historical Approach," *Signs* 14 (1988): 119–57.

3. It was reprinted five times in one year, and it was said to be translated in all neighboring countries, as well as in Scandinavia, but as yet I haven't found any translation. In 1984 it was reprinted by the Feministische Uitgeverij Sara.

4. W. H. Posthumus-van der Goot, ed., *Van moeder op dochter: Het aandeel van de vrouw in een veranderende wereld* (Leiden: Brill, 1948). In 1968 the book was reissued as a paperback which left out a good many of the illustrations. The last part was rewritten to cover "The last forty years": W. H. Posthumus-van der Goot, Anna de Waal, eds., *Van moeder op dochter* (Utrecht: Bruna 1968). In 1977 it got a reprint from a socialist press, now with a new introduction and an addendum in which Posthumus-van der Goot described the next last ten years: W. H. Posthumus-van der Goot, Anna de Waal, eds., *Van moeder op dochter: De maatsch-*

appelijke positie van de vrouw in Nederland vanaf de franse tijd (Nijmegen: SUN, 1977).

5. The National Exhibition of Women's Labor took place in the year that the young Queen Wilhelmina ascended the throne and the exhibition "De Vrouw 1813–1913" was organized as part of the celebrations for the first centennial of the Dutch Kingdom. Collective feminist memory was therefore tightly connected to national memory. See Maria Grever, Berteke Waaldijk, *Feministische openbaarheid: de Nationale Tentoonstelling van Vrouwenarbeid in 1898* (Amsterdam: Stichting Beheer IISG: IIAV, 1998).

6. Rosa Manus, longtime pivot of feminist activity, was murdered in the women's concentration camp Ravensbrück; Johanna Naber, since 1898 a chronicler and historian of the women's movement, had died of old age. For information on Rosa Manus, as well as on the fate of the IAV archives during the war, see Mineke Bosch, Annemarie Kloosterman, *Politics and Friendship: Letters from the International Woman Suffrage Alliance, 1902–1942* (Columbus: Ohio State University Press, 1990). Recently the lost archives have been traced to the Special Archive in Moscow. A microfilm of the complete collection is in the Internationaal Informatiecentrum en Archief voor de Vrouwenbeweging (International Information Center and Archive for the Women's Movement) in Amsterdam.

7. Johanna Naber had written two influential histories of the women's movement: *Na tien jaren* (Ten Years After) in 1908 and *Na XXV Jaren* (Twenty-Five Years After) in 1923. She also published in the first multilingual *Jaarboek Internationaal Archief voor de Vrouwenbeweging* (Yearbook International Archives for the Women's Movement) (Leiden: Brill, 1937): "Eerste Proeve van een Chronologisch Overzicht van de Geschiedenis der Vrouwenbeweging in Nederland" (First Attempt at a Chronological Overview of the History of the Women's Movement in the Netherlands). In the second volume (Leiden: Brill, 1938) there appeared a "Chronological List of Leading Events in the Women's Movement in Great Britain" by Ray Strachey. It may be suggested that Ray Strachey's history of the English women's movement was also a model for *Van moeder op dochter*. In both volumes the majority of articles were on the history of women's suffrage in several countries. A recent dissertation on Johanna Naber as a feminist historian is Maria Grever, *Strijd tegen de stilte: Johanna Naber (1859–1941) en de vrouwenstem in geschiedenis* (Hilversum: Verloren, 1994). The authors of *Van moeder op dochter*, however, in the choice of their title did not respect one of Johanna Naber's central metaphors in referring to feminist history as a succession of great-aunts, aunts, and nieces, which was linked up to her conviction that celibacy was a powerful motor of change.

8. For instance: Mineke Bosch, Pieternel Rol, "De ontvoogding der vrouw," *Lover* 3 (1978), no. 3.

9. Ulla Jansz, Tineke van Loosbroek, "Nieuwe literatuur over de eerste femi-

nistische golf: 'herschrijven van de geschiedenis,'" *"De eerste feministische golf."*
Jaarboek voor Vrouwengeschiedenis, 6 (Nijmegen: SUN, 1985): 10–29. Jansz has
repeated her criticism in her dissertation: Ulla Jansz, *Denken over sekse in de eerste
feministische golf* (Amsterdam: Van Gennep, 1990).

10. Joyce Outshoorn, *Vrouwenemancipatie en socialisme: Een onderzoek naar de
houding van de SDAP t.o.v. het vrouwenvraagstuk' tussen 1894 en 1919* (Nijmegen:
SUN, 1973).

11. Ulla Jansz, *Vrouwen ontwaakt! Driekwart eeuw sociaal-democratische
vrouwenorganistaie tussen solidariteit en verzet* (Amsterdam: Bert Bakker, 1983).

12. Josine Blok et al., *Vrouwen, kiesrecht en arbeid in Nederland 1889–1919*
(Groningen: OWP, 1977).

13. Tineke de Bie, Wantje Fritschy, "De 'wereld' van Reveilvrouwen, hun lief-
dadige activiteiten en het ontstaan van het feminisme in Nederland," *"De eerste
feministische golf." Jaarboek voor Vrouwengeschiedenis* 6 (Nijmegen: SUN, 1985):
30–58; Dutch historiography preserved some idea of the importance of religious
women for later feminism only through the reception of works like Olive Banks's
Faces of Feminism. A Study of Feminism as a Social Movement (Oxford, 1981). Until
recently the article received only indirect criticism. New research by Francisca de
Haan on women and prison reform is bringing the Reveil connection back into
the history of feminism. See Annemieke van Drenth, Francisca de Haan, eds., *The
Rise of Caring Power: New Perspectives on the History of Gender, Care and the 19th
Century Women's Movement. Elizabeth Fry and Josephine Butler in Britain and the
Netherlands* (Amsterdam: Stichtin University Press, 2000).

14. C. M. Werker-Beaujon, Clara Wichmann, and H. M. Werker, eds., *De
vrouw, de vrouwenbeweging en het vrouwenvraagstuk: Encyclopaedisch Handboek,* 1,
2 (Amsterdam: Elsevier, 1914, 1918). The key texts in this book revealed the three
editors to be "ethical feminists." Central to this ethical feminism is the thinking of
Gertrud Bäumer, especially her ideas on the history of feminism, which are formulated in a gendered vocabulary of binary oppositions.

15. This question is related to but not the same as another question which
haunted the first feminist historians: why feminism died after 1920.

16. Bosch, Kloosterman, *Politics and Friendship.* An earlier Dutch version was
published as: Mineke Bosch and Annemarie Kloosterman, *Lieve Dr. Jacobs: Brieven
uit de Wereldbond voor Vrouwenkiesrecht, 1902–1942* (Amsterdam: Sara, 1985).

17. The yearbook carried biographical articles on Helene Mercier, Annette Ver-
sluys-Poleman, and Wilhelmina Drucker.

18. Petra de Vries, "Alle vrouwen zijn moeders. Feminisme en moederschap
rond de eeuwwisseling," *Socialisties-Feministiese Teksten* 8 (Amsterdam: Feministische Uitgeverij Sara, 1984): 126–48.

19. Marijke Mossink, "Tweeërlei Strooming? 'Ethisch' en 'rationalistisch' femi-

nisme tijdens de eerste golf in Nederland," *Socialisties-Feministiese Teksten* 9 (Baarn: Ambo, 1986): 104–20. At the beginning of the 1980s an influential Dutch feminist group based in the Amsterdam Vrouwenhuis (Women's Center) started a campaign against "difference feminism" as embodied by Adrienne Rich's "cult of motherhood" (their term). In this campaign historical arguments played an important role. Some historical feminists (such as the ethical feminist Clara Wichmann) were labeled "protofascist." Although such ideas clearly went beyond the point of decent argumentation, in academic circles a parallel was noticed with earlier repudiations of first-wave feminism as "traditionalist." This strengthened the wish to historicize feminism and be attentive to the "use and misuse of women's history." Mossink's article is exemplary in this respect.

20. Myriam Everard, "Het burgerlijk feminisme van de eerste golf: Annette Versluys-Poelman en haar kring," *"De eerste feministische golf." Jaarboek voor Vrouwengeschiedenis* 6 (Nijmegen: SUN, 1985): 106–37.

21. Irene Stoehr, "Organisierte Mütterlichkeit: Zur Politik der deutschen Frauenbewegung um 1900," in: Karin Hausen, ed., *Frauen suchen ihre Geschichte: Historische Studien zum 19. und 20. Jahrhundert* (Munich: Beck, 1983). Ellen DuBois, *Feminism and Suffrage: The Emergence of an Independent Women's Movement in America, 1848–1869* (Ithaca, N.Y.: Cornell University Press, 1985).

22. Mieke Aerts, "Gewoon hetzelfde of nu eenmaal anders? Een feministisch dilemma," *Dilemma's van het feminisme: Te elfder Ure 39*, vol. 29, no. 1 (1986): 4–13. Joan Wallach Scott, "Deconstructing Equality-versus-Difference: Or, the Uses of Poststructuralist Theory for Feminism," *Feminist Studies*, vol. 14, no. 1 (1988): 33–50. The article was translated as: "Deconstructie van gelijkheid-versus-verschil. De bruikbaarheid van de poststructuralistische theorie van het feminisme," *"Het raadsel vrouwengeschiedenis." Jaarboek voor Vrouwengeschiedenis* 10 (Nijmegen: SUN, 1990): 96–112. Gisela Bock, "Geschiedenis, vrouwengeschiedenis en de geschiedenis der seksen," in: F. van Besouw, ed., *Balans en perspectief: Visies op de geschiedwetenschap in Nederland* (Groningen: Wolters Noordhoff, 1987), pp. 73–99. Another version of this was published as "Women's History and Gender History: Aspects of an International Debate," *Gender and History*, vol. 1, no. 1 (1989): 7–31.

23. Scott, "Deconstructing Equality-versus-Difference," p. 48.

24. This is perhaps an especially Dutch exercise since the concept of the "segmented society" (*verzuiling*) is very important in Dutch history. The *verzuiling* or segmentation of society took place in the last quarter of the nineteenth century, when Protestants and Catholics, along with a kind of coalition between socialists and liberals, managed with the help of state subsidies to organize their own cultural and social life on the basis of almost completely separate worlds, among which only the elites intercommunicated. The origin of the segmentation is to be found in the emancipation of the Dutch Catholics and the opposition of nonelite

Protestant groups to the liberal state. During the last quarter of the century until 1918 the most important political struggle in the Netherlands—apart from suffrage—was the "school struggle," the right of religious groups to have their own "special school" system, which ended in a complete victory of the religious groups. The end of this struggle is known as the "pacification."

25. Berteke Waaldijk, "De historische hypercorrecties van Ulla Jansz," *Lover* 19 (1992). This criticism, as well as Myriam Everard's, was formulated on the occasion of a public debate on the book.

26. Myriam Everard, "De woede van Wilhelmina Drucker," *Lover*, vol. 19, no. 4 (1992).

27. Mineke Bosch, *Het geslacht van de wetenschap: Vrouwen en hoger onderwijs, 1878–1948* (Amsterdam: SUA, 1994), pp. 236–39.

28. Selma L. Sevenhuijsen, *De orde van het vaderschap: Politieke debatten over ongehuwd moederschap, afstamming en huwelijk in Nederland, 1870–1900* (Amsterdam: Stichting Beheer IISG, 1987).

29. Francisca de Haan, *Sekse op kantoor: Over vrouwelijkheid, mannelijkheid en macht, Nederland 1860–1940* (Hilversum: Verloren, 1992).

30. Corrie van Eijl, *Het werkzame verschil: Vrouwen in de slag om de arbeid 1898–1940* (Hilversum: Verloren, 1994).

31. Marianne Braun, *De prijs van de liefde: De eerste feministische golf, het huwelijksrecht en de vaderlandse geschiedenis* (Amsterdam: Het Spinhuis, 1992).

32. For a general discussion of debates within Dutch women's history, see Francisca de Haan, "Women's History behind the Dykes: Reflections on the Situation in the Netherlands," in: Karen Offen, Ruth Roach Pierson, Jane Rendall, eds., *Writing Women's History* (London: Macmillan, 1990), pp. 259–77.

33. Grever, *Strijd tegen de stilte* (see note 7).

34. *"Feminisme en verbeelding": Jaarboek voor Vrouwengeschiedenis* 14 (Amsterdam: Stichting Beheer IISG, 1994).

35. It was the third seminar, organized by Mieke Aerts, Ulla Jansz, and Marijke Mossink, in which social scientists and historians met to discuss theoretical problems in relation to practical research. Especially the dissertations of Jolande Withuis and Mieke Aerts have been an inspiration for the new interest in political history: Jolande Withuis, *Opoffering an heroïek: De mentale wereld van een communistische vrouwenorganisatie in na-oorlogs Nederland, 1946–1976* (Meppel: Boom, 1990), and later articles on feminism and postwar politics. Mieke Aerts, *De politiek van de katholieke vrouwenemancipatie: Van Marga Klompé tot Jacqueline Hillen* (Amsterdam: SUA, 1994).

36. Henk te Velde, "Viriliteit en opoffering: 'Mannelijkheid' in het Nederlandse politieke debat in het fin-de siècle," *Tijdschrift voor Vrouwenstudies* 56, vol. 14, no. 4 (1993): 421–33.

37. Denise Riley, *"Am I that Name?" Feminism and the Category of "Women" in History* (London: Macmillan, 1988), p. 8.

38. Although Offen avoids the terms difference and equality, they are at the heart of relational and individual feminism. In both publications it is stressed that relational/difference arguments were used by the majority of feminists, which nevertheless leads to very different evaluations.

39. See especially the introduction to the article "Defining Feminism." In another article by Karen Offen, "Feminism and Sexual Difference in Historical Perspective," in D. L. Rhode, ed., *Theoretical Perspectives on Sexual Difference* (New Haven: Yale University Press, 1990), it becomes clear that Offen's proposal of defining feminism serves the political purpose of fighting postmodern feminism in women's studies and women's history, which definitely leads to rather questionable rhetoric.

40. Offen, "Defining Feminism," pp. 125 and 128.

Chapter 5

1. Steven C. Hause, Jennifer Waelti-Walters, eds., *Feminisms of the Belle Epoque: A Historical and Literary Anthology* (Lincoln, Neb.: University of Nebraska Press, 1994); Steven C. Hause, Anne R. Kenney, *Women's Suffrage and Social Politics in the French Third Republic* (Princeton, N.J.: Princeton University Press, 1984); Patrick Kay Bidelman, *Pariahs Stand Up! The Founding of the Liberal Feminist Movement in France, 1858–1889* (Westport, Conn.: Greenwood, 1982); Charles Sowerwine, *Sisters or Citizens? Women and Socialism in France since 1876* (Cambridge: Cambridge University Press, 1982); Claire Goldberg Moses, *French Feminism in the Nineteenth Century* (Albany: State University of New York Press, 1984); Marilyn J. Boxer, Jean H. Quataert, eds., *Socialist Women: European Socialist Feminism in the Nineteenth and Early Twentieth Centuries* (New York: Elsevier North-Holland, 1978); Marilyn J. Boxer, Jean H. Quataert, *Connecting Spheres: European Women in a Globalizing World, 1500 to the Present* (New York: Oxford University Press, 2000).

2. Eleni Varikas, "La révolte des dames: Genèse d'une conscience féministe dans la Grèce du 19ème siècle," Ph.D. diss., Université de Paris, 1986.

3. Laurence Klejman, Florence Rochefort, *L'Egalité en marche: le féminisme sous la Troisième République* (Paris: Presses de la Fondation Nationale des sciences politiques/Des femmes, 1989).

4. Laurence Klejman, Florence Rochefort, "Féminisme—Histoire—Mémoire," *Pénélope, Mémoires des femmes*, no. 12 (Spring 1985): 129–38.

5. Dominique Godineau, *Citoyennes tricoteuses: Les femmes du peuple à Paris pendant la Révolution française* (Aix en Provence: Alinea, 1988).

6. Michèle Riot-Sarcey, *La démocratie à l'épreuve des femmes* (Paris: Albin

Michel, 1994); Christine Planté, "Les féministes saint-simoniennes: Possibilités et limites d'un mouvement féministe en France au lendemain de 1830," in J. R. Debré, ed., *Regards sur le Saint-Simonisme et les Saints-Eimoniens* (Lyon: Presses Universitaires des Lyon, 1986), pp. 73–99; Claire Goldberg Moses, *French Feminism in the Nineteenth Century* (Albany: State University of New York Press, 1984); Marilyn Boxer, "'First Wave' Feminism in Nineteenth Century France: Class, Family and Religion," *Women's Studies International Forum*, vol. 12, no. 3 (1982): 551–59; Maïtè Albistur, Daniel Armogathe, *Histoire du féminisme français* (Paris: Editions des femmes, 1977); Joan Wallach Scott, *Only Paradoxes to Offer: French Feminists and the Rights of Man* (Cambridge, Mass.: Harvard University Press, 1996).

7. Karen Offen, "A Nineteenth-Century French Feminist Rediscovered: Jenny P. d'Héricourt 1809–1875," *Signs*, vol. 13, no. 11 (Fall 1987): 144–58; and Laurence Klejman, Florence Rochefort, "'Les Premières': Julie Daubié," *Bulletin Centre Pierre Léon d'histoire économique et sociale*, Université Lumière Lyon 2/CNRS, no. 2–3 (1993): 81–92. Pierre Joseph Proudhon (1809–1865) was a socialist thinker who greatly influenced the French workers' movement throughout the nineteenth century.

8. Christine Bard, *Les filles de Marianne: Histoire des féminismes 1914–1940* (Paris: Fayard, 1995).

9. Maria Deraismes, "La femme et le droit," in *Oeuvres complètes* (Paris: Côté-femmes, 1990 [1896]), vol. 2, p. 23.

10. The three preceding quotations are from Deraismes, *Eve dans l'humanité*, in: *Oeuvres Complètes*, vol. 2 (1896), p. 137.

11. Joan Wallach Scott, *Only Paradoxes to Offer: French Feminists and the Rights of Man* (Cambridge, Mass.: Harvard University Press, 1996).

12. Patrick Kay Bidelman, *Pariahs Stand Up! The Founding of the Liberal Feminist Movement in France 1858–1889* (Westport: Greenwood Press, 1982); and Laurence Klejman, Florence Rochefort, "Gloria e miseria d'un pionniere del femminismo: Léon Richer," in Ginevra Conti Odorisio, ed., *Salvatore Morelli (1824–1880)* (Milan: Edizioni Scientifiche Italiane, 1992), pp. 305–16.

13. Florence Rochefort, "Démocratie féministe contre démocratie exclusive ou les enjeux de la mixité," in Michèle Riot-Sarcey, ed., *Démocratie et représentation* (Paris: Kimè, 1995), pp. 181–202; Karen Offen, "Depopulation, Nationalism, and Feminism in fin de siècle France," *The American Historical Review* (June 1984): 648–76; Elinor A. Accampo, Rachel G. Fuchs, Mary Lynn Stewart, *Gender and the Politics of Social Reform in France, 1870–1914* (Baltimore: Johns Hopkins University Press, 1995); Florence Rochefort, "L'Égalité dans la différence: les paradoxes de la République, 1880–1940," in Marc Olivier Baruch et Vincent Duclert, eds., *Serviteurs de l'État. Une histoire politique de l'administration française 1875–1945* (Paris: La Découverte, 2000), pp. 183–98.

14. Karen Offen, "Defining Feminism: A Comparative Historical Approach," *Signs*, vol. 14, no. 1 (Aug. 1988): 119–57.

15. Maria Deraismes, "La femme dans la démocratie," in *Oeuvres complètes*, vol. 3, p. 323.

16. The expression is from the French historian and sociologist Jean Baubérot, a scholar of the history of Protestantism and the "laïcité" in France. Baubérot's notion of pact, which is close to convenant, refers to the French republican will to transform the various opponents of "laïcité" (the state's neutrality with regard to religious institutions and political groups) into partners with a shared respect for pluralism.

17. Steven C. Hause, *Hubertine Auclert: The French Suffragette* (New Haven, Conn.: Yale University Press, 1987), and Hubertine Auclert's own newspaper, *La Citoyenne 1848–1914* (Paris: Giard et Brière, 1907; preface, notes, and commentary by Edith Taïeb); Scott, *Only Paradoxes to Offer*.

18. Florence Rochefort, "Du Droit des femmes au féminisme en Europe 1860–1914," in Christine Fauré, ed., *Encyclopèdie politique et historique des femmes* (Paris: Presses Universitaires de France, 1997), pp. 551–70. We may discern the development of female individualism in France by studying legal archives, among other documents. See Anne Marie Sohn, *Chrysalides: femmes de la vie privée (19e–20e siècles)* (Paris: Publications de la Sorbonne, 1996).

19. Adrienne Avril de Sainte Croix, *Le féminisme* (Paris: Giard et Brière, 1907).

20. "Aperçu général de nos buts (General Statement of Our Goals)," written by "le Comité" and published in the first issue of *La Femme de France* (Aug. 2, 1879). Only eleven issues of the paper were printed; it was succeeded by *La Femme dans la Famille et dans la Société*, whose editorial staff was mixed. See Anne Cova, *Maternité et Droits des femmes en France* (Paris: Economica, 1997).

21. Ibid.

22. "Congrès des Oeuvres et institutions féminines" (the philanthropists) and "Congrès français et international du droit des femmes," both held in 1889.

23. Florence Rochefort, "L'Ouvrière et la Prostituée. Deux modes d'approche catholique et protestante du féminisme sous la Troisième République," in Françoise Lautman, ed., *Ni Eve ni Marie. Luttes et incertitudes des héritières de la Bible* (Geneva: Labor et Fidès, 1998), pp. 211–29; Florence Rochefort, "Féminisme et protestantisme au XIXe siècle. Premières rencontres 1830–1900," *Bulletin de la Société de l'Histoire du Protestantisme Français* (janvier–mars 2000): 69–89.

24. Hubertine Auclert, "La femme arabe," *Papers from the Congrès français et international du droit des femmes*, pp. 175–81.

25. Karen Offen, "Sur l'origine des mots 'féminisme' et 'féministe,'" *Revue d'histoire moderne et contemporaine* (July–Sept. 1987): 492–96.

26. Annie Dizier-Metz, *La Bibliothèque Marguerite Durand: Histoire d'une*

femme, mèmoire des femmes (Paris: Bibliothèque Marguerite Durand, 1992); Mary Louise Roberts, "Acting Up: The Feminist Theatrics of Marguerite Durand," *French Historical Studies*, vol. 19, no. 4 (Fall 1996): 1103–1138. (I don't think that historians like Hause and Waelti-Walters or Klejman and I have "reproduced the pariah status" of Marguerite Durand in our works, as claimed by Roberts in her article, p. 1104.)

27. Marguerite Durand, Letter to Jane Misme dated Oct. 14–15, 1930. Bibliothèque Marguerite Durand, Paris.

28. *Le Temps* was a major daily newspaper of the period; Mary Louise Roberts, "Copie subversive: Le Journalisme féministe en France à la fin du siècle dernier," *Clio: Histoire, Femmes et Sociétés*, no. 6 (1997): 230–47.

29. Marguerite Durand, "Confessions," *La Fronde* (Oct. 1, 1903).

30. Nelly Roussel, *L'Eternelle sacrifiée* (Paris: Syros, 1978; preface, notes, and commentary by Maïté Albistur and Daniel Armogathe); Madeleine Pelletier, *L'éducation féministe des filles et autres textes* (Paris: Syros, 1978; preface and notes by Claude Magnien); Elinor A. Accampo, "The Rhetoric of Reproduction and the Reconfiguration of Womanhood in the French Birth Control Movement 1890–1920," *Journal of Family History*, vol. 21, no. 3 (July 1996): 351–71; Felicia Gordon, *The Integral Feminist: Madeleine Pelletier 1874–1939* (Minneapolis: University of Minnesota Press, 1990); Charles Sowerwine and Claude Maignien, *Madeleine Pelletier, une féministe dans l'arène politique* (Paris: Les Editions ouvrières, 1992).

31. Nelly Roussel, "Qu'est-ce que le Féminisme," *Le Petit Almanach Illustré pour 1906*; Léopold Lacour, *L'Humanisme intégral* (Paris: Stock, 1897). On feminist positions regarding seduction see Florence Rochefort, "La séduction résiste-t-elle au féminisme (1880–1930)," in Cécile Dauphin et Arlette Farge, eds., *Séduction et Société* (Paris: Seuil, 2000).

32. Marbel, "Le calendrier féministe," *Le Petit Almanach Illustré pour 1906*, p. 1.

33. Florence Rochefort, "A propos de la libre-disposition du salaire de la femme mariée. Les ambiguïtés d'une loi (1907)," *Clio: Histoire, Femmes et Sociétés*, no. 7 (1998): 177–90.

Chapter 6

1. Gertrud Bäumer, *Lebensweg durch eine Zeitwende* (Tübingen: Rainer Wunderlich, 1933), p. 175.

2. Joachim Raschke, *Soziale Bewegungen: ein historisch-systematischer Grundriß* (Frankfurt/M.: Campus, 1985), p. 35.

3. Cf. Jürgen Habermas, *Theorie des kommunikativen Handelns* (Frankfurt/M.: Suhrkamp, 1982), vol. 2, pp. 578–79; idem, *Stichworte zur "geistigen Situation der Zeit"* (Frankfurt/M.: Suhrkamp, 1979), vol. 1, note 15; idem, *Die neue Unüber-*

sichtlichkeit (Frankfurt/M.: Suhrkamp, 1985), p. 159: "The struggles [of the women's movement] remain mostly latent; they move only within the microcosm of daily communication, intensify only every now and then as public discourses and intersubjectivities on a higher level."

4. Cf. Silvia Kontos, "Modernisierung der Subsumtionspolitik? Die Frauenbewegung in den Theorien neuer sozialer Bewegungen," *Feministische Studien*, vol. 5, no. 2 (Nov. 1986): 34–49; Antje Wiener, "Wider den theoretischen 'Kessel': Ideen zur Sprengung der binären Logik in der Neue Soziale Bewegungen-Forschung," *Forschungsjournal Neue Soziale Bewegungen*, vol. 5, no. 2 (May 1992): 34–43.

5. Roland Roth, Dieter Rucht, eds., *Neue soziale Bewegungen in der Bundesrepublik Deutschland* (Frankfurt/M.: Campus, 1991), p. 13.

6. Dieter Rucht, *Modernisierung und neue soziale Bewegungen* (Frankfurt/M.: Campus, 1994), p. 28.

7. As far as I know, only in Richard J. Evans, *The Feminists: Women's Emancipation Movements in Europe, America, and Australasia, 1840–1920* (London: Croom Helm 1977); Marilyn J. Boxer, Jean H. Quataert, eds., *Socialist Women: European Socialist Feminism in the Nineteenth and Early Twentieth Centuries* (New York: Elsevier, 1978); Renate Bridenthal, Atina Grossmann, Marion Kaplan, eds., *When Biology Became Destiny: Women in Weimar and Nazi Germany* (New York: Monthly Review Press, 1984); Joni Lovenduski, *Women and European Politics: Contemporary Feminism and Public Policy* (Brighton: Wheatsheaf, 1986); Ruth-Ellen Boetcher Joeres, Mary Jo Maynes, eds., *German Women in the Eighteenth and Nineteenth Centuries: A Social and Literary History* (Bloomington: Indiana University Press, 1986); Karen Offen, "Liberty, Equality, and Justice for Women: The Theory and Practice of Feminism in Nineteenth Century Europe," in Renate Bridenthal, Claudia Koonz, Susan Stuard, eds., *Becoming Visible: Women in European History* (Boston: Houghton Mifflin, 1987), pp. 335–73; Richard J. Evans, *Comrades and Sisters: Feminism, Socialism and Pacifism in Europe 1870–1945* (Brighton: Wheatsheaf, 1987); Gisela Bock, Pat Thane, eds., *Maternity and Gender Policies: Women and the Rise of the European Welfare States, 1880s-1950s* (London: Routledge, 1991).

8. Among these are the unfortunately unpublished, but early and profound dissertation by Amy Hackett, "The Politics of Feminism in Wilhelmine Germany, 1890–1918," Ph.D. diss., Columbia University, 1976; idem, "The German Women's Movement and Suffrage, 1890–1914: A Study of National Feminism," in Robert Bezucha, ed., *Modern European Social History* (Lexington, Mass.: D. C. Heath, 1976); and especially the works of Richard J. Evans, *The Feminist Movement in Germany 1894–1933* (London: Sage, 1976); idem, *The Feminists*; idem, *Sozialdemokratie und Frauenemanzipation im deutschen Kaiserreich* (Berlin: Dietz, 1979); and idem, *Comrades and Sisters*; other references in Lovenduski, *Women and European Politics*, pp. 31–32; cf. also Catherine N. Prelinger, *Charity, Chal-*

lenge, and Change: Religious Dimensions of the Mid-Nineteenth-Century Women's Movement in Germany (New York: Greenwood Press, 1987); and recently the thorough monograph by Ann Taylor Allen, *Feminism and Motherhood in Germany, 1800–1904* (New Brunswick, N.J.: Rutgers University Press, 1991).

9. Janet Saltzman Chafetz, Anthony Gary Dworkin, "Action and Reaction: an Integrated, Comparative Perspective on Feminist and Antifeminist Movements," in Melvin Kohn, ed., *Cross-National Research in Sociology* (Beverly Hills, Calif.: Sage, 1989), pp. 329–50; Janet Saltzman Chafetz, Anthony Gary Dworkin, Stephanie Swanson, "Social Change and Social Activisms: First-Wave Women's Movements Around the World," in Guida West, Rhoda Lois Blumberg, eds., *Women and Social Protest* (Oxford: Oxford University Press, 1990), pp. 302–20.

10. Cf. Chafetz and Dworkin, "Action and Reaction," p. 332: "Earlier movements, termed First Wave, tended to be ameliorative and did not challenge male privilege, whereas later movements did."

11. Chafetz, Dworkin, Swanson, "Social Change," p. 304.

12. Ibid., p. 38.

13. Cf. Gerda Lerner, *The Majority Finds its Past* (Oxford: Oxford University Press, 1979); Ulla Bock, *Androgynie und Feminismus: Frauenbewegung zwischen Institution und Utopie: Ergebnisse der Frauenforschung* (Weinheim: Beltz, 1988).

14. Only a few titles can be mentioned as examples—I make no claim to completeness. Margrit Twellmann, *Die deutsche Frauenbewegung: Ihre Anfänge und erste Entwicklung. Quellen 1843–1889*, 2 vols. (Meisenheim: Hain, 1972); Evans, *The Feminists*; and Evans, *Sozialdemokratie und Frauenemanzipation*; Barbara Greven-Aschoff, *Die bürgerliche Frauenbewegung in Deutschland: 1894–1933* (Göttingen: Vandenhoeck und Ruprecht, 1981); Marion A. Kaplan, *Die jüdische Frauenbewegung in Deutschland: Organisationen und Ziele des Jüdischen Frauenbundes 1904–1938* (Hamburg: Christians, 1981); Heinz Niggemann, *Emanzipation zwischen Sozialismus und Feminismus: die sozialdemokratische Frauenbewegung im Kaiserreich* (Wuppertal: Hammer, 1981); Sabine Richebächer, *Uns fehlt nur eine Kleinigkeit: Deutsche proletarische Frauenbewegung 1890–1914* (Frankfurt/M.: Fischer, 1982); Rita Thalmann, *Frausein im Dritten Reich* (Munich: Hanser, 1984); Doris Kaufmann, *Frauen zwischen Aufbruch und Reaktion: Protestantische Frauenbewegung in der ersten Hälfte des 20. Jahrhunderts* (Munich: Piper, 1988); Bärbel Clemens, *"Menschenrechte haben kein Geschlecht!" Zum Politikverständnis der bürgerlichen Frauenbewegung* (Pfaffenweiler: Centaurus, 1988); Theresa Wobbe, *Gleichheit und Differenz: Politische Strategien von Frauenrechtlerinnen um die Jahrhundertwende* (Frankfurt/M.: Campus, 1989); Irene Stoehr, *Emanzipation zum Staat? Der Allgemeine Deutsche Frauenverein—Deutscher Staatsbürgerinnenverband (1893–1933)* (Pfaffenweiler: Centaurus, 1990).

15. For example, Herrad-Ulrike Bussemer, *Frauenemanzipation und Bildungs-*

bürgertum: Sozialgeschichte der Frauenbewegung in der Reichsgründungszeit (Weinheim: Beltz, 1985); Ute Frevert, *Frauen-Geschichte: Zwischen bürgerlicher Verbesserung und neuer Weiblichkeit* (Frankfurt/M.: Suhrkamp, 1986), translated into English as *Women in German History: From Bourgeois Emancipation to Sexual Liberation* (Oxford: Berg, 1989).

16. Gerda Tornieporth, *Studien zur Frauenbildung* (Weinheim: Beltz, 1979); Dietlinde Peters, *Mütterlichkeit im Kaiserreich: Die deutsche Frauenbewegung und der soziale Beruf der Frau* (Bielefeld: Kleine, 1984); Christoph Sachße, *Mütterlichkeit als Beruf: Sozialarbeit, Sozialreform und Frauenbewegung 1871–1929* (Frankfurt/M.: Suhrkamp, 1986).

17. Regina Schulte, *Sperrbezirke: Tugendhaftigkeit und Prostitution in der bürgerlichen Welt* (Frankfurt/M.: Syndicat, 1979); Kristine von Soden, *Die Sexualberatungsstellen der Weimarer Republik 1919–1933: Stätten der Geschichte Berlins* (Berlin: Edition Hentrich, 1988).

18. Again only a few examples: Renate Möhrmann, ed., *Frauenemanzipation im deutschen Vormärz* (Stuttgart: Reclam, 1978); Gisela Brinker-Gabler, ed., *Frauen in der Gesellschaft: Frühe Texte* (Frankfurt/M.: Fischer, 1979); Annette Kuhn, *Frauen in der Geschichte* (Düsseldorf: Schwann, 1979); Ute Gerhard, Elisabeth Hannover-Drück, Romina Schmitter, eds., *"Dem Reich der Freiheit werb' ich Bürgerinnen." Die Frauen-Zeitung von Louise Otto* (Frankfurt/M.: Syndicat, 1979); Elke Frederiksen, ed., *Die Frauenfrage in Deutschland, 1865–1915* (Stuttgart: Reclam, 1981); Gerlinde Hummel-Haasis, ed., *Schwestern, zerreißt eure Ketten: Zeugnisse zur Geschichte der Frauen in der Revolution von 1848–49* (Munich: DTV, 1982); Karin Hausen, ed., *Frauen suchen ihre Geschichte: Historische Studien zum 19. und 20. Jahrhundert* (Munich: Beck, 1983). One should not forget the documents published by the women's movement itself around the turn of the century and the results of women's studies in the 1920s (research was interrupted in 1933). This material is of great value to current feminist historical research, especially because so many personal estates were lost as a result of two world wars. To be mentioned are: Helene Lange, Gertrud Bäumer, eds., *Handbuch der Frauenbewegung* (Berlin: Moeser, 1901); Lily Braun, *Die Frauenfrage: Ihre geschichtliche Entwicklung und ihre wirtschaftliche Seite* (Berlin: Dietz, 1979 [1901]); Else Lüders, *Der "linke Flügel": Ein Blatt aus der Geschichte der deutschen Frauenbewegung* (Berlin: Loewenthal, 1904); Hilde Lion, *Zur Soziologie der Frauenbewegung: Die sozialistische und die katholische Frauenbewegung* (Berlin: Herbig, 1926); Agnes von Zahn-Harnack, *Die Frauenbewegung: Geschichte, Probleme, Ziele* (Berlin: Deutsche Buchgemeinschaft, 1928); cf. the indispensable bibliography by Hans Sveistrup, Agnes von Zahn-Harnack, eds., *Die Frauenfrage in Deutschland: Strömungen und Gegenströmungen 1790–1930* (Burg: Hopfer, 1934).

19. Cf. Bussemer, *Frauenemanzipation*; Carola Lipp, ed., *Schimpfende Weiber und patriotische Jungfrauen: Frauen im Vormärz und in der Revolution von 1848/49*

(Moos: Elster, 1986); Elisabeth Meyer-Renschhausen, *Weibliche Kultur und soziale Arbeit: Eine Geschichte der Frauenbewegung am Beispiel Bremens 1810–1927* (Cologne: Böhlau, 1990); Sylvia Paletschek, *Frauen und Dissens: Frauen im Deutschkatholizismus und in den freien Gemeinden 1841–1852* (Göttingen: Vandenhoek und Ruprecht, 1990); Ute Gerhard, *Unerhört: Die Geschichte der Deutschen Frauenbewegung* (Reinbek bei Hamburg: Rowohlt, 1990).

20. Sydney Tarrow, "Struggle, Politics, and Reform: Collective Action, Social Movements, and Cycles of Protest," Western Societies Program, Occasional Paper no. 21, Center of International Studies, Cornell University, 1989.

21. Cf. Ute Gerhard, "Westdeutsche Frauenbewegung: Zwischen Autonomie und dem Recht auf Gleichheit," *Feministische Studien*, vol. 10, no. 2 (Nov. 1992): 35–55; idem, "Die 'langen Wellen' der Frauenbewegung: Traditionslinien und unerledigte Arbeiten," in Regina Becker-Schmidt, Gudrun-Axeli Knapp, eds., *Das Geschlechterverhältnis als Gegenstand der Sozialwissenschaften* (Frankfurt/M.: Campus 1995), pp. 247–78.

22. John D. McCarthy, Mayer N. Zald, "Resource Mobilization and Social Movements: A Partial Theory," *American Journal of Sociology*, vol. 82, no. 6 (1977): 1212–41; Mary Fainsod Katzenstein, Carol McClurg Mueller, eds., *The Women's Movement of the United States and Western Europe: Consciousness, Political Opportunity, and Public Policy, Women in the Political Economy* (Philadelphia: Temple University Press, 1987); Myra Marx Ferree, Beth Hess, *Controversy and Coalition: the New Feminist Movement* (Boston: Twayne, 1985); Steven M. Buechler, *Women's Movements in the United States: Woman Suffrage, Equal Rights, and Beyond* (London: Rutgers, 1990); Rucht, *Modernisierung*.

23. Ellen DuBois, Mari Jo Buhle, Temma Kaplan, Gerda Lerner, Carroll Smith-Rosenberg, eds., "Politics and Culture in Women's History: a Symposium," *Feminist Studies*, vol. 6, no. 1 (Spring 1980): 26–64.

24. Nancy F. Cott, *The Bonds of Womanhood: "Women's Sphere" in New England, 1780–1835* (New Haven: Yale University Press, 1977).

25. Blanche Wiesen-Cook, *Female Support Networks and Political Activism: Women Support Networks* (New York: Out & Out, 1979).

26. Hanna Hacker, *Frauen und Freundinnen: Studien zur weiblichen Homosexualität am Beispiel Österreich 1870–1938* (Weinheim: Beltz, 1987).

27. Mineke Bosch, Annemarie Klostermann, eds., *Politics and Friendship: Letters from the International Woman Suffrage Alliance, 1902–1942* (Columbus: Ohio State University Press, 1990); Philippa Levine, "Love, Friendship and Feminism in Later 19th-Century England," *Women's Studies International Forum*, vol. 13, no. 1/2 (1990): 63–79.

28. Cf. Ute Gerhard, Christina Klausmann, Ulla Wischermann, "Frauenfreundschaften—ihre Bedeutung für Politik und Kultur der Frauenbewegung,"

Feministische Studien, vol. 11, no. 2 (Nov. 1993): 21–37. In this context we are grateful to Mineke Bosch for many stimulating comments.

29. Cf. the completely different periodization for the British women's movement in: Olive Banks, *Faces of Feminism. A Study of Feminism as a Social Movement* (Oxford: Martin Robertson, 1981); and in contrast Christine Bolt, *The Women's Movements in the United States and Britain from the 1790s to the 1920s* (Hemel Hempstead: University of Massachusetts Press, 1993).

30. Gertrud Bäumer, "Die Geschichte der Frauenbewegung in Deutschland," in: Helene Lange, Gertrud Bäumer, eds., *Handbuch der Frauenbewegung* (Berlin: Moeser, 1901), vol. 1, pp. 1–158.

31. Wilhelm H. Riehl, *Die Familie* (Stuttgart, 1855).

32. Ulla Wischermann, "Sittlichkeit und Stimmrecht: Zur Politik und Kultur der Frauenbewegung um die Jahrhundertwende," unpublished MS, Frankfurt, 1996; Hilde Lion comes to the same conclusion in her book *Zur Soziologie der Frauenbewegung* regarding the proletarian women's movement (p. 13).

33. Cf. Bäumer, "Geschichte der Frauenbewegung," p. 22; Frances Magnus-Hausen, "Ziel und Weg in der deutschen Frauenbewegung des 19. Jahrhunderts," in Paul Wentzke, ed., *Deutscher Staat und deutsche Parteien: Friedrich Meinecke zum 60. Geburtstag dargebracht* (Munich: R. Oldenbourg, 1922), pp. 201–26, especially p. 202; Margrit Twellmann, *Die deutsche Frauenbewegung,* vol. 1, p. 1.

34. Twellmann, *Die deutsche Frauenbewegung;* Möhrmann, *Frauenemanzipation;* Gerhard et al., eds., *"Dem Reich der Freiheit werb' ich Bürgerinnen";* Hummel-Haasis, ed., *Schwestern, zerreißt eure Ketten;* Ute Gerhard, "Über die Anfänge der deutschen Frauenbewegung um 1848: Frauenpresse, Frauenpolitik und Frauenvereine," in Karin Hausen, *Frauen suchen ihre Geschichte* (Munich: Beck, 1983), pp. 196–220; Lipp, ed., *Schimpfende Weiber;* Paletschek, *Frauen und Dissens;* Gerhard, *Unerhört.*

35. Ute Gerhard et al., eds., *"Dem Reich der Freiheit werb' ich Bürgerinnen";* cf. the paper edited by Louise Dittmar, *Soziale Reform* (1849); cf. Möhrmann, *Frauenemanzipation* and Christina Klausmann, Louise Dittmar, "Ergebnisse einer biographischen Spurensuche," *Amsterdamer Beiträge,* vol. 28 (1989): 17–39; cf. the paper edited by Mathilde Franziska Anneke, *Frauen-Zeitung,* 1848; cf. Martin Henkel, Rolf Taubert, *Das Weib im Conflict [Konflikt] mit den socialen [sozialen] Verhältnissen. Mathilde Franziska Anneke und die erste deutsche Frauenzeitung* (Bochum: Edition Égalité, 1976).

36. Paletschek, *Frauen und Dissens,* p. 12.

37. Paletschek, *Frauen und Dissens,* p. 233; Louise Dittmar, *Das Wesen der Ehe. Nebst einigen Aufsätzen über die soziale Reform der Frauen* (Leipzig: Wigand, 1849).

38. *Frauenzeitung,* no. 31 (1849): 173.

39. Gerhard, "Anfänge der deutschen Frauenbewegung," p. 196.

40. Ann Taylor Allen, *Feminism and Motherhood*, p. 58.

41. Louise Otto-Peters, *Das erste Vierteljahrhundert des Allgemeinen deutschen Frauenvereins* (Leipzig: Schäfer, 1890), p. 4.

42. Bussemer, *Frauenemanzipation*, p. 119.

43. Louise Otto, *Das Recht der Frauen auf Erwerb* (Hamburg: Hoffmann und Campe, 1866).

44. Bussemer, *Frauenemanzipation*; Gerhard, *Unerhört*, p. 117.

45. Lion, *Soziologie der Frauenbewegung*, p. 31.

46. Twellmann, *Die deutsche Frauenbewegung*, pp. 221–23.

47. Clara Zetkin, "Für die Befreiung der Frau!" in *Ausgewählte Reden und Schriften* (Berlin: Dietz, 1957), vol. 1, p. 1. For an English translation of Zetkin's speech see Susan Groag Bell, Karen M. Offen, eds., *Women, the Family, and Freedom: The Debate in Documents* (Stanford, Calif.: Stanford University Press, 1983), vol. 2, doc. 15. During that same summer two feminist congresses were held in Paris. See pp. 88–89 in the present volume.

48. Anna Simson, *Der Bund Deutscher Frauenvereine: What It Wants and Does Not Want* (Breslau: Maruschke & Behrendt, 1895), p. 9.

49. Gertrud Bäumer, *Die Geschichte des Bundes Deutscher Frauenvereine* (Berlin: Teubner, 1921), p. 17.

50. Irmgard Remme, "Die internationalen Beziehungen der deutschen Frauenbewegung vom Ausgang des 19. Jahrhunderts bis 1933," Ph.D. diss., Berlin, 1955, p. 17.

51. Cf. Ute Gerhard, "National oder international. Die internationalen Beziehungen der deutschen bürgerlichen Frauenbewegung," *Feministische Studien*, vol. 12, no. 2 (Nov. 1994): 34–52.

52. This sample consists of the subjectively chosen women in my book *Unerhört*, who are introduced in a biographical "box" because of their special role in the women's movement around the turn of the century; only five other names (see appendix) are added afterwards. I owe many thanks to Petra Pommerenke for her assistance in the collection of these data.

53. Together with Christina Klausmann and Ulla Wischermann I participated in a DFG project at the University of Frankfurt titled "Sittlichkeit und Stimmrecht—Zur Politik und Kultur der Frauenbewegung um die Jahrhundertwende." I want to thank both for giving me permission to "give away" some of their results in this contribution. Klausmann reports on these investigations in her dissertation; Wischermann is working on a national media analysis on the same topic. Cf. Christina Klausmann, *Politik und Kultur der Frauenbewegung im Kaiserreich: Das Beispiel Frankfurt am Main* (Frankfurt/M.: Campus 1997) and Wischermann, "Sittlichkeit und Stimmrecht."

54. Twellmann, *Die deutsche Frauenbewegung*, vol. 1, p. 95.

55. Meyer-Renschhausen, *Weibliche Kultur*.

56. Monika Schmittner, "Frauenemanzipation in der 'Provinz': Entstehungsbedingungen und Entwicklungsgeschichte der bürgerlichen Frauenbewegung in Aschaffenburg vor dem Ersten Weltkrieg," Ph.D. diss., Frankfurt, 1993.

57. Christina Klausmann, *Politik und Kultur der Frauenbewegung*.

58. Wischermann, "Sittlichkeit und Stimmrecht."

59. Letter from Anna Simson to Miss Wilson, dated Feb. 4, 1899, Helene Lange Archives, Section 17 IV.

60. For Munich cf. Brigitte Bruns, "Weibliche Avantgarde um 1900. Die Münchener Moderne," in Rudolf Herz, Brigitte Bruns, eds., *Hof, Atelier, Elvira 1887–1928: Ästheten, Emanzen, Aristokraten* (Munich, 1985), as well as Gertrud Bäumer, *Lebensweg*, p. 180. For details of the three examples see Ute Gerhard, Christina Klausmann, Ulla Wischermann, "Frauenfreundschaften—ihre Bedeutung für Politik und Kultur der alten Frauenbewegung," *Feministische Studien*, vol. 11, no. 1 (May 1993): 21–37.

61. I am well aware of the fact that again the culture of the proletarian women's movement has been omitted. A separate part would be necessary here, because the organized female laborers, most of them wives or daughters of laborers, are fundamentally important for the culture of a labor movement. Cf. Dieter Langewiesche, Klaus Schönhoven, eds., *Arbeiter in Deutschland: Studien zu Lebensweisen der Arbeiterschaft im Zeitalter der Industrialisierung* (Paderborn, 1981). However, to fill this gap it would be necessary to work through already existing examinations of the female labor movement. Cf. especially Richebächer, *Uns fehlt nur eine Kleinigkeit* and Heinz Niggemann, *Emanzipation zwischen Sozialismus und Feminismus. Die sozialdemokratische Frauenbewegung im Kaiserreich* (Wuppertal: Hammer, 1981) as well as new historical and empirical research. Cf. also Klausmann, *Politik und Kultur der Frauenbewegung*.

62. Letter from Anna Simson to Miss Wilson, dated Feb. 4, 1899, Helene Lange Archives, Section 17 IV.

63. Helene Lange, *Die Frauenbewegung in ihren modernen Problemen* (Leipzig: Quelle & Meyer, 1908), p. 24.

64. Ibid., p. 19.

65. Ibid., p. 28.

66. Ibid., p. 23.

67. Helene Lange, *Kampfzeiten: Aufsätze und Reden aus vier Jahrzehnten* (Berlin: Herbig, 1928), p. 197.

68. Lange, *Frauenbewegung*, p. 121.

69. Programs of the ADF.

70. Henriette Goldschmidt, "Erklärung gegen das Frauenstimmrecht," *Die Frauenbewegung*, no. 3 (1895), p. 18.

71. Cf. Zahn-Harnack, *Die Frauenbewegung*, pp. 77–78: "Organized Motherhood . . . sends women not only into the nursery schools, kindergartens, and schools, but also into the ministeries and parliaments. . . . This is not the often-praised division of labor that links the man with the mind and the woman with the heart . . . [but rather] the humanization of work, the humanization of science, the humanization of contact among people."

72. Marie Hecht, quoted in Frances Magnus-Hausen, "Ziel und Weg," p. 224.

73. Alice Salomon, "Literatur zur Frauenfrage: Die Entwicklung der Theorie der Frauenbewegung," *Archiv für Sozialwissenschaft und Sozialpolitik*, vol. 26 (1908): 451–500, esp. p. 467.

74. Gertrud Bäumer, *Die Frau im neuen Lebensraum* (Berlin: Herbig, 1931), p. 16.

75. Lange, *Frauenbewegung*, p. 31.

76. Thus Helene Lange's reaction to the heated debate about the Bund für Mutterschutz and Sexualreform (Association for Motherhood and Sexual Reform). Cf. Gertrud Bäumer, Agnes Bluhm, Ika Freudenberg, Anna Kraußneck, Helene Lange, Anna Pappritz, Alice Salomon, Marianne Weber, *Frauenbewegung und Sexualethik, Beiträge zur modernen Ehekritik* (Heilbronn: Salzer, 1909).

77. Anita Augspurg, "Gebt acht, solange noch Zeit ist!" *Die Frauenbewegung*, no. 1 (1895): 4; for details see Gerhard, *Unerhört*.

78. Salomon, "Literatur zur Frauenfrage," p. 462.

79. Cf. Augspurg, "Gebt acht, solange noch Zeit ist!"

80. Cf. Else Lüders, *Der "linke Flügel": Ein Blatt aus der Geschichte der deutschen Frauenbewegung* (Berlin: Loewenthal, 1904).

81. Cf. Clara Zetkin, "Nur mit der proletarischen Frau wird der Sozialismus siegen. (Rede auf dem Parteitag der Sozialdemokratischen Partei Deutschlands zu Gotha am 16. Oktober 1886)," in Clara Zetkin, *Ausgewählte Reden und Schriften* (Berlin: Dietz, 1957), vol. 1, pp. 95–111; here p. 102.

82. Ibid., p. 95.

83. Cf. Gerhard, *Unerhört*, p. 195 ff.

84. Cf. the above-mentioned literature, especially the books by Evans and Gerhard; cf. Barbara Greven-Aschoff, *Die bürgerliche Frauenbewegung in Deutschland: 1894–1933* (Göttingen: Vandenhoeck und Ruprecht, 1981); Theresa Wobbe, *Gleichheit und Differenz*.

85. Magnus-Hausen, "Ziel und Weg," p. 220.

86. Marie Stritt, ed., *Der Internationale Frauenkongress in Berlin 1904* (Berlin: Habel, 1904).

87. Doris Kaufmann, *Frauen zwischen Aufbruch und Reaktion: Protestantische Frauenbewegung in der ersten Hälfte des 20. Jahrhunderts* (Munich: Piper, 1988), p. 185.

88. Ibid., p. 35; see also Elisabeth Moltmann-Wendel, *Frauenbefreiung* (Mu-

nich: 1978); and idem, ed., *Frau und Religion: Gotteserfahrungen im Patriarchat* (Frankfurt/M.: Fischer, 1983).

89. Lion, *Soziologie der Frauenbewegung*, p. 14.

90. Marion A. Kaplan, *Die jüdische Frauenbewegung*; and idem, "The Competition for Women's Lebensraum, 1928–1934," in Renate Bridenthal, ed., *When Biology Became Destiny* (New York: Monthly Review Press, 1984), pp. 174–98.

91. Karen Offen, "Liberty, Equality, and Justice."

92. Cf. Lange, *Frauenbewegung*; Salomon, *Literatur zur Frauenfrage*; Marianne Weber, *Beruf und Ehe: Die Beteiligung der Frau an der Wissenschaft* (Berlin: Hilfe, 1906); Ann Taylor Allen, *Feminism and Motherhood*, p. 12.

93. Lange, *Frauenbewegung*, p. 29.

94. Franz Wieacker, *Privatrechtsgeschichte der Neuzeit, unter Berücksichtigung der deutschen Entwicklung* (Göttingen: Vandenhoeck & Ruprecht, 1967), p. 454.

95. Gertrud Bäumer, "Lage und Aufgabe der Frauenbewegung in der deutschen Umwälzung," *Die Frau*, vol. 40, no. 7 (1933): 385–92; here p. 385. See also Gertrud Bäumer, *Die Frau im deutschen Staat* (Berlin: Juncker & Dünnhaupt, 1932).

96. Gertrud Bäumer, *Die Frau in der Kulturbewegung der Gegenwart* (Wiesbaden: Bergmann, 1904), p. 48.

Chapter 7

1. Bjørnstjerne Bjørnson in *Nylænde* 1899, pp. 130–31.

2. For a comprehensive short history of Norway (with a few references to women's history), see Rolf Danielsen et al., *Norway: A History from the Vikings to Our Own Times*, translated from the Norwegian by Michael Drake (Oslo: Scandinavian University Press, 1995). For a national Norwegian history with a gender perspective, see Ida Blom and Sølvi Sogner, eds., *Med kjønnsperspektiv på norsk historie—fra vikingtid til 2000–årsskiftet* (Oslo: Cappelen Akademisk Forlag A/S, 1999). For an evaluation of this book in English, see *Historisk tidskrift*, 2000, no. 2.

3. Anna Caspari Agerholt, *Den norske kvinnebevegelses historie* (Oslo: Gyldendal Norsk Forlag, 1973 [1937]).

4. For a comprehensive bibliography of research in Norwegian women's history, see Ingeborg Fløystad, "Kvinnehistorie i Norge. En bibliografi," *Historisk tidskrift*, 1990, no. 4, pp. 598–621. An introduction to this research is found in Ida Blom, "Women's History in Norway," in Jan Eivind Myhre, William B. Hubbard, Trond Nordby, Sylvi Sogner, eds., *The Making of an Historical Culture* (Oslo: Universitetsforlaget, 1995).

5. See Tayo Andreasen, Anette Borchorst, Drude Dahlerup, Eva Lous, Hanne Rimmen Nielsen, eds., *Moving On: New Perspectives on the Women's Movement* (Aarhus: Acta Jutlandica LXVII: 1. Humanities Series 66, Aarhus University Press),

in particular the Introduction, pp. 8–17; Jane Rendall, "Nineteenth Century Feminism and the Separation of Spheres: Reflections on the Public/Private Dichotomy," pp. 17–37; Hanne Rimmen Nielsen, "Christian and Competent Schoolmistresses: Women's Culture at the Aarhus Training College for Women Teachers 1909–1950," pp. 90–123; Kari Melby, "Women's Ideology: Difference, Equality or a New Femininity: Women Teachers and Nurses in Norway 1912–1940," pp. 138–54.

6. Torill Steinfeld, "Gjør sommeren blid for svalerne: Camilla Collett," in Irene Engelstad, Jorunn Hareide, Irene Iversen, Torill Steinfeld, Janneken Ÿverland, eds., *Norsk kvinnelitteraturhistorie*, vol. 1 (Oslo: PaxForlag A. S., 1988), pp. 77–83.

7. Eva Pedersen, "Refleksjon og emansipasjon: Essayistikk fram til århundreskiftet," in Irene Engelstad et al., eds., *Norsk kvinnelitteraturhistorie*, pp. 129–36. Bente Nilsen Lein, *Furier er også kvinner: Aasta Hansteen 1824–1908* (Oslo: Universitetsforlaget, 1984).

8. Agerholt, *Den norske*, pp. 32–53. Ida Blom, ed., *Cappelens kvinnehistorie*, vol. 3 (Oslo: J. W. Cappelen forlag, 1993), p. 188.

9. Aslaug Moksnes, *Likestilling eller særstilling? Norsk Kvinnesaksforening 1884–1913* (Oslo: Gyldendal Norsk forlag, 1984), p. 45. Where no other sources are mentioned, the following is based on Moksnes 1984 and Agerholt 1973.

10. The right to study at the university had been obtained in 1882, two years before the women's movement started organizing. In 1884, women also got the right to pass university exams. The efforts of one woman, Cecilie Thoresen, assisted by a small group of men, were behind these changes. Exams at university level opened up new career possibilities for women, moving into areas so far clearly masculine. But it was not till 1912 that exams gave women the same possibilities as men. Only then were the diplomatic services and high-level government positions opened to women. Female candidates of theology had to wait until 1956 before they were accepted into the clergy. See Agerholt, *Den norske*; and Ida Blom, " . . . uden dog at overskride sin naturlige Begrænsning. Kvinner i akademia 1882–1932," in Suzanne Stiver Lie and Maj Birgit Rørslett, eds., *Alma Maters Døtre—Et århundre med kvinner i akademisk utdannelse* (Oslo: Pax Forlag A/S, 1995), pp. 19–32.

11. Moksnes, *Likestilling*; Agerholt, *Den norske*, pp. 163–83.

12. Moksnes, *Likestilling*, pp. 157–63; Vera Espeland Ertresvaag, "Arbeiderkvinnenes faglige og politiske organisering 1889–1901," in Ida Blom, Gro Hagemann, eds., *Kvinner selv . . . Sju bidrag til norsk kvinnehistorie* (Oslo: H. Aschehoug, 1980), pp. 47–70, esp. pp. 53–9.

13. Ertresvaag, "Arbeiderkvinnenes," p. 47. For the following, see also Ertresvaag.

14. Kirsten Flatøy, "Utviklingslinjer innen Arbeiderpartiets Kvindeforbund fra 1901 til 1914," in Blom and Hagemann, eds., *Kvinner selv*, p. 71. The following is based on Flatøy, pp. 71–94. See also Ida Blom, "A Double Responsibility: Women, Men and Socialism in Norway c. 1918—c. 1940," in Helmuth Gruber and Pamela

Graves, eds., *Women and Socialism, Socialism and Women: Europe between the Two World Wars* (New York: Berghahn Books, 1998), pp. 450–77.

15. Agerholt, *Den norske*, pp. 184–201 and pp. 207–32; Moksnes, *Likestilling*, pp. 183–86, 193, 203–09, and 254–60; Ida Blom, "The Struggle for Women's Suffrage in Norway, 1885–1913," *Scandinavian Journal of History*, vol. 8, no. 1: 3–22.

16. Ida Blom, "Equality and the Threat of War in Scandinavia, 1884–1905," in T. G. Fraser and Keith Jeffery, eds., *Men, Women and War* (Dublin, 1993, Historical Studies 18), pp. 100–118.

17. Moksnes, *Likestilling*, pp. 199–212; Agerholt, *Den norske*, pp. 191–99.

18. Ida Blom, "Nation—Class—Gender: Scandinavia at the Turn of the Century," *Scandinavian Journal of History*, vol. 21 (Spring 1996): 1–16.

19. Blom, "The Struggle for Women's Suffrage," pp. 16–17; and Blom, ed., *Cappelens kvinnehistorie*.

20. *Nylænde* 1898. Quoted from Gro Hagemann, "Særvern av kvinner—arbeidervern eller diskriminering?" in Blom, Hagemann, eds., *Kvinner selv*, p. 115.

21. The following is based on Hagemann, "Særvern," in Blom, Hagemann, eds., *Kvinner selv*, pp. 95–121.

22. Lise Rosenberg has analyzed the discussions in her Ph.D. thesis, "Hagar og Ismael i Sarahs telt: Holdninger til familie og ekteskap id ebatten om de Castbergske barnelover 1901–1915," unpublished thesis, Department of History, University of Bergen, 1981.

23. Moksnes, *Likestilling*; Agerholt, *Den norske*; Blom, "The Struggle for Women's Suffrage."

24. Reidun Klokkersund, "'. . . hjemmet først og fremst, men det andre ikke forsømmes.' Kirkas kvinnesyn belyst med utgangspunkt i debatten om kvinners adgang til presteembetet i perioden 1891–1912," Ph.D. diss., University of Bergen, Department of History, 1986, esp. p. 74.

25. Ida Blom, *"den haarde Dyst"—Fødsler og fødselshjelp gjennom 150 år* (Oslo: J. W. Cappelens forlag, 1988), pp. 183–95.

26. Reidun Klokkersund, "Kirkas kvinnesyn 1891–1912," pp. 107–37.

27. Ida Blom, "Changing Gender Identities in an Industrialising Society," *Gender and History*, vol. 2, no. 2 (Summer 1990): 131–47.

28. Katti Anker Møller in *Nylænde* 1902: 135–37.

29. Ibid.

30. Blom, "Nation—Class—Gender."

31. Ida Blom, *Barnebegrensning—sund eller sunn fornuft?* (Bergen: Universitetsforlaget, 1980), p. 121. The quotation is from an anonymous contributor to *Husmoderen*, the journal of Hjemmenes Vel, 1910, p. 23.

32. Blom, "Changing Gender Identities," esp. p. 138.

33. Agerholt, *Den norske*, p. 150; Moksnes, *Likestilling*, p. 265.

34. Blom, "Nation—Class—Gender."

35. Gro Hagemann, *Skolefolk: Lærernes historie i Norge* (Oslo, 1992), pp. 172–73.

36. Agerholt, *Den norske*, pp. 119–25, esp. p. 119.

37. Blom, *Barnebegrensning*, pp. 93–4.

38. Agerholt, *Den norske*, p. 120.

39. Mathilde Schjøtt married P. O. Schjøtt, government member in the 1880s; Frederikke Marie married Anton Qvam, and Randi Blehr married Otto Blehr, the two last men at times prime ministers. Gina Krog was the sister-in-law of Cecelie Thoresen Krog. Ragne Nielsen was the sister of Viggo Ullman. Their mother was Vilhelmine Ullman, born in 1816, but still very active within the women's movement in the 1880s and 1890s. She was one of the few divorced women, and was still working as the manager of a children's asylum when she had passed 70 years of age. Other complete families were sometimes involved, the most important of which was probably the Qvam family. Frederikke Marie Qvam, the eminent organizer of the Sanitary Association and of the National Suffrage Association, was married to Anton Qvam, an outstanding liberal politician who strongly supported the women's movement. Their daughter, Anne Qvam, was very active in the struggle for the vote. Family ties also connected Katti Anker Møller to Johan Castberg (her brother-in-law).

40. Anna Bugge formed a common-law marriage with Knut Wicksell, an ardent Swedish proponent of family planning. Margrete Vullum, daughter of one of the leading Danish liberal politicians of the period, married a Norwegian artist and herself became a prominent cultural journalist. Of three Danish sisters, two, Mix and Ida Bojsen, found Norwegian husbands within the Liberal Party. Ida was active in the more conservative part of the women's movement, and among Mix's ten children was Katti, later Katti Anker Møller. The third of the three sisters was Jutta Bojsen Møller, president of the Danish Women's Association. See Moksnes, *Likestilling*, esp. pp. 21–32.

41. Blom, "Nation—Class—Gender."

42. Moksnes, *Likestilling*, p. 60.

43. Marit Tokheim, *Norske Kvinners Nasjonalråd 1904–1914*, in: Blom, Hagemann, eds., *Kvinner selv*, pp. 122–50.

Chapter 8

1. For overviews see Gunnar Qvist, "Policy Towards Women and the Women's Struggle in Sweden," *Scandinavian Journal of History*, vol. V (1980): 51–74; Christina Carlsson Wetterberg, "Equal or Different—That's Not the Question: Women's Political Strategies in a Historical Perspective," in Drude van der Fehr, Anna G. Jonasdottir, Bente Rosenbeck, eds., *Is There a Nordic Feminism? Nordic Feminist*

Thought on Culture and Society (London, 1998). See also Barbara Hobson, "Feminist Strategies and Gendered Discourses in Welfare States: Married Women's Right to Work in the United States and Sweden," in Seth Koven, Sonya Michel, eds., *Mothers of a New World: Maternalist Politics and the Origins of Welfare States* (New York, 1993), pp. 396–429, about the women's movement and the concern for married women's right to work during the thirties. For a general view of the development of the women's vote see Appendix in Caroline Daley, Melanie Nolan, eds., *Suffrage and Beyond: International Feminist Perspectives* (New York, 1994), pp. 349–52.

2. The local representation was on an individual basis. In 1905 local branches of the FBF got started. The FBF had around 900 members in 1884 and around 2,600 members in 1920. See Ulla Manns, *Den sanna frigörelsen: Fredrika-Bremer-förbundet 1884–1921* (True Emancipation: The Fredrika Bremer Association 1884–1921) (Stockholm/Stehag, 1997), p. 256.

3. Adlersparre got married in 1869. She did not become chairperson of the FBF. The first chairperson, 1884–1903, was Hans Hildebrand, director-general of the Central Board of National Antiquities. His successor was the social reformer Mrs. Agda Montelius. Adlersparre was the editor of the journal but withdrew in 1887 owing to internal conflicts concerning moral matters in relation to emancipation. See Manns, *Den sanna frigörelsen*, p. 97.

4. Cited from Manns, *Den sanna frigörelsen*, p. 65.

5. Sophie Adlersparre (Esselde), "En öfverblick af arbete på den svenska qvinnans framåtskridande" (An Overview of the Progress of Swedish Women), *Tidskrift för hemmet* (Home Journal), vol. XXVII (1885), p. 17.

6. The naturalistic ideas received from both Drysdale and Nordau had a large impact on the author August Strindberg, who was crucial for the young, mainly male generation of authors of the 1880s. See Ulf Boëthius, *Strindberg och kvinnofrågan* (Strindberg and the Woman Question) (Uppsala, 1969). See also Inger-Lise Hjordt-Vetlesen, "Modernitetens kvinnliga text: Det moderna genombrottet i Norden" (The Female Text of Modernity: The Modern Breakthrough in the Nordic Countries), in: *Nordisk kvinnolitteraturhistoria* (A History of Women's Literature in the Nordic Countries), vol. II (Höganäs, 1993); and Ingeborg Nordin Hennel, Christina Sjöblad, "Lyckligare ungdom har aldrig funnits: Det moderna genombrottet i Sverige" (Happier Youth Has Never Existed: The Modern Breakthrough in Sweden), in *Nordisk kvinnolitteraturhistoria*.

7. Manns, *Den sanna frigörelsen*, chap. 3.

8. See Valery Bryson, *Feminist Political Theory* (London, 1992); Alison M. Jaggar, *Feminist Politics and Human Nature* (Totowa, N.J. 1983); and Karen Offen, *European Feminisms, 1700–1950: A Political History* (Stanford: Stanford University Press, 2000). The FBF was particularly inspired by the English women's movement; see articles by Jane Rendall and Christine Bolt in this book; see also

Barbara Caine, *Victorian Feminists* (Oxford, 1992); and Philippa Levine, *Victorian Feminism* (London, 1987).

9. The first board consisted of fourteen women and ten men, but by 1920 the number of men had decreased considerably; only one was left. The new statutes of 1921 did not mention cooperation with men any more. See Manns, *Den sanna frigörelsen*, pp. 212–13.

10. Hjalmar Strömer, "Bidrag till belysande af kvinnans själsbegåfning" (A Contribution to the Elucidation of the Mental Capacity of Women), *Tidskrift för hemmet*, vol. XXI (1879), pp. 113–37; Sophie Adlersparre, "Reaktionen mot det af qvinnofrågan framkallade äktenskapsidealet" (The Reaction Against the Ideal of Marriage within the Woman Question), *Dagny*, vol. II (1887), pp. 18–25; Oscar Montelius, "Huru länge har kvinnan betraktas som mannens egendom?" (How Long Have Women Been Considered the Property of Men?), *Nordisk tidskrift* (Nordic Journal), vol. XI (1898), pp. 1–30, 95–122. Mill's book *The Subjection of Women* was translated into Swedish immediately after publication.

11. Manns, *Den sanna frigörelsen*, pp. 80–102.

12. Elisabeth Grundtvig, *Nutidens sedlige jemnlikhetskraf* (The Contemporary Claim for Equality within Sexual Morals) (Helsinki, 1888), p. 21. The pamphlet was originally published in the journal of *Dansk Kvindesamfund* (the Danish Women's Association), *Kvinden og Samfundet* (Woman and Society), one year earlier.

13. The idea of self-help was also significant in the early philanthropy movement in which several members of the FBF were active. See Ingrid Åberg, "Revivalism, Philanthropy and Emancipation. Women's Liberation and Organisation in the Early Nineteenth Century," *Scandinavian Journal of History*, vol. XIII (1988).

14. For a full description of the activities within the FBF, see Manns, *Den sanna frigörelsen*.

15. Associations for women office employees and for women at the state telegraph and state post offices were started in 1903. In 1908 *Föreningen kvinnor i statlig tjänst* (Association for Female State Employees) was founded, also with help from the FBF.

16. Numerous groups used the FBF as an information channel. They included: *Föreningen för välgörenhetens ordnande* (Association for the Organization of Charity Work), the Association for Married Women's Property Rights, *Handarbetets vänner* (Friends of Handicraft), *Kristliga föreningen af unga kvinnor* (YWCA), *Gymnastiska centralinstitutet* (Institute for Gymnastics), *Drägtreformföreningen* (Dress Reform Association), *Vita bandet* (White Ribbon: WCTU), discussion clubs like *Nya Idun* (New Idun) and *Kvinnoklubben* (Women's Club), and *Kvinnliga fredsföreningen* (Women's Peace Association). When the suffrage movement became organized it soon used both the journal and the bureau. During 1908–1911 the journal *Dagny* was a joint publication of the suffrage movement and the FBF. Advice service was

given to all women, not only members, for a fee that was affordable to them, in some cases for free.

17. According to the FBF the numbers of women participating in municipal elections in Stockholm grew from 131, representing 3,912 votes in 1886, to 462, representing 10,290 votes the following year. See *Dagny*, vol. I (1886), pp. 125–26, *Dagny*, vol. II (1887), p. 135.

18. Manns, *Den sanna frigörelsen*, pp. 79–80.

19. See Manns, *Den sanna frigörelsen*, chap. 3; and the writings of Anna Sandström, especially the article "Kvinnoarbete och kvinnolycka" (Women's Work and Women's Happiness) in *Dagny*, vol. XI (1896), which was a reply to the criticism of Ellen Key concerning women's emancipation and gender.

20. See Carlsson Wetterberg, "Equal or Different," pp. 37–41 about the visionary maternalism represented by Ellen Key and Frida Stéenhoff. The latter did not see women and men as biologically different to the extent that Key did, but she was nevertheless regarded as an important representative of maternalism at the turn of the century.

21. Manns, *Den sanna frigörelsen*, p. 229. A similar development was seen in both Norway and Denmark. Were moral questions to be given priority or should the organizations concentrate on social and legal matters? Sweden and Norway chose to concentrate on *Realpolitik*, while Denmark after thorough discussions decided that the moral question was an integral part of the work for emancipation and therefore essential. See Gro Hagemann, "Bohemer, kvinnesakskvinner og hanskemoral" (Bohemians, Feminists, and Sexual Morals), in Gro Hagemann, Anne Krogstad, eds., *Höydeskrekk: Kvinner og offentlighet* (Acrophobia: Women and Public Space) (Oslo, 1994); and Gyrithe Lemche, *Dansk Kvindesamfunds historie gennem 40 aar* (Forty Years in the History of the Danish Women's Association) (Copenhagen, 1939). It is important to notice that the internal conflicts in the 1880s did not seem to have to do with different views about emancipation but with strategy vs. ideals.

22. The suffrage organization dissolved in 1921.

23. The intense work and cooperation is shown by Bertil Björkenlid, *Kvinnokrav i manssamhälle* (Women's Demands in a Society of Men) (Uppsala, 1982). Concerning social policy and the close relationship to many feminists of the time, see Sven E. Olsson, "Before Social Democracy: The Early Formation of a Social Policy Discourse in Sweden," chap. 1 of his book *Social Policy and Welfare State in Sweden* (Lund, 1990); and James Rössel, *Kvinnorna och kvinnorörelsen i Sverige 1850–1950* (Women and the Women's Movement in Sweden 1850–1950) (Stockholm, 1950), pp. 60–62.

24. On the clashes between the FBF and Ellen Key concerning emancipation see Ulla Manns, "Kvinnofrigörelse och moderskap: En diskussion mellan Fredrika-

Bremer-förbundet och Ellen Key" (Women's Emancipation and Motherhood: A Discussion between the Fredrika Bremer Association and Ellen Key), in Ulla Wikander and Ulla Manns, eds., *Det evigt kvinnliga: En historia om förändring* (Eternal Femininity: A History of Change) (Stockholm, 2001). The fight against the prohibition of women's night work is analyzed by Lynn Karlsson, "The Beginning of a 'Masculine Renaissance': The Debate on the 1909 Prohibition against Women's Night Work in Sweden," in Ulla Wikander, Alice Kessler-Harris, Jane Lewis, eds., *Protecting Women: Labor Legislation in Europe, the United States, and Australia, 1880–1920* (Urbana, 1995), pp. 235–66.

25. See Björkenlid, *Kvinnokrav i manssamhälle.*

26. The Swedish women's movement sought alliances on several questions during the suffrage years. Apart from suffrage, cooperation took place concerning pension funds, labor legislation, a new marriage law, peace, and domestic education. See Manns, *Den sanna frigörelsen,* chap. 5 and 6.

27. Joan W. Scott, "Gender: A Useful Category of Historical Analysis," p. 42, in her book *Gender and the Politics of History* (New York, 1988); and Yvonne Hirdman, "Genussystemet—reflexioner kring kvinnors sociala underordning" (The Gender System—Reflexions on the Social Subordination of Women), *Kvinnovetenskaplig tidskrift* (Women's Studies Review), no. III (1988). A brief presentation in English is given in Hirdman, "The Gender System," in Tayo Andreasen et al., eds., *Moving On: New Perspectives on the Women's Movement* (Aarhus, 1991).

28. See Manns, *Den sanna frigörelsen.* On the suffrage movement and the Social Democratic women see Björkenlid, *Kvinnokrav i manssamhälle* and Wetterberg, "Equal or Different." One of the few who exclusively claimed suffrage as a natural right was Frida Stéenhoff in *Hvarför skola kvinnorna vänta?* (Why Must Women Wait?) (Stockholm, 1905).

29. This is further elaborated upon in Manns, "Kvinnofrigörelse och moderskap."

30. One prominent member of the board, Ellen Fries (Ph.D. in history), left the board. She explicitly declared that the reason for this was an ideological change within the FBF. She could not remain in a board that focused exclusively on practical matters. See Manns, *Den sanna frigörelsen,* p. 146.

31. Kjell Östberg, *Efter rösträtten: Kvinnors utrymme efter det demokratiska genombrottet* (After Suffrage: Women's Space after the Emergence of Democracy) (Stockholm/Stehag, 1997). The organizations were *Moderata kvinnoförbundet* (Conservative Women's Association), 1911, *Föreningen frisinnade kvinnor* (Liberal Women's Union), 1914, *Allmänna Valmansförbundets centrala kvinnoråd* (Women's Central Council of the Conservative Party), 1920, *Socialdemokratiska kvinnoförbundet* (Social Democratic Women's Association), 1920, and *Landsbygdens kvinnoförbund* (Women's Association of the Rural Party), 1921.

32. Olsson, "Before Social Democracy," pp. 64–74. The CSA did not represent any consistent ideology on women's questions. There existed, for example, different ideas about protective labor legislation among feminists within the CSA. Different ideas about moral matters and sexuality were also represented. See Lynn Karlsson, "The Beginning of a 'Masculine Renaissance.'"

33. See Thomas Laqueur, *Making Sex: Body and Gender from the Greeks to Freud* (Cambridge, Mass., 1990) and Cynthia Russet, *Sexual Science: The Victorian Construction of Womanhood* (London, 1989). A Swedish contribution about gender in science, especially in medicine, is Karin Johannisson, *Den mörka kontinenten: Kvinnan, medicinen och fin-de-siècle* (The Dark Continent: Women, Medicine, and the Fin-de-siècle) (Stockholm, 1994).

34. The explicit purpose of the FBF in 1921 was "to gather Swedish women for joint community work, to promote their abilities and sense of responsibility as citizens, educators and workers in various fields, and act to improve the position of women in the home, in the community, and in the state." Annual report from 1921, here cited from *I Fredrika Bremers spår: Fredrika-Bremer-förbundet 1884–1944* (In the Footsteps of Fredrika Bremer: The Fredrika Bremer Association 1884–1914), ed. by the board of the FBF (Stockholm, 1944), p.160. See also *Vad vill Fredrika-Bremer-förbundet?* (What Does the FBF Want?), ed. by the board of the FBF (Stockholm, 1919), pp. 2–3; and Gertrud Törnell, *Sveriges kvinnor och Fredrika-Bremer-förbundet* (Swedish Women and the FBF) (Stockholm, 1920), pp. 14–15.

35. See Ulla Wikander, "Some 'Kept the Flag of Feminist Demands Waving': Debates at International Congresses on Protecting Women Workers," in Ulla Wikander, Alice Kessler-Harris, Jane Lewis, eds., *Protecting Women*, pp. 29–62; and Offen, *European Feminisms*.

Chapter 9

1. Richard J. Evans, *The Feminists: Women's Emancipation Movements in Europe, America and Australasia 1840–1920* (London: Croom Helm, 1977), pp. 96–8.

2. Katherine David, "Czech Feminists and Nationalism in the Late Habsburg Monarchy: 'The First in Austria,'" *Journal of Women's History*, vol. 3, no. 2 (1991): 27.

3. Helena Volet-Jeanneret, *La femme bourgeoise à Prague, 1860–1895: De la philanthropie à l'émancipation* (Genève: Editions Slatkine, 1988), pp. 275–84.

4. In 1999, three books were published dealing with the 19th-century history of Czech women, which, however, are not taken into consideration in this article, written in 1995: Pavla Horská, *Naše prababičky feministky* (Our Great-Grandmothers the Feminists) (Prague: NLN, 1999); Milena Lenderová, *K hříchu i k modlitbě: Žena y minulém století* (For Sin and Prayer: Woman in the Last Century) (Prague:

Mladá Fronta, 1999); Marie L. Neudorflová, *České ženy v 19. století: Usilí a sny, úspěchy i zklamáni na cestě k emancipaci* (Czech Women in the Nineteenth Century: Efforts and Dreams, Successes and Disappointments on the Way to Emancipation) (Prague: Janua, 1999). Especially Marie Neudorflová's extensive work includes detailed information on the women's movement. See also Jitka Malečková, "Nationalizing Women and Engendering the Nation: The Czech National Movement," in Ida Blom, Karen Hagemann and Catherine Hall, eds., *Gendered Nations: Nationalisms and Gender Order in the Long Nineteenth Century* (Oxford and New York: Berg, 2000), pp. 293–310.

5. See Pavla Horská, "K ekonomické aktivitě žen na přelomu 19. a 20. století" (Příklad Českých zemí) (On the Economic Activity of Women at the Turn of the 19th and 20th Centuries [The Example of the Czech Lands]), *Československý časopis historický*, vol. 21, no. 5 (1983): 711–42.

6. *Ottův slovník naučný* (Otto's Encyclopedia), vol. 21 (Prague: J. Otto, 1908), pp. 808–11.

7. Vlasta Kučerová, *K historii ženského hnutí v Čechách (Amerlingova éra)* (On the History of the Women's Movement in Bohemia [Amerling's Era]) (Brno: Ženská revue, 1914), pp. 1–2.

8. Stanley Z. Pech, *The Czech Revolution of 1848* (Chapel Hill: The University of North Carolina Press, 1969), p. 326; *Ottův slovník naučný*, p. 809; Volet-Jeanneret, *La femme*, pp. 61, 74, and 161.

9. David, "Czech Feminists," p. 30.

10. Evans, *The Feminists*, p. 96.

11. Vladimír Macura, *Znamení zrodu: České obrození jako kulturní typ* (A Sign of Emergence: the Czech Revival as a Cultural Type) (Prague: Československý spisovatel, 1983), pp. 128–35.

12. Kučerová, *K historii*, p. 19 and pp. 8–21; Volet-Jeanneret, *La femme*, pp. 67–71.

13. Magdalena Dobromila Rettigová, *Věneček pro dcerky vlastenské* (A Garland for Patriotic Daughters) (Hradec Králové: Jan Host. Pospíšil, 1825), pp. 7–8.

14. *Ottův slovník naučný*, p. 808.

15. Volet-Jeanneret, *La femme*, p. 71; Kučerová, *K historii*, pp. 31–3. On Rajská's marriage see *Z let probuzení, III, Vzájemné dopisy Antonie Čelakovské (Bohuslavy Rajské) a Boženy Němcové, 1844–1849* (From the Years of Awakening, III, Correspondence of Antonie Čelakovská [Bohuslava Rajská] and Božena Němcová, 1844–1849) (Prague: J. Otto, 1873), pp. 8–10.

16. For example, the poems "Ženám českým" (To Czech Women) and particularly "Slavné ráno" (A Glorious Morning), both from 1843.

17. The former, aimed at promoting women's education, was founded by Honorata z Wiśniowskych-Zapová, assisted by Amerling's wife and Rajská's sister Jo-

hana Fričová. Volet-Jeanneret, *La femme*, p. 75; *Ottův slovník naučný*, p. 809; Pech, *The Czech Revolution*, p. 325.

18. The next meeting proposed the foundation of a women's patriotic club and girls' school. See Pech, *The Czech Revolution*, pp. 320–25.

19. Ibid., pp. 321 and 323.

20. Otto Urban, *Česká společnost 1848–1918* (Czech Society 1848–1918) (Prague: Svoboda, 1982), pp. 142–326.

21. Volet-Jeanneret, *La femme*, pp. 101–34; Pavla Horská, "Za práva žen" (For Women's Rights), *Dějiny a současnost*, vol. 14, no. 1 (1992): 29–30.

22. Volet-Jeanneret, *La femme*, pp. 101–10; Horská, "Za práva," p. 30.

23. Among the activities of the Club, particularly popular were lectures, ranging from such topics as socialism and idealism to industry, science and technology, from astronomy and geography to national history and literature, with an emphasis on achievements of outstanding Czech and foreign women. See Stanislav Kodym, *Dům u Halánků: Vzpomínky na Vojtu Náprstka* (The House U Halánků: Memories about Vojta Náprstek) (Prague: Československý spisovatel, 1955), pp. 72–89.

24. *Ottův slovník naučný*, pp. 810–12.

25. Horská, "K ekonomické aktivitě," pp. 715–25.

26. *Ottův slovník naučný*, p. 810.

27. See, for example, Věnceslava Lužická, *Žena ve svém povolání* (Woman in Her Profession) (Prague: Ženský svět, 1872).

28. Introduction to the first volume of *Ženská bibliotéka* (Women's Library) (Prague: J. Otto, 1872), pp. 7–8.

29. Horská, "Za práva," pp. 30–31.

30. Jana Brabencová, "Pražské ženy v procesu vývoje českého dívčího vzdělání ve 2. polovině 19. století" (Prague Women in the Process of Development of Czech Girls' Education in the Second Half of the 19th Century), in Jiří Pešek and Václav Ledvinka, eds., *Žena v dějinách Prahy* (Woman in the History of Prague) (Prague: Scriptorium, 1996), pp. 203–11.

31. Eliška Krásnohorská, *Ženská otázka česká* (The Czech Woman Question) (Prague: Nákladem dr. Grégra, 1881), p. 28.

32. Horská, "K ekonomické aktivitě," p. 734; *Ottův slovník naučný*, pp. 810–11.

33. *Ottův slovník naučný*, p. 811; Miloslava Turková, "Pražské ženy na I. sjezdu žen českoslovanských" (Prague Women at the First Congress of Czechoslavic Women), *Žena v dějinách Prahy*, pp. 301–5.

34. See, for example, *Zpráva Vlasty, spolku paní a dívek v Hlinsku, za léta 1893 až 1919* (The Report of Vlasta, an Association of Women and Girls in Hlinsko, from the Years 1893 to 1919) (Hlinsko: Vlasta, 1919).

35. In 1903, the 50,000 members of Sokol included nearly 9,000 women. *Ottův slovník naučný*, vol. 23 (Prague: J. Otto, 1905), pp. 623–26.

36. *Ottův slovník naučný*, p. 811.

37. Albína Honzáková, "Studie práce a osobnosti F. F. Plamínkové" (A Study of the Work and Personality of F. F. Plamínková), in: Albína Honzáková, ed., *Kniha života: Práce a osobnost F. F. Plamínkové. Sborník k 60. narozeninám* (The Book of Life: The Work and Personality of F. F. Plamínková. A Festschrift on the Occasion of Her 60th Birthday) (Prague: Melantrich, 1935), pp. 63–7.

38. In 1910, Wiedermannová became a secretary of the "Progressive Organization of Women in Moravia," which united regional clubs of progressive orientation and fought against clericalism, alcoholism, and prostitution. In 1911 she founded a political weekly *Právo ženy* (A Woman's Right), promoting female suffrage. See Miroslava Dorazilová, *Vývoj pokrokového ženského hnutí na Moravě* (The Development of the Progressive Women's Movement in Moravia) (Vyškov: Zemská organisace pokrokových žen moravských, 1928), pp. 3–6.

39. On women's work see Horská, "K ekonomické aktivitě," pp. 711–17.

40. Ibid., p. 735.

41. In 1898, a conference of Brno Social Democratic women asked for protection of women's work, shorter working time, and voting rights for women. The working-class women's movement was appreciated, for example, by Pavla Buzková and Tereza Nováková.

42. By 1903, the Frauenfortschritt had over 1,200 members from the Czech Lands and from abroad. See Horská, "K ekonomické aktivitě," p. 734.

43. See Urban, *Česká společnost*, pp. 456–89.

44. Horská, "K ekonomické aktivitě," p. 735.

45. Honzáková, "Studie," p. 65; David, "Czech Feminists," p. 36.

46. On Masaryk's views about women see Marie L. Neudorfl, "Masaryk and the Women's Question," in Stanley B. Winters, ed., *T. G. Masaryk (1850–1937)*, vol. 1: *Thinker and Politician* (New York: St. Martin's Press, 1990), pp. 258–82.

47. Jarmila Mourková, *Růžena Svobodová* (Prague: Melantrich, 1975), pp. 109–15.

48. Teréza Nováková, "Volební právo žen u nás" (Women's Voting Rights in Our Country), in Teréza Nováková, *Ze ženského hnutí* (From the Women's Movement) (Prague: Jos. R. Vilímek, 1912), pp. 309–26.

49. In 1913, *Moravský svaz pro volební právo žen* (Moravian Union for Women's Voting Rights) was founded. See Dorazilová, *Vývoj*, p. 6.

50. Honzáková, "Studie," pp. 69–70.

51. Ibid., pp. 63–7.

52. Ibid., p. 61.

53. Jiří Kořalka, "Zvolení ženy do českého zemského sněmu roku 1912" (Election of a Woman to the Czech Diet in 1912), *Žena v dějinách Prahy*, pp. 307–20.

54. Ibid.

55. Dorazilová, *Vývoj*, p. 6.

56. *Ženský list*, vol. 21, no. 22 (1912): 2.

57. On the split see Urban, *Česká společnost*, pp. 552–64.

58. Quoted in Kořalka, "Zvolení ženy."

59. A. M. Marek, "Rovnoprávnost ženy" (The Equality of Women), in *Ženský list*, vol. 21, no. 20 (1912): 3–4; Nováková, "Volební právo," p. 323; Pavla Buzková, *Pokrokový názor na ženskou otázku* (A Progressive View on the Woman Question) (Prague: Pokrok, 1909), pp. 13–15, 22.

60. *Ženský list*, vol. 21, no. 20 (1912): 2–3, and no. 22: 2.

61. Honzáková, "Studie," pp. 58–9.

62. Marie Tůmová, *Pro volební právo žen* (For Women's Voting Rights) (Královo Pole u Brna: Právo ženy, 1911), p. 11.

63. Buzková gave up her brief career of a teacher when she married in 1907.

64. Buzková, *Pokrokový názor*.

65. Quoted in *Ženský list*, vol. 21, no. 21 (1912): 4.

66. Božena Viková-Kunětická, *Dál!* (Onward!) (Prague: Dr. Ed. Grégr a syn, nakl. Českého čtenáře, 1912).

67. Teréza Nováková, "Svazy žen a nacionalismus" (Women's Unions and Nationalism), in: *Ze ženského hnutí*, pp. 357–60.

68. Honzáková, "Studie," pp. 102–3.

Chapter 10

1. See especially the following pioneering studies: Gábor Gyáni, *Család, háztartás és a városi cselédség* (Family, Household, and the Urban Domestic Servants) (Budapest: Magvető, 1983); Gábor Gyáni, "Női munka és család Magyarországon 1900–1930" (Women's Work and the Family in Hungary), *Történelmi Szemle*, no. 3, 1987–88: 366–78; Gábor Gyáni, *Hétköznapi Budapest: Nagyvárosi élet a századfordulón* (Everyday Budapest: Urban Life at the Turn of the Century) (Budapest: Városháza, 1995), especially pp. 12–27; and Beáta Nagy, "A nők kereső tevékenysége Budapesten a 20. század első felében" (Women's Wage-Earning Work in the First Half of the Twentieth Century), in Miklós Hidas, ed., *Férfiuralom* (Budapest: Replika Kör, 1994): 155–75.

2. An example of the genre is Matild B. Tóth, *A magyar nők jogainak fejlődése* (The Progress of Hungarian Women's Rights) (Budapest: Táncsics, 1964). Despite its limited focus on legal and political history, Katalin Szegvári Nagyné, *Ut a nők egyenjogúságához* (The Path to the Equality of Women) (Budapest: Kossuth:

MNOT, 1981) provides an informative overview of the history of women's rights in Hungary.

3. Péter Hanák, ed., *Magyarország története 1890–1918* (The History of Hungary) (Budapest: Akadémiai, 1978), vol. VII.

4. Mária Neményi, "Miért nincs Magyarországon nőmozgalom?" (Why Is There No Women's Movement in Hungary?), in Hidas, *Férfiuralom*, pp. 235–45.

5. Rózsa Bédy-Schwimmer, *A magyar nőmozgalom régi dokumentumai* (The Old Documents of the Hungarian Women's Movement) (Budapest: Kunossy, Szilágyi és társa, 1907), pp. 1–6.

6. Andor Máday, *A magyar nő jogai a multban és jelenben* (The Rights of the Hungarian Woman in the Past and the Present) (Budapest: Atheneum, 1913), especially pp. 129–96.

7. See Rózsa Bédy-Schwimmer, *A magyar nőmozgalom régi dokumentumai*, pp. 7–38.

8. The best source to consult for the program, membership, organization, and activities of the feminists is the collection of the Feministák Egyesülete (Association of Feminists) at the Országos Levéltár, the Hungarian National Archives, font P 999 (hereafter FE).

9. The words "feminist" and "emancipation of women" had positive connotations for leading liberal journalists and authors of the era, for instance, Géza Kenedi, *Feminista tanulmányok* (Feminist Essays) (Budapest: Lampel, no date); and Ignotus, *Emma asszony levelei: Egy nőimitátor a nőemancipációért* (The Letters of Mrs. Emma: A Woman-Imitator for the Emancipation of Women), ed. by Péter Kardos (Budapest: Magvetö, 1985).

10. References to their role models abroad came up in almost every issue of *A Nő és a Társadalom* (The Woman and Society).

11. For the short-lived alliances of the feminists with the Social Democratic Party and the Independent Socialist Party, see *A Nő és a Társadalom*, May 1907, November 1907, September 1908, and the unpublished manuscript of Janka Gergely, one of the feminist leaders, on the early history of the Feministák Egyesülete, esp. pp. 6–7, FE, file 19, item 33.

12. For the temporary alliance with the right-of-middle Democratic Party, see *A Nő és a Társadalom*, 5 March 1913.

13. There are no biographies available in Hungarian on the two leaders of Hungarian feminism. Well-known and respected in the international women's movement before the war, they both emigrated after 1919 and held important posts in the international women's organizations. Rózsa Bédy-Schwimmer's collection is at the New York Public Library. See also the unpublished manuscript of Janka Gergely, esp. pp. 3–6, FE, file 19, item 33; Marcell Benedek, "Schwimmer Rózsa," *Huszadik Század*, no. 5–6 (1948): 347–49; and Mariska Gárdos, *A nő a*

történelem sodrában (The Woman in the Current of History) (Budapest: Népszava, 1942).

14. See Máday, "A feminizmus mint osztályharc" (Feminism as Class Struggle), *A Nő és a Társadalom*, vol. 1, no. 2 (1 Feb. 1907): 18–19.

15. Rózsa Bédy-Schwimmer, "A magyar nő különb helyzete" (The Privileged Situation of the Hungarian Woman), *A Nő és a Társadalom*, vol. 2, no. 12 (Nov. 1908): 194–96; the editorial "A választójog" (The Suffrage), ibid., vol. 2, no. 4 (Apr. 1908): 53–55; and Andor Máday, *A magyar nő jogai a multban és jelenben*, pp. 25–31, 35–65, 99–112.

16. Articles such as "Nők uj foglalkozásokban" (Women in New Professions), *A Nő és a Társadalom*, vol. 4, no. 8 (Aug. 1910): 138, appeared in almost each number of the feminist newspaper. See also Feministák Egyesülete, Petition to the Hungarian Parliament, 26 March 1910, FE, file 2, item 6.

17. See, among other articles, "A női választójog hatása" (The Effect of Women's Suffrage), *A Nő és a Társadalom*, vol. 2, no. 9 (Sept. 1908): 155; "Adatok a nők választójoga köréböl" (Facts on Women's Suffrage), ibid., vol. 4, no. 8 (Aug. 1910): 138; and Feministák Egyesülete, Petition to the Minister of Interior, 22 February 1908, FE, file 2, item 6.

18. The feminists addressed the parliament in petitions signed by groups of professional women. FE, file 16, item 15.

19. Mrs. Péter Agoston, *A magyar szocialista nőmozgalom története* (The History of the Hungarian Socialist Women's Movement) (Budapest: Népszava, 1947), and the memoirs of the socialist women's leader, Mariska Gárdos, *Százarcu élet* (Life of a Hundred Faces) (Budapest: Szépirodalmi, 1975), provide insider's views on the beginnings of the Social Democratic women's movement. For similar conflicts within the German and Austrian Social Democratic Parties, see Richard Evans, *Comrades and Sisters: Feminism, Socialism and Pacifism in Europe 1870–1945* (Sussex: Wheatsheaf Books; New York: St. Martin's Press, 1987), pp. 66–92.

20. For a summary of the feminist stand on the question of the night shift, see Rózsa Bédy-Schwimmer, "Az éjjeli munka kérdés" (The Question of the Night Shift), *A Nő és a Társadalom*, vol. 5, no. 3 (March 1911): 39–42.

21. See *A Nő és a Társadalom*, especially the year 1910 and Mariska Gárdos, *Százarcu élet*.

22. A short English overview of the political counter-culture of the Hungarian turn of the century is provided in Péter Hanák, ed., *The Corvina History of Hungary* (Budapest: Corvina, 1991), pp. 148–54.

23. See "Választójogi nép(?)gyülések" (Mass [?] Meetings for the Suffrage), *A Nő és a Társadalom*, vol. 5, no. 7 (July 1911): 110–11.

24. For a feminist viewpoint of the radicals' agenda, see Rózsa Bédy-Schwimmer, "A Haladás bajnokai" (The Champions of Progress), *A Nő és a Társadalom*,

vol. 4, no. 11 (Nov. 1910): 171–3; and "Allomások" (Stations), ibid., vol. 5, no. 6 (June 1911): 87–9. For the opposite perspective, see G. Sz., "A feminista mozgalom" (The Feminist Movement), *Huszadik Század* (Twentieth Century), vol. 14 (July–December 1913), pp. 66–74.

25. *A Nő és a Társadalom*, 1912–1913 and FE, file 17, item 21.

26. According to some sources, philanthropic women's organizations at the turn of the century numbered close to 800. Their umbrella organization, the Magyar Nőegyesületek Szövetsége (Federation of Hungarian Women's Associations), joined the International Council of Women. See Rózsa Bédy-Schwimmer, "Nömozgalom Magyarországon" (Federation of Hungarian Women's Associations), draft of petition, FE, file 16, item 15.

27. The best study on the domestic servants is Gábor Gyáni, *Család, háztartás és a városi cselédség*.

28. See Rosika Bédy-Schwimmer, *Zentralhaushaltung* (Leipzig, 1907), and the regular contributions on the subject in *A Nő és a Társadalom*.

29. Janka Gergely, unpublished manuscript, pp. 10–12, FE file 19, item 33.

30. See note 18.

31. Victor Karady, "Jewish Over-schooling in Hungary: its Sociological Dimensions," in Victor Karady and Wolfgang Mitter, eds., *Education and Social Structure in Central Europe in the 19th and 20th Centuries* (Köln: Böhlau, Deutsches Institut für Internationale Pädagogische Forschung, 1990), vol. 42, pp. 209–46.

32. See, for instance, the correspondence of Laura Polányi, a typical representative of this new type of woman, with her cousin, the sociologist and socialist theoretician Ervin Szabó, in György Litván and László Szücs, eds., *Szabó Ervin levelezése* (The Correspondence of Ervin Szabó) (Budapest: Kossuth, 1977), vol. 1, pp. 296, 302–3, 415–17 and 560. Gábor Gyáni cites the first examples of marriage contracts that acknowledge the equal status of the wife as proof for the emerging modern marriage among the representatives of the urban intelligentsia. Gábor Gyáni, *Hétköznapi Budapest*, pp. 14–15.

33. See, for instance, the letter of the renowned Hungarian historian Henrik Marczali to his student, Laura Polányi, congratulating her on her recent marriage: "Your 'new career' means that I will lose my dear student; nevertheless we hope to keep you as our dear friend." Letter of Henrik Marczali on 8 September 1904, Polányi collection, Manuscript Division, Széchényi National Library, Budapest.

34. Jelentés az 1910. évi müködésről (Report on the Activities of the Year 1910), FE, file 2, item 2.

35. Electoral speech of Laura Polányi in January 1919, manuscript, courtesy of Eva Zeisel.

Chapter 11

1. Whether women's duties to others as opposed to themselves stemmed from the traditional familial model, or the newer civic one, is beyond the scope of this essay. In general, Polish nineteenth-century society stressed individual responsibility while saying little about the individual's rights within society. An interesting departure from that is the case of Narcyza Żmichowska, whose emphasis on personal liberty is discussed by Grazyna Borkowska in her "Literatura i 'geniusz kobiecy': wiek xix, wiek x," in *Kobieta i kultura* (Wydawnictwo DIG, 1996), pp. 29–43. Brian Porter's incisive essay on the course of liberal ideology in Poland during this period makes the point that "there was a national agenda behind the initial deployment of liberal rhetoric, and this in turn implied that some concept of 'society' would have to balance enthusiasm for the individual. Liberalism to be national, also had to be social." "Construction and Deconstruction of 19th century Polish Liberalism," presented at the 5th Congress of the International Council for Central and Eastern European Studies, Warsaw, 1995.

2. Piotr S. Wandycz, *The Lands of Partitioned Poland, 1795–1918* (Seattle: University of Washington Press, 1974), pp. 208–9.

3. R. F. Leslie, *The History of Poland since 1863* (Cambridge: Cambridge University Press, 1983), p. 47.

4. When the Historical Institute at the University of Warsaw published a volume of essays on Polish women, in 1990, it launched them as subjects in Polish history. The editors, Anna Zarnowska and Andrzej Szwarc, have since edited other volumes with essays on women and education, politics, and culture. Thus far the scholarship has remained in the 19th and 20th century; we hope that other periods will also get their due. The first English volume of essays on Polish women was published in 1992 by Eastern European Monographs. It was edited by Rudolf Jaworski and Bianka Pietrow-Ennker, and who is an editor of this volume. Unfortunately the title, *Women in Polish History*, is quite misleading since only the introductory essay by Bianka Pietrow-Ennker delves earlier than the 19th century (the editors had no control over the title).

5. Piotr S. Wandycz, *The Lands of Partitioned Poland*, p. 117.

6. Piotr Chmielowski, *Autorki Polskie wieku XIX*, Polska Akademia Umiejętnosci, Archiwum Komisji do Dziejow Oświaty i Szkolnictwa w Polsce, no. 5, p. 229.

7. Ibid. Some notable Enthusiast women were Narcyza Żmichowska, Wincenta Zabłocka, Kazimiera Ziemiecka, Faustyna Morzycka, Bibianna Moraczewska, Tekla Dobrzyńska, and Anna Skimborowicz, whose husband edited the journal.

8. E. Ziemiecka, *Myśli o wychowaniu kobiet* (Warsaw, 1843).

9. Sabina Grzegorzewska, "Wpływ kobiet na rozwój duchowy czlowieczeństwa," *Biblioteka Warszawska*, 1855: 236–37.

10. Stanisław Bogusławski, "Lwy i lwice," Komedia w 3 aktach wierszem, in Stanisław Bogusławski, *Komedie oryginalne*, vol. 2 (Warsaw, 1846); August Wilkoński, "Emacypacja Sabiny ze stanowiska absolutnego," Komedia w dwoch aktach, in *Ramoty i ramotki literackie*, vol. 2 (Warsaw, 1845).

11. A. Mińkowska, *Organizacja spiskowa 1848r. w Królestwie Polskim* (Warsaw, 1923); Mieczysława Romankówna, "Sprawa Entuzjastek," *Pamiętnik Literacki*, z. 2 (1957), pp. 516–17.

12. The 1863 Uprising in Russian-controlled Poland was the second and last attempt to regain independence through force of arms. Poland regained independence after World War I. Adam Winiarz, "The Woman Question in the Kingdom of Poland," *Women in Polish Society* (Boulder, Colo.: East European Monographs, 1992), pp. 177–219.

13. J. Hulewicz, *Sprawa wyższego wyksztalcenia kobiet w Polsce w XIX wieku* (Cracow, 1939), pp. 152–56.

14. Norman Davies, *God's Playground: A History of Poland*, vol. 2 (New York: Columbia University Press, 1982), p. 44.

15. Piotr S. Wandycz, *The Lands of Partitioned Poland*, p. 208.

16. According to R. F. Leslie, "the theory, which went by the name of 'Warsaw Positivism,' and drew freely upon the writings of August Comte, J. S. Mill, Herbert Spencer, Darwin and Buckle, had its roots in the obvious facts of Polish subjection. Its principal exponent, Alexander Świętochowski, might condemn through the periodical *Przegląd Tygodniowy* the outmoded ethos of the szlachta and demand a leading role for the entrepreneur and the industrialist, but theory and practice were unhappy bedfellows. Economic expansion brought new problems in its train." Leslie, *History of Poland*, p. 47. In *Liberalizm po Komunizimie* (Społeczny Instytut Wydawniczy Znak, 1994), Jerzy Szacki asserts that there never was fertile ground for liberalism in Poland during the nineteenth century because of economic backwardness, while earlier, the highly touted Golden Freedoms of the szlachta, which some see as precursors of liberal ideology, were actually the opposite of it. Poland before the partitions was too backward economically and lacked the centralized political authority which is the backbone of liberalism. Szlachta wanted freedom for the noble estate and fought all efforts to strengthen the position of the monarchy.

17. This topic is treated in Winiarz, "The Woman Question."

18. Liliana, *Kobieta na katedrze in Rodzina*, 1866, p. 6.

19. Aleksandra Borkowska, "Kilka mysli wstępnych o emancypacji kobiet," *Kronika Rodzinna*, 1871/1872: p. 15; H. Stuve, "O emancypacji kobiet," *Kronika Rodzinna*, 1867/1868: pp. 49 and 65.

20. Antoni Nowosielski, "O przeznaczeniu i zawodzie kobiet," in *Tygodnik Ilustrowany*, no. 166 (1862); idem: "O kwestji kobiet," *Gazeta Polska*, no. 126 (1870).

21. Roman Bierzyński, *Somatologie de la femme, etudes physiologiques* (Paris, 1869).

22. Roman Bierzyński, *Jeszcze słówko o kobiecie* (Warsaw, 1870); Roman Bierzyński, *Nieco o prawie kobiety do nauki i pracy* (Warsaw, 1871).

23. Stanisław Bronikowski, *Emancypacja i równouprawnienie kobiety* (Poznań, 1877).

24. Rudolf Jaworski, "Kilka refleksji nad dziejami wielkopolanek w 19. i na poczatku 20. wieku," in Anna Żarnowska, A. Szwarc, eds., *Kobieta i społeczenstwo na ziemiach polskich w 19. wieku* (Warsaw, 1990), p. 24; Bianka Pietrow-Ennker, "Tradycje szlachecki a dążenia emancypacyjne kobiet w społeczenstwie polskim w dobie rozbiorów," in Anna Żarnowska, A. Szwarc, *Kobieta i edukacja*, vol. 2, part 1 (Warsaw, 1992), pp. 23–4.

25. B. Czajecka, "Z domu w szeroki swiat . . . ," in *Droga kobiet do niezależnosci w zaborze austriackim w latach 1890–1914* (Cracow, 1990), pp. 13–14.

26. Z. Filar, Anna Tomaszewicz-Dobrska, *Karta z dziejów polskich lekarek* (Warsaw, 1959); C. Walewska, *Ruch kobiecy w Polsce*, cz. 1 (Warsaw, 1909), p. 33 and passim; R. Pachucka, *Pamiętniki 1886–1914* (Wroclaw, 1958), p. 18.

27. Dioniza Wawrzykowska-Wierciochowa, *Od prządki do astronautki: Z dziejów kobiety polskiej, jej pracy i osiagnięc* (Warsaw, 1963), pp. 243–44 and 248–49. Other radical women were Stefania Sempolowska, Iza Moszczeńska, Maria Turzyma, Kazimiera Bujwidowa, Maria Wysłuchowa, Waleria Gąsiorowska, Janina Jahołowska, Teodora Męczkowska, Zofia Golińska-Daszyńska, and Maria Paszkowska.

28. Wawrzykowska-Wierciochowa, *Od prządki do astronautki.*

29. Cecylja Walewska, "Ruch kobiecy w Polsce," *Bluszcz*, no. 13 (1924): 158 (this article is an expanded version of the previously cited *Ruch kobiecy w Polsce*, part 1 and 2, Warsaw, 1909).

30. Ibid.

31. M. Hulewiczowa, "Ilnicka Maria," in *Polski Slownik Biograficzny*, vol. 10 (1962–1964): 155–56.

32. Antoni Krzyżanowski, "Kobieta angielska, jej cele i dążenia," *Bluszcz*, no. 30, 1898.

33. Cecylja Walewska, *Ruch kobiecy w Polsce*, p. 158.

34. Iza Moszczeńska, "Męszczyzna i kobieta," in *Glos kobiet w kwestii kobiecej* (Cracow, 1903); Teodora Męczkowska, *Słuzace a prostytucja* (Warsaw, 1905).

35. Odo Bujwid, *Osamotnienie: Pamiętniki lat 1932–1942*, edited by Danuta

and Tadeusz Jaroskiński (Cracow, 1990), p. 8 and passim; B. Czajecka, *Z domu*, pp. 41–6.

36. K. Kapłanski, *Przeciw emancypacji kobiet czyli supremacji kobiet nad mężczyznami* (Lvov, 1898), p. 6.

37. Romana Pachucka, *Pamiętniki*, pp. 203–4.

38. Wawrzykowska-Wierciochowa, *Od prządki do astronautiki*, pp. 259–60.

39. Ibid., pp. 260–61.

40. Iza Moszczeńska, "Mężczyzna i kobieta," in *Glos kobiet w kwestii kobiecej* (Cracow, 1903), p. 140.

41. *Kobieta wpólczesna* (Warsaw, 1904).

42. Winnicka, "Plaskowicka Filipina," *Polski Słownik Biograficzny*, vol. 26 (1981): 765–66. Wawrzykowska-Wierciochowa, *Plaskowicka: Opowieść biograficzna* (Warsaw, 1979).

43. The most important members were Aleksandra Jentysówna, Witolda Krupowicz-Rechniewska, Zofia Onufrowicz-Płoska, and Zofia Płaskowicz-Dziewanowska.

44. In addition to Bohuszewiczówna, Ludwik Waryński, Stanisław Kunicki, and Maria Jankowska, there were: Cecylia Wojnarowska, Barbara Waligórska, and Stefania Motzówna.

45. A. Próchnik, *Kobieta w walce o niepodleglosc i socjalizm w Polsce* (Warsaw, 1938); see also his *Kobieta w ruchu socijalistycznym* (Warsaw, 1948); M. Bohuszewiczówna, *Pamiętnik*, edited by Wawrzykowska-Wierciochowa (Warsaw, 1954). More information on Bohuszewiczówna is contained in Wawrzykowska-Wierciochowa, "Maria Bohuszewiczówna ostatnia działaczka Proletariatu," *Wiedza i Zycie*, no. 1 (1954).

46. *Przedświt*, no. 9–12 (1886).

47. R. Pachucka, *Pamiętniki*, pp. 144–45.

48. *Gazeta Kaliska*, no. 218 (1909).

49. *Bluszcz*, no. 40 (1912).

50. Zenon Kmiecik, "Prasa Polska w Krolestwie Polskim I Imperium Rosyjskim w latach 1865–1904, in *Prasa Polska w latach 1864–1918* (Warsaw, 1976), p. 82.

51. Davies, *God's Playground*, p. 48.

Chapter 12

1. See, for example, Joan B. Landes, *Women and the Public Sphere in the Age of the French Revolution* (Ithaca, N.Y.: Cornell University Press, 1988). See also her edited anthology, *Feminism, the Public and the Private* (Oxford: Oxford University Press, 1998), for a wide range of essays on this theme.

2. Carole Pateman, *The Sexual Contract* (Stanford: Stanford University Press, 1988), p. 95.

3. I have examined this question in more detail in "Women's Rights, Gender and Citizenship in Tsarist Russia: the Question of Difference," in Patricia Grimshaw, Katie Holmes, and Marilyn Lake, eds., *Women's Rights and Human Rights: International Historical Perspectives* (Basingstoke, Hampshire and New York: Palgrave, 2001).

4. Karen Offen, "Defining Feminism: A Comparative Historical Approach," *Signs: Journal of Women in Culture and Society,* vol. 14, no. 1 (1988): 119–57.

5. This was the All-Russian Union of Equal Rights for Women (*Vserossiiskii soiuz ravnopravnosti zhenshchin*).

6. Barbara Caine has argued the case for "feminism" succinctly and persuasively in the introduction to her study, *Victorian Feminists* (Oxford: Oxford University Press, 1992), pp. 4–7.

7. The last years of czarism saw the beginnings of a feminist recovery of women's history. Most notable are a four-volume work on the history of female education, E. Likhacheva, *Materialy dlia istorii zhenskogo obrazovaniia v Rossii* (St. Petersburg: Tipografiia M. M. Stasiulevicha, 1890–1901), and E. N. Shchepkina's extended collection of essays and lectures on women in Russian history, *Iz istorii zhenskoi lichnosti v Rossii* (St. Petersburg: Tipografiia B. M. Vol'fa, 1914). The 1920s saw a proliferation of memoirs and documentation of the history of the prerevolutionary period, focused naturally on political radicals. Accounts of the nonrevolutionary women's movement were not favored: Shchepkina's own article on the Union of Equal Rights for Women in the 1905 Revolution (she had been a leading figure in the union) was advertised for publication in 1926 but never appeared. Over the following half-century, little historical research on women was published, and none that did not adhere to the Soviet line on women's emancipation.

8. For a vivid example of this work, the result of Russian-American collaboration, see Barbara Alpern Engel and Anastasia Posadskaya-Vanderbeck, *A Revolution of Their Own: Voices of Women in Soviet History* (Boulder, Colo.: Westview Press, 1998). For a sample of recent oral history on women and their families in Russia, see Marina Malysheva, "Migranty v krupnom gorode: istoriia sem'i Shinelevykh," in V. Semenova and E. Foteeva, *Sud'by liudei: Rossiia XX vek. Biografii semei kak ob'ekt sotsiologicheskogo issledovaniia,* Moscow, 1996, Institut sotsiologii RAN, pp. 70–98. During the 1990s, Svetlana Aivazova published a number of challenging articles on Soviet interpretations of the women's movement. One has been published in English as "Feminism in Russia: Debates from the Past," in Anastasia Posadskaya, ed., *Women in Russia. A New Era in Russian Feminism* (London, New York: Verso, 1994), pp. 154–63.

9. For notable exceptions, see G. A. Tishkin, who in addition to being the first

Soviet historian to publish a serious work on the woman question in nineteenth-century Russia, convened a series of conferences during the 1990s entitled "Russian Women and European Culture" in St. Petersburg. See G. A. Tishkin, *Zhenskii vopros v Rossii v 50–60 gody XIX veka* (Leningrad: Izdatel'stvo Leningradskogo universiteta, 1984); *Rossiiskie zhenshchiny i evropeiskaia kul'tura. Tezisy dokladov 13–15 dekabria 1993 g.* (St. Petersburg, 1993). Among the few studies of this period published before 1991 are E. A. Pavliuchenko, *Zhenshchiny v russkom osvoboditel'nom dvizhenii: ot Marii Volkonskoi do Very Figner* (Moscow: Mysl', 1988); and Svetlana Kaidash, *Sila slabykh: zhenshchiny v istorii Rossii (XI–XIX vv.)* (Moscow: Sovetskaia Rossiia, 1989). N. L. Pushkareva, an authority on women in medieval and early-modern Russia, is the first to have published a survey of women's history, spanning ten centuries: Natalia Pushkareva, *Women in Russian History. From the Tenth to the Twentieth Century*, translated and edited by Eve Levin (Armonk, N.Y.: M. E. Sharpe, 1997).

10. For some of the mid-1990s works in English, all invaluable, see Catriona Kelly, *A History of Russian Women's Writing 1820–1992* (Oxford: Oxford University Press, 1994), and its companion, edited by Kelly, *An Anthology of Russian Women's Writing 1777–1992* (Oxford: Oxford University Press, 1994); and Marina Ledkovsky, Charlotte Rosenthal, and Mary Zirin, eds., *A Dictionary of Russian Women Writers* (Westport, Conn.: Greenwood Press, 1994); Toby W. Clyman and Diana Greene, eds., *Women Writers in Russian Literature* (Westport, Conn.: Praeger, 1994).

11. See Stephanie Sandler, "The Canon and the Backward Glance. Akhmatova, Lisnianskaia, Petrovykh, Nikolaeva," and Nicholas Zekulin, "Soviet Russian Women's Literature in the Early 1980s," both in Helena Goscilo, ed., *Fruits of Her Plume. Essays on Contemporary Russian Women's Culture* (Armonk, N.Y.: M. E. Sharpe, 1993), pp. 113–33 and pp. 33–58 respectively.

12. This admittedly is an oversimplification of the claim, as historians have always recognized the movement's antecedents, including Catherine the Great's educational reforms, the inspirational example of the self-sacrificing wives of the Decembrists, the enthusiasm for George Sand among the "dissidents" of the 1840s, and other phenomena.

13. Catriona Kelly's history dates from the 1820s, though in her anthology she includes one work from the 1770s. See note 10.

14. The discovery of the writer Nadezhda Durova and her highly colored gender-bending "autobiography" has been almost as inspiring to modern Western feminist literary scholars as the equally romanticized legend of the Decembrist wives was to Russians in the nineteenth century. See Nadezhda Durova, *The Cavalry Maiden. Journals of a Russian Officer in the Napoleonic Wars*, translated, introduced and annotated by Mary Zirin (Bloomington, Ind.: Indiana University Press, 1988).

15. See Irina Paperno, *Chernyshevsky and the Age of Realism. A Study in the*

Semiotics of Behavior (Stanford: Stanford University Press, 1988). For further thoughts on these male radicals, see Linda Edmondson, "Women's Emancipation and Theories of Sexual Difference in Russia, 1850–1917," in Marianne Liljeström, Eila Mäntysaari, Arja Rosenholm, eds., *Gender Restructuring in Russian Studies, Slavica Tamperensia*, vol. 2 (University of Tampere, Finland, 1993), pp. 39–52.

16. This is the approach taken by Richard Stites, who deliberately bridges the chasm of 1917 in his pioneering book, *The Women's Liberation Movement in Russia. Feminism, Nihilism and Bolshevism, 1860–1930* (Princeton: Princeton University Press, 1978).

17. See an unpublished article by Rochelle Ruthchild, "Feminism Re-examined: Gender, Class and the Women's Equal Rights Union in 1905," and her current research. See also my unpublished paper, "The Women's Movement and the State in Russia before 1917," given at a conference entitled "Rethinking Women and Gender Relations in the Modern State," held at the University of Bielefeld on 2–6 April 1993.

18. See, for example, the three biographies of Kollontai: Barbara Clements, *Bolshevik Feminist: The Life of Alexandra Kollontai* (Bloomington, Ind.: Indiana University Press, 1979); Beatrice Farnsworth, *Aleksandra Kollontai: Socialism, Feminism, and the Bolshevik Revolution* (Stanford: Stanford University Press, 1980); Cathy Porter, *Alexandra Kollontai* (London: Virago, 1980); see also R. C. Elwood, *Inessa Armand. Revolutionary and Feminist* (Cambridge: Cambridge University Press, 1992).

19. At the time feminists in Russia were celebrating their first victory, obtaining access to public lectures for women. Mill's letter was reproduced (in Russian translation) in *Sankt-Peterburgskie vysshie zhenskie kursy za 25 let. Ocherki i materialy* (St. Petersburg, 1903), p. 34.

20. Indeed, the political climate of the 1880s closely resembled the reign of Alexander's predecessor, Nicholas I, who had created a virtual police state which drove much of the intelligentsia into voluntary or imposed exile.

21. As a point of comparison, it should be noted that women at Oxford, first admitted as students in the 1870s, could not graduate until the 1920s, and at Cambridge not until 1948. Bonnie S. Anderson and Judith P. Zinsser, *A History of Their Own. Women in Europe from Prehistory to the Present* (Harmondsworth, Middlesex: Penguin Books, 1988), vol. 2, p. 497.

22. Women also received training in pedagogical courses at the girls' gymnasia (themselves an innovation of the Great Reforms) and later in the century at newly established three-year pedagogical courses for women. Female teachers have long been neglected by historians. A 1994 study by Christine Ruane admirably fills the gap: *Gender, Class and the Professionalization of Russian City Teachers, 1860–1914* (Pittsburgh: Pittsburgh University Press, 1994).

23. See ibid., and Ruane's article, "The Vestal Virgins of St. Petersburg: School-teachers and the 1897 Marriage Ban," *Russian Review*, vol. 50, no. 2 (1991): 163–82.

24. For domestic servants in Russia, see Angela Rustemeyer, *Dienstboten in Petersburg und Moskau 1861–1917. Hintergrund, Alltag, soziale Rolle* (Stuttgart: Steiner, 1996). See also an unpublished article by Catriona Kelly, "On Occasion Glad to Serve: Representations of Servants and Domestic Service in Russia, 1890–1914."

25. For a history of women in philanthropy, see Adele Lindenmeyr, "Public Life, Private Virtues: Women in Russian Charity, 1762–1914," *Signs*, vol. 18, no. 3 (1993): 562–91.

26. See Bianka Pietrow-Ennker, *Rußlands "neue Menschen". Die Entwicklung der Frauenbewegung von den Anfängen bis zur Oktoberrevolution* (Frankfurt/Main: Campus, 1999).

27. The literature in this field is now growing rapidly. For a detailed and provocative study, with an acknowledged debt to Foucault, see Laura Engelstein, *The Keys to Happiness. Sex and the Search for Modernity in Fin-de-Siècle Russia* (Ithaca, N.Y.: Cornell University Press, 1992). For an excellent collection of essays, see Jane T. Costlow, Stephanie Sandler, Judith Vowles, eds., *Sexuality and the Body in Russian Culture* (Stanford: Stanford University Press, 1993). For "The Kreutzer Sonata" and contemporary debates about sexual morality, see Peter Ulf Møller, *Postlude to the Kreutzer Sonata. Tolstoj and the Debate on Sexual Morality in Russian Literature in the 1890s* (Leiden: E. J. Brill, 1988). On the same subject, see also Kelly, *History of Women's Writing*, pp. 127–29.

28. Laurie Manchester takes the remarkable number of priests' sons who became part of the radical intelligentsia of the 1860s as a starting point for a detailed investigation into the formation of an ascetic *mentalité* that distinguished these young men and that may have influenced the character of the Russian intelligentsia to a far greater degree than has been recognized. Laurie Manchester, "Secular Ascetics: The Mentality of Orthodox Clergymen's Sons in Late Imperial Russia" (Ph.D. diss., Columbia University, 1995).

29. For more detail, see Rochelle Lois Goldberg (now Ruthchild), "The Russian Women's Movement 1859–1917" (Ph.D. diss., University of Rochester, New York, 1976); Stites, *Women's Liberation Movement*; Linda Edmondson, *Feminism in Russia, 1900–1917* (London and Stanford: Heinemann Educational Books and Stanford University Press, 1984).

30. One, Anna Shabanova, maintained an intermittent correspondence with Lady Aberdeen and other members of the International Council of Women during the 1920s. These letters are in the Council archives held by the Public Archives of Canada in Ottawa. Personal contacts between Russian and western feminists have so far hardly been explored and should reveal much illuminating information.

31. For more detail on the Russian women's movements' relations with the outside world, see chapter five of Edmondson, *Feminism in Russia*, pp. 107–31. The prime mover in the scheme to create a national council was Anna Filosofova, one of the initiators of the women's movement in the late 1850s. Although she was made an honorary vice-president of the ICW, she died in 1912 without seeing her dream realized.

32. The exhibit was apparently devoted to the achievements of Russian women in higher education. It was never seen, as it disappeared in transit to America. Vladimir Stasov, *Nadezhda Vasil'evna Stasova* (St. Petersburg, 1899), pp. 411–12.

33. A home reading circle survived only four years and a seminar group disappeared two years later. See Edmondson, *Feminism in Russia*, pp. 20–21.

34. Mass communication in itself, of course, does not inevitably produce more open societies or easier international contact.

35. See Olga Crisp and Linda Edmondson, eds., *Civil Rights in Imperial Russia* (Oxford: Clarendon Press, 1989), especially the essays by S. A. Smith, "Workers and Civil Rights in Tsarist Russia, 1899–1917" (pp. 145–69), and Linda Edmondson, "Was There a Movement for Civil Rights in Russia in 1905?" (pp. 263–285).

36. The union was the Union of Equal Rights for Women (Soiuz ravnopravnosti zhenshchin), one of fourteen affiliates to the Union of Unions.

37. *Trudy pervogo vserossiiskogo zhenskogo s"ezda pri Russkom Zhenskom (Vzaimno-Blagotvoritel'nom) Obshchestve v S-Peterburge 10–16 dek. 1908 goda* (St. Petersburg, 1909). For the congress, see chapter four of Edmondson, *Feminism in Russia*, pp. 83–106.

38. Separatist criticism of the mainstream was formalized at the end of 1905. Mariia Pokrovskaia, a dedicated feminist who had anticipated the politicization of the women's movement by setting up a journal, the *Women's Messenger* (Zhenskii vestnik), in September 1904, announced that she was leaving the Mutual Philanthropic Society to form the Women's Progressive Party (Zhenskaia progressivnaia partiia). Pokrovskaia distanced herself from the male-led liberation movement and from liberal politics, but nonetheless envisaged working within the political system. The initiative was not a success, though she may have had many more sympathizers than were willing to join a party.

39. Many male liberals in 1905 argued the reverse, however. In opposing the inclusion of women's suffrage in the Constitutional-Democratic Party program, they claimed that a dogmatic insistence on sexual equality was endangering the liberals' appeal to sections of the population deeply opposed to women's emancipation. For a discussion of the relationship between liberals and feminists, see my article, "Women's Rights, Civil Rights and the Debate over Citizenship in the

1905 Revolution," in Linda Edmondson, ed., *Women and Society in Russia and the Soviet Union* (Cambridge: Cambridge University Press, 1992), pp. 77–100.

40. Outside Russia, a number of historians have been studying women in Ukraine and Poland. See Martha Bohachevsky-Chomiak, *Feminists Despite Themselves. Women in Ukrainian Community Life, 1884–1939* (Edmonton, Alberta, Canadian Institute of Ukrainian Studies, 1988); Rudolf Jaworski and Bianka Pietrow-Ennker, eds., *Women in Polish Society* (Boulder, Colo.: East European Monographs, 1992).

41. The search for a definition of the Russian woman and the nature of femininity has been a recurrent preoccupation of Russian philosophers, usually male. There has been a resurgence of interest in this topic since 1991, closely related to the issue of Russian national identity and anxiety about Russia's destiny. For a history of the philosophy of femininity in Russia, see O. V. Riabov, *Russkaia filosofiia zhenstvennosti (XI–XX veka)* (Ivanovo: Izdatel'skii tsentr "Iunona," 1999).

42. See, for example, Barbara Evans Clements, Barbara Alpern Engel, Christine D. Worobec, eds., *Russia's Women. Accommodation, Resistance, Transformation* (Berkeley: University of California Press, 1991).

Chapter 13

1. Carmen de Burgos, *La mujer moderna y sus derechos* (Valencia: Ed. Sempere, 1927); Carmen de Burgos, *Misión social de la mujer*, Conferencia pronunciada el día 18 de febrero de 1911 (Bilbao: Imp. José Rojas Núñez, 1911). Also Paloma Castañeda, *Carmen de Burgos "Colombine,"* (Madrid: Horas y Horas, 1994).

2. Gabriella Bonacchi, Angela Groppi, eds., *Il dilemma della cittadinanza* (Rome: Laterza, 1993); Mary Nash, "Experiencia y aprendizaje: la formación de los feminismos en España," *Historia Social*, no. 20 (Autumn 1994); Karen Offen, "Defining Feminism: a Comparative Historical Approach," *Signs. Journal of Women in Culture and Society*, vol. 14, no. 1 (1988): 119–57.

3. Mary Nash, "Political Culture, Catalan Nationalism and the Women's Movement in Early Twentieth Century Spain," *Women's Studies International Forum* (special issue: *Links across Differences: Gender, Ethnicity and Nationalism*), vol. 19, no. 1/2 (Apr. 1996): 45–54; Caroline Daley, Melanie Nolan, eds., *Suffrage and Beyond: International Feminist Perspectives* (New York: New York University Press, 1994).

4. Mary Nash, *Political Culture*.

5. Mary Nash, Susana Tavera, *Experiencias desiguales: Conflictos sociales y respuestas colectivas (siglo 19)* (Madrid: Síntesis, 1994).

6. Ana M. Aguado, Rosa M. Capel, Teresa Gónzalez Calbet, Cándida Mártinez López, Mary Nash, Gloria Nielfa, Margarita Ortega, Maria D. Ramos,

Maria X. Rodriquez Galdo, Susanna Tavera, Mercedes Ugalde, *Textos para la historia de las mujeres en España* (Madrid: Cátedra, 1994).

7. Benito Jerónimo Feijoo, *Teatro crítico universal* (Pamplona: Benito Cosculla, 1784). See Sally-Ann Kitts, "La prensa y la polémica feminista en la España del siglo 17," *Estudios de Historia Social,* no. 52–53 (June 1990): 265–73.

8. See Victora López Cordón's introduction to Josefa Amar y Borbón, *Discurso sobre la educación física y moral de las mujeres* (Madrid: Cátedra, 1994); also C. A. Sullivan, "Josefa Amar y Borbón (1749–1833)," in L. G. Levine, E. E. Marson, G. F. Waldman, eds., *Spanish Women Writers: A Bio-bibliographical Source Book* (Westport: Greenwood Press, 1993).

9. Bernardo Clavero, "Cara oculta de la Constitución: sexo y trabajo." *Revista de las Cortes Generales,* no. 10 (1987): 11–25.

10. Gloria Nielfa Cristóbal, "La revolución liberal desde la perspectiva de género," *Ayer,* no. 17 (1995): 103–20.

11. Susan Kirkpatrick, *Las románticas: Escritoras y subjetividad en España 1835–1850* (Madrid: Crítica, 1989), pp. 56–62.

12. "Freedom! Is it not a sarcasm / that makes us bleed / repeating this cry / in front of our irons?" Quoted in Kirkpatrick, *Las románticas,* p. 47.

13. Kirkpatrick, *Las románticas,* p. 264.

14. Antonio Elorza, "Feminismo y socialismo en España (1840–1868)," *Tiempos de Historia,* no. 1/3 (Feb. 1976); Antonio Elorza, *El Fourierismo en España* (Madrid: Ed. Revista del Trabajo, 1975).

15. Pere Sánchez i Ferré, "Els orígens del feminisme a Catalunya: 1870–1920," *Revista de Catalunya,* no. 45 (Oct. 1990): 33–49.

16. Paloma Villota, "Los motines de Castilla la Vieja de 1856 y la participación de la mujer: Aproximación a su estudio," *Nuevas perspectivas sobre la mujer,* Actas de las Primeras Jornadas de Investigación Interdisciplinaria (Madrid: Universidad Autónoma, 1982); Paloma Villota, "La mujer castellano-leonesa en los orígenes del movimiento obrero (1855)," *La mujer en la Historia de España (siglos (XVI–XX),* Actas de las Segundas Jornadas Investigación Interdisciplinaria (Madrid: Universidad Autónoma, 1984).

17. Josep Benet, Casimiro Martí, *Barcelona a mitjan segle 19: El moviment obrer durant el Bienni Progressista (1854–1856)* (Barcelona: Curial, 1976), pp. 356, 422, 669–70.

18. Concha Fagoaga, *La voz y el voto de las mujeres: 1877–1931* (Barcelona: Icaria, 1985), pp. 45–49.

19. Mary Nash, "Two Decades of Women's History in Spain: A Re-appraisal," in Karen Offen, Ruth Roach Pearson, Jane Rendall, *Writing Women's History: International Perspectives* (London: Macmillan, 1991), pp. 381–415.

20. Antón Costas Comesaña, "Apogeo del liberalismo," in *"La Gloriosa":*

La reforma económica en el Sexenio liberal (1868–1874) (Madrid: Siglo 19, 1988); José M. Jover Zamora, ed., *La Era Isabelina y el Sexenio Democrático. Historia de España de Menéndez Pidal. 34* (Madrid: Espasa-Calpé 1981); M. Victoria López Cordón, *La revolución de 1868 y la 1. República* (Madrid: Siglo 19, 1976); Concepción Saiz, *La Revolución del 68 y la cultura femenina: Apuntes al natural, Un episodio nacional que no escribió Pérez Galdós* (Madrid: Librería General de Victoriano Pérez, 1929).

21. José Francos Rodríguez, *La mujer y la política españolas* (Madrid: Pueyo, 1920), p. 146.

22. Francisco Pi y Margall, *La misión de la mujer en la sociedad* (Madrid: Rivadeneyra, 1869).

23. Giuliana di Febo, "Orígenes del debate feminista en España: La escuela Krausista y la Institución Libre de Enseñanza (1870–1890)," *Sistema: Revista de Ciencias Sociales*, no. 12 (Jan. 1976), p. 61.

24. Francisco Pi y Margall, *La República de 1873: Apuntes para escribir su historia* (Madrid, 1980), cited in Agustí Colomines i Companys, "Amunt! Amunt! Vida i benestar social a la Barcelona de la segona meitat del segle 19," *Afers*, no. 8, 1988–1989, p. 511.

25. Francisco Pi y Margall, "Discurso leído en el Centro Federal de Madrid. 4-11-1899," reproduced in Ana. M. Aguado et al., *Textos para la historia de las mujeres en España*, pp. 363–64.

26. di Febo, "Orígenes del debate feminista," p. 61.

27. Mary Nash, "Experiencia y aprendizaje: la formación histórica de los feminismos en España," *Historia Social* (Oct. 1994): 151–72.

28. Javier Tusell, "El sufragio universal en España (1891–1936)," *Ayer*, no. 3, 1991.

29. José M. Jover Zamora, "La época de la Restauración: Panorama político-social, 1875–1902," in Manuel Tuñón de Lara, ed., *Historia de España: Revolución burguesa, oligarquía y constitucionalismo* (Barcelona: Labor, 1981); José Luis García Delgado, ed., *La España de la Restauración: Política, economía, legislación y cultura* (Madrid: Siglo 19, 1985).

30. For a detailed analysis see Mary Nash, "Political Culture" and Mary Nash, "Experiencia y aprendizaje."

31. Mary Nash, "Experiencia y aprendizaje."

32. María Glória Núñez Pérez, *Trabajadoras en la Segunda República: Un estudio sobre la actividad económica extradoméstica (1931–1936)* (Madrid: Ministerio de Trabajo, 1989).

33. Mary Nash, "Experiencia y aprendizaje."

34. Guadalupe Gómez-Ferrer Morant, "La imagen de la mujer en la novela de la Restauración: ocio social y trabajo doméstico," in Rosa M. Capel Martínez, ed., *Mujer y sociedad en España 1700–1975* (Madrid: Ministerio de Cultura, 1982),

pp. 179–206; Mary Nash, "Identidades, representación cultural y discurso de género en la España Contemporánea," in Julio Aróstegui Sánchez, Pedro Chalmeta, Fernando Checa Cremades, Ferran García-Oliver, Manuel González Portilla, Alfredo Jiménez, Anthony McFarlane, Francisco de Luis Martin, Emilio Mitre Fernández, Mary Nash, Adriano Prosperi, Manuel Reder San Román, Jose Luis Sánchez Lora, eds., *Cultura y culturas en la Historia* (Salamanca: Universidad de Salamanca, 1995).

35. Mª. José Lacalzada de Mateo, *Mentalidad y proyección social de Concepción Arenal* (Ferrol: Cámera Oficial de Comercio, Industria y Navegación, 1994).

36. Concepción Arenal, "La mujer del porvenir," cited in Concepción Arenal, *La emancipación de la mujer en España*, ed. by Mauro Armiño (Madrid: Jucar, 1974), pp. 106–17.

37. Therese de Coudray, "Defensa del Bello Sexo," *La Muger*, 30 March 1882.

38. François Furet, Jacques Ozouf, *Reading and Writing: Literacy in France from Calvin to Jules Ferry* (Cambridge, Eng.: Cambridge University Press, 1982); Carmela Covato, *Sapere e pregiudizio: L'Educazione delle donne fra '700 e '800* (Rome: Archivio Guido Izzi, 1991).

39. Rosa M. Capel, *El trabajo y la educación de la mujer en España 1900–1936* (Madrid: Dirección General de la Juventud y Promoción Socio-cultural, 1982).

40. Concepción Arenal, "Estado actual de la mujer en España," *Boletín de la Institución Libre de Enseñanza* (31 Aug. 1895).

41. Mary Nash, *Defying Male Civilization: Women in the Spanish Civil War* (Denver: Arden Press, 1995).

42. José Lacalzada de Mateo, *Mentalidad y proyección social de Concepción Arenal*, p. 199.

43. José L. Abellán, *La cultura española* (Madrid: Edicusa, 1971).

44. Pilar Ballarín, "La construcción de un modelo educativo de 'utilidad doméstica,'" in Georges Duby and Michelle Perrot, *Historia de las mujeres en Occidente* (Madrid: Taurus, 1993), vol. 4; Geraldine Scanlon, *La polémica feminista en la España contemporánea* (Madrid: Akal, 1986).

45. di Febo, "Orígenes del debate feminista."

46. Fernando de Castro, *Discurso Inaugural de las Conferencias Dominicales sobre la educación de la mujer* (Madrid: Imprenta de Rivadeneyra, 1869), p. 8. Cited in di Febo, "Orígines del debate feminista."

47. Tomas Tapia, *La religión en la conciencia y en la vida*, Universidad de Madrid: Conferencias Dominicales sobre la educación de la mujer (Madrid: Imprenta de M. Rivadeneyra, 1869), p. 4.

48. Ballarín, "La construcción de un modelo educativo."

49. Emilia Pardo Bazán, "La educación del hombre y la de la mujer: Sus relaciones y diferencias (Memoria leída en el congreso pedagógico el día 16 de octubre

de 1892)," *Nuevo Teatro Crítico*, no. 22 (Oct. 1892): 14–82, reproduced in Leda Schiavo, ed., *Emilia Pardo Bazán: La mujer española y otros artículos feministas* (Madrid: Ed. Nacional, 1976), pp. 71–97.

50. Pardo Bazán, "La mujer española," *La España Moderna*, no. 17 (May 1890): 101–13, reproduced in *La mujer española y otros artículos feministas*, pp. 26–70.

51. Rosa M. Badillo Baena, *Feminismo y educación en Malaga: El pensamiento de Suceso Luengo de la Figuera 1898–1920* (Malaga: Universidad de Malaga, 1992).

52. Suceso Luengo de la Figuera, *Pedagogía Social: Conferencia dada en la Sociedad de Ciencias de Malaga* (Malaga: Tipografía el Cronista, 1902). Cited in Badillo Baena, *Feminismo y educación*, pp. 121–22.

53. Berta Wilhelmi, "La aptitud de la mujer para todas las profesiones," *Boletín de la Institución Libre de Enseñanza*, no. 388 (1893), p. 101. Cited in Ballarín, "La construcción de un modelo educativo," p. 611.

54. On the development of gender discourse in Spain, see Mary Nash, "Un/contested Identities: Motherhood, Sex Reform and the Modernization of Gender Identity in Early Twentieth Century Spain," in Victoria Lorée Enders and Pamela Beth Radcliff, eds., *Constructing Spanish Womanhood: Female Identity in Modern Spain* (New York: SUNY Press, 1999).

55. Arenal, "La educación de la mujer," in Arenal, *La emancipación*, p. 67.

56. Arenal, "La mujer de su casa," in Arenal, *La emancipación*, pp. 248–49.

57. Arenal, "La mujer de su casa," in Arenal, *La emancipación*, p. 249.

58. Arenal "La mujer del porvenir," in Arenal, *La emancipación*, p. 185.

59. Arenal, "La mujer del porvenir," in Arenal, *La emancipación*, p. 185.

60. Arenal, "La mujer del porvenir," in Arenal, *La emancipación*, p. 104.

61. John Stuart Mill, *La esclavitud femenina* (Madrid: Biblioteca de la Mujer, 1891).

62. Emilia Pardo Bazán, "La mujer española," *La España Moderna*, no. 17 (May 1890).

63. Mary Nash, "Experiencia y aprendizaje."

64. Therese de Coudray de Arámburu, "La mujer proletaria," *La Muger* (10 Apr. 1882).

65. Adolfo Posada, *Feminismo* (Madrid: Librería de Fernando Fé, 1899), p. 221.

66. Rosalía de Castro, *Follas Novas*, 1880, reproduced in Ana M. Aguado et al., *Textos de Historia de las mujeres*, p. 331.

67. Therese de Coudray de Arámburu, "La mujer proletaria," *La Muger*, 10 Apr. 1882.

68. Fagoaga, *La voz y el voto*, pp. 72–76.

69. Guillermo A. Tell y Lafont, *Comentarios al movimiento feminista* (Barcelona: Imprenta Elziviriana de Borrás, 1915).

70. Mary Nash, "Political culture."

71. Mary Nash, ed., *Més enllà del silenci: Les dones a la història de Catalunya* (Barcelona: Generalitat de Catalunya, 1988); Mercedes Ugalde Solano, *Mujeres y nacionalismo vasco: Génesis y desarrollo de Emakume Abertzale Batza 1906–1936* (Bilbao: Universidad del País Vasco, 1993).

Chapter 14

1. See S. Ziogou-Karasteryiou, *Secondary Education in Greece 1830–1893* (Athens, 1986), p. 32.

2. See A. Dimaras, *The Unaccomplished Reform* (Athens, 1973, 1974), vol. 1, p. 7.

3. Quoted by Sotiria Aliberti, *The Heroines of Greek Revolution* (Athens, 1933), p. 304 (in Greek).

4. Quoted by G. Veloudis, *Jacob Philipp Falmerayer and the Genesis of Greek Historicism* (Athens, 1982), p. 29 (in Greek).

5. See J. P. Falmerayer, *Geschichte der Halbinsel Morea während des Mittelalters* (Stuttgart, 1830), and *Fragmente aus dem Orient* (Stuttgart and Tübingen, 1845).

6. Ibid.

7. In less than four decades, traditional culture and institutions totally disappeared from Athens and the few big urban centers: traditional architecture gave way to German neoclassic style, monophonic music to military bands, the shadow theater to Italian operettas, vestmentary habits to European dress. See Eleni Varikas, *The Revolt of the Ladies: Formation of a Feminist Consciousness in 19th-Century Greece* (Athens, 1987) (in Greek).

8. Quoted by G. Kerofyllas, *Athens and Athenian Women* (Athens, 1982), p. 10.

9. Concerning the impact of westernization on Greek women's social position, see my article "Trop archaïques ou trop modernes? Les citadines grecques face à l'occidentalisation (1833–1875)," *Peuples Méditerranéens*, no. 44–45 (1988): 269–92.

10. On the contradictory dynamics of such oppositions see Varikas, *The Revolt of the Ladies*.

11. Jean Psychari, *My Voyage* (Athens, 1971), p. 39 (in Greek).

12. See Eleni Varikas, "Vertus privées dans l'espace public: Le cas des institutrices grecques au XIX siècle," in M. Pavillon, F. Vallotton, eds., *Lieux des femmes dans l'espace public: 1800–1930* (Lausanne: Univ. de Lausanne, 1992), pp. 123–42.

13. *Ladies' Newspaper*, March 8, 1892.

14. *Ladies' Newspaper*, January 1, 1893.

15. Sapho Leondias, "Woman in the Greek Tragedy," *Ladies' Newspaper*, August 21, 1888.

16. Callirhoi Parren, "Women and Municipal Elections," *Ladies' Newspaper*, November 15, 1887.

17. Parren, "Lascarina Bouboulina," *Ladies' Newspaper*, March 29, 1887.

18. Parren, "The Woman Question," *Ladies' Newspaper*, October 11, 1901.

19. See Raoul Girardet, *Mythes et mythologies politiques* (Paris: Seuil, 1990), p. 104. Girardet emphasizes the importance of what he calls "the affirmation of a renaissance" in the development of national movements. "It is in relation to the ideologically reconstructed image, of a nation lost in history, whose memory is reactivated and glory celebrated, that the struggle for its resurrection is legitimated." See also Eric Hobsbawm, *Nations et nationalisme depuis 1780* (Paris: Gallimard, 1992), pp. 99–101.

20. Parren, "The Woman Question," *Ladies' Newspaper*, December 19, 1900.

21. *Ladies' Newspaper*, December 3, 1900.

22. Ibid.

23. Ibid.

24. See Eleni Varikas, "Droit naturel, nature féminine et égalité des sexes," in *L'homme et la Société* (1987), 3/4, pp. 107–108.

25. Ernst Bloch, *Droit naturel et dignité humaine* (Paris: Payot, 1976), p. 199.

26. Ibid., p. 198.   27. *Ladies' Newspaper*, May 25, 1899.

28. Ibid., May 23, 1888.   29. Ibid.

30. Ibid.

31. Costis Palamas, "War dances," in Palamas, *Works*, vol. 1, p. 158–9.

32. Quoted in *Ladies' Newspaper*, December 24, 1900; see also the newspaper *Estia*, December 15, 1900. My emphasis.

33. *Estia*, December 15, 1900.

34. Parren, "The Woman Question," in *Ladies' Newspaper*, February 17, 1901.

35. "Women's Emancipation and Criminality," in *Ladies' Newspaper*, February 11, 1896. My emphasis.

36. "Women and Marriage," in *Ladies' Newspaper*, October 11, 1897.

37. "The International Conference of Women," in *Ladies' Newspaper*, May 14, 1900. My emphasis.

38. Walter Benjamin, "Sur le concept d'histoire," in: *Ecrits Français* (Paris: Gallimard, 1991), pp. 338–56.

39. "Woman in the Future," in *Ladies' Newspaper*, February 21, 1887. My emphasis.

40. Max Weber, *Economy and Society* (Berkeley: University of California Press, 1978), p. 491.

41. See ibid., pp. 491–99, and the famous essay by Friedrich Nietzsche, *La généalogie de la morale* (Paris: Gallimard, 1972).

42. See, for instance, the article "Old Ideas," in *Ladies' Newspaper*, October 14, 1901.

43. See Max Weber's example of the proletarian movement, *Economy and Soci-*

ety, p. 492. See also the example of Periclis Yannopoulos, the famous bard of the Great Idea, who appealed to the Greeks to follow the example of Alexander the Great: "Now that the decadence of Western civilization is becoming visible, there is only one race [*sic*] who can attain the summit of universal good: *our race*, sleeping and besotted; on the condition that it wakes up to fulfill its destiny." Periclis Yannopoulos, *Appeal to the Panhellenic Community* (Athens, 1907).

44. "The New Contract," *Ladies' Newspaper*, December 16, 1901.

45. See Eleni Varikas, "Les dernières seront les premières: potentiel utopique et apories d'une révolte paria dans la morale," in: Fabienne Gambelle, Michel Trebitch, eds., *Révolte et Société* (Paris: Publications de la Sorbonne, 1988), p. III.

46. Weber, *Economy*, p. 491. Author's emphasis.

47. "Subjects and Objects of Injustice," *Ladies' Newspaper*, October 10, 1898.

48. "Women and Politics," *Ladies' Newspaper*, February 28, 1899.

49. Ibid.

50. See "Women against the Decline of Humanity," *Ladies' Newspaper*, May 7, 1895.

51. Weber relates this claim to what he calls "proletarian, petty-bourgeois and pariah intellectualism," which includes people with inferior education, elementary-school teachers of all sorts, and the self-taught intelligentsia of the disprivileged strata. See Weber, *Economy and Society*, p. 507. A similar analysis is made by Hannah Arendt, who speaks about the "telescopic gaze" of the "pariah rebel." See *The Jew as a Pariah: A Hidden Tradition* (New York, 1978).

52. "An Answer to the 'Friend of Women' of the Newspaper *Estia*," in *Ladies' Newspaper*, April 4, 1900.

53. Nietzsche, *La généalogie*, p. 45.

Chapter 15

1. See, for instance, Gisela Bock and Pat Thane, eds., *Maternity and Gender Policies: Women and the Rise of the European Welfare States, 1880s–1950s* (London: Routledge, 1994); Seth Koven and Sonya Michel, eds., *Mothers of a New World: Maternalist Politics and the Origins of Welfare States* (New York: Routledge, 1993); Karen Offen, Ruth Roach Pierson, and Jane Rendall, eds., *Writing Women's History: International Perspectives* (London: Macmillan, 1991).

2. Gisela Bock and Susan James, eds., *Beyond Equality and Difference: Citizenship, Feminist Politics and Female Subjectivity* (London: Routledge, 1992), p. 2. I do not accept this European/Anglo-American divide but it has no doubt come about because of the early emergence of American and British women's movements; their close links and common heritage; and the early influence of liberal ideas on both movements.

3. Christine Bolt, *The Women's Movements in the United States and Britain from the 1790s to the 1920s* (Hemel Hempstead: University of Massachusetts Press, 1993); and Christine Bolt, *Feminist Ferment: "The Woman Question" in the USA and England, 1870–1940* (London: UCL Press, 1995).

4. See, for instance, Mary Fainsod Katzenstein and Carol McClurg Mueller, eds., *The Women's Movements of the United States and Western Europe: Consciousness, Political Opportunity, and Public Policy* (Philadelphia: Temple University Press, 1987), especially the article by Joyce Gelb, pp. 267–89.

5. Blanche Glassman Hersh, *The Slavery of Sex: Feminist Abolitionists in America* (Urbana, University of Illinois Press, 1978), pp. 166–7; Clare Midgley, *Women Against Slavery: The British Campaigns, 1780–1870* (London: Routledge, 1992), chap. 6; Frank Thistlethwaite, *America and the Atlantic Community* (New York: Harper and Row, 1959).

6. Arthur Mann, "British Social Thought and American Reformers of the Progressive Era," *Mississippi Valley Historical Review*, vol. 42, no. 4 (1955–56): 672–92.

7. Barbara Leigh Smith Bodichon, *An American Diary* (London: Routledge, 1972), edited from the manuscript by Joseph W. Reed, Jr.; Sheila R. Herstein, *A Mid-Victorian Feminist: Barbara Leigh Smith Bodichon* (New Haven, Conn.: Yale University Press, 1985).

8. Elizabeth Cady Stanton, *Eighty Years and More: Reminiscences, 1815–1897* (New York: Oxford University Press, 1984).

9. Harold Goldman, *Emma Paterson: She Led Women Into a Man's World* (London: Lawrence and Wishart, 1974).

10. Hilda Martindale, *From One Generation to Another, 1839–1944* (London: George Allen and Unwin, 1944); Mary Drake McFeely, *Lady Inspectors: The Campaign for a Better Workplace, 1893–1921* (Oxford: Basil Blackwell, 1988).

11. Nancy Cott, ed., *A Woman Making History: Mary Ritter Beard Through Her Letters* (New Haven, Conn: Yale University Press, 1991), p. 7.

12. Anna A. Gordon, *The Beautiful Life of Frances E. Willard* (London: Samson Low, 1898), p. 210 (source of quotation); Kathleen Fitzpatrick, *Lady Henry Somerset* (London: Jonathan Cape, 1923).

13. See Dorothy Clarke Wilson, *Lone Woman: The Story of Elizabeth Blackwell, the First Woman Doctor* (Boston, Mass.: Little and Brown, 1970); Ida Husted Harper, *The Life and Work of Susan B. Anthony*, 3 vols. (Salem, N.H.: Ayer Company, 1983 [1898]), vol. 2; "Sarah Parker Remond," in Matthew Davenport Hill, ed., *Our Exemplars, Poor and Rich* (London: Cassell, Petter and Galpin, 1861), pp. 276–86; Alreda M. Duster, ed., *Crusade for Justice: The Autobiography of Ida B. Wells* (Chicago: University of Chicago Press, 1970); Vida D. Scudder, *On Journey* (J. M. Dent, 1937); Jane Addams, *Twenty Years at Hull House* (New York: Signet Classics, New American Library, 1981 [1910]); Mary Ray Peck, *Carrie Chapman*

Catt (New York: Octagon, 1975 [1944]); Angela John, *Elizabeth Robins: Staging a Life, 1862–1952* (London: Routledge, 1995); Charlotte Perkins Gilman, *The Living of Charlotte Perkins Gilman* (New York: Appleton-Century, 1935); Margaret Sanger, *My Fight for Birth Control* (London: Faber, 1932).

14. Sandra Stanley Holton, "'To Educate Women into Rebellion': Elizabeth Cady Stanton and the Creation of a Transatlantic Network of Radical Suffragists," *American Historical Review*, vol. 99, no. 4 (Oct. 1994): 1112–36.

15. Harriot Stanton Blatch and Alma Lutz, *Challenging Years: The Memoirs of Harriot Stanton Blatch* (New York: G. W. Putnam's Sons, 1940).

16. David Rubinstein, *A Different World for Women: The Life of Millicent Garrett Fawcett* (Hemel Hempstead: Harvester Wheatsheaf, 1991), pp. 75–6.

17. Gerda Lerner, *The Creation of Feminist Consciousness: From the Middle Ages to Eighteen-seventy* (New York: Oxford University Press, 1993), pp. 231–2; Kate Flint, *The Woman Reader, 1837–1914* (Oxford: Clarendon Press, 1993), p. 249.

18. See, for instance, Shirley Foster, *American Women Travellers to Europe in the Nineteenth and Early Twentieth Centuries* (Keele: Keele University Press, 1994, for British Association for American Studies: BAAS Pamphlet 27); Leila J. Rupp, "Constructing Internationalism: The Case of Transnational Women's Organizations, 1888–1945," *American Historical Review*, vol. 99, no. 5 (Dec. 1994): 1571–1600.

19. Theodore Stanton, ed., *The Woman Question in Europe: A Series of Original Essays With an Introduction by Frances Power Cobbe* (New York: G. P. Putnam's Sons, 1884), pp. 6, 18.

20. Midgley, *Women Against Slavery*, p. 161.

21. Theodore Stanton, "Eighty Years and More," in Elizabeth Cady Stanton, Susan B. Anthony, Matilda Joslyn Gage, eds., *History of Woman Suffrage*, 6 vols. (New York: Fowler and Wells, 1886), vol. 3, pp. 943–4.

22. Mary Erhart, *Frances Willard: From Prayers to Politics* (Chicago: University of Chicago Press, 1944), p. 335; Fitzpatrick, *Lady Henry Somerset*, p. 163.

23. Bolt, *The Women's Movements*, p. 203.

24. Peck, *Carrie Chapman Catt*, p. 298; *English Suffrage Journal*, vol. 15, no. 169 (1 Jan. 1884): 5.

25. Quoted in Marcus Cunliffe, *The Literature of the United States* (Harmondsworth: Pelican Books, 1980), p. 230.

26. Frances Power Cobbe, *The Duties of Women: A Course of Lectures* (London: Williams and Norgate, 1888), pp. 10, 16.

27. Harriet Beecher Stowe, *Uncle Tom's Cabin or, Life Among the Lowly* (New York: Penguin Books, 1986 [1852]), pp. 11–12.

28. *Englishwoman's Review*, no. 14 (Apr. 1873): 126.

29. Midgley, *Women Against Slavery*, chap. 7.

30. Seymour Drescher, "Whose Abolition? Popular Pressure and the Ending of the British Slave Trade," *Past and Present*, no. 143 (May 1994): pp. 136–66, esp. pp. 165–6.

31. Midgley, *Women Against Slavery*, pp. 167–8.

32. See Ellen Carol DuBois, *Feminism and Suffrage: The Emergence of an Independent Women's Movement in America, 1848–1869* (Ithaca, N.Y.: Cornell University Press, 1985).

33. Kathryn Kish Sklar, "The Historical Foundations of Women's Power in the Creation of the American Welfare State, 1830–1930," in Koven and Michel, eds., *Mothers of a New World*, especially pp. 51–63; Bolt, *The Women's Movements*, p. 43.

34. Frances Willard, *Glimpses of Fifty Years: The Autobiography of an American Woman* (Chicago: WCTU Publications, 1889), p. 433; see also Ian Tyrrell, *Woman's World, Woman's Empire: The Women's Christian Temperance Union in Woman's International Perspective, 1880–1930* (Chapel Hill, N.C.: University of North Carolina Press, 1991).

35. Elizabeth Cady Stanton et al., *History of Woman Suffrage*, vol. 4, p. 124; Harper, *The Life and Work of Susan B. Anthony*, vol. 2, pp. 627–45; Edith F. Hurwitz, *Women in a Changing World: The Dynamic Story of the International Council of Women since 1888* (London: Routledge, 1966).

36. Regine Deutsch, *The International Woman Suffrage Alliance: Its History from 1904 to 1929* (London: International Alliance for Suffrage and Equal Citizenship, 1929).

37. See letter of Mrs. Catt to Mrs. Alice Park, 13 April 1916, and a general, money-raising letter of 11 May 1916, in *Autograph Letter Collection*, Fawcett Library, London; and in ibid., letter of Miss Mary Sheepshanks to Miss Alice Park, n.d., on suffragist progress in New York, and of 16 October 1916 and 12 July 1917 asking for details of American suffrage activities.

38. Pat Thane, "Women in the British Labour Party and the Construction of State Welfare, 1906–1939," in Koven and Michel, eds., *Mothers of a New World*, pp. 343–77.

39. Lori D. Ginzberg, "Moral Suasion is Moral Balderdash: Women, Politics and Social Activism in the 1850s," *Journal of American History*, vol. 73, no. 3 (Dec. 1986): 601–22; also Ginzberg, *Women and the Work of Benevolence: Morality, Politics and Class in the Nineteenth-Century United States* (New Haven, Conn.: Yale University Press, 1990).

40. David Morgan, *Suffragists and Democrats: The Politics of Woman Suffrage in America* (East Lansing, Mich.: Michigan State University Press, 1972).

41. Archibald Prentice, *History of the Anti-Corn-Law League* (London: Frank Cass, 1968 [1853]), vol. 1, pp. 170–3.

42. George M. Frederickson, *The Inner Civil War: Northern Intellectuals and*

the Crisis of the Union (New York: Harper and Row, 1965); see also John Higham, *From Boundlessness to Consolidation: The Transformation of American Culture* (Ann Arbor, Mich.: University of Michigan Press, 1969); Carroll Smith-Rosenberg, *Disorderly Conduct: Visions of Gender in Victorian America* (New York: Oxford University Press, 1985), pp. 170–6.

43. Brian Harrison, "A Genealogy of Reform in Modern Britain," in Christine Bolt and Seymour Drescher, eds., *Anti-Slavery, Religion and Reform: Essays in Memory of Roger Anstey* (Folkestone: Dawson, 1980), pp. 138–45.

44. Lilian Lewis Shiman, *Women and Leadership in Nineteenth-Century England* (London: Macmillan, 1992), pp. 171–205; Leslie Walker, "Party Political Women: A Comparative Survey of the Liberal Women and the Primrose League, 1890–1914," in Jane Rendall, ed., *Equal or Different: Women's Politics, 1800–1914* (Oxford: Blackwell, 1987), pp. 165–91; Martin Pugh, *Women and the Women's Movement in Britain, 1914–1959* (London: Macmillan, 1992), p. 124.

45. Pamela M. Graves, *Labour Women: Women in British Working-Class Politics, 1918–1939* (Cambridge, Eng.: Cambridge University Press, 1994).

46. See report of Alice Scatcherd, "A British Suffragist of Liberal-Radical Persuasion," in Stanton, ed., *History of Woman Suffrage*, vol. 4, p. 140.

47. Patricia Hollis, *Ladies Elect: Women in English Local Government, 1865–1914* (Oxford: Clarendon Press, 1987).

48. See, for instance, Paula Baker, "The Domestication of Politics: Women and American Political Society, 1780–1920," *American Historical Review*, vol. 89, no. 3 (June 1984): 620–47; Mary P. Ryan, *Women in Public: Between Banners and Ballots, 1825–1880* (Baltimore: Johns Hopkins University Press, 1990); Glenna Matthews, *The Rise of the Public Woman: Woman's Power and Woman's Place in the United States, 1630–1970* (New York: Oxford University Press, 1992), chaps. 7–9.

49. Harper, *Life and Work*, vol. 2, p. 641.

50. Jo Freeman, "Whom You Know versus Whom You Represent: Feminist Influence in the Democratic and Republican Parties," in Katzenstein and Mueller, *The Women's Movements*, pp. 215–19.

51. Stanton, ed., *The Woman Question*, p. 6.

52. Sklar, *To Educate Women*, pp. 1118, 1126.

53. Catharine Waugh McCulloch to the editor of the *Record Herald*, 25 March 1902, in *McCulloch Papers*, Schlesinger Library, Radcliffe College, Massachusetts.

54. This collective emphasis is highlighted by Philippa Levine. See her *Feminist Lives in Victorian England: Private Roles and Public Commitment* (Oxford: Blackwell, 1990).

55. Bolt, *Women's Movements*, pp. 201–4.

56. Mari Jo Buhle, *Women and American Socialism 1870–1920* (Urbana: University of Illinois Press, 1981).

57. Ellen Carol DuBois, "Working Women, Class Relations, and Suffrage

Militance: Harriot Stanton Blatch and the New York Woman Suffrage Movement, 1894–1909," in Vicki L. Ruiz and Ellen Carol DuBois, *Unequal Sisters: A Multi-Cultural Reader in U.S. Women's History* (London: Routledge, 1994), pp. 228–46.

58. Peck, *Carrie Chapman Catt*, p. 434.

59. Catt quoted in *Jus Suffragii*, vol. 2, no. 3 (15 Nov. 1907).

60. See, for instance, Levine, *Feminist Lives*, pp. 177–9; Carol Dyhouse, *Feminism and the Family in England, 1880–1939* (Oxford: Basil Blackwell, 1989); Susan Kingsley Kent, *Sex and Suffrage in Britain, 1860–1914* (London: Routledge, 1990); Nancy Cott, *The Grounding of Modern Feminism* (New Haven, Conn.: Yale University Press, 1987); William Leach, *True Love and Perfect Union: The Feminist Reform of Sex and Society* (Middletown, Conn.: Wesleyan University Press, 1989).

61. Rosalind Rosenberg, *Beyond Separate Spheres: Intellectual Roots of Modern Feminism* (New Haven, Conn.: Yale University Press, 1982), chap. 8 and epilogue.

62. For example Rene Denfeld's *The New Victorians: A Young Woman's Challenge to the Old Feminist Order* (Allen and Unwin, 1995).

63. Katzenstein and Mueller, eds., *The Women's Movements*, chap. 1.

64. Bock and James, eds., *Beyond Equality and Difference*, especially p. 11; Karen Offen, "Defining Feminism: A Comparative Historical Approach," *Signs*, vol. 14, no. 1 (1988): 119–57; and June Purvis, "Women's History in Britain: An Overview," *The European Journal of Women's Studies*, vol. 2, no. 1 (Feb. 1995): 7–19, especially pp. 14–16.

65. Both the British and American women's movements did, of course, change over time: see Jane Rendall's article in this collection; Bolt, *The Women's Movements*; and Cott, *The Grounding of Modern Feminism*.

66. Description of the ICW's purpose by Fannie Fern Andrews, 1925, in *Fannie Fern Andrews Papers*, Schlesinger Library.

67. Rebecca L. Sherrick, "Toward Universal Sisterhood," *Women's Studies International Forum*, vol. 5, no. 6, p. 657.

68. Graves, *Labour Women*, pp. 138–51.

69. See Cott, *Grounding*, on the debate, especially chap. 4; and Susan D. Becker, *The Origins of the Equal Rights Amendment: American Feminism Between the Wars* (Westport, Conn.: Greenwood Press, 1981).

70. Rupp, *Constructing Internationalism*, pp. 1574–5, 1587–9.

71. Stanlie M. James and Abena P. A. Busia, eds., *Theorizing Black Feminists: The Visionary Pragmatism of Black Feminisms* (London: Routledge, 1993), p. 2.

72. Eileen Boris, "The Power of Motherhood: Black and White Activist Women Redefine the 'Political,'" in Koven and Michel, eds., *Mothers of a New World*, pp. 213–45.

73. Katzenstein and Mueller, eds., *Women's Movements*, p. 27.

74. James and Busia, *Theorizing Black Feminists*; Boris, *The Power of Motherhood.*

75. Ray Strachey, *The Cause: A Short History of the Women's Movement in Great Britain* (London: Virago, 1989 [1928]), p. 245.

76. Margaret Strobel, *Gender, Sex and Empire* (Washington, D.C.: American Historical Association, 1993), pp. 6–7.

77. See Christine Bolt, *Feminist Ferment*, chap. 2.

78. Catherine Hall, *White, Male and Middle-Class: Explorations in Feminism and History* (Cambridge: Polity Press, 1992), pp. 18–19.

Chapter 16

1. Ray Strachey, *The Cause: A Short History of the Women's Movement in Great Britain* (1928; reprinted London: Virago, 1978); Helene Lange, Gertrud Bäumer, *Handbuch der Frauenbewegung*, Vol. 1, Berlin: Moeser, 1901; Johanna Naber, *Na tien jaren* (Ten Years After), 1908; idem, *Na XXV Jaren* (Twenty-Five Years After), 1923; *Jaarboek Internationaal Archief voor de Vrouwenbeweging* (Yearbook, International Archives for the Women's Movement), 1937; Wilhelmijn Hendrika Posthumus-van der Goot, ed., *Van moeder op dochter: Het aandeel van de vrouw in een veranderende wereld* (Leiden: Brill, 1948). See also the articles by Rendall and Bosch in this volume.

2. Karen Offen, *European Feminisms 1700–1950. A Political History* (Stanford: Stanford University Press 2000), p. 7.

3. Cf. the catalog of the Gerritsen Collection on Women's History; cf. H. J. Mehler, *La Femme et le féminisme* (Paris: Giard & Brière, 1900). Eliska Vincent collected material on the French women's movement since the 1890s, but unfortunately it has been lost. Further important documentation can be found in the Fawcett Library in England, the Helene-Lange-Stiftung in Berlin, and the bibliography published in 1934 by Agnes von Zahn-Harnack and Hans Sweistrup, *Die Frauenfrage in Deutschland. Strömungen und Gegenströmungen 1790–1930* (reprinted Munich: Sauer, 1984). The Internationaal Archief voor de Vrouwenbeweging (International Archive for the Women's Movement, IAV) was founded in Amsterdam in 1935 by Dutch feminists. Cf. Offen, *European Feminisms*, pp. 3–17 on the efforts to reconstruct and hand down one's own history.

4. Rendall, p. 34.   5. Rendall, p. 33.
6. Rochefort, p. 100.   7. Varikas, p. 268.
8. Ibid.

9. Malečková, p. 167. The female figures were discovered by the early Czech nationalist movement and became part of national mythology. Male intellectuals praised the achievements of the Hussite women in order to encourage women to support the national movement.

10. This danger still exists: "Amnesia, not lack of history, is feminism's worst enemy today." Offen, *European Feminisms*, p. 17.

11. Maria Grever, "The Pantheon of Feminist Culture: Women's Movements and the Organisation of Memory," *Gender & History* 9 (1997): 364–74; idem, "Rivals in Historical Remembrance. Wollstonecraft and Holy Women as Loci of Feminist Memory," *European Journal of Women's Studies* 3 (1996): 101–103; Bonnie G. Smith, *The Gender of History: Men, Women, and Historical Practice*, Cambridge, Mass: Harvard Univ. Press, 1998.

12. Gerhard, p. 104.

13. Rochefort, p. 78.

14. Posthumus-van der Goot, *Van moeder op dochter.*

15. Bosch, p. 65. There has been almost been no treatment in modern German research of the *Handbuch der Frauenbewegung*, which was published in 1901 by Helene Lange and Gertrud Bäumer. Volume 1, written by leading European feminists of the time, deals with the history of the different European women's movements.

16. Bosch, p. 67.

17. Ibid., p. 69.

18. Bolt, p. 296.

19. Karen Offen, "Defining Feminism: A Comparative Historical Approach," *Signs: Journal of Women in Culture and Society*, 14 (1988): 119–57.

20. For a basic critique of this concept—re-creation of insurmountable dichotomies, lack of contact with the contemporary political discourse in Europe, the historian's problematic power of definition—cf. the arguments by Mineke Bosch in this volume, p. 70.

21. Offen, "Defining Feminism," p. 135.

22. This sharp turn towards gender history and to discursive practice explains why there has been little work done recently on the history of women's emancipation movements.

23. It was shown, for example, that almost all feminist issues were related to matrimonial laws.

24. Bosch, p. 72.

25. Szapor, p. 190.

26. Ibid.

27. Edmonson. p. 226.

28. Ibid.

29. Ibid. p. 227. There is a dearth of research about the women's movement within the multinational Russian empire. Besides undertaking research on the rhetoric of the movement, one should examine how political equality was supposed to be put into practice: "Because of the severe restrictions on the activities and concerns of the Russian women's movement before 1900, the issue of political power was debated only in generalities and clichés, although it underlay every discussion of female emancipation." Ibid. p. 238.

30. Ibid. p. 223.

31. Nash, pp. 243–244. This problem is clearly shown in the case of the Spanish women's movement. Although there were clearly male and female precursors and pioneering projects in the nineteenth century, the real organizational phase first began in the 1920s. Thus, the First World War cannot be presented as a turning point in this case, and Spain does not fit into the usual chronology which describes the years between 1880 and the First World War as a peak phase of European feminism.

32. Cf. the article by Karen Offen in this reader.

33. It was not the first time women's associations had been founded. Charitable religious women's associations already existed which were usually supported by women from the upper classes. But this was the first time women had supported a political movement where they collected money, scraped lint, or took care of the wounded.

34. On the scope for action for women during the European revolutions of 1848/49 see Gabriella Hauch, "Frauen-Räume in der Männer-Revolution 1848," in Dieter Dowe, Heinz-Gerhard Haupt, Dieter Langewiesche, eds., *Europa 1848. Revolution und Reform* (Bonn: Dietz, 1998), pp. 841–900.

35. Gerhard, p. 312.

36. Cf. Bianka Pietrow-Ennker, *"Rußlands neue Menschen". Die Entwicklung der Frauenbewegung von den Anfängen bis zur Oktoberrevolution* (Frankfurt: Campus, 1999); and Natalie Stegmann, *Die Töchter der geschlagenen Helden. "Frauenfrage", Feminismus und Frauenbewegung in Polen 1863–1919* (Wiesbaden: Harrassowitz, 2000).

37. Rochefort, p. 92.

38. Rendall, p. 34.

39. Szapor, p. 194.

40. Before and during the First World War women's suffrage had been granted in Finland (1906), Norway (1907), Denmark (1915), and Russia (1917). In 1918 suffrage was granted in Austria, Germany, Czechoslovakia, Hungary, Poland, and England, followed in 1919 by the Netherlands and Sweden, and in 1920 by Belgium. Thus women had achieved suffrage in most of Europe, although sometimes it was limited by age and property restrictions. Turkey granted suffrage in 1931, Spain in 1931 (rescinded 1936), Portugal in 1933, France in 1944, Bulgaria and Italy in 1945, Rumania and Yugoslavia in 1946, Greece in 1952, Switzerland in 1971. Data from Caroline Daley, Melanie Nolan, eds., *Suffrage and Beyond. International Feminist Perspectives* (New York: New York University Press, 1994), pp. 349 ff.

41. Up to now there has been hardly any research on the social supporters of the women's emancipation movement, and the existing research usually only looks

at the leaders, not the grassroots participants. The German and English women's movements are the best known with respect to social composition.

42. Rendall, p. 41.

43. Gerhard, p. 114.

44. Rochefort, p. 97.

45. Szapor, p. 193.

46. Rochefort, pp. 90–91.

47. Blom, p. 150.

48. Gisela Bock, "Frauenwahlrecht. Deutschland um 1900 in vergleichender Perspektive," in Michael Grüttner et al., eds., *Geschichte und Emanzipation: Festschrift für Reinhard Rürup* (Frankfurt: Campus, 1999), pp. 95–136.

49. See especially the articles by Offen, Rochefort, Gerhard, Blom, Malečková, and Bolt.

50. Bolt, p. 297.

51. Ibid. p. 299.

52. Ibid, p. 298.

53. Rochefort, p. 78.

Supplementary Bibliography

Chapter 2

Anderson, Bonnie S. *Joyous Greetings: The First International Women's Movement, 1830–1860*. New York: Oxford University Press, 2000.

Cova, Anne. *Au service de l'Eglise, de la patrie et de la famille: femmes catholiques et maternité sous la IIIe République*. Paris: L'Harmattan, 2000.

———. *Maternité et droits des femmes en France (XIX–XXe siècles)*. Paris: Anthropos Historiques, 1997.

Daskalova, Krasimira. *Ot sjankata na istorijata: Ženite v balgarskoto obštestvo i kultura (1840–1940)*. Sofia: Dom na naukite za čoveka i obštestvoto, 1998.

McFadden, Margaret H. *Golden Cables of Sympathy: The Transatlantic Sources of Nineteenth-Century Feminism*. Lexington: University of Kentucky Press, 1999.

Chapter 3

Bolt, Christine. "The Ideas of British Suffragism." In June Purvis and Sandra Stanley Holton, eds., *Votes for Women*, pp. 34–56. London: Routledge, 2000.

Brown, Heloise. "An Alternative Imperialism: Isabella Tod, Internationalism and 'Good Liberal Unionist.'" *Gender & History* 10 (1998): 358–80.

Crawford, Elizabeth. *The Women's Suffrage Movement: A Reference Guide 1866–1928*. London: Routledge, 1999.

Hannam, June. "'An Enlarged Sphere of Usefulness': the Bristol Women's Movement c. 1860–1914." In Madge Dresser and Philip Ollerenshaw, eds., *The Making of Modern Bristol*, pp. 184–209. Tiverton: Redcliffe Press, 1996.

Holton, Sandra Stanley. "British Freewomen: National Identity, Constitutionalism, and Languages of Race in Early Suffragist Histories." In Eileen Janes Yeo, ed., *Radical Femininity: Women's Self-Representation in Nineteenth- and Twentieth-*

Century Social Movements, pp. 149–71. Manchester: Manchester University Press, 1998.

Howarth, Janet. "Mrs Henry Fawcett (1847–1929): the Widow as a Problem in Feminist Biography." In June Purvis and Sandra Stanley Holton, eds., *Votes for Women*, pp. 84–108. London: Routledge, 2000.

John, Angela, and Claire Eustance, eds. *The Men's Share. Masculinities, Male Support and Women's Suffrage in Britain*. London: Routledge, 1997.

Kelly, Audrey. *Lydia Becker and the Cause.* Lancaster: Centre for North-West Regional Studies, University of Lancaster, 1997.

Kent, Susan Kingsley. *Gender and Power in Britain, 1640–1990.* London: Routledge, 1999.

Midgley, Clare. "Anti-slavery and the Roots of 'Imperial Feminism.'" In Clare Midgley, ed., *Gender and Imperialism*, pp. 161–79. Manchester: Manchester University Press, 1998.

Pugh, Martin. *The March of the Women: A Revisionist Analysis of the Campaign for Women's Suffrage, 1866–1914.* Oxford: Oxford University Press, 2000.

Purvis, June, ed. *Women's History. Britain 1850–1945. An Introduction.* London: UCL Press, 1995.

Rendall, Jane. "The Citizenship of Women and the Reform Act of 1867." In Catherine Hall, Keith McClelland, and Jane Rendall, *Defining the Victorian Nation. Class, Race, Gender and the Reform Act of 1867*, pp. 119–78. Cambridge: Cambridge University Press, 2000.

———. "Who was Lily Maxwell? Women's Suffrage and Manchester Politics, 1866–7." In June Purvis and Sandra Stanley Holton, eds., *Votes for Women*, pp. 57–83. London: Routledge, 2000.

Smith, Harold. *The British Women's Suffrage Campaign, 1866–1928.* London: Longman, 1998.

Yeo, Eileen Janes. "Protestant Feminists and Catholic Saints in Victorian Britain." In Eileen Janes Yeo, ed., *Radical Femininity: Women's Self-Representation in Nineteenth- and Twentieth-Century Social Movements*, pp. 127–48. Manchester: Manchester University Press, 1998.

———. *The Contest for Social Science. Relations and Representations of Gender and Class.* London: Rivers Oram Press, 1996.

Chapter 5

Bard, Christine, ed. *Un siècle d'antiféminisme.* Paris: Fayard, 1999.

Margadant, Jo Burr, ed. *The New Biography: Performing Femininity in Nineteenth-Century France.* Berkeley: University of California Press, 2000.

Chapter 6

Bereswill, Mechthild, and Leonie Wagner, eds. *Bürgerliche Frauenbewegung und Antisemitismus*. Tübingen: edition diskord, 1998.

Berneike, Christiane. *Die Frauenfrage ist Rechtsfrage. Die Juristinnen der deutschen Frauenbewegung und das Bürgerliche Gesetzbuch*. Baden-Baden: Nomos, 1995.

Breuer, Gisela. *Frauenbewegung im Katholizismus. Der Katholische Frauenbund 1903–1918*. Frankfurt/M.: Campus, 1998.

Fassmann, Irmgard Maya. *Jüdinnen in der deutschen Frauenbewegung: 1865–1919*. Hildesheim: Olms, 1996.

Geisel, Beatrix. *Klasse, Geschlecht und Recht. Vergleichende sozialhistorische Untersuchung der Rechtsberatungspraxis von Frauen- und Arbeiterbewegung (1894–1933)*. Baden-Baden: Nomos, 1997.

Gerhard, Ute. *Atempause. Feminismus als demokratisches Projekt*. Frankfurt/M.: Fischer, 1999.

Herlitzius, Anette. *Frauenbefreiung und Rassenideologie: Rassenhygiene und Eugenik im politischen Programm der "Radikalen Frauenbewegung" (1900–1933)*. Leverkusen: Deutscher Universitäts-Verlag, 1995.

Ley, Ulrike. *Einerseits und andererseits: das Dilemma liberaler Frauenrechtlerinnen in der Politik. Zu den Bedingungen politischer Partizipation von Frauen im Kaiserreich*. Pfaffenweiler: Centaurus, 1999.

Mues, Ingeborg, ed. *Was Frauen bewegt und was sie bewegen. 26 Originalessays*. Frankfurt/M.: Fischer, 1998.

Sack, Birgit. *Zwischen religiöser Bindung und moderner Gesellschaft. Katholische Frauenbewegung und politische Kultur in der Weimarer Republik (1918/19–1933)*. Münster: Waxmann, 1998.

Wawrzyn, Heidemarie. *Vaterland statt Menschenrecht: Formen der Judenfeindlichkeit in den Frauenbewegungen des Deutschen Kaiserreichs*. Marburg: Diagonal-Verlag, 1999.

Chapter 7

Blom, Ida. "A Double Responsibility: Women, Men and Socialism in Norway c. 1918–c. 1940." In Helmuth Gruber and Pamela Graves, eds., *Women and Socialism, Socialism and Women: Europe between the Two World Wars*, pp. 450–77. New York: Berghahn Books, 1998.

———. "Fra det moderne til det postmoderne subjekt: En historikers refleksjoner." *Nytt Norsk Tidskrift* 12, no. 2 (1995): 137–45.

———. "A Gendered Approach to the History of the Welfare State: Reflections on a Study of the Fight against Tuberculosis in Norway." In Terry Brotherstone and Debbie Simonton, eds., *Gendering Scottish History: An International Perspective*, pp. 84–97. Glasgow: Cruithne Press, 1999.

Blom, Ida, and Sølvi Sogner, eds. *Med kjønnsperspektiv på norsk historie—fra vikingtid til 2000-årsskiftet.* Oslo: Cappelen Akademisk Forlag, 1999.

Haavet, Inger Elisabeth. "Et respektabelt liv—arbeiderfamiliene og arbeiderbevegelsen under industrialiseringsprosessen." In Bente Alver and Lisbeth Mikaelsson, eds., *Kvinne Minnebok. Bok til Ida Blom.* Universitetet i Bergen. Senter for humanistisk kvinneforskning, 1991.

Hagemann, Gro. "Protection or Equality? Debates on Protective Legislation in Norway." In Ulla Wikander et al., eds., *Protecting Women: Labor Legislation in Europe, the United States, and Australia, 1880–1920.* Urbana, Ill.: University of Illinois Press, 1995.

———. "Seksualmoral og samfunnsmoral: Konkurrerende diskurser i sedelighetsdebatten." In Tarald Rasmussen and Trygve Wyller, eds., *Kristelig og borgerlig offentlighet i Norge.* Oslo. KULTs skriftserie nr. 53, Norges Forskningsråd, 1996.

Hagemann, Gro, and Anne Krogstad, eds. *Høydeskrekk: kvinner og offentlighet.* Oslo: Ad notam Gyldendal, 1994.

Melby, Kari. *Kvinnelighetens strategier. Norges Husmorforbund 1915–1940 og Norges Lærerinneforbund 1912–1940.* Trondheim: Senter for kvinneforskning, Skriftserie 4/97. Universitetet i Trondheim, 1997.

Viken, Lisbeth. "'Der besluttedes at gi . . .' Kvinner og lokal foreiningsverksemnd. Ein studie av fem kvinneforeiningear på Høylandet 1885–1940." Ph.D. thesis in history, NTNU Trondheim, 1997.

Chapter 9

Horská, Pavla. *Naše prababičky feministky* (Our Great-Grandmothers the Feminists). Prague: NLN, 1999.

Lenderová, Milena. *K hříchu i k modlitbě: Žena v minulém století* (For Sin and Prayer: Woman in the Last Century). Prague: Mladá Fronta, 1999.

Malečková, Jitka. "Nationalizing Women and Engendering the Nation: The Czech National Movement." In Ida Blom, Karen Hagemann, and Catherine Hall, eds., *Gendered Nations: Nationalisms and Gender Order in the Long Nineteenth Century*, pp. 293–310. Oxford: Berg, 2000.

Neudorflová, Marie L. *České ženy v 19. století: Úsilí a sny, úspěchy i zklamání na cestě k emancipaci* (Czech Women in the Nineteenth Century: Efforts and Dreams, Successes and Disappointments on the Way to Emancipation). Prague: Janua, 1999.

Pešek, Jiří, and Václav Ledvinka, eds. *Žena v dějinách Prahy* (Woman in the History of Prague). Prague: Scriptorium, 1996.

Chapter 10

Fábri, Anna. *"A szép tiltott táj felé": Magyar irónők a két századforduló között, 1795–1905* ("Towards the beautiful, forbidden land": Hungarian woman writers between the two turns of the century, 1795–1905). Budapest: Kortárs, 1996.

———, ed. *A nő és hivatása. Szemelvények a magyarországi nőkérdés történetéből, 1777–1865* (The woman and her vocation. Selections from the history of the Hungarian woman question). Budapest: Kortárs, 1999.

Gács, Anna. "Beteljesületlen várakozások. Nőirók egy kis irodalomban" (Unfulfilled expectations. Woman writers in a small literature). *Beszélő*, April 2000: 108–15.

Nagy, Beáta, and Margit S. Sárdi, eds. *Szerep és alkotás: Női szerepek a társadalomban és az alkotóművészetben* (Role and creativity: female roles in society and the creative arts). Debrecen: Csokonai, 1997.

Pető, Andrea. *Nőhistóriák. A politizáló magyar nők történetéből, 1945–51.* Budapest: Seneca, 1998. In English: *Women in Hungarian Politics, 1945–51.* Boulder, Col.: East European Monographs, 2003.

Pető, Andrea, and Mark Pittaway, eds. *Women in History—Women's History: Central and Eastern European Perspectives.* Central European University, History Department, Working Papers Series I. Budapest: Central European University, 1994.

Zimmermann, Susan. "Hogyan lettek feministák?" (How did they become feminists?). *Eszmélet* 32 (1996 tél): 57–92.

———. "How They Became Feminists: The Origins of the Women's Movement in Central Europe at the Turn of the Century." In *CEU History Department Yearbook, 1997–1998*, pp. 195–236. Budapest: CEU, 1999.

———. *Die bessere Hälfte? Frauenbewegungen und Frauenbestrebungen in Ungarn der Habsburgermonarchie 1848 bis 1918.* Vienna: Promedia. Budapest: Napvilág, 1999.

Chapter 11

Borkowska, Grażyna. *Cudzoziemki.* Warsaw, IBL, 1996. This study of Polish nineteenth-century women writers includes a discussion of Western feminist theory. For more details see the review in *Women East-West* (May 1998): 9.

Chamerska, Halina. "Women of the Petty Nobility in the Polish Kingdom During the 19th Century." *Acta poloniae historica* 74 (1996): 91–96.

Jakubiak, K. *Partnerka, Matka, Opiekunka: Status kobiety w dziejach nowożytnych.* Bydgoszcz: Wydawnictwo Uczelniane Wyższej Szkoły Pedagogicznej w Bydgoszczy, 2000. Examines Polish women as partners, mothers, and caregivers.

Kitzwalter, T. "Modernization Processes and Emancipation of Women in Polish Territories in the 19th Century." *Acta poloniae historica* 74 (1996): 91–96.

Lorence-Kot, Bogna, and Adam Winiarz. "Preschool Education in Poland." In Roberta Lyn Wollons, ed., *Kindergartens and Cultures.* New Haven: Yale University Press, 2000.

Stegmann, Natali. *Die Töchter der geschlagenen Helden. "Frauenfrage," Feminismus und Frauenbewegung in Polen 1863–1919.* German Historical Institute, Warsaw, Vol. 11. Wiesbaden: Harrassowitz, 2000

Winiarz, A., and K. Jakubiak, eds. *Wychowanie w rodzinie polskiej od schyłku XVIII do połowy XX wieku.* Bydgoszcz:Wydawnitwo Uczelniane Wyższej Szkoly Pedagogicznej w Bydgoszczy, 2000. Charts Polish motherhood in all of its dimensions from the eighteenth century onward.

Zarnowska, A., and A. Szwarc have published a series about Polish women. Their volumes include such topics as education, culture, politics, and daily life. Volumes I and II were published by Instytut Historyczny Uniwersytetu Warszawskiego (Warsaw, 1995); Volumes III, IV, and V were published by Dig (Warsaw) in 1996 and 1997.

Chapter 12

Clements, Barbara Evans. *Bolshevik Women.* Cambridge: Cambridge University Press, 1997.

Edmondson, Linda, ed. *Gender in Russian History and Culture.* Basingstoke: Palgrave, 2001.

Gheith, Jehanne, and Barbara Norton, eds. *An Improper Profession: Women, Gender and Journalism in Late Imperial Russia.* Durham, N.C.: Duke University Press, 2001.

Kelly, Catriona, and David Shepherd, eds. *Introduction to Russian Cultural Studies.* Oxford: Oxford University Press, 1998.

Wagner, W. G. *Marriage, Property and Law in Late Imperial Russia.* Oxford: Clarendon Press, 1994.

Chapter 13

Jagoe, Catherine, Alda Blanco, Cristina Enríquez de Salamanca, eds. *La mujer en los discursos de género. Textos y contextos en el siglo XIX.* Barcelona: Icaria, 1998.
Sánchez, Francisco. *Literatura feminina e feminista da seguda mitade do século XIX. Antoloxía.* Vigo: A nosa terra, 1996.

Chapter 15

Alexander, S. *Becoming a Woman and Other Essays in Nineteenth and Twentieth Century Feminist History.* London: Virago, 1994.
Banks, O. *The Politics of British Feminism, 1918–1970.* Aldershot: Edward Elgar, 1993.
Bland, L. *Banishing the Beast; English Feminism and Sexual Morality, 1885–1914.* London: Penguin, 1995.
Bruley, S. *Women in Britain Since 1900.* Basingstoke: Macmillan, 1999.
Burton, A. *At the Heart of Empire. Indians and the Colonial Encounter in Late-Victorian Britain.* London: California University Press, 1998.
Caine, B. *English Feminism, 1780–1980.* Oxford: Oxford University Press, 1997.
Chaudhuri, N., and M. Strobel. *Western Women and Imperialism. Complicity and Resistance.* Bloomington: Indiana University Press, 1992.
Clark, A. *The Struggle for the Breeches. Gender and the Making of the British Working Class.* Berkeley: University of California Press, 1995.
Davidoff, L., et al. *The Family Story. Blood, Contract and Intimacy, 1830–1960.* Harlow: Addison, Wesley, Longman, 1999.
Dyhouse, C. *No Distinction of Sex? Women in British Universities, 1870–1939.* London: UCL Press, 1995.
Giles, J. *Women, Identity and Private Life in Britain, 1900–50.* London: Macmillan, 1995.
Grant, J. *Women, Migration and Empire.* Stoke-on-Trent: Trentham Books, 1996.
Hannam, June, et al. *British Women's History. A Bibliographical Guide.* Manchester: Manchester University Press, 1996.
Holton, S. S. *Suffrage Days. Stories from the Women's Suffrage Movement.* London: Routledge, 1996.
Jarrett-Macaulay, D. *Reconstructing Womanhood, Reconstructing Feminism. Writings on Black Women in Britain.* London: Routledge, 1996.
Joannou, M., and J. Purvis, eds. *The Women's Suffrage Movement. New Feminist Perspectives.* Manchester: Manchester University Press, 1998.
Law, C. *Suffrage and Power. The Women's Movement, 1918–1928.* London: I. B. Tauris, 1997.

Midgley, C., ed. *Gender and Imperialism.* Manchester: Manchester University Press, 1998.

Mirza, H. S., ed. *Black British Feminism. A Reader.* London: Routledge, 1997.

Purvis, June, ed. *Women's History. Britain, 1850–1945.* London: UCL Press, 1995.

Purvis, June, and S. S. Holton, eds. *Votes for Women.* London and New York: Routledge, 2000.

Rupp, L. J. *Worlds of Women. The Making of an International Women's Movement.* Princeton: Princeton University Press, 1997.

Scott, J. W., ed. *Feminism and History.* New York: Oxford University Press, 1996.

Sharpe, P., ed. *Women's Work. The English Experience.* London: Arnold 1998.

Webster, W. *Imagining Home. Gender, "Race" and National Identity, 1945–64.* London: UCL Press, 1998.

Index of Names

Cott, Nancy, 66
Coudray, Therese de, 254, 261
Cova, Anne, 27
Cox, W. H., 61
Cracow, 215, 218
Craig, Isa, 348
Craigen, Jessie, 47
Czech Lands, 167–88 *passim*, 302, 320, 322, 329, 408. *See also* Bohemia; Moravia

d'Alembert, Jean Le Rond, 17
d'Aurevilly, Barbey, 82
d'Héricourt, Jenny P., *La Femme affranchie: réponse à MM Michelet, Proudhon, E. de Girardin, Legouvé, Comte et autres innovateurs*, 81
Darlington, 41
Darwin, Charles, 385
Daubié, Julie, *La Femme pauvre*, 81
David, Katherine, 168
Davies, Emily, 35f, 41, 46
Davies, Norman, 211, 220
Davis, Natalie Zemon, 13
Defense of the Participation of Women in the Government of the Country (P. B. von W.), 19
"Defining Feminism: A Comparative Historical Approach" (Offen), 22, 24, 54, 75, 305
Defoe, Daniel, 17
Dekker, Eduard Douwes, *see* Multatuli
Demar, Claire, 80
Dembowska, Anna, 209
Dembowski, Edward, 209
Denken over sekse in de eerste feministische golf (Jansz), 69, 72
Denmark, 131, 329, 371, 374, 408
Deraismes, Maria, 81ff, 85f, 89, 91
Deroin, Jeanne, 80
Deuxième Sexe, Le (Beauvoir), 16, 83
Dickenson, Sarah, 348
Dijon, 20
Discurso sobre la educación física y moral de las mujeres (Amar y Borbón), 245
Dobrzyńska, Tekla, 384
Doll's House, A (Ibsen), 129
Douglas, Ann, 287
Drescher, Seymour, 288
Dresden, 111

Dreyfus, Alfred, 85, 90, 94–95
Drucker, Wilhelmina, 57f, 62, 70, 73, 353
Drysdale, George, 153, 372
DuBois, Ellen, 68
Duby, Georges, 13
Dulebianka, Maria, 215
Dumas, Alexander, *L'Homme-femme*, 91
Duoda, Spanish writer, 245
Dupin, Amandine-Lucie-Aurore (Baroness Dudevant), *see* Sand, George
Durand, Marguerite, 93, 94, 100
Durova, Nadezhda, 389
Dworkin, Anthony Gary, 103
Dyhouse, Carol, 295

Eckenstein, Lina, *Woman under Monasticism*, 33f
Edinburgh, 46f
Edmondson, Linda, 307
Eijl, Corrie van, 70
Eliot, George (Marian Evans), 287
Ellis, Sarah Stickney, 25
Elmy, Ben, 47
Elmy, Elizabeth Wolstenholme, 44ff
Emancypacja i równouprawnienie (Bronikowski), 212–13
Emancypacja Sabiny ze stanowiska absolutnego (Wilkoński), 210
England, *see* Great Britain
European Feminisms, 1700–1950 (Offen), 15, 17
Evans, Richard J., *The Feminists: Women's Emancipation Movements in Europe, America and Australasia, 1840–1920*, 11–13, 14, 168, 339
Everard, Myriam, 68f
L'évolution du mariage et de la famille (Letourneau), 271

Faithfull, Emily, 41
Falmerayer, J. P., 265
Fawcett, Millicent Garrett, 36, 50–51, 285
Feijoo, Benito Jerónimo, *Teatro crítico universal*, 245
Feminismo (Posada), 262
Feminist Lives in Victorian England (Levine), 35–36, 40–45 *passim*
Feminists: Women's Emancipation Movements in Europe, America and Australa-